Journal of
CHINESE
LITERATURE
and CULTURE

T0311029

Volume 9 · Issue 1 · April 2022

Critical Theory and Premodern Chinese Literature
STEPHEN J. RODDY and ZONG-QI CAI, Special Issue Editors

Introduction

STEPHEN J. RODDY

This special issue of the *Journal of Chinese Literature and Culture* has brought an exceptionally accomplished group of scholars together to reflect on the impact of theoretical and methodological trends on our field. Surveying the past achievements, current state, and future prospects of the study of premodern Chinese literature from broadly cosmopolitan theoretical and comparative perspectives, these scholars address, inter alia, the following questions: What place do works written in a Western language and/or from perspectives informed substantially by non-Chinese scholarship occupy within the full ambit of Chinese literary studies? If scholarship written in English or other Western languages is for the most part pitched primarily to non-Chinese audiences, what are its strengths and weaknesses for native-speaking readers? And, how has theoretically informed work complemented and drawn upon the rapidly expanding body of Chinese- and other East Asian–language research in these fields? Finally, what is the current state of the dialogue between scholarship on Chinese literature—whether in Western languages or not—and that of other literatures? Has it resulted in any significant impacts on the latter, or on the literary field as a whole?

Each of the nine articles in this issue takes a slightly different tack in treating their respective genres, fields, or texts. While the first four engage primarily in retrospective surveys of previous scholarship, the remaining five introduce and apply relatively novel conceptual and interpretive models to Chinese examples. Although this division is far from absolute—all of the articles engage to some degree in both of these exercises—we have organized the chapters into two sections to reflect their relative differences in emphasis. In aggregate, all nine authors both argue for and demonstrate the value of the

The Journal of Chinese Literature and Culture · 9:1 · April 2022
DOI 10.1215/23290048-9681124 · © 2022 by Duke University Press

application of theory to Chinese literary works while also reflecting on the shortcomings, detours, or disappointments of some approaches as well as the controversies that have arisen among their practitioners.

Needless to say, we have not attempted to survey all of the genres and periods in which theoretical interventions have made an impact. A more exhaustive project would require several volumes and a significantly larger cadre of contributors. Our hope is that future scholars will fill in the gaps that we have left unexplored, in areas such as narrative theory, mixed media (e.g., illustrated fiction, drama, or other works), commentarial traditions, and the heterogeneous materials that fall under categories such as *biji* 筆記 or other compendia, as well as orally recited and other demotic literature. We also wish to stress that, while we have framed this overall endeavor in the terminology of theory that, as François Jullien and others have argued, imposes dualisms alien to Chinese epistemological as well as exegetical habits, our contributors have benefited from and participated in the revival of philological inquiry of recent years, in both China and the West. A felicitous complementarity between textually grounded, philologically informed scholarship and literary theory is evident in all of the articles contained herein.

Paula Varsano sketches an illuminating overview of the postwar zeitgeist of Anglophone academic Sinology and the debates that have taken place around its relationship with and place within the disciplines of both literature and history. Her discussion begins with the exchanges published in two issues of *Journal of Asian Studies* (1961 and 1962) among four China historians—Frederick Mote, Denis Twitchett, Joseph Levenson, and Mary Wright—that illustrate the divisions between those who would "fence off" Chinese studies from other specializations (Mote and Twitchett) and others who sought greater dialogue with and integration within their disciplines (Levenson and Wright). She finds strong echoes of this dispute in the subsequent reception of James J. Y. Liu's pathbreaking books on Chinese poetics and traditional literary criticism of the late 1960s and early 1970s, which in turn leads her into the heart of her article: the seminal studies of Chinese poetics coauthored by Yu-kung Kao and Tsu-lin Mei of the 1970s that redefined the study of Chinese poetry, and subsequent contributions by Stephen Owen and Pauline Yu, among others, that complemented or built on these achievements.

Xinda Lian hones in on the insights of Stephen Owen and of the Mei-Kao collaboration discussed by Varsano, elaborating their significance to the field of poetry studies through meticulously delineating both their readings of specific poems and the overall conceptual architecture of their arguments. Moreover, he traces the further development of their discoveries in some of Kao's later single-authored essays on Tang and Song *ci*, as well as in multiple essays and monographs by Zong-qi Cai about poetic prosody, syntax, and structure published over the past three decades. By freeing themselves from the bonds of the European-language-based classification of parts of speech imposed on the Chinese language that prevailed in much Western-oriented scholarship, and applying instead the topic-comment linguistic paradigm first elaborated by Yuen Ren Chao (Zhao Yuanren) and others to the analysis of poetry, the contributions of Kao, Mei, and Cai have opened a new horizon for the study of Chinese poetry. While demonstrating the novelty of these approaches, Lian also draws attention to their points of similarity and connection to the New Critical tradition of close reading that, both for its original proponents and for Cai as well, proves highly productive as a methodology of systematic study and analysis.

Lucas Klein turns his lens toward European and American poststructuralist writers who have laid some claim to knowledge of China (such as Julia Kristeva and her contemporaries in the 1970s journal *Tel Quel*) to explore their impact on various representatives of academic Sinology over the past four decades. Dividing the latter into two groups based on the degree to which they either deconstructed or reinforced European tendencies to reify East-West divisions (exemplified by Jacques Derrida's infamous othering of Chinese philosophical writings as "thought"), he argues that the most successful poststructural decentering occurs when Sinologists themselves decenter French theory and disseminate this decentering through a more dissipated poststructuralism. Whereas influential figures like Stephen Owen and Pauline Yu have simultaneously adhered to and dissented from poststructuralism, nodding to its critique of Western dualism while also carving a space outside of that dualism, a considerable proportion of such literary scholarship ultimately reproduces Derrida's positioning of Chinese as "outside of all logocentrism" through the pretense of offering a "gaze coming from the inside." Instead, Klein finds in some exemplary recent scholarship the production of knowledge that is not centered on a binary opposition of China and the West, which he calls, after Roland Barthes, a "sideways glance" that has absorbed influences of poststructuralism without succumbing to its blind spots.

In her retrospective portrait of the rise of feminist perspectives in literary scholarship over the past several decades, Grace S. Fong draws attention to the obstacles such work had to overcome even (or perhaps especially) within the academy and specifically the largely conservative, theory-averse domain of Sinology. Thanks to the valiant efforts of pioneering scholars like Maureen Robertson, Ellen Widmer, Kang-i Sun Chang, Haun Saussy, and Fong herself, vigorous theorization and analysis of premodern Chinese women's writing came to the fore in the late 1990s and has blossomed since then. She notes how such work was motivated not only by purely academic concerns but also the feminist desire for the advancement and equality of women socially, politically, and intellectually. And thanks to the fairly recent discoveries and research of significant but previously neglected or unknown troves of women's writing from the last two dynasties, Fong shows how much the study of women's writings has demonstrated that a women's literary tradition flowered during the seventeenth and again in the nineteenth centuries, even if "contending views expressing both support for and opposition to women's participation in learning and writing by both men and women persisted to the end of the imperial period."

In a path-breaking reappraisal of the textual history of the *Lisao* 離騷 (Encountering Sorrow), Martin Kern mines insights from cultural memory theory, pioneered in the 1990s by Jan Assmann and Aleida Assmann. The approach of the Assmanns and their successors diverges from both history and tradition: from history in that its stated focus of interest lies not in the past as such but in its successive retrospective configuration, and from tradition in that it is not static or conservative but, because of its responsiveness to an ever-evolving present, dynamic and innovative. Kern brings this methodology to bear on what he calls the "distributed Qu Yuan Epic," the narrative of a composite Qu Yuan 屈原 (trad. 340–278 BCE) persona that is distributed across multiple prose and poetic texts within and beyond the *Chuci* 楚辭. Based on his close and original analysis of the *Lisao* as a discontinuous and nonlinear sum total of parallel discourses of separate origins and diverse literary idioms, Kern argues that the model of a paragon of loyalty in an unappreciative and self-destructive royal court emerged from the Han literati's refashioning of a Chu aristocratic poetic hero into a heroic poet, a new ideal of authorship advanced by Liu An 劉安 (179–122 BCE), Sima Qian 司馬遷 (ca. 145–ca. 85 BCE), and Liu Xiang 劉向 (77–6 BCE). Rather than being a stable historical entity, this Qu Yuan was developed as a textual configuration through which events and ideals were "inscribed in the discourse of the nation," a continuous process that allowed for destabilization, reconfiguration, or expungement.

The concept of *mouvance,* articulated by European medievalists to analyze and indeed embrace the fluidity of pre-Gutenberg scribal culture, is deployed to great effect in Christopher Nugent's discussion of the mid-Tang florilegium *Xinji wenci jiujing chao* 新集文詞九經抄 (New Compilation of Phrases Excerpted from the Nine Classics, ca. 755–883), a manuscript found in at least sixteen fragments at Dunhuang. While the value of this conceptual framework has already been demonstrated by scholars working on early Chinese texts, which recent archeological finds have shown to be much less stable than what was believed just a few decades ago, Nugent shows its relevance to later eras in his careful comparisons of passages from the Confucian *Analects* and a few other classical texts quoted in these manuscripts. Memory and memorization clearly functioned in ways parallel to the "joyful appropriation" that characterizes medieval texts, with materials rearranged, paraphrased, reattributed, or even invented, for works like *Analects*, whose textual uniformity was promoted and enforced by the state through institutional mechanisms such as the examination system. Nugent's work opens up possibilities for postulating the contours of a literate population beyond, and much larger than, the examination-taking elite, for whom these variorum texts served as the principal medium by which they knew and appreciated the values and their attendant practices across multiple segments of society. Their understandings of the "classics" may well have differed substantially from our own conceptions of such works.

Manling Luo surveys the expansive terrain of what she separates into two categories of spatiality, "general theories" and "local theories," and their potential for application to Chinese examples from the medieval period. She notes the distinction between space (a geometrically quantified raw material) and place, the latter preferred by humanistic geographers as the product of human activity, enabling the "seeing, knowing, and understanding [of] the world." Discussing Edward Soja's Thirdspace, feminist traditions of urban design, Edward Said, bell hooks, and numerous other examples, Luo contemplates their potential relevance to the historical excavation of medieval Chinese conceptions and practices of spatiality. She gives us a broad sampling of recent scholarship on, inter alia, medieval urban spaces such as Chang'an, the landscapes of the poetry of Xie Lingyun 謝靈運 (385–433), sacred mountains and pilgrimage sites, qualities like *feng* 風 and *qi* 氣, "meta-geographies of ecumenical regionalism," and her own work on the sixth-century *Luoyang qielan ji* 洛陽伽藍記 (Records of Buddhist Monasteries in Luoyang), providing a comprehensive palette of possibilities for geographical theorizing about and interpreting the vast range of writings and topics that are relevant to understanding space/place in Chinese contexts.

As with the expansive view of theoreticians and their writings in Manling Luo's article, Patricia Sieber gives us a similarly wide-ranging and thought-provoking survey of contemporary developments in theater studies with potential applicability to Chinese theatrical texts and performance studies. Taking note of the methodological pluralism that characterizes theoretical writings and the considerable range of opinion even over what constitutes theatricality, she then turns to the historical reception of Chinese theater in Europe and North America, beginning with its relegation to the category of opera, as well as other preconceptions that became attached to it thanks in part to Jesuit moral preoccupations. Sieber discusses the exceptionally rich variation in language registers and their rhetorical manipulation in all three of the early theatrical genres (*zaju* 雜劇, *nanxi* 南戲, and *chuanqi* 傳奇) and notes how the attention to language use in which recent Western scholarship (including her own) has excelled can contribute to the cross-cultural studies of mixed-register literature as a whole. Concluding with Brecht's famous engagement with Chinese theater and the continuing controversy over whether his conception of the alienation effect stems from misunderstanding of that tradition, she cites several provocative recent efforts to revisit fundamental questions of theatricality in its Chinese contexts.

Alexander Des Forges brings a novel perspective to late imperial literary history through the application of the concept of involution, including both aesthetic and sociopolitical ramifications, to the understanding of classical prose, specifically the genre of examination prose known popularly as the "eight-legged essay" or, in its normative name, the "prose of our time" (*shiwen* 時文). Beginning with involution's history of use in debates over late imperial Chinese economic development, Des Forges demonstrates its potential for illuminating the "complex interiority" of the formally intricate examination essays that evolved continuously from the mid-Ming to the late Qing. Institutionally, involution was evident among government departments of the imperial bureaucracy that were balanced against one another, duplicating their functions, and also within departments where bipartition into parallel, virtually redundant units occurred, and was further replicated by commercial brokers whose development mirrored their bureaucratic counterparts. Des Forges then reminds us that involution originated as a critical term in the field of art history, and only much later appropriated by Clifford Geertz to describe the division of Javanese rice paddies in increasingly granular fashion. This mutual imbrication between the aesthetic, political, and institutional dimensions of involution make it a useful tool in examining the parallels between dissatisfaction expressed by critics of such institutional subdivision and reduplication, on the one hand, and criticism of the allegedly superfluous doubling that characterizes the eight-legged essay, on the other. Des Forges argues that we can attribute these processes to the "industrialization of the subjectivity production process" that is not unlike the alchemy by which our "free time" activity is transmuted into data mined so profitably by the algorithmic wizards of Silicon Valley and elsewhere.

In conclusion, we wish to acknowledge the contributions of Yuan Xingpei 袁行霈, director of the International Academy for Chinese Studies (IACS) at Peking University and leader of the multilingual project History of the Dissemination of Chinese Civilization (*Zhonghua wenming chuanboshi* 中华文明傳播史) based there. Along with other volumes devoted to the Western reception of Chinese literary and philosophical texts, Yuan and his collaborator Zong-qi Cai of Lingnan University and the University of Illinois first conceived the idea for a collection of articles devoted to the application of Euro-American theoretical or methodological tools to the study of traditional Chinese literature. The authors presented papers at a preparatory virtual workshop in July 2021, and the present volume represents the fruit of their efforts. We offer our heartfelt gratitude to Dr. Yuan and the faculty and staff members of IACS for their encouragement and support of this project and, indeed, for their steadfast and energetic commitment to the dissemination of knowledge about Chinese literature and culture throughout the world.

 STEPHEN J. RODDY   斯定文
University of San Francisco
roddys@usfca.edu

The Elusiveness of Commonality: Late Twentieth-Century Sinology and the Search for a Shared Lyric Language

PAULA VARSANO

Abstract As the study of what we now call "premodern" China gained traction among students in the postwar United States, the question of how it should be approached emerged as a divisive issue among interested scholars, perhaps nowhere as much as it did among those with a particular interest in Chinese poetry. From the 1960s to the 1980s, the stakes seemed high as scholars confronted their passionate disagreements about things as fundamental as the proper subject of study and the most fruitful methodology. Is China a coherent and self-sufficient subject of study? Can it be rightly and accurately characterized as a civilization so separate from the West, and so perfectly integrated within itself, as to render impossible—and even damaging—an approach to any aspect of its civilization that enables comparison? What is lost and what is gained if one chooses to focus more on Chinese poetry as poetry and less on Chinese poetry as Chinese? Is it really necessary—or possible—to choose? Or is it possible to find balance along a continuum? Of particular interest is the discourse of scholars who saw in the rise of formalist studies of literature either an opportunity or a threat. This article traces just some of the lines of resistance and exploration, convergence, and bifurcation that developed in this period, observing that the disagreements that were exercising these camps, while quite real, were not as absolute as their rhetoric would suggest.

Keywords Chinese literary studies, Sinology, comparative literature, formalism, Chinese poetry

As the study of what we now call "premodern" China gained traction among students in the postwar United States, the question of how it should be approached emerged as a divisive issue among interested scholars, perhaps nowhere as much as it did among those with a particular interest in Chinese poetry. From

The Journal of Chinese Literature and Culture • 9:1 • April 2022
DOI 10.1215/23290048-9681137 • © 2022 by Duke University Press

the 1960s to the 1980s, the stakes seemed high as scholars confronted their passionate disagreements about things as fundamental as the proper subject of study and the most fruitful methodology. Is China a coherent and self-sufficient subject of study? Can it be rightly and accurately characterized as a civilization so separate from the West, and so perfectly integrated within itself, as to render impossible—and even damaging—an approach to any aspect of its civilization that enables comparison? What is lost and what is gained if one chooses to focus more on Chinese poetry as poetry and less on Chinese poetry as Chinese? Is it really necessary—or possible—to choose? Or is it possible to find balance along a continuum?

At the very heart of these debates, which took place between those simplistically but conveniently labeled "Sinologists," on the one hand, and, eventually, "comparatists" on the other, lay the question of language itself: how much is language capable of revealing about the world in which it is used, and how should it be read in order to accurately discern the lineaments of the world woven into its fabric?

What follows is in no way a literature survey but, rather, a discussion of how these questions came to be formulated and answered by some of the writers who were most actively engaged with them. Of particular interest is the work of scholars during the early period of these debates, who first saw in the rise of formalist studies of literature either an opportunity to bring Chinese poetry into the broader conversations about literature per se or a threat to the integrity of their chosen field of study. In the process, I trace just some of the lines of resistance and exploration, convergence and bifurcation, observing that the differences in substance between these camps, while quite real, were not as absolute as their rhetoric would suggest.

A Question of Integrity

In 1964, Denis Twitchett, best known today for his conception and coeditorship of the magisterial *Cambridge History of China*, was barely ten years out from having received his PhD when he published the article "A Lone Cheer for Sinology," which he characterizes as a "plea for the unity of Chinese Studies," a unity that he conceives as threatened by the field's fragmentation into disparate disciplines. Pointing out that he himself held a PhD in "physical geography," was conducting research in economic history, and at the time was "administering a department of languages and literature (chairing the Department of Far Eastern Languages at the University of London)," Twitchett establishes his standing to make his case: he is, after all, someone who understands, both by training and by professional practice, the extent to which China, in its organic integrity, warrants—and indeed requires—treatment as an organic whole, in what we might call today an "interdisciplinary" approach.[1] Another scholar publishing in the same issue, Frederick Mote, who was already a professor at Princeton and would later coedit the *Cambridge History of China* with Twitchett, shows that Twitchett's "lone cheer" was not as alone as he may have thought. In "The Case for the Integrity of Sinology," Mote issues an even more impassioned cri de coeur, formulated as an extended metaphor in which Sinology is likened to a map bounded on all sides by natural boundaries, boundaries set by the presumably shared cultural and historical knowledge of those who built its textual tradition. The "disciplines" of our own time and place, believes Mote, can only be superimposed on that map like so many arbitrary (or, at best, politically motivated) boundaries, delineated with only the thinnest of dotted lines.[2]

Both of these respected scholars are arguing for what they see as the preservation of the integrity—in the sense of indivisible, organic wholeness—of their subject, imperial China, a subject they felt constituted a field in itself. Twitchett, more than Mote, recognizes the need for a degree of specialization in approaching this vast subject, as long as those specialties aren't defined in arbitrary, self-defeatingly rigid terms. For him, the goal was "the imaginative restoration of [China's] past in all its infinite variety,"[3] so a concomitant openness to the application of a wide range of materials and methods was both good and necessary. The plaintive tone of the title of his brief essay notwithstanding, his stated goals are as forthright as they are unobjectionable: to counter the "caricatural" (and he does use this word) thinking that falsely pits the gains made by Sinological (read: philological) research against the methodological advantages being developed in the disciplines. For Twitchett, all honestly acquired methodological discoveries and advances can and must converge in the united effort of bringing China's otherwise vanished and inaccessible past to life, provided that one does not abandon the whole for the part.

Mote's position is close to but more absolute (and thus more easily caricatured) than Twitchett's. Introducing the question of language as a way of clarifying the boundaries of his Sinological map, he betrays the proposed naturalness of his topographical metaphor by tellingly including a feature that is anything but: the (despotically constructed) Great Wall: "Language study is the only pass leading through the Great Wall and into the *chung-yuan*. Those who fail to enter through this pass must remain more or less tame barbarians basking in the partial glow that is reflected into the outer border regions."[4] Mote may well have been deliberately ironic, even erecting in the above passage his own "Great Wall" through his use of the untranslated word *chung-yuan* 中原 (Central Plains), the meaning and connotations of which will be understood only by those who have already "entered through this pass." In any case, Mote's point is clear. The goal of the Sinologist, ambitious (and, from today's perspective, naïve) though it may be, is to shed his status as "barbarian" (another word whose connotations can only be grasped by fellow Sinologists) and acquire the depth and breadth of textual knowledge that would have been assumed among those living in that world during the period in question—those people he calls "the natives." In that world, he notes, there is no room for the alien, anachronistic, fragmentary (and fragmenting), and ultimately arbitrary constructs known as the disciplines. The Sinologist must therefore "go native" himself, applying what Mote calls "a native standard of integrity": "Perhaps the only way to penetrate the unusually broadly-informed and broadly-interested minds of the persons who created most of the records of Chinese civilization is to attempt to acquire a similar breadth."[5] These statements can be roundly critiqued, and indeed, they have been. Sinology—or, more accurately, a caricatured version of it—continues today in some quarters to play its part as the useful bogeyman, even as most of us who study premodern China avail ourselves, and teach the use of, its hard-won tools. Few of us today would take issue with a notion of integrity that asserts the vital interconnectedness of the disciplinary precincts that fall within the bounds of premodern Chinese studies.

Furthermore, just as Twitchett and Mote argued for the importance of maintaining an integral view on their chosen subject, so we are bound to duly recognize the larger picture of which their views formed a part. They were formulated and articulated in the context of the 1964 annual meeting of the Association of Asian Studies, in a panel discussion called "Sinology and the Disciplines," itself a response to the pressures of the times. Indeed, its perceived significance was such that the *Journal of Asian Studies* saw fit to dedicate sections of two separate issues—in August and November 1964—to the remarks of several of the panelists, including (besides Twitchett and Mote) Benjamin Schwartz, Joseph Levenson, and Mary Wright. Pressure was clearly growing to interrogate, reconfigure, and even expand the boundaries of the humanistic study of premodern China, potentially fracturing or even marginalizing the domain of Sinology in the process.

The drawing and redrawing of boundaries, in academic endeavors as in electoral politics, is a regular and necessary—albeit fraught—process. This may be one reason that the nondogmatic, conciliatory view of even as respected a figure as Twitchett can become submerged in a tide of divisive rhetoric. As often happens, both sides of this then-nascent feud between the Sinologists and what we might call the comparatists (in lieu of the rather comical "disciplinarians") invoked the same ideals as the basis for their respective positions: integrity (in all senses of the word) and, implicitly, respect. And, equally consistent with feuds of this nature, each side appeared to its adversary as having betrayed those ideals. Mote's brief essay is especially easy to condemn as an example of the binary thinking—the objectifying, self-other/West-China construct—that has rendered the term *Sinology* so objectionable to so many.

But, just as clearly, in a glass-half-full mode, we also see in these protective gestures an understandable response on the part of individuals whose immersion in the endlessly imbricated Chinese textual heritage taught them what stands to be lost if scholars were to confine their inquiry within prescribed subdomains—history, literature, and philosophy being the most obvious candidates—to which the texts do not necessarily adhere. We can, if we allow ourselves, notice a respect (not just fetishization) of that textual heritage so profound that the Sinologists wildly sought to bracket their own cultural heritage in the interest of immersing themselves in a world to which they could lay no claim other than a desire to accurately interpret and transmit its threatened riches to future generations. They believed, no less than their perceived adversaries, that knowledge and understanding could most nearly be obtained by adhering to a disinterested stance of scholarly objectivity. The difference is that, unlike the comparatists in their midst (and in their surrounding environs), the Sinologists believed that such an achievement required nothing less than taking on the subjectivity of their object, a goal that they conceded was daunting but still thought doable. What looks to some of us today like the arrogant appropriation and transformation of a self-servingly designated other was intended to be the very opposite: a desire to be appropriated and transformed by a culture that lay beyond oneself.

Whatever thoughts these scholars were having, the arguments they put forward in the name of the integrity and wholeness of a Chinese tradition were framed not so much ethically as intellectually. It is here, perhaps, that lay what we can now perceive as their blind spot. Still, with the boundaries of their subject so carefully drawn and so assiduously guarded, they inadvertently revealed the delimiting weakness of their own argument, even in academic terms. That is, even if it were possible for human beings to utterly abandon their own cultural and linguistic perspective (while still dwelling and working in the same world that formed it), and even if the herculean task of achieving the requisite encyclopedic knowledge were feasible, who, in the end, were the envisioned beneficiaries of the fruits of that labor? Who, many began to ask themselves, are the intended—and real—readers of the books we "naturalized" Sinologists write? If we were to thus, somewhat miraculously, cast off our "barbarian" status, would the "natives" living in contemporary China ever welcome us and our work in their midst, or even be interested? And if not, how long can we go on just producing these works for our tiny in-group of outsiders? Of what value is this whole if, from everyone else's perspective, it is only a part—and a negligible one at that?

Clearly, the intellectual dead end toward which Sinology (thus conceived) was heading was already coming into view in the 1960s, well before the emergence of the ethical scruples that would be leveled at it later. Another participant on the same panel, the influential UC Berkeley history professor Joseph Levenson, articulated the coming crisis quite clearly in his contribution to the symposium. Here we see him taking aim at the Great Wall that his colleagues had built around Sinology for its own protection:

> The sum of the matter is this: the world is a world, not the sum of -ological areas. Sinology as a conception will not do, not because China ought to be bleached out of its individual significance, but because, as an individual, China belongs now in a universal world of discourse. The Sinologist is entitled to be very reserved about easy universal analogies, but he should entertain comparisons, if only to give his particular field a universal context. Only then, when the creative life of China is studied in something more than the Sinological spirit, will Chinese civilization seem not just *historically* significant but historically *significant*. A purely "Sinological" form of admiration of Chinese culture may amount to denigration.[6]

Levenson's call to dismantle the barriers that had been built around Sinology and to situate Chinese civilization in an open-ended "something more" announces the change that the defenders of Sinology saw on the horizon and feared. The protective lines drawn around China as an -ology, as a coherent discipline, are thus revealed as paradoxically detrimental to its most treasured object, dooming it to historical insignificance. And if the boundaries set by Sinology are in fact no more "natural" than those imposed by any other discipline, and possibly even less so, then how is a China scholar to proceed? What does it mean to insert this infinitely complex object of study into the even more infinitely complex "universal world of discourse," subjecting it to alien languages of comparison over which it has no dominion?

One answer seems to have been suggested, if only implicitly, by the disciplinary composition of the scholarly panel itself. All of its members were close colleagues, collaborating on various projects or working in the same departments. Notably, and of particular significance to a discussion about "the disciplines," all were historians. Only Mary Wright's intervention, "Chinese History and the Historical Vocation," tacitly acknowledges this fact, and posits it not as happenstance but as revelatory of the nature of Sinology. Arguing that the study of history and the study of China are not just mutually beneficial but, in fact, mutually necessary, Wright ends up showing that the two "disciplines" are in effect coeval and complementary in both their approach and their ultimate goals. Quintessentially humanistic, both Sinology and history, she argues, encompass all of the texts produced by their target civilizations (in their indigenous languages). Both are shaped primarily by an overarching awareness of time, and while eschewing the tools of the abstract models and logical deduction of the social sciences, both allow the received texts to dictate not just the answers to questions but the questions themselves.[7]

In effect, by thus constituting the study of China and the study of history as methodologically and practically of a piece, and by emphasizing dynamism and expansiveness over philological analysis, Wright came the closest of all the panelists to addressing the fear of fragmentation that was animating their conversation and of pointing to the possibility of a larger audience for their work.

It is telling that the title of Wright's essay dubs history not as a particular discipline but as a "vocation" that should be embraced and practiced "without fear." Such is the investment of these scholars; such is their belief in the nature of the contribution they were making.

The Common Ground of Literature (or, The Devil in the Details)

Of course, it was not just the historians who worried about the future of Chinese studies (even if they abandoned the fraught term *Sinology*), seeking ways to shift and broaden its defining boundaries in an effort to increase the number of interlocutors. At the same time that the "Sinology and the Disciplines" panel convened and published its comments, other "Sinologists" who were more inclined toward the study of China's literary writings—poetry in particular— were fashioning their own answers to these questions. Like the historians Levenson and Wright, they nurtured the hope of disseminating their hard-won knowledge of China to a non-China-focused readership, ideally transforming that readership's intellectual parameters in the process. Although no one would attempt to apply Wright's idea and argue that the study of China and the study of literature were coeval, interest was growing in figuring out how to make good use of both Sinological/philological and Euro-American "disciplinary" methodologies, and thereby enter into—to quote Levenson one last time—the "universal world of discourse" of the times.

It was no coincidence that this perspectival shift (I hesitate to call it a movement) among students of China occurred at a time when scholars of European and American literary traditions, too, were looking to justify the study of literature as such, rather than as evidentiary documentation of the larger currents of history. And so, by virtue of a combination of historical serendipity and particular features of a particular form of Chinese poetry, it was the rise in interest in linguistic analysis, formalism, structuralism, and New Criticism that both inspired and seemed to provide answers to the question of how to insert Chinese literature into the literary discourse of the time.

In 1962, around the time that the "Sinology and the Disciplines" panel was organized, James J. Y. Liu, then professor of Chinese at the University of Hawaii, published a book that would set in motion a bold attempt to both carve out a method of study of Chinese poetry per se and at the same time reach a readership beyond the accustomed audience of specialized scholars in the field of Chinese studies: *The Art of Chinese Poetry.* Early days as these were, this goal naturally demanded some justification, and Liu obliges by penning a notably commonsensical opening paragraph:

> In recent years, a fair amount of Chinese poetry has been translated into English, and there have even been a few English biographies of individual Chinese poets, but little has been written in English in the way of criticism. This is not surprising in view of the obvious difficulties of criticizing poetry in a language far removed from the one in which it is written. Nevertheless, the English-speaking reader who has acquired some knowledge of and taste for Chinese poetry through translations might well wonder at times: How should one approach Chinese poetry critically? Could one apply to it the technique of verbal analysis now prevailing in English and American literary criticism? What critical standards did Chinese critics in the past adopt? And what does Chinese poetry sound like? What are the principles of versification and the major verse forms and poetic devices? Difficult as some of these questions admittedly are, the fact that most English-speaking readers interested in Chinese poetry, of whom there appear to be quite a few apart from professional sinologues, cannot devote years to the study of the Chinese language, seems to justify an attempt, quixotic perhaps, but much needed, to answer them, if only partially and tentatively.[8]

One of the most remarkable things about this paragraph, which amounts to the inauguration of a new field of study, is its simplicity, its enumeration of the kinds of questions that any reader of European and American poetry at that time would have been likely to ask. For Liu, Chinese poetry is, in fact, *poetry* as much as if not more than it is *Chinese*. As such, it is meant to be read by other lovers of poetry, and could be, if only they had the critical tools to do so. The gate through Mote's Great Wall of language learning has thus been opened—or, at least, was being held ajar. And most radically, it was being held ajar specifically so that nonreaders of Chinese could have access to what are arguably the most (Chinese) language-specific texts of all: poetry.

To be sure, Liu does not go so far as to suggest that the tools he offers to the non-Sinological audience can substitute for direct knowledge of the poetry itself. What Liu does is take the first step toward establishing the groundwork for a comparative discourse that includes China. His first chapter thus offers, in terms that strive to be concrete and empirically verifiable, an extended description not of Chinese poetry but of "the Chinese language as a medium of poetic expression, *as compared with English*."[9]

For all of his confidence in the benefits and feasibility of an eventual umbrella theory of poetic expression under which all of Chinese poetic writing too might be subsumed, Liu cautions that this first "quixotic" effort to enable the fruitful reading of Chinese poetry exclusively in translation is unlikely to be anything more than "partial" or "tentative."[10] Still, this first, provisional attempt to remove classical Chinese language as an absolute, exclusionary filter and to push back against the grudging view of translation as terminally inadequate and even impossible was nothing less than groundbreaking. Confronting head on, rather than sidestepping, the "obvious difficulties of criticizing poetry in a language far removed from the one in which it is written," Liu asserts that to write about Chinese texts in English is to engage in a particularly complex act of interpretation and that all interpretation (including, implicitly, those enacted by Sinologists) is a form of translation. Indeed, to engage in interpretations that are both accurate and comprehensible, the literary scholar must, no less than the Sinologist, train his eye on the workings of language itself.

Consistent with this position, *The Art of Chinese Poetry* deploys what we might call radical translation at every stage of analysis (not just of the poems themselves), from the description of the Chinese language in part 1 to the critical categories that he extracts, rationalizes, and translates from the works of traditional Chinese critics in part 2, and finally to his own synthetic creation of a critical system combining Western and Chinese concepts and ideas in part 3. The allies he enlists in this effort, most famously, are William Empson and I. A. Richards, whose efforts to lay bare the workings of poetic language writ large (as separate from discursive language, but encompassing all national languages) would also help form the basis of the establishment of literary studies as a discipline in its own right, quite apart from the debates that were beginning to swirl around the future of Sinology.

It is as much a measure of this book's daring as it is of its shortcomings that *The Art of Chinese Poetry* was barely noticed by a large segment of Liu's target audience: the non-Chinese-reading reader of poetry. The book was, as far as I can discover, hardly reviewed in any non-Sinological journals, and where it was covered, it was mentioned but briefly.[11] These were early times indeed, and the assumption that Chinese literature was impenetrable—best left to "natives" and experts—was widely held and even expressed directly in a dismissive mention by D. J. Enright in *New Statesman*. The book was, however, reviewed in most Sinological journals, including two branches of the *Royal Asiatic Society*, the *Journal of the American Oriental Society, Harvard Journal of Asiatic Studies* (*HJAS*), *Artibus Asiae*, *T'oung Pao*, and the *Journal of Asian Studies*. Most of these reviews, perhaps because they were constrained by space limitations, made simple note of the book's appearance, accompanied by generic praise, schematic description, and finally, as was expected at the time, a list of errors of fact, analysis, and, most commonly, points of disagreement regarding translation. However, two review articles, one written by Hans Frankel and published in *HJAS*, and the other by Donald Holzman, published in *Artibus Asiae*, stake out the two poles at either end of the Sinological spectrum: poles that nevertheless reveal telling commonalities.

Frankel, a professor at Yale whose doctoral training at the University of California, Berkeley was in the Romance languages and literatures, with a particular focus on Spanish, opens his article with a long paragraph that echoes Liu's own, reaffirming the necessity—even the inevitability—of this book's existence:

> This is an important book on a vital but hitherto neglected subject. It meets the needs of the growing number of readers of Chinese poetry in English translation who want authentic information on technical and aesthetic aspects of Chinese poetry and who wish to be guided toward a critical evaluation of Chinese poetry. At the same time, Chinese studies in the West have now reached a stage beyond the all-encompassing Sinology of a few decades ago, a stage where the student of Chinese literature, aware of his dual allegiance to Chinese studies and to literary studies, must modify and apply to Chinese literature the tools and techniques that have proved effective in the study of other literatures, and investigate Chinese literature in such a way that the results will be significant also for the understanding of literature in general. Mr. Liu's monograph makes substantial contributions in all three of these areas, and he is to be congratulated for addressing himself to a broad audience—all lovers of poetry—while saying much that will be of interest to specialists in Chinese literature.[12]

Like Liu, Frankel feels the pressure of a growing number of readers of Chinese poetry in translation and has enthusiastically embraced, as a vocation, the responsibility to answer the call. But he also makes explicit what Liu did not: that such a work, in attempting to give nonspecialists access to these poems (as poems), must say something of import to specialists as well, specialists who were beginning to feel torn by their "dual allegiance" to Chinese and literary studies, respectively. That something, of course, would need to be the basis for the kind of fruitful comparison that might bring the two camps together, and it is no surprise that Frankel, whose own writings on Chinese poetry were peppered with comparative assertions and references to European poetic traditions, would be among the first and most vocal supporters of Liu's efforts. It is a testimony to Frankel's support of this larger cause that he appreciates Liu's attempt at the systematization of this vast and unwieldy corpus of material, given its stark differences with his own work.[13] At several points, he praises Liu for his "common sense,"[14] in a veiled rebuke of what he deems to be a defunct and arcane "all-encompassing Sinology,"[15] standing alongside him in the effort to pull Chinese poetry out from under that restrictive dome and into the open air of the literature of a world of common (and not-so-common) readers.

Where Frankel does express some disappointment—and this is revelatory—is around the specifics of Liu's interpretive translation of the tradition. He is troubled by the flattenings and oversimplifications (and, by extension, inaccuracies) imposed by Liu's attempt to translate rich, context-sensitive complexity into transportable schemata. The issue for him is not the distortions that will inevitably arise from Liu's transcultural and translingual imposition of language-specific terms and literary categories. Rather, he worries about the impact of (over) generalization. Systems do tend to obscure details, and while Frankel seems to appreciate the practical advantages that Liu's system offers, he is frustrated by the loss of specificity that it incurs. He does not seem to accept Liu's apparent judgment that too much detail on one or another topic (for example, the workings of tonal parallelism or the overlapping views among the different types of traditional critical stances) would likely have undone the whole project and would have confirmed rather than dissolved the dominant impression of China's inaccessibility, ultimately repelling the very audience that Liu was most interested in reaching.

Frankel's critique raises the question, then, of how much detail is too much. How useful is a critical model once it excludes the myriad particularities of the material that it attempts to rationalize? On what basis are some maintained and others ignored? And what happens to those particularities, and how they shape the whole, once that model is in place?

Donald Holzman's critical review of the book is animated by just such questions, driven by the same concerns we sense that would later motivate the yet-to-be-conceived "Sinology and the Disciplines" panel for the Association of Asian Studies annual meeting. He considers Liu's project to be a direct threat to the accurate understanding of the texts in question and possibly everything that he values as a scholar of China. Holzman, whose rich studies of medieval Chinese poetry cohere closely with the Sinological ideals outlined by Twitchett and, most especially, Mote, shows little patience for Liu's approach.[16] He opens his review article with a passionate description of what a true critic of Chinese poetry should strive to accomplish:

> The critic of poetry must tell us in our own cultural terms what the poem "feels like," how it "vibrates" in its Chinese cultural context, what it means there. To do this he

must himself be at home in that culture, he must have nurtured in himself, in his sensitivity, those thousands or millions of pores or taste buds that respond to the allusions, the prejudices, the landscape, the social conventions, in short to the whole complex of Chinese culture.[17]

For Holzman, Chinese poetry is an all-encompassing, infinitely rich and complex sensorial realm—something that cannot be merely understood but that must be felt, heard, and savored. Frankel would certainly not have objected to this assertion, and it is fair to say that few students of Chinese poetry—or any poetry—would deny that acquiring this degree of readerly sensitivity was also a goal of their own work. Holzman's goal, in this way reminiscent of Twitchett's, is not so much to insist on the intractability of an East-West poetic divide as to assert the need to respect the Chinese tradition on its own terms—to accord it the same respect one would the tradition of a Baudelaire or a Mallarmé. And to further contextualize his words, note that in his later years, writing an introduction to a retrospective volume of his own collected works, Holzman shows that he is as apt to engage in comparative thinking and rhetoric as anyone and that the application of non-native categories of understanding (such as "landscape" and "spirituality") at times could come quite naturally to him.[18]

It is, in fact, not comparison and certainly not "translation" that Holzman objects to. Rather, it is (what he sees as) Liu's shoehorning of the holistic, organic, fine-grained nature and texture of the Chinese textual world into an incompatible and hopelessly transcendent analytical schema. For him, Liu "has decided to study Chinese poetry from a very high level of abstraction, withdrawn from history. In such a short book this general approach can perhaps be defended, but the decision of the author to cut Chinese poetry up into images, symbols, allusions and simple illustrations of various prosodic forms or 'Chinese ways of thinking' can definitely not be defended."[19] It is unnecessary to delve any further into the details of this review, the dismissive tone of which at some points makes it nearly unreadable, fueled as it is by disdain for the literary critics, Richards and Empson, and by a potent disrespect for any critic of Chinese poetry who would feel the need to cite Western critics at all. Frankel may have appreciated the value of Liu's book, and Holzman may have panned it, but in the end both of these scholars experienced the same sense of dissatisfaction. They wished for more detail and greater depth—a greater degree of engagement with what makes a poem a poem. Where Frankel sees (potentially correctible) omission, Holzman sees fatal fragmentation and deracination. Either way, these are concerns about the consequences of a decontextualized reading of the literature, and they must be answered.

An answer would quietly appear just a few years later, in 1968, in the form of an article by Kao Yu-kung and Mei Tsu-lin, titled "Tu Fu's 'Autumn Meditations': An Exercise in Linguistic Criticism," published in the *HJAS*. Kao and Mei make no secret of the sources of their inspiration, citing at the outset not only the work of Empson and Richards but also that of Northrop Frye. Like James Liu, they see in Empson's, Richards's, and Frye's extension of structural linguistics to literary theory an approach that could render Chinese poetry accessible to scholarly readers of literature at large, Sinologists and non-Sinologists alike.

But, if Kao and Mei had such ambitions at the time, they took care not announce them. Unlike Liu's *Art of Chinese Poetry*, this new work was launched as a modest article, not a ground-breaking book, making it unlikely that a dedicated critical review would appear anywhere. In addition, it was published in a premier Sinological journal, with little prospect of being read by anyone outside of that field. In contrast with the ambitious scope and high-level perspective of Liu's project, Kao and Mei trained their sights on the narrow terrain of a single, if crucial and notoriously complex, poem cycle composed by one poet, albeit the poet universally thought of as standing at the peak of the tradition: Du Fu 杜甫 (712–770). Rather than claim that their project fulfilled a pressing, overarching need, they state their goals in the narrowest of terms: to find out whether they could uncover the uniqueness of Du Fu's "late style" by subjecting it to the rigorous application of linguistic criticism. As a matter of methodological thoroughness, the authors further justify their choice, going out of their way to explain that these specific poems' length and complexity make them especially apt subjects for such a treatment. They also point to contextual evidence (specifically, both the known formal generic particularities of these poems and Du Fu's own writings about poetry), which would be available and of interest to Sinologists alone in order to further legitimize their approach, explaining:

> In addition to verbal complexity, there are other factors which make the "Autumn Meditations" ideal subject matter for close analysis. Poems written in septasyllabic regulated verse, the most exacting form of T'ang poetry, are poetry consciously written and meant to be read or heard with constant attention. We also know from Tu Fu's own statements that he strove for striking effects and took considerable pride in the refinements of his craftsmanship, and from a chronological study of his works, that he had been experimenting with various forms and styles shortly before he wrote the "Autumn Meditations." These external considerations increase the possibility that the verbal structures discerned will be those which the poet consciously put in and which an attentive reader is expected to notice—*that is, not just something invented by an ingenious critic.*[20]

Strategically and rationally, Kao and Mei are clearly taking pains to situate this essay well within the "natural" bounds of responsible Sinological practice, even invoking the less palpable but equally important contemporaneous assumptions about the "constant attention" accorded by poetry readers in the Tang (618–907). The humble tone of the authors—that these "external considerations increase the possibility" (rather than, say, definitively demonstrate) that the poetic features they scrutinize were consciously integrated into the poem—is emphasized by the title of the article itself, which cautions its readers that it is only an "exercise." Their stated goal couldn't be more sharply circumscribed: to establish the uniqueness, not even of Du Fu's entire corpus, but (merely) of his late style.

We cannot know, of course, whether Kao and Mei had any particular Sinologists in mind when they wrote this introductory passage, noting simply that Yu-kung Kao and Frederick Mote were already colleagues in the same department at Princeton at the time. Regardless, we can certainly see that care is being taken to firmly ground the poems in the Chinese tradition, in such a way that affirms the importance of, in the words of Holzman, telling "us in our own cultural terms what the poem 'feels like,' how it 'vibrates' in its Chinese cultural context."[21] Kao's training as a historian no doubt also played a role in the fashioning of this integrative approach, such that the joint authorship of a historian and a linguist succeeds in giving this article its overall impression of methodological balance.

Whatever the reasoning that gave rise to this article, we do know from the trajectory of the ensuing two *HJAS* articles that Kao and Mei would publish (1971, 1978), and from the writings that Kao continued to publish independently thereafter, that Kao would take years to feel comfortable generalizing, explicitly, about the correspondence between the particular linguistic features of Chinese poetry and the broader categories of what he would eventually call "Chinese lyric aesthetics." In the end, his work grew out of—and always hearkened back to—the case study, rather than leaping to the level of high abstraction, successfully guarding against attacks of deracination, denaturalization, and fragmentation.

Kao and Mei's sustained respect for the organic, integral nature of Chinese textual traditions, while integrating Chinese poetry into the larger discourse of poetry as such, also manifested in this first article in another important way: their stated method for identifying the central ambiguities of the "Autumn Meditations." For Kao and Mei, inspired as they are by Empson, ambiguity is the very locus of poetry's signature complexities. Rather than simply assert on the basis of linguistic analysis their own understanding of where the ambiguities of "Autumn Meditations" lay, they acknowledge that they cannot, given their own distance in time and place from their composition, be the sole arbiters. Respect for the world that gave rise to the poems, and care for what would have been the real experience of attentive readers in that world, would have to prevail. Therefore, "whenever the organic unity of a poem demands a more circuitous route, we shall also let [traditional Chinese] literary criticism take the helm away from literary theory, if only temporarily."[22] Specifically, building on the 1966 book that the formidable scholar Yeh Chia-ying dedicated in its entirety to elucidating these same eight poems, they "canvas" the traditional commentators who have weighed in on the poems' meaning over centuries in order to "rectify [their] intuition," explaining: "For whatever their shortcomings as analysts, they are closer to Tu Fu in time and in literary habits. Thus, when an overwhelming majority of them react the same way, our task is simply that of pinpointing the linguistic features which in the given context trigger this reaction. And when they do not agree and there is no clear-cut evidence tipping the balance either way, we can almost he sure that the word or sentence under litigation is inherently ambiguous."[23]

Clearly, although they seem to share Liu's ultimate goal of integrating the world of Chinese poetry into the broader realm of literary studies in the Euro-American academy, they are still willing to sacrifice (or perhaps don't believe in the existence of) the broader academic audience that Liu actively sought to attract. Kao and Mei supplant Liu's comforting (to some) "commonsense" approach with a method of reading unencumbered by any illusions that non-Sinologically trained readers will delve into its complexities. That may be one reason they offer no translations of the poems they discuss. But a more important reason may be their recognition that to offer translations as part of a linguistic analysis would risk undercutting the nature of the project itself.

And so, the revolutionary nature of this article becomes all the clearer: Kao and Mei are thinking historically, not just of the works they analyze but also of their own contribution as situated in the long arc of Chinese literary scholarship. At this stage, they are deploying Western critical tools to unearth the riches of classical Chinese poetry, not for the benefit of the hoped-for (but as yet merely imagined) larger audience of comparative-minded Western scholars interested in including China in their world of universal literary discourse, or for contemporary Chinese scholars of Chinese literature working in China and Taiwan (although it would not be long before his work would be translated and published there, to great acclaim). This article's realistically envisioned audience is exclusively a very restrained subset of their immediate colleagues: scholars trained in the Western-based field of Sinology, with a particular interest in poetry.

What makes this decision revolutionary is, paradoxically, its conservative nature. Kao and Mei realize that, if Chinese poetry is going to enter the stage of world literature as an object of comparative discourse, the audience that must first be persuaded of both the value and feasibility of doing so is that of the

Sinologists who created the tools that made such a project possible in the first place. For all that "Tu Fu's 'Autumn Meditations'" withholds translations of these most powerful poems, it is still a work of translation, thinly veiled and potent, a work concerned first and foremost with the question of how to read the poems.

Discerning a Chinese Theory of Literature

By the middle of the next decade, the variety of approaches to Chinese literature among scholars writing in European languages, along with the genres they studied, had proliferated. I do not replicate here the exhaustive and detailed account of this burgeoning that was published by none other than James J. Y. Liu in 1975.[24] Judging from the books and articles catalogued therein, the simple bifurcation between the Sinologists and the discipline-based literary scholars seems to have become more apparent than real, at least insofar as they both shared a belief in Chinese literature's specificity (if not its absolute uniqueness). As approaches to the material proliferated and diversified, Liu celebrated in this article the growth of what he saw as a community of scholars of Chinese literature in the West working toward a shared goal through different means. At the same time, he apparently still felt the need to address the persistent fractural lines that threatened that imagined community, and so he ventures this definition of the integrated field his article covers:

> This survey, therefore, will be limited to the study of Chinese literature in the Western world, which, however, is not to be understood in a strictly geographical sense but rather in a cultural-linguistic one. Thus, works written in or translated into a Western language, and with a predominantly "Western" orientation, may be included irrespective of the author's nationality or the place of publication-whereas works by Chinese, Japanese, Soviet, and Eastern European scholars in their own languages will not be discussed.[25]

This is, to my knowledge, one of the earliest if not the earliest acknowledgment of differences in nationality among the scholars working in the field, a group that included both Western-born, ethnically Caucasian scholars and Chinese who had immigrated to the United States and Europe. Liu makes explicit the cohesiveness of a scholarly community that was already in place by expressly minimizing those differences, emphasizing what they share: an undefined "'Western' orientation," which amounts to the practice of writing and teaching about traditional Chinese literature in European languages, especially English, French, and German. Consistent with his general stance of openness, and aiming in this survey for ecumenical coverage, he then takes aim squarely at what he sees as the most counterproductive of all binaries, that which exiles the discipline of literary scholarship from the realm of Sinology:

> Together with the quantitative growth of the field, there has been a growing tendency (at least in the U.S.A.) to recognize the study of Chinese literature as a discipline in itself rather than a part of Sinology. To avoid any misunderstanding, let it be made clear that those (including myself) who prefer to think of themselves as literary critics or literary historians specializing in Chinese literature rather than as Sinologists do not belittle the importance of other disciplines (such as philology and history) that have traditionally also been covered by the term Sinology; on the contrary, they consider philological and historical knowledge a prerequisite for the study of Chinese literature itself. Nonetheless, they conceive their central concern to be the study of the intrinsic qualities of Chinese literature and its development as an autonomous-though not independent-cultural phenomenon, not the study of literary texts as social documents or linguistic data.[26]

For some, this distinction between belittling philology and history (as charged, for example, by a Mote or a Holzman) and considering them to be (some would read "merely") essential "prerequisites" for the reading of a literary text is a subtle one indeed, perhaps too subtle. But Liu is attempting to defuse tensions by arguing that the difference between scholars of Chinese literature and of Sinology is one of emphasis, not of kind. Given the radical nature of his project and the little space he himself devotes to philological considerations, one might be forgiven for perceiving this argument as tactical, if not disingenuous. However, one chapter in *The Art of Chinese Poetry* had already given evidence of his sincerity in identifying some real, defensible, and ultimately fertile common ground, and that was his discussion of traditional, indigenous literary criticism. This would then become the subject of his 1977 book, *Chinese Theories of Literature*.

As Liu points out in his survey article, Western scholarly interest in traditional Chinese literary criticism—a response to the growth of the subfield of literary theory in the West—was on the rise at this time, driving a surge in translations and studies of key Chinese literary treatises.[27] The identification, analysis, and translation of classical Chinese writings on the nature of literature could satisfy the Sinologists' demand for cultural integrity while also providing a culturally indigenous lexicon in which to articulate, for a discipline- or comparative-focused audience, a higher-level, if not transcendent, view on literature. Writings such as the "Da xu" 大序 (Great Preface), Lu Ji's 陸機 (261–303) "Wenfu" 文賦 (Rhymeprose on Literature), Liu Xie's 劉勰 (ca. 465–ca. 532) *Wenxin diaolong* 文心雕龍 (The Literary Mind Carves Dragons), the best-known *shihua* of the Song dynasty (960–1279), and beyond presented a solid rationale for comparing Chinese literary thought with those theories being developed in Western traditions, bringing China into the "universal discourse" that had long been imagined. And so, Liu himself would go on to publish a book-length study on this very subject. Having failed to attract the non-Sinological audience that he had hoped to reach with *The Art of Chinese Poetry*, Liu shifted to what may have seemed more promising territory. Hoping to contribute to "an eventual universal theory of literature by presenting the various theories of literature" that had been developed by the Chinese, he published *Chinese Theories of Literature* in 1977.[28]

The framework he developed applies a modified version of the model proposed by M. H. Abrams in *The Mirror and the Lamp*, putting into productive play the three agents of the "work," the universe, and the author. Blending that schema with what he identifies as the six types of Chinese theory while trying to avoid unnatural fragmentation of the whole, Liu takes care to show that individual critics could and did belong to more than one of the categories he identifies. Despite these precautions, however, his book once again missed its mark. Reviewed this time in widely read non-Sinological literary journals, albeit by Sinologically trained scholars (for example, in *MLN* by Stephen Owen and in the *Journal of Aesthetics and Art Criticism* by Karen J. Lee), as well as in journals dedicated to Chinese studies (in *HJAS* by Chow Tse-tsung and in *Monumenta Serica* by J. Timothy Wixted), this project, too, was roundly criticized. Indeed, the criticisms echoed, by and large, those issued in response to *The Art of Chinese Poetry*. Critics bridled at the artificiality of imposing order on a tradition that was anything but orderly, and at the even greater artificiality of imposing categories drawn from an entirely separate tradition. Lee, a particularly trenchant critic, objects (somewhat snarkily) that Liu would have been well advised to first ask himself whether a synthesis of Chinese literary thought (decidedly not "theory") as such is even possible before inserting it into a comparative framework—or, more to the point, whether a universal literary theory was even possible (or, remaining unasked: desirable) in the first place.[29]

Once again, the lacunae and overgeneralizations that resulted from Liu's high-level approach were enumerated and lamented by many. Ironically, it may have been Liu's perceived denaturing of Chinese literature's proprietary attributes that was most effective in uniting traditional Sinologists with the growing number of China-focused literary scholars. Nevertheless, his book also laid the groundwork for an approach that at least had the potential to join these camps in a more productive way, in his chapter on what he called "metaphysical theory"—the one chapter that received unanimous praise.

From Linguistics to Metaphysics

Liu coined the term *metaphysical theory* to refer to the features of Chinese literature, poetry in particular, that were anchored in or at least resonated with the cosmological or "metaphysical" strands of Chinese thought. This area of focus appeared in studies by others as well, beginning in the 1970s and continuing strong through the 1980s. This lens, instead of transposing a con-stellation of critical categories onto the Chinese tradition, offered the possibility of peering into its particularities, looking at them holistically, and finding the bases of comparison already present therein. Linguistic analysis would remain central but not as an end in itself. Rather, it would be deployed to reveal the natural links between language and the cultural paradigms as expressed in indigenous writings, with the aid of what we might call, in the broadest terms, semiotics. The unifying potential of this approach lay in its ability to investigate the nature of Chinese literature within its own conceptual framework and with reference to its own language, while translating its operative concepts for pos-sible use in a comparative, if not universal, discourse.

Once again, as in the previous decade, Kao Yu-kung and Mei Tsu-lin published an apparently modest (at least in terms of scope and target audience) article that resonated with Liu's ambitions while avoiding its pitfalls, in this case even before the appearance of Liu's own work. In 1971, well before the appearance of Liu's *Chinese Theories of Literature*, Kao and Mei took a further step toward uncovering and articulating the specific linguistic features that gave Tang dynasty regulated poetry its rich meaning-making capabilities. This time, they drew on a broader range of Western theorists (including Suzanne Langer, T. J. Hulme, Ernest Fenollosa, and Ernst Cassirer) whose fields of inquiry extend well beyond linguistic analysis, also inserting comparisons with Western poetry as needed. This technically titled 88-page article (not much shorter than Liu's 140-page book), titled "Syntax, Diction, and Imagery in T'ang Poetry," consti-tutes a significant leap in precisely the kind of expansive thinking that Liu had been calling for.

This article demonstrates, in the most technical and analytic way possible, how imagery—the sine qua non of poetry—is grounded in the multilayered interactions among carefully chosen words created by different syntactic arrangements, which are themselves determined by choices of diction. Kao and Mei dig deeply into the intricate workings of particular poems, unearthing the most complex of patterns in order to render the whole understandable, not through simplification but through its opposite, the practice of close reading. Where this article manifests its compatibility with Liu's evolving program and where it goes further than their own article on Du Fu's "Autumn Meditations," however, is in its willingness to develop their findings in the area of linguistics into generalizations about Tang poetry and, by implicit extension, to Chinese poetic writing.

To their mind, such generalizations cannot be made meaningfully without some basis of comparison, even if the comparisons remain largely implicit. (As discussed below, consistent with their careful, gradualist approach, they address the uses of comparison explicitly, if briefly, in their third and final joint article.) Recognizing that a central part of this comparative perspective inheres in their demonstration of Chinese poetry's specificity, their observations about Chinese poetic writing exist within the larger ecosystem of Chinese culture; they link some of the technicalities of poetic language and Daoist and Confucian thought.[30] It would be misleading to suggest that these points constitute the centerpiece of their argument—one does not need to have studied Daoism and Buddhism to read these poems in this way. But a belief in the existence of a "metaphysical" connection is there nevertheless. In the end, insistent as they are on the primacy of language, a kind of metaphysicality—admittedly taking the form of a psychocultural awareness more than one of spirituality—is pointed to as a basis for the linguistic patterning that makes Chinese regulated poetry what it is, in all of its particularity.

In a further contrast with their first article, the patient reader need no longer be a trained Sinologist to understand the discussion; Kao and Mei seem to be aiming for a slightly larger readership, one that has the potential to encompass both Sinologists and comparatists (beyond the world of linguistics). One senses this in their attempt to blend together two traditionally distinct models of integrated, holistic thinking about their subject of study: one within the boundaries of a heuristically unified "China," and one beyond those boundaries, integrating "China" into the universal world of poetic language. On an obvious level, that larger world is integrated in part through the simple fact that the authors now provide translations of the poems they analyze. Then, at the deeper level of the argument itself, the article presumes—or perhaps creates—a readership that is endowed with both the meticulous attentiveness of the philologically trained Sinologist and the daring of the comparatist. It is these readers, in the end, who will be rewarded with a conclusion that is itself poetic, especially insofar as poetry rests on associative thinking.

This conclusion, which appears almost abruptly in the last few pages of the article, intriguingly invites the reader to read and then modify an extended quote from Ernst Cassirer's *Language and Myth*, a key work referenced at several points in the article, by a philosopher whose views emphasizing the overarching unity of opposing intellectual traditions (particularly between the sciences and humanistic study) held obvious attractions for Kao and Mei. In the quote, which warrants full reproduction here, Cassirer contrasts two modes of thinking: the unanticipated, visceral, concentrating spirit of "mythical thinking" and the rational and expansive "conceptual" or "theoretical" mode of thinking:

> For in this [i.e., mythical] mode, thought does not dispose freely over the data of intuition in order to relate and compare them to each other, but is captivated and

enthralled by the intuition which suddenly confronts it. It comes to rest in the immediate experience. . . . The ego is spending all its energy on this single object, lives in it, loses itself in it. Instead of a widening of intuitive experience, we find here its extreme limitation; instead of expansion that would lead through greater and greater spheres of being, we have here an impulse toward concentration; instead of extensive distribution, intensive compression. This focusing of all forces on a single point is the prerequisite for all mythical thinking and mythical formulation.[31]

Kao and Mei offer this passage from Cassirer as the crescendo of their own argument, as a far-reaching psychopoetic rationale for the organic workings of syntax, diction, and most importantly, the image making that results therefrom. The culturally presumed mental state that they had described in their first article as readerly (and writerly) "attentiveness" to language has here been expanded into a shared cultural psyche that is at once more specific and more universal. In that spirit, the authors instruct us to now reread it, replacing Cassirer's "mythic thinking" with "imagistic language." Perhaps their replacement of the first term, *mythic*, with *imagistic* seems unsurprising, flowing naturally from a discussion that grounds imagery in an atemporal, nondiscursive mode of human experience, but their more central and innovative point is the replacement of "thinking" with "language," a rhetorical move that, almost counterintuitively, effaces (or perhaps reverses) their presumed hierarchy and raises literature (or, perhaps, just Tang poetry) to the highest plane of universal human experience.

What Kao and Mei have done is to continue building an edifice, brick by brick, that imbues a very specific type of poetic writing with a fundamentally human, if culturally shaped, aspect of psychological experience. In the process, they converge the microspecificity of a particular Chinese poetic form, the Tang dynasty "regulated poem," with the universality of human thought, even as they ground it in Daoist and Buddhist metaphysics. Rather than borrow and adapt a metaphysical structure (such as that developed by M. H. Abrams) to accommodate a Chinese literary mode (transforming the understanding of both), they have been working to build out, into the realm of the intangible, from carefully observed indigenous habits of writing.

Shaping their investigation and its articulation at a time when worries around the proper orientation of Chinese studies in general, and Chinese literary studies in particular, were becoming increasingly divisive, Kao and Mei display a skill at keeping programmatic concerns at bay. This would be key to the effectiveness of their contribution. By honing as closely as possible to the empirical evidence, they effectively fly under the radar of either side of the divide.

Seven years later, Kao and Mei would publish one final article together, "Meaning, Metaphor, and Allusion in T'ang Poetry." In their first footnote, they identify this article as the "sequel" to the preceding one, and so it is. Once again, the pair applies a structuralist method of analysis to draw together ever more tightly the bond between universal modes of thought and mental states (if not metaphysics per se) and particular structures of literary expression. Yet, even as they continue to focus on the "Recent Style" or "Regulated" poetry of the Tang, they extend the applications of their findings ever more explicitly toward something essentially human. Yes, it is something of a coup that they bring the fine points of Chinese poetry to bear on Roman Jakobson's theory of equivalence relation at least as much as they bring Jakobson to bear on Chinese poetry. This accomplishment alone fulfills precisely the kind of goals that Liu foresaw as lying within reach of linguistic analysis, and it even surpasses Levenson's integrative vision. But, given their by now well-established prudence, it is at least as remarkable that, toward the end of this piece, they directly address the underlying assumption of their work to date, responding to a challenge that might easily have been posed by scholars on both sides of the Sinology/comparatist divide. And so, to the question "is structuralism a passing fashion, or does it have something of permanent value to say about the relation between linguistics and poetics?," Kao and Mei choose the latter. Arguing that poetry is "language writ large," they further assert that poetry and the language in which it is written will be mutually illuminating, contributing to our understanding of how poetic language works as a common human phenomenon. With this, they finally state the obvious: while they have been relating "facts about a specific language with characteristic features of the poetry written in that language," they are "also engaged in a comparative study of Recent Style poetry and English poetry."[32]

It is also at this moment in the article that they choose to make a fundamental and illuminating distinction, albeit almost in passing, as if it were a minor caveat. They assert that the juxtaposition of two historically unrelated languages and poetic traditions should not, in fact, be seen as "comparative" (a process one reserves for languages that have something in common) but as "contrastive." And in that regard, they say, their "primary focus is the relation between Chinese language and Chinese poetry. English is used as a way to set forth contrast."[33]

Whether or not it was intended, there is something amusing in this candid clarification, as Kao and Mei—who have been conscientiously treading the fraught path of applying Western theory to Chinese texts—turn the table on their readers, ever so slightly. By explicitly decentering English poetry, identifying it as merely the tool they are using to highlight the workings of Chinese, and even stating that any other European language would have done just as well,[34] they effectively ward off any accusations of a Eurocentric approach to Chinese poetry. It is as if, in one sentence, they sweep away the Sinologists' justification of isolating "China" as an object of study while confirming their practice of centering it within what might be the most encompassing of humanistic fields of inquiry:

the nature of linguistic expression—all this through the judicious application and adjustment of Western theory. Recall Mary Wright's argument of just a few years earlier: if, as she proposed, the discipline of history can be thought of as methodologically coeval with the discipline of Sinology, perhaps the structuralist study of Chinese poetry is methodologically coeval with the discipline of linguistics. Perhaps, to paraphrase and tweak her original point, scholars whose vocation it is to study language need to integrate into their knowledge base an understanding of Chinese poetry, just as scholars of Chinese poetry need to understand the functioning of language.

After "Meaning, Metaphor, and Allusion," Kao Yu-kung would continue his own investigation into the broader implications of Tang poetry, still armed with, but branching out from, the technicalities of linguistic analysis. Having empirically forged a link between language, mental states, and culturally specific rhetorical form, he ventured into an exploration of the most abstract, and yet the most fundamental, feature of the literary tradition: what he would call the "underlying aesthetics" of the Chinese lyric. This work culminated in his article "The Aesthetics of Regulated Verse," which would be published almost a decade later in the concertedly (and refreshingly) eclectic volume edited by Stephen Owen and Shuen-fu Lin, *The Vitality of the Lyric Voice:* Shih *Poetry from the Late Han to the T'ang*, the first volume to cover this topic in English.

In "Aesthetics," likely his most frequently cited and influential essay, Kao has come to acknowledge both the centrality and the limitations of a formalist approach to poetry, clearly recognizing that it is but a means to an end, with the end being that even more intangible, elusive, yet essential aspect of any poem, its "total artistic effect": "Although any study of a schematized verse form should begin with its basic technical requirements, the study should not end there. A schematized form can be considered artistically significant only if its formal components contribute substantially to the total artistic effect of the poem."[35]

Kao's journey from grammar to metaphysics ultimately led him to write directly about aesthetics. His gradual and careful trajectory ensured his credibility, such that the approach he developed would be adopted and adapted by a succeeding generation of scholars in the field, both in the United States and in Taiwan. Indeed, all of his writings in English would also be translated into Chinese, where they (alongside many articles he wrote directly in Chinese) would prove influential, breaking through the boundary encircling the field of Western-oriented Chinese scholarship described by Liu in 1975.

From Metaphysics to Metaphor

The metaphysical approach to Chinese poetry had champions beyond the borders of the United States. In 1977, just before the publication of Kao and Mei's last article, François Cheng, who emigrated from China to France, where he studied under Roland Barthes and Julia Kristeva, published his *Ecriture poétique chinoise-Suivi d'une anthologie des poèmes des T'ang* (Chinese Poetic Writing—with an Anthology of Tang Poems) with the prestigious publishing house Seuil in Paris. One readily perceives the kinship of this work with the transcendental approach of Liu's work, as well as with the structuralist method of Kao and Mei's articles. Like Kao and Mei, Cheng took the formal features of Tang dynasty regulated poetry as representative of something quintessentially Chinese and performed analyses that incorporated syntax into the production of imagery. Like them, too, he held the results up in a purely contrastive relationship with Western language poetry. But unlike them, and even different than James Liu, Cheng's intended audience was not strictly academic. He endeavored to transmit the beauty of Chinese poetry to a broad non-Sinological audience of intellectuals and literate readers of poetry, specifically sensitizing them by appealing to constructs they already understood. One may fault him (and many have) for being overzealous in his efforts to proselytize and being less rigorous in his explanations than he should have.

In any event, for reasons that owe at least as much to the habits of French readers as they do to the qualities of Cheng's work per se, his book succeeded in becoming something of a popular phenomenon in that country. Indeed, it would initiate a career of cultural and aesthetic translation that would eventually make of him something of a celebrity. *Ecriture* responded to the age-old desire, especially among lovers of poetry, to find a linguistic mode of expression that incarnated meaning rather than mediated it, and some of Cheng's views—particularly his surprising (and for some fatal) echo of Ezra Pound's theory about the pictorial nature of Chinese writing—suggest the intensity of his wish to indulge that desire.

Without rehearsing the various criticisms that were leveled at Cheng's work once it was first translated into English in 1982 (among the harshest of which was Liu),[36] Cheng's basic thesis was well received: the assertion, guided by his training in semiology, of a primary and unerring correspondence between the formal elements of language, particularly poetry (especially the development of parallelism as evidenced in the Tang), and the cosmological structures favored in Chinese thought. This thesis argues for the rootedness of language in culture and, by extension, for the possibility of discerning the metaphysical disposition of a culture through the close reading of its poetry. His vision of the uniqueness and specificity of Chinese poetics was distilled into an article titled "Some Reflections on Chinese Poetic Language and Its Relation to Chinese Cosmology," translated by Stephen Owen and published in the same volume as Kao's "Aesthetics," forming an interesting counterpoint.

But by the time of that publication, another "metaphysical" approach to Chinese poetry with comparative intent—perhaps directly inspired by Liu but grounded in the specific workings of Chinese poetic language and thought in ways that resonate with Kao—had already begun to make itself felt in the early work of another scholar in the United States, who also reached a non-Sinological audience: Pauline Yu. In 1978 and 1979, Yu published two exploratory articles in this vein, not in the usual Sinological journals, as had been the norm, but in two of the most prestigious and widely read journals in the growing field of comparative literature: *Comparative Literature* and *PMLA*. It is the first of these two articles that interests us here, for it cites Liu's category of the metaphysical at the outset. "Chinese and Symbolist Poetic Theories" attempts to show that the "metaphysical" school of Chinese critical theory (as delineated by Liu) and modern symbolist poets in the West both assert a transcendent nonduality between self and world.

This essay is comparative literature at its plainest, engaging in great detail both literary history and language analysis as the grounds for its argument. Overriding Kao and Mei's criteria for distinguishing between comparison and contrast, she embarks on the comparison of two unrelated traditions, giving Chinese traditional theory and modern symbolist theory equal weight and equal time. Indeed, "putting aside the question of their direct relation," for Yu, "comparative poetics possesses values in its own right."[37] Not only does their mutual illumination demonstrate that "the similarities between Chinese and Western theories outweigh the differences," but their "careful comparison offers several advantages, the most salient being that, in order to execute it, we must isolate the salient and comparable features in the theories."[38] She further recognizes that doing so in this particular case is no easy matter, not because the cultural grounds in which these theories grew are fundamentally incomparable but because both sets of ideas "are embedded and embodied in highly poetic language, often metaphors of metaphors, paradoxes, or outright contradictions."[39]

The essay is a tour de force, and the erudition therein displayed a resounding indictment of the belief that the time required to attain deep knowledge of the Chinese textual tradition does not allow for an equivalent level of familiarity with Western traditions, and vice versa. But when she presents her ultimate goal and explains why it is important to point out the resemblances, there is a faltering, an ambivalence, which I think is revelatory of the problem facing the field at that time:

> An awareness of these resemblances may not only illuminate the two critical traditions, but more importantly, may also lay the groundwork for a cross-cultural poetics of the short lyric. Such a theory could not, of course, embrace all of Western or

Chinese poetry, yet it would provide a new entrance into the works of several major figures of the Tang dynasty—the period of greatest literary florescence in China—and of the late nineteenth and twentieth centuries in the West.[40]

Yu's conclusion bespeaks her hard-earned ambivalence about the scope of comparison and its ultimate aims: is the goal something as encompassing as a "cross-cultural poetics of the short lyric" or is it merely a matter of attaining "a new entrance into the works of several major figures of the Tang dynasty . . . and of the late nineteenth and twentieth centuries in the West"? Indeed, the title of the essay itself reveals an imbalance between the vast realm of what is "Chinese" and the exceedingly restrained referent of "symbolist." She stops short of embracing Liu's hopes for an all-embracing theory, but she shares with Kao and Mei the conviction that the most precise analysis has the potential to be the most expansive, and that the greatest degree of expansiveness can only be realized in the act of comparison or contrast. In retrospect, one senses that Yu, whose training in both traditions is unimpeachable, felt a degree of discomfort, and we now know that she would not take up such studies of similarities again.

Instead, she would shift the emphasis to the language of difference and, judging from her subsequent work, never look back. This shift accompanied an evolution in focus as well. Whereas Kao proceeded from the formal study of poetry to the metaphysical (without using that term, of course), and Cheng went so far as to subsume poetry under the dome of metaphysics, one might say that Yu's trajectory took her from the metaphysical back to the formal. And so, in 1981, she published an article in *CLEAR* (*Chinese Literature: Essays, Articles, Reviews*) that would, along with a sequel in *HJAS* in 1983, assert the consonance between cosmogony and the evolution of rhetorical form, taking much of her inspiration from Eric Auerbach and Paul Ricoeur. In the first of these two oft-cited and groundbreaking articles, "Metaphor and Chinese Poetry," Yu opens with an assertion that stands as a powerful counterpoint to her earlier "Chinese and Symbolist Poetic Theories." After acknowledging that the precise meaning of the word *metaphor* as used in Western literary criticism is contested at best, she turns to the possibilities of its application in the Chinese tradition, observing that, while "most critics have taken for granted the existence of tropes equivalent to those which pass for 'metaphor' in the West," the differences between these and the Western tropes are "even more crucial" than those found among the Western tropes themselves. Furthermore, the import of these differences extends well beyond the realm of rhetorical figures and poetic analysis to "*the conventions and world-view underlying them* and in some basic assumptions about the poetic act."[41]

In direct engagement with, and refutation of, Kao and Mei's "Meaning, Metaphor, and Allusion" article, Yu holds that, although analogical constructs abound in Chinese poetry, none of them are truly "metaphorical" as understood in the West and, indeed, that the Chinese worldview makes it unlikely that such a thing would be conceived. Drawing on a wealth of critical and poetic sources (from Plato and Aristotle to Wordsworth and Coleridge, and onward to Culler and Derrida), Yu meticulously demonstrates that the signal factor unifying various conceptions of "metaphor" is its analogical construction across two different planes of existence: one concrete and one abstract, transcendent, metaphysical. In an argument strongly reminiscent of Eric Auerbach's *Mimesis* and mirroring (yet affirming) Kao and Mei's replacement of Cassirer's "thinking" with "language," Yu echoes Aristotle's point that, in her words, "metaphor is not just a linguistic phenomenon, it is a mode of cognition" and, going further, that it is fundamentally an act of creation (or making, consonant with the meaning of the word *poeisis* itself) ex nihilo,[42] a point that had recently been addressed by Stephen Owen in his essay "Transparencies: Reading the T'ang Lyric," discussed below. The existence of two planes across which to analogize and create meaning recapitulates both Platonic theories of duality between the noumenon and the phenomenon and Judeo-Christian dichotomies between matter and spirit.[43]

Giving equal time and attention to an equally venerable lineage of critical and literary Chinese sources, Yu makes her famous and controversial argument that all analogical tropes in the Chinese tradition happen on the contiguous plane of the experienced, observable world that readers and writers were presumed to share; the Aristotelian or Judeo-Christian notions of immanence are absent. Rather, she affirms Pound's statement that, "for the Chinese poet, 'The natural object is always the *adequate* symbol.'"[44] "Movement beyond a Chinese poem is metonymical. . . . It does not head toward another, transcendent realm that is autonomous and different in kind from the sensory world of the poet and his readers, simply because such a realm was not held to exist."[45]

In 1983, Pauline Yu extended her argument of difference, emphasizing the relative incommensurability of Western rhetorical terminology and Chinese poetics in her article "Allegory, Allegoresis, and the *Classic of Poetry.*" In this essay, the nonfictional aspect of the unitary plane of lived reality is developed further, but the point is familiar. That is, traditional commentators who, with a typically didactic bent, interpreted poems thematizing courtship or the harvest in the *Classic* as referring to political or moral issues were not engaging in *allegoresis* as understood in the West. These critics "are not making the poems refer to something *fundamentally* other—belonging to another plane of existence—than what they say, but are revealing them to be specifically referential. The process is one of *contextualization*, not allegorization. . . . Thus the moral lesson is not accidental or arbitrary, but one that arises from a specific context, and for a specific historical reason."[46]

Both of these essays, like the previous articles and books discussed here, deserve to be read carefully and in their entirety. Even better, one would be well advised to read Yu's 1987 monograph, *The Reading of Imagery in the Chinese Poetic Tradition*, which both refined and extended the scope of her argument. Its publication represents a milestone in the field, and not just as the first book-length treatment of the evolution of Chinese poetic criticism that meticulously develops a language and a rationale whereby readers can begin to encompass that tradition into a universal discourse of poetry.

One can see where Yu was inspired by, but also saw the shortcomings of, her mentor James Liu, sensitive as she clearly was to the dangers of over-generalizing, whether for the sake of ease of comprehension by a nonspecialized audience or of establishing the legitimacy of Chinese literature as a self-conscious literary tradition in its own right. Her work carries forward his broad attention to the connection between metaphysics and literature, while remaining deeply cognizant of the importance of precision and detail in matters of language (the comparative potential of which had been clearly demonstrated by Kao and Mei). She thus produced a book that marshaled her deep and rare knowledge of two traditions—ultimately arguing for commonality—for the integrity of human expression—by engaging in direct, sustained comparison. For Yu, in direct contradiction with Kao and Mei, literary comparison is possible across unrelated cultures because they are not unrelated. What connects them is the fact that they both produce literature.

As far as I could learn, only one review of Yu's *Reading of Imagery* was published for a comparative literature audience (by Michelle Yeh for *Comparative Literature*); all of the others appeared in the usual Sinological journals. This is especially surprising given that both articles that led up to this publication were published in comparative literature journals. Reading those reviews, one would never imagine the general respect it has garnered since then. The critiques are, in some ways, reminiscent of those that had been directed at Liu. Holzman, who admires her erudition and is unable to fault her for over-generalizing, is dismayed by the framing of the argument, characterizing it as "a book about books."[47] He is puzzled as to why she makes critics "the heroes of the book" when, in fact, it should be the poems themselves that are studied; at one point he throws up his hands and asks, "Are these questions really interesting?"[48] Ronald Miao, for his part, objects in his extensive and detailed critical essay that it is wrongheaded to extrapolate "a theory about Chinese poetic imagery from these philosophical texts, whose chief concern was the clarification of the metaphysical relationship between cosmos, earth, and man."[49]

There does seem to be a certain lack of generosity in these criticisms, and it would be easy to write them off as generally—and perhaps, to a degree, willfully—uninformed about the Western theories that inspired Yu. However, if we are to exercise our own capacity for generosity, note that what seems to be lacking in Yu's book, as far as these two Sinologically inclined scholars are concerned, is also something that at least some self-described comparatists care about deeply: the experience of the reader of the poems themselves, what Holzman called the poetry critic's obligation to "tell us in our own cultural terms what the poem 'feels like,' how it 'vibrates' in its Chinese cultural context, what it means there."[50]

Yu is not doing this, but it is not her stated goal. One can easily see that part of her goal in hammering down the particular, deep structure of analogical thinking in the Chinese context, is to get at what the resulting poems must have "felt like" in their own context. The connections she draws in her articles, but even more clearly in her book, between the nondualism of Chinese thought and what she argues is the nonfictionality of Chinese poetry gestures quite clearly toward the contemporaneous readers' presumed reading practices and experiences—and is perhaps even intended to function as a guide for readers approaching those works in our own times. The reason it is difficult for Holzman and Miao to recognize this rests only in part with Yu's work per se.

Looking back at our sampling of scholarly work across these two decades, we can see that, for all that they engaged with a blend of structuralism, semiotics, aesthetics, and metaphysics, their prime goal was to recapture and translate the elements of Chinese poetry that made it, from the readers' perspective, poetic. They all strove to tie the specificities of poetic language into the larger ecosystem of Chinese language and thought: to check their own readings of poems against the responses of the traditional commentators who, they felt, better approximated what a poem meant to readers in its own context. And they were all hard at work doing what Holzman recommended: making themselves "at home in that culture, . . . [nurturing] those thousands or millions of pores or taste buds that respond to the allusions, the prejudices, the landscape, the social conventions, in short to the whole complex of Chinese culture."[51]

Where they differed from the imaginings and yearnings of the Sinologists was in their desire to redraw Mote's map of the field and to redefine what constituted its "natural" boundaries—not by superimposing arbitrary "dotted lines" onto his unalterable cartography but by attempting to append a key that would render that map legible as part of the larger world. They did not deny the particularities of the Chinese textual tradition but, rather, sought to translate those particularities for the benefit of a larger audience in a bid to transmit its riches to the readership among whom they now live, through the medium of English. Nor did they deny the validity or the importance of a "native" readership but, rather, rejected the idea that the only alternative was a readership composed of illiterate "barbarians."

To this group of scholars, thinking of Chinese and Western literature as literature first was possible solely because they saw between them enough similarity to warrant a discussion (rather than the assumption or even the denial) of difference. This perception of what we might call "sufficient" similarity was in fact what scholars on the "disciplinary" side of the old Sinology/Disciplines debate had been working toward establishing all along: first through the transcendent schemas proposed by Liu, then through meticulous linguistic analysis, and finally through the link between literary expression and native metaphysics and aesthetics. One may well emphasize what is similar or what is different, but it is simply a fact that any discussion in this context will necessarily involve some conception of both.

Ultimately, then, the elusive commonality that unites the community of Western-oriented scholars of traditional Chinese poetry is not to be conceived as a hidden thread running through their varied methodologies nor even as a manifest interest in China (something that is clearly true but ultimately somewhat arbitrary). What we share is the recognition of sufficient similarity in the face of felt difference and a desire to figure out the best way to use it to illuminate the poetry we all love and try to understand and preserve: to nurture and awaken our own preprogrammed taste buds, such as they are (not just as we wish they could be), and to guide others toward being able to do the same.

Reading ~~in~~ *as* Translation

By now it should be apparent that behind all this debate and analysis and abstraction lies the (usually hidden) practice of translation. Recall that James J. Y. Liu pointed to the increase in the translation of Chinese poetry into English as having motivated the interpretations he offers in *The Art of Chinese Poetry.* Further, he insisted that this interpretive project, like all such projects, was nothing more or less than an act of translation.[52] This vision naturally situates the (poetry) reader at the center, as the necessary component for the longevity of any poetic tradition. All scholars of traditional Chinese literature, then, especially if they are working in a modern, non-Chinese-reading world, are by definition translators—not just of the individual texts they choose to discuss but also, and essentially, of the reading practices that bring those texts alive. And, like all translations, they anticipate a particular readership—what translators routinely call their "target audience."

Perhaps the most consistent and effective practitioner of this vision is Stephen Owen. His body of work, the foundation of which was being developed during the period covered in this article, resonates with (and in some cases utilizes) the linguistic, structuralist, semiotic, and metaphysical methods set in motion by Liu, not to mention the philological expertise so jealously defended by Sinologists. What Owen has sought to do almost from the first—and this goal unifies all of his work—was to recreate the readerly habits of premodern China and articulate assumptions most likely held by those readers, not as a matter of historical record but as a way of instructing a modern, literate audience, whether schooled in Chinese or not, in methods of reading poems from across Chinese history that would prove meaningful to interested readers today.

Although evidence of this perspective can be found throughout his work, two pieces, both of which appeared in 1979, remain to my mind the quintessential expression of this project: "Transparencies: Reading the T'ang Lyric" and "A Defense." It is a tribute to the burgeoning creativity of the moment that they appeared in this period. To situate them on our very rough timeline, they were published just after Kao and Mei's "Meaning" and Yu's "Chinese and Symbolist Poetics" articles, and just before Yu's own article on metaphor. It is no coincidence that metaphor became the touchstone of these writers, for if literary thinkers from across the fields could agree on nothing else, they could find common ground in the understanding that the kind of associative thinking it expresses is precisely where the technical capacities of language and the shaping structures of (particular) culture converge.

"Transparencies" aspires to be a field guide to readers of Tang poetry (that is, both a guide for aspiring readers of the poems and a guide to understanding the readers of that time). And with this publication, Owen makes two important points: first, that to have access to the poetry of a given civilization, one must be schooled in its codes; and second, that those codes can be inferred and articulated for that purpose. Like the works by Liu, Cheng, Kao and Mei, and Yu discussed here, "Transparencies" is a classic in the field, often referenced and, perhaps even more often, integrated into the work of later scholars. While it is not the first piece of writing to mention the importance of reading practice (for Kao Yu-kung cared enough about Tang readers to point out the presumed intensity of their attention to language, fine-tuned enough to warrant the kinds of close-reading practices that he advocated and demonstrated), it is the first to make this kind of instruction its purpose. For Owen, it was not enough to mention that intense levels of attention were assumed; he set out to qualify the precise disposition toward poetry that shaped the nature of that attention. He refers to this as the "art of reading," replete with its own unspoken "rules," or what he calls "shared norms" that are particular to specific literary traditions:

> In every literary civilization there is an art of reading which is as much a part of literary experience as the inert elements of the text itself. That learned art of reading is the means by which a reader can aesthetically know a literary text. Even within a single culture there is great variety in the rules of reading, differing by the age, the class of readers, and the genre read. However, there are also certain shared norms, the fundamental presumptions in the process of forming meaning, and these must be understood before one can consider more specific rules, such as generic expectations.
>
> Language is not only a set of conventional signs and generative rules of combination, it is also a set of instructions for use, a set of operations for understanding. The most consistent trait of literature and literary language is that the processes of forming meaning (rules of reading) operate differently than in nonliterary language.[53]

In Owen's view, the two central rules of reading Tang poetry are to read the poems with the understanding that the "poet" is conveying something real and true about his (for they are almost always men) experience, and that the "conventional signs and generative rules of combination" should not be read as metaphorical but, rather, as tending toward the metonymical. Note this argument was published almost two years before Yu's "Metaphor and Chinese Poetry," which offers similar observations but, as we have seen, offers a metaphysical context to explain why they are so.[54] Instead, Owen's approach is close to Kao and Mei's, building outward from the "exercise" of close reading. In a sense, the argument itself can be read as performative, as he elucidates not just how the poems he selects (one by Wang Wei 王維 [ca. 701–61] and one by Du Fu) function as organic wholes but also how they are metonymically connected to the larger whole of the Tang lyric, which itself is metonymically connected to the poetic practices of Chinese poetry. Left implicit in this article, but borne out in his other publications, is the understanding that these, too, are of a piece with the larger workings of thought and society in Tang China and—as Pauline Yu would show—long-standing Chinese notions of the world.

Owen's work during this period is clearly aimed primarily at the "Western-oriented" reader, although it would prove to be of interest to scholars of Chinese poetry in China and Taiwan as well. It is, more than most, a work of translation, in both the narrowest and the broadest sense, even as it is grounded in a philological understanding of the texts and is carefully embedded in its context. With its emphasis on the poetic experience of the reader, it posed a particular challenge to other practitioners of translation who felt the value of the poems just as deeply but who equated its particular transformations of the original (since all translation involves this) as destructively accommodating. Owen's second book, *The Poetry of the Early T'ang*, would, as a case in point, occasion a review by Paul Kroll in *CLEAR*, which took issue with, among other things, some instances of Owen's practice of translation. Although Kroll himself states that the main of his disagreements are merely matters of "personal preference," Owen understands Kroll's critiques to be more pointed than that. He reads them as representative of the translation practices—indeed, of the view of poetic language itself—of scholars commonly associated as being among those "Sinologists," who continued to disdain attempts to insert Chinese literature into a world context.[55]

Owen responds, therefore, with an essay simply titled "A Defense." At the conclusion of a detailed justification of his own philosophy of translation, he situates his and Kroll's disagreement at the very heart of what he sees as a fundamental and "irreconcilable" bifurcation in the field regarding "the nature of language," stating starkly, "One group believes in stable definition or the etymon; the other group believes in function."[56]

Owen aligns himself with the latter group, and Kroll with the former— Owen sees himself as a practitioner of literary translation, and sees Kroll as the practitioner not of literal translation (as one might have expected) but of a "third form" of translation, one that his readers would recognize as having its roots in the work of such scholars as Peter Boodberg and Edward Schafer. Owen explains:

> "Literary" translation means adapting a Chinese poem to the aesthetic values of English poetry; "literal" translation means using the full range of the English language to "carry over" as much of the original poem as possible. I consider Kroll's views to represent a third form, neither literal nor literary, which seeks to create a new language out of English words to represent poetic Chinese. In some ways it is a noble endeavor, and its novel use of English has a certain appeal. But ultimately I feel that the charms of this language are thin and sacrifice the real pleasures of poetry to the bright image and quick surprise. The language fails because it lacks what both Chinese and real English possess—a complicated range of style, nuance, and association that can only come from a long history of memorable use.[57]

Owen's appeal to "the real pleasures of poetry" comes straight out of the world of those who, like Levenson back in the early 1960s, were defenders of the "disciplines," but his emphasis on the importance of integrating "a long history of memorable use" into his translations of poetry could just as easily have been uttered by Donald Holzman, or even Denis Twitchett and Frederick Mote, except perhaps for the fact that he was referring here not just to the Chinese source language but to the target language of English as well. The point is, as he states in "Transparencies," to establish and teach the rules of reading that would make the poems comprehensible on their own terms. It would stand to reason that the translations he produced would be designed to facilitate this experience.

For all that he declares the divide irreconcilable, in this formulation the methodology Owen is espousing looks an awful lot like a bridge between Sinology and the disciplines. It is a methodology that announces itself in all of his most thought-provoking and influential work, from his provocative article "The Self's Perfect Mirror: Poetry as Autobiography" to his judiciously selected and annotated anthology of traditional writings on literary expression, *Readings in Chinese Literary Thought*. Indeed, his is an approach that harmonizes particularly well with the efforts made by Kao Yu-kung and Mei Tsu-lin, designed to build a pathway outward from texts as they seem to have lived in their native world, into theoretical contexts in the worlds of others—and then, implicitly, inviting others to follow the pathway back to the source. No one thinks the path, in either direction, is perfectly constructed, but one can argue that the approximations are meaningful as such, a kind of added value, saying much about how understanding is attempted and achieved, across time, language, and cultures.

Toward an Elusive Commonality

What is one to take away from this account of such a brief segment of the history of the field of Chinese literary studies? It would be fatuous and glib declare that the scholars involved—who sought to both conserve and communicate the uniqueness *and* the universality of China's literary legacy—were in fundamental agreement about what mattered; or that, in short, commonality was less elusive than they thought. Disagreements were keenly felt and vigorously enacted, and the stakes were deemed to be high. And so, it is perhaps all the more remarkable that it was the formal, linguistic approach to literature, in all its guises, that would open up a commodious two-way passage through the Great Wall of Chinese language and, by extension, of poetry. The applied discernment of fine-grained semantic, syntactic, and semiotic patterning is ultimately what made it possible to notice and articulate literary elements of both sufficient similarity and instructive contrast, to situate the resulting works in worlds both contemporaneous and contemporary, and then to think about how those elements project meaning beyond the words themselves.

Messy as it is, this is the stuff that inspires one to believe in the possibility of a united field of study. After all, all attentive reading—which is what the reading of poetry must be—carries the reader across boundaries of one kind or another. All such reading is translation, and there is integrity in that very recognition.

PAULA VARSANO   方葆珍
University of California, Berkeley
pvarsano@berkeley.edu

Notes

1. Twitchett, "Lone Cheer," 109.
2. Mote, "Integrity of Sinology," 534.
3. Twitchett, "Lone Cheer," 111.
4. Mote, "Integrity of Sinology," 533.
5. Ibid.
6. Levenson, "Humanistic Disciplines," 512.
7. Wright, "Chinese History."
8. Liu, *Art of Chinese Poetry*, xiii.
9. Ibid., xiii; emphasis added.
10. Ibid.
11. See, e.g., the poet D. J. Enright's dismissive mention—almost an aside (appended tellingly to a composite review of Black-authored works titled "Negro Special")—in the *New Statesman* and F. N. Lees's admittedly more thoughtful review in the *British Journal of Aesthetics*, as well as a review by Marjorie Sinclair in the *Western Humanities Review* and one by Roy E. Teele in *Books Abroad*.
12. Frankel, review, 260.
13. Frankel's own writings on Chinese poetry would, in turn, be criticized for their loose structure and impressionistic comparisons. See, for example, A. R. Davis's review of Frankel's *Flowering Plum and the Palace Lady* in *HJAS*. Although Davis's main point of contention is Frankel's supposed rejection of history as an aid to poetic appreciation (another example of caricatural criticism) and praises him for his "good sense and clarity" and "the absence of ill-conceived theories and clumsy neologisms," he also says that, "apart from the particular concentration on the stylistic feature of parallelism, there is little depth on any one topic with a resulting discursiveness and repetitions of often-made generalizations" (205).
14. Frankel, review, 269.
15. Ibid., 260.
16. For a most thorough appreciation of Holzman's contribution to the field, see the review of his body of work by Alan Berkowitz in *Early Medieval China*.
17. Holzman, review of *The Art of Chinese Poetry*, 359–60.
18. In his introduction to a volume of his collected essays, *China in Transition*, summarizing his own synthetic view of his life's work, Holzman wrote, "I have attempted to show that, in the changes in their attitudes towards literature and in their appreciation of landscape, during the Han and the first four centuries of the Christian era, we can see signs of a turning inward and the birth of new forms of spirituality that can truly be considered akin to those that also arose in the West during the same period" (quoted in Berkowitz, review, 143).
19. Holzman, review of *The Art of Chinese Poetry*, 360.
20. Kao and Mei, "Tu Fu's 'Autumn Meditations,'" 44–45; emphasis added.

21. Holzman, review of *The Art of Chinese Poetry*, 359.
22. Ibid., 46.
23. Ibid., 45–46.
24. See Liu, "Study of Chinese Literature in the West."
25. Ibid., 21.
26. Ibid., 22.
27. Such work was initiated in China as early as the 1930s, with the publication of Guo Shaoyu's *Zhongguo wenxue piping shi* (History of Chinese Literary Criticism) in 1934.
28. Liu, *Chinese Theories of Literature*, 2.
29. Lee, review, 506. Liu does go on to address this very question in his 1977 article, "Towards a Synthesis of Chinese and Western Theories of Literature."
30. See their remarks regarding the integration of the Confucian and Daoist awareness of "vital process" in nature into poetic language: Kao and Mei, "Syntax," 95. Note that they do this in connection with a discussion of Ernst Fenollosa's theory about the transfer of power as enacted in grammatical transitivity.
31. Cassirer, *Language and Myth*, 32–33, quoted in Kao and Mei, "Syntax," 132.
32. Kao and Mei, "Meaning, Metaphor, and Allusion," 352.
33. Ibid.
34. Ibid., 353.
35. Kao, "Aesthetics," 332–33.
36. See Liu, review.
37. Yu, "Chinese and Symbolist Poetic Theories," 300.
38. Ibid., 312.
39. Ibid.
40. Ibid.
41. Yu, "Metaphor and Chinese Poetry," 205. She cites both Stephen Owen and Wai-lim Yip as sharing similar views, if developed on different grounds (209).
42. Yu, "Metaphor and Chinese Poetry," 207.
43. Ibid., 210.
44. Ibid., 220.
45. Ibid. For a most recent exploration of this observation, see Stephen Owen's 2016 essay, "Synecdoche of the Imaginary."
46. Yu, "Allegory," 406.
47. Holzman, review of *The Reading of Imagery*, 365.
48. Ibid., 366.
49. Miao, review, 727.
50. Holzman, review of *The Art of Chinese Poetry*, 359.
51. Ibid., 359–60.
52. He recapitulates this position in his brief reply to a negative review of his book by C. H. Wang: "Interpretation, by its very nature, entails 'translating' an author's words into different terms; otherwise all interpretations would be either impossible or tautological." See Liu, "Reply," 452.
53. Owen, "Transparencies," 232.
54. At first glance, this seems somehow surprising, insofar as the article reads as the practical application of theoretical principles that have already been described elsewhere. Yu does indeed cite this article in "Metaphor," and the clear affiliation between her work and

Owen's led David McCraw, in his review of *Reading of Imagery*, to dub it "correct, but hardly novel" (130).

55.   Kroll, review, 126.

56.   Owen, "Defense," 261.

57.   Ibid.

References

Abrams, M. H. *The Mirror and the Lamp: Romantic Theory and the Critical Tradition*. New York: Oxford University Press, 1953.

Berkowitz, Alan J. Review of *Chinese Literature in Transition from Antiquity to the Middle Ages* and *Immortals, Festivals and Poetry in Medieval China*, by Donald Holzman. *Early Medieval China* 6 (2000): 139–46.

Cassirer, Ernst. *Ecriture poétique chinoise-Suivi d'une anthologie des poèmes des T'ang* (Chinese Poetic Writing—with an Anthology of Tang Poems). Paris: Seuil, 1977.

———. *Language and Myth*. Translated by Susanne K. Langer. New York: Dover, 1946.

———. "Some Reflections on Chinese Poetic Language and Its Relation to Chinese Cosmology." Translated by Stephen Owen. In *The Vitality of the Lyric Voice: Shih Poetry from the Late Han to the T'ang*, edited by Stephen Owen and Shuen-fu Lin, 32–48. Princeton, NJ: Princeton University Press, 1987.

Chow Tse-tsung. Review of *Chinese Theories of Literature*, by James J. Y. Liu. *Harvard Journal of Asiatic Studies* 37, no. 2 (1977): 413–23.

Davis, A. R. Review of *The Flowering Plum and the Palace Lady*, by Hans H. Frankel. *Harvard Journal of Asiatic Studies* 37, no. 1 (1977): 203–7.

Enright, D. J. Review of *The Art of Chinese Poetry*, by James J. Y. Liu. *New Statesman* 6 (1962): 743–44.

Frankel, Hans H. Review of *The Art of Chinese Poetry*, by James J. Y. Liu. *Harvard Journal of Asiatic Studies* 24 (1962–63): 260–70.

Guo Shaoyu 郭绍虞. *Zhongguo wenxue piping shi* 中国文学批评史 (History of Chinese Literary Criticism). Shanghai: Shangwu yinshuguan, 1934.

Holzman, Donald. Review of *The Art of Chinese Poetry*, by James J. Y. Liu. *Artibus Asiae* 26, no. 3/4 (1963): 359–61.

———. Review of *The Reading of Imagery in the Chinese Poetic Tradition*, by Pauline Yu. *Journal of Asian Studies* 47, no. 2 (1988): 365–67.

Kao Yu-kung, "The Aesthetics of Regulated Verse." In *The Vitality of the Lyric Voice: Shih Poetry from the Late Han to the T'ang*, edited by Stephen Owen and Shuen-fu Lin, 332–86. Princeton, NJ: Princeton University Press, 1987.

Kao Yu-kung and Tsu-lin Mei. "Meaning, Metaphor, and Allusion in T'ang Poetry." *Harvard Journal of Asiatic Studies* 38, no. 2 (1978): 281–356.

———. "Syntax, Diction, and Imagery in T'ang Poetry." *Harvard Journal of Asiatic Studies* 31 (1971): 49–136.

———. "Tu Fu's 'Autumn Meditations': An Exercise in Linguistic Criticism." *Harvard Journal of Asiatic Studies* 28 (1968): 44–80.

Kroll, Paul W. Review of *Poetry of the Early T'ang*, by Stephen Owen. *Chinese Literature Essays, Articles, Reviews (CLEAR)* 1 (1979): 120–28.

Lee, Karen J. Review of *Chinese Theories of Literature*, by James J. Y. Liu. *Journal of Aesthetics and Art Criticism* 34, no. 4 (1976): 505–6.

Lees, F. N. Review of *The Art of Chinese Poetry*, by James Liu. *British Journal of Aesthetics* 4, no. 3 (1964): 278–79.

Levenson, Joseph R. "The Humanistic Disciplines: Will Sinology Do?" *Journal of Asian Studies* 23, no. 4 (1964): 507–12.

Liu, James J. Y. *The Art of Chinese Poetry*. Chicago: University of Chicago Press, 1962.

———. *Chinese Theories of Literature*. Chicago: University of Chicago Press, 1975.

———. "A Reply to Professor Wang." *Journal of Asian Studies* 39, no. 2 (1980): 452.

———. Review of *Chinese Poetic Writing*, by François Cheng, Donald A. Riggs, and Jerome P. Seaton. *Journal of Asian Studies* 44, no. 1 (1984): 157–58.

———. "The Study of Chinese Literature in the West: Recent Developments, Current Trends, Future Prospects." *Journal of Asian Studies* 35, no. 1 (1975): 21–30.

———. "Towards a Synthesis of Chinese and Western Theories of Literature." *Journal of Chinese Philosophy* 4, no. 1 (1977): 1–24.

McCraw, David. Review of *The Reading of Imagery in the Chinese Poetic Tradition*, by Pauline Yu. *Chinese Literature: Essays, Articles, Reviews (CLEAR)* 9, no. 1/2 (1987): 129–39.

Miao, Ronald. Review of *The Reading of Imagery in the Chinese Poetic Tradition*, by Pauline Yu. *Harvard Journal of Asiatic Studies* 51, no. 2 (1991): 726–56.

Mote, Frederick W. "The Case for the Integrity of Sinology." *Journal of Asian Studies* 23, no. 4 (1964): 531–34.

Owen, Stephen. "A Defense." *Chinese Literature: Essays, Articles, Reviews (CLEAR)* 1, no. 2 (1979): 257–61.

———. *The Poetry of the Early T'ang*. New Haven, CT: Yale University Press, 1977.

———. *Readings in Chinese Literary Thought*. Cambridge, MA: Council on East Asian Studies, Harvard University, 1992.

———. Review of *Chinese Theories of Literature*, by James J. Y. Liu. *MLN* 90, no. 6, (1975): 986–90.

———. "The Self's Perfect Mirror: Poetry as Autobiography." In *The Vitality of the Lyric Voice: Shih Poetry from the Late Han to the T'ang*, edited by Stephen Owen and Shuen-fu Lin, 71–102. Princeton, NJ: Princeton University Press, 1987.

———. "Synecdoche of the Imaginary." In *The Rhetoric of Hiddenness in Traditional Chinese Culture*, edited by Paula Varsano, 261–77. Albany: SUNY Press, 2016.

———. "Transparencies: Reading the T'ang Lyric." *Harvard Journal of Asiatic Studies* 39, no. 2 (1979): 231–51.

Sinclair, Marjorie. Review of *The Art of Chinese Poetry*, by James J. Y. Liu. *Western Humanities Review* 18, no. 1 (1964): 75.

Teele, Roy E. Review of *The Art of Chinese Poetry*, by James J. Y. Liu. *Books Abroad* 37, no. 2 (1964): 219.

Twitchett, Denis. "A Lone Cheer for Sinology." *Journal of Asian Studies* 24, no. 1 (1964): 109–12.

Wixted, J. T. Review of *Chinese Theories of Literature*, by James J. Y. Liu. *Monumenta Serica: Journal of Oriental Studies* (1977): 466–71.

Wright, Mary C. "Chinese History and the Historical Vocation." *Journal of Asian Studies* 23, no. 4 (1964): 513–16.

Yeh, Michelle. Review of *The Reading of Imagery in the Chinese Poetic Tradition*, by Pauline Yu. *Comparative Literature* 42, no. 3 (1990): 285–87.

Yip, Wai-lim. *Chinese Poetry: Major Modes and Genres*. Berkeley: University of California Press, 1976.

Yu, Pauline R. "Allegory, Allegoresis, and the *Classic of Poetry*." *Harvard Journal of Asiatic Studies* 43, no. 2 (1983): 377–412.

———. "Chinese and Symbolist Poetic Theories." *Comparative Literature* 30, no. 4 (1978): 291–312.

———. "Metaphor and Chinese Poetry." *Chinese Literature: Essays, Articles, Reviews (CLEAR)* 3, no. 2 (1981): 205–24.

———. *The Reading of Imagery in the Chinese Poetic Tradition.* Princeton, NJ: Princeton University Press, 1987.

Secret Laid Bare:
Close Reading of Chinese Poetry

XINDA LIAN

Abstract In the most exciting results of linguistic criticism of poetic function in classical Chinese poetry, one sees an ideal integration of microattention to texts and macroinvestigation of grammars of Chinese poetics. The greatest contribution of this close reading of the sinologist brand is the laying bare—in plain analytical language—of the mechanism of Chinese poetics, long grudgingly guarded as some ineffable (*zhike yihui buke yanchuan* 只可意會不可言傳) secret.

Keywords close reading, topic + comment construction, the paradigmatic vs. the syntagmatic

Suppose I. A. Richards, famously known for his experiment of teaching poetry "by isolating the text from history and context,"[1] gives his students the following poem:

> The phoenix cover and the lovebird curtain are nearby
> Where I would go if I could get there.
> Shrimp whisker brushes the floor and double doors are still.
> I recognize the shuffle of embroidered slippers
> Invisible in the bedroom,
> Her forced laugh, her voice
> Light and lovely, like a woodwind.
>
> Her makeup done,
> She idly holds a lute.
> Love songs she likes to relish.

The Journal of Chinese Literature and Culture • 9:1 • April 2022
DOI 10.1215/23290048-9681150 • © 2022 by Duke University Press

Into every note she seems to put her fragrant heart.
Listening outside the curtain
Gets me so much heartbreak!
Misery such as this
Only she could share.[2]

What kind of interpretation would Richards expect from his students?

The first thing students would try to do is to "*mak[e] out the plain sense* of the poetry," as this is the "chief difficult[y]" their teacher told them to tackle when reading a poem.[3] Students will find without difficulty that the poem is about a male persona overhearing a female character's singing. The situation, however, is not so plain. Even though the singer is said to "relish" the love songs in a "light and lovely" voice, and even though her intermittent laughter can be heard, there is something wrong. The word used to describe her laughter—"forced"—arouses students' suspicion about the sincerity of the words she is singing. The genuineness of her tone is instantly called into question.

This should alert students to an instruction from their teacher. "The tone of [a character's] utterance," says Richards, "reflects . . . his sense of how he stands toward those he is addressing."[4] For the singer to have a clear target toward whom she could reflect her unwillingness to sing, there has to be an unwanted listener in her presence. This pitiable listener cannot be the persona, since he is "listening outside the curtain." Obviously, a third character, not mentioned in the poem, sits squarely or reclines languidly on the other side of the "lovebird curtain."

And three's a crowd. The situation becomes interesting. While the invisible listener—whom the singer is "forced" to entertain—will take the singer's melodious words as genuine, the eavesdropper persona is not so sure about this. Since the singer's "fragrant heart" only seems to be true, it can be untrue. Excited by their new finding, Richards's students might be able to gather enough internal evidence (from the meticulously detailed description of the singer's boudoir) to conclude that, in all likelihood, the persona himself has been there before, on the other side of the curtain ("where I would go if I could get there"). Precisely for this reason, the ambiguity in the singer's voice both encourages and devastates him. The misery and desperation the persona expresses at the end carries more than a ring of truth. It seems to be genuine to his audience, the readers of this poem, a love song of his own.

Irony, paradox, ambiguity, and tension, crisscrossed, interloped, or overlapped with one another at different levels of the meaning of words—every ingredient for an intense close reading is there. For students from Richards's class, the mission of interpretation seems to be accomplished.

For Stephen Owen, however, whose shrewd and close reading of the poem we went over above,[5] the examination of the "internal evidence" found in the poetic text itself is far from enough. Reading the poem in its original Chinese certainly helps with a more intimate understanding of the formal features of the poem:

> 咫尺鳳衾鴛帳，
> 欲去無因到。
> 蝦鬚窣地重門悄。
> 認繡履頻移，
> 洞房杳杳。
> 強笑語。
> 逞如簧、再三輕巧。
>
> 梳妝早。
> 琵琶閒抱。
> 愛品相思調。
> 聲聲似把芳心告。
> 隔簾聽，
> 贏得斷腸多少。
> 恁煩惱。
> 除非共伊知道。[6]

But it is the examination of the poem in a rich context, instead of focusing on the text as such, that enables Owen to make the best of close reading as a powerful interpretive tool. By reading the poem as an integral piece in a poetic tradition, he retraces the trajectory of Chinese literati's adoption, reformation, and eventual appropriation of a poetic form with a special folk origin and reveals the mechanism of the generic features of this poetic subgenre to which this poem belongs.

A fundamentalist close reader from the New Criticism camp, who insists in excluding any outside evidence from the interpretive probing, will not know that the poem under discussion is not just another poem but a song lyric, or *ci* 詞, originally meant to be sung by an entertainer at banquets or pleasure quarters. Its title, "Listening outside the Curtain," is the title of a song tune, the musical prosody of which shapes the formal structure of the lyric. The author of the piece, Liu Yong 柳永 (ca. 987–ca. 1053), a member of the Northern Song literati well known for his morally dubious experiences on both sides of many "curtains," might just try to enliven an old tune title by creating a mini poetic drama. Like numerous versions of the same song before this one, Liu's "Listening outside the Curtain" had been, and would be, performed repeatedly in many other occasions by different "fragrant hearts." The genuineness of the feeling it expresses is further complicated.

> The love song is both the stylized imitation of love and at the same time the words in which a truth of love can be spoken. The singer is both a professional, paid to enact passion, and a human being, to whom love, longing, and loss can actually happen. We would be overly credulous to believe every statement of love-longing is indeed love; we would be foolishly cynical to believe that every statement of love-longing is purely professional or part of a hollow game. And we can't tell the difference. (38)

Instantly, many questions and doubts arising from the preliminary reading of this song lyric can be answered. More important, Owen's close reading serves as a brief yet clear explanation of the *ci* genre's musical origin and the drive behind the development of the genre.

Owen does not stop here. Whereas he calls into serious question the genuineness in the singer's voice, on one hand, he pays even more attention, on the other hand, to the expressive potential he detects in the seemingly genuine tone in the eavesdropper's yearning at the end of the lyric. "As he persuasively dramatizes his own 'genuine' concern for the genuineness of the beloved's song words," observes Owen, "he drives the reading of song lyric toward being more like that of *shih* [*shi* 詩]" (45). Inevitably, Owen finds himself bringing *shi* into consideration in his search for "truth."

A time-honored poetic form for personal expression, *shi* "could make the *assumption* of genuineness. . . . In contrast, genuineness was a *problem* in the song lyric" (45–46). When one hears a singing girl performing "her" love song created by a male *ci* writer, one is listening to a formulaic duet "in the voice of others" (or *daiyan* 代言). This voice of others, however, was so "light and lovely" (*zaisan qingqiao* 再三輕巧). Its expressive melodious tone attracted the attention of the literati, who used to express their heart's intent, or *zhi* 志, in the comparatively more straightforward *shi* form. Unable to resist the artistic appeal of this novel poetic voice, they wanted to make it their own. To achieve that, they just needed to try every means to turn what was formulaic in the *ci* into something specific and concrete, to turn the unreliable reliable and the categorical particular. Seen in this light, what literary history describes as the evolution of the *ci* genre between the beginning of the Northern Song period and the time of Su Shi 蘇軾 (1037–1101) is "a transformation from a normative and typological song form to a highly circumstantial form" (45).

It is the clues hidden in Liu's ditty that leads Owen to his conclusion. However, had he not expanded the scope of his close reading, he would not have been able to elicit the generic formal features of the *ci* in its maturity, which allow the literati poets "a genuineness of voice almost impossible in *shi*" (69). Unlike early practitioners of close reading, Owen does not take the text under scrutiny as a self-contained and self-referential enclosure. His suspicion about the genuineness of the poetic expression of the *ci*, aroused by "Listening outside the Curtain," urges him to reach out to other song lyrics by the same author, then to similar works in the same tradition by other poets, and further, to works in the genre forms other than that of *ci* for a comprehensive comparative study.

Of course, we cannot pretend that Owen, as a critic of Chinese poetry, does not know about the transformational history of the *ci* genre before he picks up this poem. What is really going on is that, besides being the learned narrator in this act of close reading, he also needs to play the role of an innocent reader. The most challenging job for this double role is to defamiliarize—not exactly in the Russian formalist sense of the word—what his learned narrator knows so as to provide an exciting unfamiliar world of words for his innocent reader to make new discoveries. Actually, even the learned narrator himself can be surprised by the insight yielded by the new look of the all too familiar texts under the exacting pressure of this defamiliarization. A good example of this is seen in Owen's discovery of the workings of poetic clichés in the song lyric. Like most discussions of this poetic form, known as the long and short lines (*chang duan ju* 長短句), Owen's probing of its generic features also involves an examination of the genre's most distinctive formal features: its asymmetries (59). Unlike other studies of this subject, however, Owen does not limit his attention merely on the expressive sound effects created by the asymmetric line formation. Instead, he tries to find out why a cluster of stylized poetic expressions, or clichés, once embedded in a set of irregular lines, gain refreshing vividness.

His finding is thought provoking. "This is a question of *taxis* ('arrangement,' the sequencing of words and periods)" (58). "Song lyric works with clichés, normative responses, and commonplace categories of feeling" (62) by arranging these highly stylized and hackneyed—yet recognized as "classical"—poetic gestures in "more discursive, often vernacular" syntactic units (58). When a poetic cliché is thus qualified by the vernacular context of the specific and particular, it gains new life. It could stand as an isolated phrase representing a unique mind state, could add to another utterance "as if an after-thought," or "formally enact a sudden shift, an odd association, a flashback, an image left hanging" (59), among other things. If poetic clichés are none other than poetic emotions stylized in categorical or normative words, then "the verbal embodiment of subjectivity was achieved not 'in' words but 'in between' words" (58).

In Owen's vocabulary, *cliché* is not a pejorative. In another place, he declares that "poetry will always try to speak the difficult truths of the heart, and to break free of the tribe's clichés that involuntarily rise to the lips to take the place of everything that is hard to say. But a successful poetry recognizes that this process is a struggle, that such words do not come easily. As a culture acquires more history, credibly simple words seem more and more difficult to achieve."[7] This is tantamount to saying that cliché is a necessity in Chinese poetry. Specifically, in the case of song lyric, "to speak the difficult truths of the heart" is to embed clichés in particular situations with detail and nuance. Suddenly, Owen's understanding of the interplay between cliché and the *ci* context in which it is embedded sounds like T. S. Eliot's well-known theory on the relationship between feeling (condensed in the poetic tradition) and emotion (issuing from personal experience).[8] Yet since Owen is not bent on, as Eliot is, belittling the role of the individual talent in the preservation and development of poetic traditions, his assessment of the interactive relations between the old and the new seems more balanced and hence more helpful for a practical explanation of one of the important elements of the mechanism of the *ci* as a poetic subgenre distinctively different from the *shi*.

As an interpretive approach, close reading seems to be extremely natural and congenial to sinologists working in the field of classical poetry. When Hans Frankel used this method in 1964 to make new discoveries in Cao Zhi's 曹植 (192–232) poems, he had to carefully title his article "An Attempt at a New Approach."[9] Today, close reading is still one of the most convenient and necessary tools for researchers and academicians in the field of Chinese poetry. One just needs to look at Owen's example to see to what extent close reading has advanced from an analytical tool, unconditionally committed to tenets of New Criticism (seen in Frankel's case), to a sophisticated exegetical device in the study of classical Chinese poetry. It empowered its practitioners to perform their duties, that is, to enlighten and delight generations of readers and students of Chinese literature and to dig out hidden meanings in scholarly pursuits.

Ironically, Owen's success also reveals a limitation inherent in the use of close reading as an interpretive tool. So much depends on the critical sensitivity of an ideal close-reader and on the salient readable features of an individual ideal text to be close-read. Imagine a reader, lacking Owen's caliber of critique, facing a song lyric that does not present a suggestive curtain between the persona and the singing girl. There must be a reason that close reading both makes New Criticism and also breaks, in a way, New Criticism. One might well wonder whether it is possible to develop this effective interpretive tool into a stable, reliable, always accountable, or even predictable critical approach that can be applied indiscriminately to the study of poetic texts in general (as opposed to selected texts only). To use an example close at hand, is there a way to examine the interplay between poetic clichés and its "vernacular" *ci* context—the observation by Owen mentioned above—in light of the theoretical investigation of the coexistence of concreteness in sensory impression and the abstractness in reference in the Chinese poetic imagery?

In fact, this was precisely the kind of question posed by the pioneers in their early experimentation with close reading in the study of Chinese literature. Not long after Frankel's trial of this critical method on Cao Zhi, Yu-kung Kao and Tsu-lin Mei started their collaboration in the application of close reading to the study of Tang poetry. "By choice and by habit," the two young scholars declared with emphasis, their critical orientation was Empsonian "linguistic criticism." They also took note of Northrop Frye's *Anatomy of Criticism* and Roman Jakobson's 1958 call for linguistic approach to literature also ringed in their ears.[10] No matter what -ism caught their attention, they never wavered in their determination to "indicate how specific linguistic features are multiply effective in a poem."[11] In other words, they took it as their mission to reveal the secret of the "underlying aesthetics" of Chinese poetry.[12] The vision is systematic, the scale all-encompassing, and the methodology linguistic, hence "scientific"—nothing short of an ambitious critical scheme informed with, among other things, the principles and ideals of close reading.

Specifically, what is the "underlying aesthetics" this grand scheme of linguistics-based criticism aims to elucidate? In a retrospective explanation Kao defines it as follows:

> This aesthetics is basically an interpretative code, through which a poet can go beyond the textual meaning and the reader can understand its contextual significance. Through this code the poet and reader can communicate and exclude the uninitiated. This aesthetic code cannot be acquired as a mere set of rules, prescriptions, and proscriptions; it is learned only by internalizing models, with or without the assistance of explicit interpretation and prescription. Precisely because it always presents itself indirectly, it is difficult to articulate this aesthetics as a code, but the very fact that it never becomes fully explicit protects its power to suggest, to change, and to develop. The fact that I attempt to outline this implicit code in the following pages indicates that I do believe the code can be made explicit to a certain degree. Nevertheless, we should never forget the level on which this code always presents itself—submerged in and integrated with particular texts.[13]

The passage can be read as the manifesto of an "investigator," instead of a "critic," of the secret of Chinese poetics. Although the self-admonition at the end promises an emphasis on the close reading of "particular texts," the passage is much more than a simple pledge to the doctrines of New Criticism. By defining his coinage "aesthetics" (*meidian* 美典)[14] as an "interpretive code," Kao echoes Jakobson. For a message to get across in any verbal act, says Jakobson, it requires "a CODE fully, or at least partially, common to the addresser and addressee (or in other words, to the encoder and decoder of the message)."[15] However, before Kao commits himself to Jakobson's belief that this code can function as a "metalanguage," or "a scientific tool" in the study of literature,[16] he finds it imperative to acknowledge the complex and nearly "indescribable" nature of this code. Like Jakobson, Kao also believes that one should not confuse "literary studies" with "literary criticism": the former, in Jakobson's words, is "the description of the intrinsic values of a literary work,"[17] while the latter is characteristic of "a subjective, censorious verdict" based on "a critic's own tastes and opinions on creative literature."[18] Yet unlike Jakobson, he does not believe that embracing the former necessarily implies the rejection of the latter. Being reflective and introvert, the intuitive "knowing" of a literary critic is prone to be imagistic or even metaphorical, refusing to be pinpointed in analytical language. Nevertheless, this empirical knowing might have followed a logic or certain "objective" criteria of its own. There is a reason that most traditional commentators and not a few modern critics of Chinese poetry like to emphasize the "comprehendible yet ineffable" (*zhike yihui buke yanchuan* 只可意會不可言傳) property of the esoteric "aesthetics."[19] After all, "the very fact that it never becomes fully explicit protects its power to suggest, to change, and to develop."[20] With this understanding, we will be in a better position to know what Kao means when he declares that he would make the implicit code explicit "to a certain degree" by "outlining" it. Outlining the implicit in analytical language does not need to be an oxymoron.

Kao's first serious effort in eliciting this interpretive code is seen in his collaboration with Mei Tsu-lin in a close reading of Tang dynasty regulated style poetry. The material for the study, Du Fu's "Autumn Meditations" series, is carefully chosen to fit their purpose. The verse form Du Fu uses is the most regulated and exacting form, a "poetry consciously written and meant to be read or heard with constant attention."[21] In addition, thanks to Du Fu's obsession with the "striking effects" of poetic craftsmanship,[22] his works offer themselves as ideal artifacts for "a New Critical 'reading,'" "an exercise in reverse engineering: the examination of an artifact to see how it was made and how it worked."[23]

Possibly influenced by Jakobson's emphasis on the phonetic features in poetry,[24] Kao and Mei spend much effort discussing the "figure of sounds." The results are mixed. For example, it is quite convincing to show how Du Fu's design of overly reduplicative sound patterns "betrays a weariness" from facing beautiful scenery for too long.[25] However, based on the sound effects, the reading of the following example,

> . . . A disdained K'uang Heng, as a critic of policy;   匡衡抗疏功名薄，
> As a promoter of learning, a Liu Hsiang who failed.   劉向傳經心事違。

may be farfetched: "The punctuated repetition of *kong*-like sounds and the jostling of vela nasals convey some of the agitation" resulting from "the poet's failure in his moral and official career" (48). Then, in another example,

The clouds roll back, the pheasant-tail screens open before the throne;	雲移雉尾開宮扇,
Scales ringed by the sun on dragon robes! I have seen *His Majesty's* face.	日繞龍鱗識聖顏。

it is true that a careful modern reader, who has some knowledge of "alliteration," might notice that "there we have two rhyming syllables followed by two alliterative syllables in the leading line, and then, in the matching line, three alliterative pairs in a row." However, one might find it hard to believe that "the exuberant display of phonic patterns and especially in the cloying concentration in the third couplet is the kind of hubris portending decline [of the Tang empire]" (50). Here Kao and Mei might be overzealous in their effort to emulate Cleanth Brooks and Robert Penn Warren's meticulous analysis of the relation between sound and sense in *Understanding Poetry*. Since Chinese does not have consonant concatenation, to say the least, and the prosody of recent style poetry is highly regulated and therefore forbids much license in rhythm, the formulas provided by Brooks and Warren will not work well. To examine how sound effects serve meaning in recent style verse, one needs a different strategy.

When Kao and Mei base their investigation of poetic functions on exploiting the intrinsic features of Chinese language, the result is remarkable. This can be seen in their detailed analysis of a special type of productive ambiguity, which is possible only in Chinese language. The first example they examine is a couplet from the first poem in the "Autumn Meditations," which can be read "as it is" at first glance—

Clustered chrysanthemums have twice opened tears of other days;	叢菊兩開他日淚
The forlorn boat, once and for all, tethers my homeward thoughts.	孤舟一繫故園心

A different reading, which requires both the poet and the reader to pause and dwell longer on their meditation of the images in front of them, is no less arresting:

Clustered chrysanthemums have twice opened, and tears of other days are shed;	叢菊兩開，他日淚

> The forlorn boat is tied up for good, and my   孤舟一繫，故園心
> thoughts go home.

We have here an example of "ambiguous parallelism," in which "a couplet whose two lines each have two grammatical structures, and the structures pair off two by two" (54). Then, in a couplet taken from the second poem in the same series, we have a different kind of poetic configuration, more commonly seen than the ambiguous parallelism above:

> It is true then that tears start when we hear the   聽猿實下三聲淚
> gibbon cry thrice;
> Useless my mission adrift on the raft which came by   奉使虛隨八月槎
> this eighth month.

This is a typical example of "pseudo-couplet," *pseudo* because—in the original, but lost in the translation—what is "paralleled" is the form, not the content. In other words, this is "a couplet whose two lines are grammatically parallel at the level of words, compounds, and phrases, but not at the level of deep structure" (55). This will become clear once we set the "meaning" right:

> 聽猿三聲實下淚
> 奉使虛隨八月槎

The parallelism is lost, and the reader is allured to turn the "correct" word order in the initial line back to its "incorrect" form so as to enjoy the aesthetic effect of the desirable parallel structure. The desirable communications on different planes are thus realized between the poet's choice and the reader's appreciation, between message and grammar, and between superficial structure and deep structure, amid the welcome noises of "variety, dissonance, contrast."[26]

Kao and Mei are not satisfied with merely revealing how the ambiguous and the pseudoparallel work but also want to explain in plain language many *why*s behind the functions of these two devices of poetic rhetoric. First, "it is the couplet as a structural unit that provides the natural environment in which ambiguity and pseudo-parallelism flourish." The evolution of the couplet structure, in turn, is affected by an increasing tendency in the development of the recent style poetry "to dispense with grammatical particles in exchange for economy of expression" (55). The driving factors behind this tendency can trace to the unique properties of Chinese as a noninflectional analytical language.

On the concluding page of their exercise, Kao and Mei acknowledge unapologetically that nothing they say is likely to alter the generally accepted opinion about Du Fu's art. However, they believe that the criteria and values presupposed on the study of Du Fu before their thesis are, "without exception, peripheral to the central concern of poetry." "This exercise in linguistic criticism," the two authors say with confidence, "has provided some evidence" for the achievement of Du Fu's verbal artifacts (73).

If the first product of Kao and Mei's research is a modest "exercise," then the ensuing projects of their joint effort are meant to be methodological steps toward a much more ambitious goal. For example, although their 1971 thesis states by its title, "Syntax, Diction, and Imagery in T'ang Poetry," that it is an investigation of the constituent elements of recent style poetry, it has a grand plan, inspired by Northrop Frye's insight: the study of the larger structural principles, the recurrent general stylistic features, or the "aesthetics," of recent style poetry. The roadmap for the study looks like this: "We will begin with the simplest linguistic unit capable of assuming a poetic function in itself, namely, nouns or noun phrases. Next come the attributive sentence (noun followed by stative verb), the intransitive sentence, the transitive sentence, etc."[27] The approach is decisively linguistic and can be carried out only through close reading. The seemingly meticulous—almost to the point of being trivial—examination of the "minimal components of a poem" (62) is conducted in a well-controlled manner in the context of the antithesis and interaction between "texture" and syntax. By *texture* Kao and Mei mean "the local interaction of words—once the eminent domain of Empsonian criticism" (61). The language used in recent style poetry is already weak in syntax. In addition, the linguistic and prosodic features such as the natural pause after every disyllabic phrase at the beginning of a five-syllable or seven-syllable line, the independence of each verse line, and the autonomy of the parallel couplet unit in recent style poetry also conspire to impede the forward-moving syntactic drive (63–64). "When syntax is weak, textural relations abound"; hence, "ambiguity is the norm instead of the exception" in recent style poetry (91). Keeping this in mind, the authors subject to scrutiny a series of poetic functions of Chinese language in recent style poetry at the level of words and sentences. At one end of this series, the convenient juxtaposition of nouns, the "simplest linguistic unit capable of assuming a poetic function in itself," is explained as the result of the "discontinuity" of verse lines caused by their "having too little grammar" (64). At the other end, the reason for the following fact becomes self-evident: the unifying syntax, typically absent in the middle section of a poem, is often expected in the concluding couplet, where—and when—a discursive conclusion is needed. The discussion of the poetic functions thus proceeds along the related axes in the highly regulated discourse of recent style poetry: the imagistic language versus the propositional language, the discontinuous versus the continuous, the objective versus the egocentric, the sensory awareness versus intellectual understanding, the spatial versus the temporal, and so forth (59).

The approach Kao and Mei adopt is not in everyone's favor. One of the faults found by its detractors is its alleged confirmation bias. As Stanley Fish puts it, "I found that in the practice of stylisticians of whatever school that relationship [between description and interpretation] was always arbitrary, less a matter of something demonstrated than of something assumed before the fact or imposed after it."[28] Kao and Mei's practice is free from the blame. Although the two authors customarily declare that they always have their interpretive intuition verified by the views of traditional commentators, and that the task of their linguistic inquiry "is simply that of pinpointing" the consensus of those commentators,[29] they have no need to make their analysis fit conclusions preconceived or already known. Two examples can be used to illustrate this. The first is Kao and Mei's revelation of the "characteristic copresence of concreteness in sensory impression and abstractness in reference in recent style poetry" (94), due to the well-known facts that simple images in Tang poetry have a strong orientation toward qualities instead of specific things, and that recent style poetry as a whole might impress one as being "pervaded by the dreamy abstractness, the suffused vagueness" (83), which W. K. Wimsatt discusses in his *Verbal Icon*.[30] Notwithstanding, by combing through numerous examples, Kao and Mei notice that simple images in recent style poetry has a way—"through its plenum of quality-evoking words" (94)—to create a different kind of concreteness. Concreteness in "sensory impression ('vivid')" is no less desirable than concreteness in "centrifugal reference ('specific')" (94). The two authors are not dismayed to find that their finding "may be regarded as a significant counter example to the Imagist theory of image making" (94).

The second example comes from their study of the "dynamic image" in Tang poetry. Thanks to the Chinese worldview, Chinese art criticism always holds in high regard the keen awareness of the dynamic vital process in nature. As a result, a dynamic image can be understood as a static image "coming alive," and not merely one of active transference of power through the agent-action-object causative relationship. Because of this, certain rules regulating the "universal" grammar are challenged by the uniqueness of Chinese language. To discuss the "dynamic images," Kao and Mei found that they had to do something not required of a student of European language and literature: come up with "a typology of Chinese verbs and their varying degrees of dynamism" (98). The first thorny issue they address is to clarify the meaning of a misnomer *static verb*, which refers not only to the copula *shi* 是 but also to adjectives playing the role of predicate. A better way to solve the problem, they say, might be to replace the label *static verbs* with "static verbs and the static aspect of other verbs" (98).

Then there are "verbs of perception and cognition" (99) or "superfluous verbs" (100), such as *see* (*jian* 見) or *know* (*zhi* 知), which "do not present an additional fact but serve to emphasize the facts already presented" (100).

The significance of Kao and Mei's practice cannot be overemphasized. What they do—without claiming so—is to upset the system of classification of parts of speech, a more or less "foreign" system imposed on Chinese language. On the surface, they seem to be trying to change the size label on a procrustean bed, but actually they are putting the old label on a new bed they create. In their study, the poetic function of "dynamism words" are examined more in the "vital processes happening in nature and dynamic interconnection between individual agents" (96) than merely in the process of action. This way, words denoting posture, location, connection, simile making, changes in time and place, and so on, all have active roles to play in the making of dynamic images (100–101, 108–9). So do various stylistic choices and rhetorical devices like the manipulation of "word classes," novel observation, the creation of similarity and contrast, inversion, resultative complements, and personification (103–14, 116–18). Kao and Mei demonstrate that dynamism is not only created through analytical syntax but very much also generated from the texture of interword relationships.

Having finished their investigation of the basic constituent elements at the level of words and sentences, which serve as artistic materials of recent style poetry, Kao and Mei go a step further and focus their attention on how these constituent parts work together to generate meaning at a higher level. The result of this study is found in their 1978 thesis "Meaning, Metaphor, and Allusion in T'ang Poetry."

The critical theory they adopt for this study is the principle of equivalence put forward by Roman Jakobson. The origin of the theory traces to Ferdinand de Saussure's thoughts on the syntagmatic and the paradigmatic relations in his semiotic system, but it is Jakobson who raises the possibility of applying the theory to the study of literature:

> What is the indispensable feature inherent in any piece of poetry? To answer this question we must recall the two basic modes of arrangement used in verbal behavior, selection and combination. . . . The selection is produced on the base of equivalence, similarity and dissimilarity, synonymity and antonymity, while the combination, the build up of the sequence, is based on contiguity. *The poetic function projects the principle of equivalence from the axis of selection into the axis of combination.* Equivalence is promoted to the constitutive device of the sequence.[31]

The poetic functions Jakobson finds suitable for his approach are formal elements, especially those represented in prosody. Kao and Mei, however, believe that they can apply the theory to the study of meaning. What comes to mind is the equivalent relationship between the vehicle and tenor in a metaphor and the pairing of a contemporary topic and a past event in a typical case of allusion. For example, in the following couplet,

Floating cloud, wanderer's mind;	浮雲遊子意
Setting sun, old friend's feeling,	落日故人情

the wanderer's mind is compared to the floating cloud, and an old friend's feeling to the setting sun. The metaphors conjure up in the poet's mind paradigms of equivalence along a vertical axis, the axis of selection. When the poetic thoughts are realized in language, it necessarily has to express itself in the sequence of a time flow, along the horizontal axis of syntagms, but—very important—*without* grammatical "connectors." No poetry in any other language can "materialize" Jakobson's theoretical module in such a perfect manner! Thanks to the lack of restrictive syntax in Chinese, the "vertical" equivalence relation can be kept almost intact in the "horizontal" line of combination, in which the component parts are "loosely," if not often ungrammatically, connected.

The similar projection of Jakobson's "principle of equivalence from the axis of selection into the axis of combination" can also be seen in allusion of various types, abundant in recent style poetry. Take the following example:

If Winged General of Dragon City were present,	但使龍城飛將在
He would not let the Hunnish cavalry cross Mount Yin.	不教胡馬度陰山

"The implication is that the present dynasty, lacking a general of Li Kuang's stature, has a border defense that is altogether too porous"; conversely, say Kao and Mei, "the further implication is that although the present is unlike the past in military prowess, it would be comforting if the two were more alike."[32] Being a linguistic principle, "equivalence" places within its jurisdiction both the similarity and its opposite, the dissimilarity.

Again, Kao and Mei do not just describe how but also try to explain why Western theories work in the study of Chinese poetry. Through a close reading of numerous examples, they find that two unique features of the "refined" language used in recent style poetry that account for the characteristics of its texture and other poetic elements in local organization, and also contribute to the flourish of the equivalence relation in Tang poetry. The first of these is the quality-oriented nature of nouns and noun images (295, 298, and 346), which favors the equivalence relationship between members in the same or similar "quality categories" (316). The other feature has to do with syntax: "Since Chinese is a language weak in syntax to begin with, and syntax is further weakened by various conventions in Recent Style poetry, the result is that the metaphoric relation dominates over its complement, the analytic relation" (287). And "metaphoric relation" is nothing but another name for *equivalence*. It is not surprising that "Jakobson's theory can account for the facts of Recent Style poetry with greater ease than for those of Western poetry" (287). At the same time Kao and Mei also conclude that, though remarkably powerful in accounting for the phonological aspects, the principle of equivalence would not work well, or at all, in the study of grammatical and referential meaning in Western poetry, almost for the same type of reasons that it works in recent style poetry (347).

Taking an overview of Kao and Mei's linguistic investigation of the aesthetics of recent style poetry, one will notice an organizing methodological pattern that allows examinations of various poetic functions at different levels and from different angles to inform and interpret one another. The mainstay of this pattern is a cross-reference system of the paradigmatic versus the syntagmatic. We have seen how the local organization of words and sentences are affected by the tension between texture and syntax ("texture is the inverse of syntax!"),[33] how new meanings are generated through the projection of metaphorical relation from the axis of selection into the axis of combination, and how recent style poetry as a tightly regulated verbal structure become the site for the "war of words"[34] between imagistic language and propositional language, between the searching for "the centripetal relations among words"[35] and the drive for centrifugal reference to the specific time, place, and experience. Indeed, even the methodological choice of Kao and Mei's linguistic probe itself should be understood in the framework of the complementary relationship between the metaphorical and the analytical. The two authors are fully aware that their critical mode "is alien to the Chinese tradition," and yet they can take the hint dropped by traditional critics—such as Liu Xie's 劉勰 (ca. 465–ca. 532) poetic "awareness" of certain "premises rooted in the Chinese tradition"—and "provide the structural analysis of the working of those premises" (323–24).

This organizing methodological pattern later allows Kao a vantage holistic point of view, from which he can examine the poetic functions in Chinese poetry in the light of his reconsideration of the most distinctive features of Chinese language. The convenient binary division between spoken and written languages, Kao observes, is inadequate for a true understanding of Chinese language. He therefore proposes an audacious and probably controversial concept: the antithesis between a "character language" (*wenzi yuyan* 文字語言 or *ziyu* 字語) and a "voice language" (*shengchuan yuyan* 聲傳語言 or *shengyu* 聲語).[36]

Neither depends on the other to exist. As an ontological entity, character language is not to be confused with a written language, defined as the written form of a language. The relationship between the character language and the voice language reminds one of the antithesis between the paradigmatic and the syntagmatic.

With this insight, Kao turns his attention to the *ci*, a poetic form originating from the voice language tradition, "voiced" in the form of singing and performing by folk musicians and entertainers in their outward expression of experiences with references to specific times and places.[37] Perhaps not coincidentally, the blossoming of this melodiously "fluid" (*xuanlü* 旋律 in Kao's term) (8) poetic form coincided with the heyday of recent style poetry, whose highly regulated physical structure (*tuwei* 圖位) (8) was created—in writing, by literati members—to accommodate their inward-looking reflection of personal sentiments at a focused lyrical moment (10). Just as happened several centuries before, when the Han dynasty literati appropriated the *yuefu* 樂府 folk songs, literati poets from Tang through Song, who became fascinated by the expressive power of the *ci* form, tried their hand at it. Eventually they transformed the originally musical art form into a refined verbal structure strongly informed with the aesthetics of the character language. On the basis of his comparison between the formal features of the folk *ci* and the literati *ci*, and the study of the connections between the poetic functions of the languages of literati *ci* and that of the literati recent style poetry, Kao concludes without hesitation that the formation of the literati *ci* is not the result of "natural" historical evolution but the product of the joint efforts of literati poets in their conscious pursuit for a new aesthetics.[38] What is most noteworthy in the long process of this genre transformation, Kao says, is the evolution of the *xiaoling* 小令 (small *ci*) form, a "transitional" genre between the early song lyrics of the voice language folk tradition on one end and the character language literati *ci* on the other. Through a close reading of the structure of *xiaoling* in various types, Kao is able to trace how the rhythmic temporal flow of sound (*jielü* 節律) and the spatial structure of character (*tushi* 圖式) compete with and intermingle into each other, and how the "horizontal forward drive of voice language" and the "vertical juxtaposition of character language" merge and join forces.[39]

Comparing the structure of *ci* against that of recent style poetry, Kao points out the most fundamental difference between the two. The important role played by couplets in recent style poetry is taken over in *ci* by "concentricity" (*tongxin jiegou* 同心結構), a term Kao creates to refer to the basic structural unit that connects neighboring lines (16). Kao finds that while Jakobson's model of coordination versus equivalence can well describe the relationship between the two lines forming a couplet, it is not sufficient to account for the interline relations in a concentricity (15–16). What connects the lines in a concentricity is a common thematic center or focus (*zhongxin* 中心 or *jiaodian* 焦點), which can be a word, an image, or just an idea, around which each line in the unit can describe or narrate "from a different angle or at a different point in time, involving various kinds of mental activities in addition to sense-impressions" (16). The integral structure of a *ci* poem consisting of several units of concentricity can be called one of "stratification" (16). This structure of concentricity/stratification works at more than one level. While each unit has its own center, all the units within a *ci* poem share a common center at a higher level. In this way, the whole poem is sustained by an "incremental structure" (18–19).

The "common center," therefore, functions as a "topic" (19), and the poetic acts performed by the lines in a concentricity unit serve as comments on the topic. What Kao is doing here is explicating the most distinctive formal feature of *ci*, using the "topic + comment" construction, one of the most distinctive linguistic features of Chinese language. The poetic function of this linguistic structure has attracted the attention of Kao and Mei in their study of the language of Tang poetry at the level of local organization, especially the noun + noun configuration.[40] Now Kao begins to see the potential of its application beyond the examination of syntax. Characteristic of the "character language," topic + comment construction is actually a mode of thinking in which a sense impression generated in the mind is perceived and appreciated repeatedly from different angles, receiving attention that keeps dwelling on, lingering on, and turning back to it (*yichang santan* 一唱三嘆).[41] It is a reflective mode in the literal sense of the word.

What we have here is a tell-tale example of the linguistics-based literary study at its best. First, the function of topic + comment construction (in opposition to the "normal" subject + predicate construction) as a unique feature of Chinese language catches the attention of linguists.[42] When Kao and Mei notice in recent style poetry the unusually abundant presence of this construction, they found it apt to use the paratactic feature of this construction to account for the three characteristic stylistic features of recent style poetry at the syntactic level: discontinuity, dislocation, and ambiguity.[43] Then, in his investigation of the development of the *ci* genre, Kao becomes aware of the analogous relationship between this linguistic construction and the poetic structure of a song lyric.

The tapping of the rich potential of the topic + comment construction does not stop here. More exciting results are seen in the use of this originally syntactic construction as a theoretical framework in the study of classical Chinese poetry. It is here that Zong-qi Cai's holistic structural investigation of the aesthetics of

Chinese poetry claims our attention. In Cai's practice, the topic + comment construction not only serves as an effective tool but also functions as the framework of a self-contained critical approach or, so to speak, becomes the structure of his critical vision.

Focusing on its poetic function, Cai defines the topic + comment construction as follows:

> Instead of an agent responsible for some action or condition, *topic* refers to an object, scene, or event "passively" observed. *Comment* refers to an implied observer's response to the topic. As a rule, this response tells us more about the observer's state of mind than about the topic. The absence of a predicative verb between the topic and the comment aptly underscores their relationship as noncontiguous, nontemporal, and noncausal. The topic and comment are yoked together by the implied observer through analogy or association, in a moment of intense observation. The result is quite different from that of a temporal cognitive process. Topic + comment tends to reactivate the vortex of images and feelings, previously experienced by the observer, in the mind of the reader.[44]

The definition itself deserves a close reading. The first thing to take note is the reciprocal relationship between the topic and the comment. The topic should be attractive enough to generate meaning by inviting observation. The comment, touched off by the topic, should react toward the topic. According to Jakobson's linguistic module thinking, the two are metaphorically "equivalent" to each other. The fact that the two are copresent "in a moment of intense observation" implies that the relationship between them is simultaneous, spontaneous, and synecdochical (as the observed's and the observer's feelings and attitudes intermingle and become parts of each other). Their relationship along the paradigmatic axis is also confirmed in negative terms. There is no predicative verb to yoke the two together, and so their relationship is "noncontiguous, nontemporal, and noncausal"—in short, not syntagmatic. All the above instantly calls forth a spatial coordinate system of what Jakobson describes as the projection of "the principle of equivalence from the axis of selection into the axis of combination" mentioned earlier in this essay.[45] The poetic effect which the topic + comment construction is capable of evoking is captured in the well-chosen image "vortex of images and feelings," which vivifies the force of suction from the direction of the topic to be commented, and the rapid centripetal inward-looking force of the comment toward the topic.

Verse lines in the topic + comment formation are abundant in the *Shijing* 詩經 (The Book of Poetry). Cai uses the first two lines from "The Peach Tree Tender" to illustrate this construction:

Tender but sturdy, the peach tree,   桃之夭夭
Bright and lustrous, its flowers.   灼灼其華

[Mao no. 6, *Mao shi zhengyi* 1:279]

The peach tree and its flowers are the topics, and the two reduplicatives *yaoyao* 夭夭 and *zhuozhuo* 灼灼, with their radiating thriving liveliness, are pleasantly sensuous responses, or comments, touched off in the mind of the implied observer. The external objects and the inward responses are juxtaposed without any grammatical connective.

Thanks to its "extraordinary evocative power,"[46] the topic + comment construction not only works with *shijing* verse lines but also continuously plays its special role in the evolution of verse line patterns as various poetic genres transform and develop in later ages. Its operative machinery, so primordially detectable in the *shijing* verses, becomes more and more complicated and sophisticated.

The predominant line pattern in *Shijing* is a tetrasyllabic verse consisting of two disyllabic segments. Later, when the pentasyllabic pattern comes onstage with an additional syllable, the rules of the poetic game are fundamentally changed. Loathing its loneliness, the extra syllable tends to form alliances with existing syllabic combinations in the line, thus destabilizing the intraline balance of power. The unstable loyalty of the monosyllable to other members in the line and the multiple possibilities of permutation of syllable segments further complicate the situation. One of the consequences is the emanation of new sentence constructions capable of generating a plenum of new meanings.

Fascinated by the aesthetic effects thus generated, Cai focuses his attention on the formation of the new verse line patterns. What he discovers in the "unsurpassable" (*dengfeng zaoji* 登峰造極) artifice in an example like the following is "simply shocking" (*rangren zhenhan buyi* 讓人震撼不已):[47]

[In] the morning wind I cherish my bitter heart;   晨風懷苦心
[Amid] the sound of crickets I lament the shortness   蟋蟀傷局促
    of time.

The translation reads the couplet in the surface context of the poem. Since the two prepositions ("in" and "amid") are understood in the original, the "morning wind" and the "crickets" are not qualified. That is to say, the role they play in the two sentences becomes uncertain. Because of this, the morning wind and the crickets seem to presume the role of the subject and vicariously feel what the persona feels in his imagination:

| The morning wind cherishes a bitter heart; | 晨風懷苦心 |
| The sound of crickets laments the shortness of time. | 蟋蟀傷局促 |

An example of the pathetic fallacy, this interpretation is possible only when we read "morning wind" (*chenfeng* 晨风) and "crickets" (*xishuai* 蟋蟀) metaphorically (for, literally, the wind does not cherish feelings and crickets cannot lament). Cai therefore calls it "ambiguous reading," or *xuyi* 虛義. Just as we marvel at the poetic effect of this somewhat equivocal reading, we are surprised by the revelation that "morning wind" and "crickets" happen to be titles of two poems in the *Book of Poetry*.[48] One of them does "cherish a bitter heart," and the other "laments the shortness of time." The syntax of the verbatim reading—which Cai dubs *shiyi* 實義—of this *shijing*-related subtext,

| "Morning Wind" cherishes a bitter heart; | 《晨風》懷苦心 |
| "Crickets" laments the shortness of time | 《蟋蟀》傷局促 |

matches the grammatical structure of the *xuyi* reading above. As the wind and the crickets from the earlier texts urge a more *xuyi* reading of the present text, the "exact meaning" of these two seemingly simple lines becomes indeterminate.[49] Indeed, if we find it difficult to fit this example into one or more of William Empson's seven types of ambiguity,[50] he probably would create an eighth type to accommodate it. For uninitiated readers, the *xuyi* reading is good enough to enjoy the poetic beauty of the couplet, but for those who have ideas about its *shijing* connection, they can bring their knowledge into their more intense appreciation of poetic art.

Cai might not be the first to notice the *Shijing* origin of the "morning wind" and the "crickets," but he is the first to detect, and to explain in plain language, the subtle interaction between the *shiyi* and the *xuyi* illustrated above. In the *shiyi* reading, one sees a logical and affirmative statement in the subject + predicate format, whereas in the *xuyi* reading the relationship between the imagined subjects and their predicates is ambiguous. The morning wind and crickets function not really as agents of actions but, rather, as outside stimuli that induce the persona's feelings.

Cai's analysis of the overlapping of *xuyi* and *shiyi* here is about the intense interaction between metaphorical language and analytical language, between the analogical-associative relation and the temporal-logical relation, that is, between the topic + comment and subject + predicate constructions. Without using the terms, Cai demonstrates in his illustration that, in the best examples from the "Nineteen Ancient Style poems," even in sentences apparently belonging to the "simple subject + predicate" category,[51] one can still sense the verve of the topic + comment syntactic structure so prevalent in the *Shijing* verse lines.

An even more illuminating discovery by Cai, however, is the poetic function of the topic + comment versus subject + predicate framework at the level of stanza and the overall organization of a poem. To understand how this works, we can take another look at the two *Shijing* lines examined earlier, this time in the stanza where they are embedded:

Tender but sturdy, the peach tree,	桃之夭夭
Bright and lustrous, its flowers.	灼灼其華
This girl is going to marry,	之子于歸
Good for her house and family.	宜其室家

In contrast with the first two lines, the next two are in the subject + predicate form, with line 3 a declarative announcement and line 4 a subjective judgment. While the topic + comment at the top of the stanza displays a contemplative representation of scenery, the subject + predicate at the bottom expresses subjective thoughts and feelings.[52] There seems no logical connection between the two. The flourishing peach tree has nothing to do with the coming marriage of the young lady; they are just "yoked together." The relationship between the two parts in the stanza is "noncontiguous, nontemporal, and noncausal."

If we take a closer look, however, we can see that the first two lines present a mini drama, in which the implied observer is excited by a peach tree in full blossom. For the persona, who is lost in a moment of observation, some analogy between a productive tree and a young lady going to be married does not seem totally unlikely. In this way, the topic + comment construction on top serves as the topic, or an outside stimulus, which prompts an associative response, or a comment, represented in the subject + predicate construction at the bottom. Suddenly this sounds like a discussion of *bixing* 比興 (literally "compare and evoke"), a perennial topic of debate in the study of Chinese poetry.

And not just sounds like—it is: "We may contend that a topic + comment constitutes an analogical-associative framework" (563). Through a close syntactic analysis of the analogical-associative mode of representation, Cai pins down the elusive mechanism of *bixing*. The replacement of the translation of the term "comparing and evoking" by that of "analogical-associative mode" is not a small change (563). It marks a shift from the appreciative to the descriptive, from the metaphorical to the analytical.

The word *mode* in the new translation of *bixing* also tells us that Cai does not limit the use of the analogical-associative framework to the examination of syntactic or stanzaic choice—he takes it more for a mode of thinking. For example, when we see a poem consisting of a juxtaposition of a topic in the form of a stanza (or stanzas) and a comment in stanzaic form, we have a poem in the binary topic + comment structure. A good example Cai uses to illustrate this structure is "The Gourd Has Bitter Leaves" (*Bao you kuye* 匏有苦葉; Mao no. 34, *Mao shi zhengyi* 1:302–3), a poem "marked by neatly balanced external depiction and inner reflection, with a transitional couplet (lines 9–10) placed in between" (565). The scaffold of the form mirrors the structure of the lyrical act, with the topic + comment construction extended to the compositional organization of the poem.

In his further exploration, Cai finds that, because of its effectiveness in the organization of depictions of external scenes and expressions of inner feelings, the binary poetic structure based on the topic + comment configuration "became the dominant structure in pentasyllabic poetry during the Han and the Six dynasties."[53] The structure is found in fourteen of the "Nineteen Ancient-Style poems."[54] Later, the structure was codified in recent style poetry, the most typical structure of which "features nature description in the first two couplets and emotional expression in the other two couplets."[55] The capacity of the binary formation can be expanded in various ways, such as arranging a "parallel, yet progressive clusters of the scene-emotion combination," resulting in an "aggregated" formation. Together with the linear structure, the binary and the aggregated formations "have become archetypal structures of Chinese poetry, with numerous variants developed in different genres after the *Book of Poetry*."[56]

In this way, Cai develops a self-consistent theory on poetic structure, which germinates from, and take as its base, the topic + comment principle. The theory will bring fundamental changes to the methodology in the study of generic structural features of poetic genres, the interconnections among different genre structures, the intragenre transformation and evolution of poetic forms, and so forth.

Productive results brought about by the application of Cai's theory have already been seen in his own research. We can see this in two examples. The first shows how the creative use of the topic + comment principle in the close reading of an individual song lyric contributes to the study of the organizational functions of a key generic element of *ci* poetry. This is a case of moving from the small to the big, and from the local to the whole, or, to use a fancy phrase for a particular reason that will come up later, from the concrete to the universal.

The variety of archetypal structures mentioned in Cai's theory are not the products of certain manipulation of the topic + comment and the subject + predicate modes by means of mechanical stacking and attaching. The persistent search for the most appropriate poetic forms for variegated lyrical expressions always involves a thoughtful matching, coordination, and adjustment of structural components of different shapes and tones. To exemplify the working of this intense interaction between the thematic demand and the formal necessity from converse directions, Cai dissects as follows the structure of Liu Yong's song lyric "Facing Swishing and Splashing Evening Shower Sprinkling from the Sky over River" in the tune of "Basheng ganzhou" 八聲甘州：

對	⇒	瀟瀟、暮雨灑江天，一番洗清秋。
漸	⇒	霜風悽慘，關河冷落，殘照當樓。
是處	⇒	紅衰翠減，苒苒物華休。唯有長江水，無語東流。
不忍	⇒	登高臨遠，
望	⇒	故鄉渺邈，歸思難收。
嘆	⇒	年來蹤跡，何事苦淹留。
想佳人、	⇒	妝樓顒望，
誤幾回、	⇒	天際識歸舟。
爭知我，	⇒	倚闌杆處，正恁凝愁。

Horizontally, each lead word at the beginning of a line and the lyrical acts it leads form a topic + comment relationship, representing one step in the persona's reflective experience at a specific lyrical moment. Vertically, the series of lead words shows a progression of the persona's thoughts and feelings. What Cai calls "the interlocking aggregate structure"[57] is almost graphically mapped—*almost* because, while the paradigmatic relationship between different layers of experience is clearly visible, the difficulties in typesetting (on the part of this essay) do not allow the imaging of the syntagmatic relationship between the lead words— a step-by-step linear poetic process along the axis of time, which should look like this:

對 ⇒ 漸 ⇒ 是處 ⇒ 不忍 ⇒ 望 ⇒ 嘆 ⇒ 想佳人 ⇒ 誤幾回 ⇒ 爭知我

The concentricity/stratification structure Yu-kung Kao conceives of, mentioned above, finds a perfect match in Cai's elucidation and analysis here.[58] The ingenuity of this poetic form, Cai explains further, does not stop here. This "interlocking aggregate" structural design allows the lyrical act to occur on two planes. On one plane the persona loses himself in the contemplation of a poetic "inscape." On the other plane, he observes and traces the twists and turns of the lyrical experience from the viewpoint of an "other," following the hints dropped by the series of leading words, hence the "double subjectivity" structure not seen before or later in the Chinese poetic tradition.[59]

It is close reading that enables Cai to make his insightful discoveries of this kind. Close reading is not just reading closely. As John Crowe Ransom says, close reading is the methodology of a "systematic" study.[60] Cai's close reading of Liu Yong's art is not meant to be an exegesis of a particular poem. By applying the topic + comment versus subject + predicate framework to his examination of lead words, Cai advances onto a higher level the study of the poetic functions of a key element in the development of the *ci* genre. The specimen to dissect is small, but the holistic vision of his linguistic investigation is always at the back of mind.

The second example shows how the holistic perspective provided by the same framework helps explain the cause and effect behind the intragenre transformation of poetic forms. So, this is a case of using the whole and the overall to reveal the small and the local, or going from the total to the individuals. "If we trace the development from Han *yuefu* to Late Tang regulated verse, or from the early short *ci* to the late long *ci* poems on objects," Cai observes, "we can perceive a clear intra-generic trajectory from orality to literacy."[61] Then, history can repeat itself time and again, and sometimes in a reverse manner: "Interestingly, an obsessive pursuit of textuality (diction) and intertextuality (allusion) often marks the last great glory of a thoroughly 'literatified' [*wenren hua* 文人化] genre and heralds the rapid ascendancy of a new genre of oral folk origin."[62] The drive behind these two trends from different directions can be explained in light of the interaction epitomized in the topic + comment versus subject + predicate framework. As the stylistic features of the oral tradition are characteristic of the subject + predicate relationship, and those of the written tend to be topic + comment oriented, it is only fitting to think of the "process of imitating, and eventually transforming an oral tradition into a purely literary one by the literati"[63] as the aesthetics of the paradigmatic winning over that of the syntagmatic. Cai's earlier study of the evolution of the pentasyllabic poetry, together with his "afterthoughts" in later works along the same line, is a good example of this.[64] His "aesthetics-conscious" perspective is also notable in the idea of *shibian* 詩變 (the change of poetic form), which defines his study of the *xiaoling*'s evolution from recent style poetry as the literati's quest for a new poetic form.[65] In fact, the overall editorial scheme for Cai's landmark anthology *How to Read Chinese Poetry* is informed with his reflective considerations on intragenre development.

Cai's approach to his research target, therefore, is no less enlightening than his findings. Enthralled by the poetic effects produced by the intricate play between the topic + comment and the subject + predicate modes, traditional critics and commentators have made numerous comments on it. At their best, these comments and observations seem to come close to a certain understanding of the workings of its poetic function yet still fell short of pinning that down in specific language. Most of the commentators can only be content with their ineffable impressionistic responses, or expressed amazement. The following comment on the syntax, and perhaps also on its impact on the structural organization, of the Nineteen Ancient Style poetry is an interesting example: "There are no syntactic rules in the 'Nineteen Ancient-Style Poems,' some people say. That is not true. Those poems surely follow syntactic rules of their own, but leave no signs of their distinctions for us to trace."[66] The rules are there and yet are not there. The comment does not seem to be helpful. The next comment, by Fang Dongshu 方東樹 (1772–1851), seems to have noticed some "signs of their distinctions," which the first commentator fails to see:

> When these ancient people wrote, if there was a forward movement there must have been a backward movement; if there was a thrust downward there must be a thrust back upward. To soar like a startled wild goose or to wind along like a swimming dragon: this is the way we follow their rules of composition and the way we seek to understand their meaning. Having grasped this point, we will understand why these poems are thought to be "seamless like clothes made by heaven."[67]

Cai obviously likes the comment, as he offers this generous compliment: "In this single passage Fang sums up all I have said about the two aesthetic movements."[68] But does Fang? He certainly describes in imagistic language the impression made on him by the poetic beauty in question. And yet, "unexplained beauty arouses an irritation in me"[69]—we share this typical New Criticism complaint from William Empson and would like to have that unexplained beauty explained. A comparison is in order between Fang's remarks and what Cai says about the two aesthetic movements.

Credit should go to Fang for his intuitive feeling of the interaction between two forces in the organization of a poem, the "forward movement" and the "backward movement." Unable to grasp the intangible movement of the forces represented in language, however, he has to resort to comparison. What he can see in the nearly visible kinesthetic—hence more or less tangible—movement of a calligrapher's brush seems comparable to the intangible feeling he experiences in his psyche when reading a poem. Exactly what the shape of that feeling is depends totally on Fang's readers' acumen in their understanding of the movements of some "startled wild goose" or that "swimming dragon."

Reading Cai's comment on the same subject side by side with Fang's, one wonders whether the two critics use the same language:

> In the "Nineteen Ancient-Style Poems" both the binary structure and the multilateral texture are born of the constant movement back and forth between the outer and inner world in the poets' process of imagining. In turn, they activate similar movements of the temporal and spatial imagination of the silent reader. In the mind of poet

and reader alike, the intensification of these two aesthetic movements will lead to a point where the boundary between the outward and the inward dissolves and a timeless and spaceless poetic vision emerges.[70]

The language is unadorned, with words trimmed down to the very essence. The only word that looks beautiful is *aesthetic*, but that is exactly what the passage is about. Of course, to fully understand what Cai means, it takes a good understanding of the binary structure, together with its underlining framework of topic + comment versus subject + predicate construction discussed above. All this, in turn, is sustained by Cai's close reading of various linguistic elements of poetic language, exemplified in his meticulous categorization and tabulation of various types of syllables and syllabic units, their combinations, syntactic types, prosodic patterns, organizational structures, and so forth.

As Cai continues, he does need some help from the figurative language—a "common phrase"—to describe what Fang refers to as the seamless "clothes made by heaven": "While this aesthetic principle was established with the 'Nineteen Ancient-Style Poems,' it became the ultimate matrix for all the intricate rules of temporal progression and spatial correspondence—in rhythm, meter, grammatical category, and semantic meaning—in T'ang regulated verse. Later this aesthetic principle is often spoken of with this common phrase 'moving in a circle; going and returning' [*hsünhuan wang-fu* 循環往復], and is observed as a golden rule for writing and reading Chinese poetry."[71] Recalling Yu-kung Kao's dialectic attitude toward what Jakobson labels as the "subjective, censorious verdict" based on "a critic's own tastes and opinions on creative literature,"[72] we can see that Fang and other traditional commentators belong to the camp of the critic. According to Kao, appreciative criticism by these literary critics is creative in nature.[73] Endowed with a sharp insight and equipped with a logic of its own, the traditional metaphorical criticism serves as a rich resource anyway. To draw on this resource, one needs "to analyze objectively the subjective critical experiences."[74] Cai does just that: going over his research, one cannot but marvel at the sincere respect he pays to the subjective traditional criticism. However, in his negotiation with the wisdom of traditional critics, Cai never satisfies with repeating or paraphrasing them, or simply translating their language from the classical into the vernacular, or from the Chinese into the foreign, passing the ineffability of their intuitive ideas to his own readers. His dialogue with Fang Dongshu seen above is but one of many good examples. When he explains how "Fang sums up all I have said," he is using his plain analytical language to lay bare what Fang can feel only metaphorically. Actually, his innovative interpretation of *bixing*, discussed earlier, is another product of an intense dialogue with some of the best critical minds in Chinese literary history, such as Liu Xie, Zhong Rong 鍾嶸 (ca. 469–518), Kong Yingda 孔穎達 (574–648), and Zhu Xi 朱熹 (1130–1200).[75]

If the metaphorical understanding of traditional critics smacks of—to stretch the use of now the most familiar module used in this survey—the topic + comment principle, then Cai's analytical discourse is a cool-minded demonstration of the subject + predicate, which is specific, down to earth, and nearly "scientific." The complementary relationship between the two types of mindset and the two modes of discourse reminds us of the clever remarks on one—or more than one—key concept left for us by Wimsatt, one of the most outspoken New Critics, while he ponders over the meaning of the paradox of "the concrete universal":

> A modern literary critic, John Crowe Ransom, speaks of the argument of a poem (the universal) and a local texture or tissue of concrete irrelevance. Another literary critic, Allen Tate, manipulating the logical terms "extension" and "intension," has arrived at the concept of "tension" in poetry. "Extension," as logicians use the word, is the range of individuals denoted by a term (denotation); "intension" is the total of qualities connoted (connotation). In the ordinary or logical use of the terms, extension and intension are of inverse relationship—the wider the one, the shallower the other. A poem, says Tate, as I interpret him, is a verbal structure which in some peculiar way has both a wide extension and a deep intension.[76]

Judging from the "figure of sounds" in Wimsatt's voice, we can tell that, no matter how "peculiar" the way the poetic functions function, the ideal poetry he envisages can live only in a poet's wishful dream—unless he composes in Chinese, and unless he uses not only voice language but also character language, a verbal structure in the physical-material sense of the term. As to the antithesis between denotation and connotation, or between the individuals and the total, Yu-kung Kao has already proved that the relationship between the two does not always need to be inverse. An image in Chinese poetry can at the same time be vividly specific and abstract, or concrete and universal (a good time to recall the function of poetic clichés in the song lyric). And now, Zong-qi Cai has just demonstrated that the theoretical framework of the topic + comment paradigm versus the subject + predicate syntagm can be projected from the poetic texts to the critics who close-read the poems—just as Stephen Owen shows at the beginning of this article how a learned narrator and an innocent yet curious novice reader can inform each other in an intense act of close reading. Maybe we should not feel surprised to see that, in the semantic field of Chinese, poets, texts and close readers are a perfect match, and the framework of the topic + comment plus the subject + predicate is omnipresent.

XINDA LIAN 連心達
Denison University
lian@denison.edu

Notes

1.   Barry, *Beginning Theory*, 5.
2.   English translation of Liu Yong's 柳永 (ca. 987–ca. 1053) "Gelianting" 隔簾聽 (Listening outside the Curtain) from Hightower, "Songwriter Liu Yung," 375.
3.   Richards, *Practical Criticism*, 13.
4.   Ibid., 182.
5.   Owen, "Meaning the Words," 30–35. Hereafter references to this work are given in parentheses in text.
6.   Liu, "Gelianting."
7.   Owen, "Anxiety of Global Influence," 30.
8.   Eliot, "Tradition and the Individual Talent," 9–10. "The business of the poet," says Eliot, "is not to find new emotions, but to use the ordinary ones and, in working them up into poetry, to express feelings which are not in actual emotions at all" (10).
9.   Frankel, "Fifteen Poems by Ts'ao Chih."
10.   At the 1958 University of Indiana conference on style in language, Jakobson said this at the conclusion of his now well-known closing statement: "All of us here, however, definitely realize that a linguist deaf to the poetic function of language and a literary scholar indifferent to linguistic problems and unconversant with linguistic methods are equally flagrant anachronisms" ("Linguistics and Poetics," 377).
11.   Kao and Mei, "Syntax," 90.
12.   Kao, "Aesthetics," 332.
13.   Ibid., 333–34.
14.   Kao ("Aesthetics," 332n1) states that he follows Owen's usage of the term aesthetic (in Owen's *Great Age of Chinese Poetry* [1981], 14). The Chinese equivalence of the term, *meidian* 美典, however, tells that it is a new concept Kao creates for his purpose.
15.   Jakobson, "Linguistics and Poetics," 353.
16.   Ibid., 356.
17.   Ibid., 351–52.
18.   Ibid., 352.
19.   Kao, "Wenxue yanjiu de lilun jichu," 17.
20.   Kao, "Aesthetics," 334.
21.   Mei and Kao, "Tu Fu's 'Autumn Meditations,'" 44.
22.   Ibid., 44–45. Du's obsession can be seen in the famous line "yu bu jingren sibuxiu 語不驚人死不休" in his "江上值水如海勢聊短述 (A Short Poem Written While River Water Is Surging like Ocean)" (*Quan Tang shi* 7:226.2443).
23.   Smith, "What Was 'Close Reading'?," 60.
24.   This term is from Hopkins, *Journals and Papers*, 289. In his 1958 closing speech, Jakobson quotes Hopkins to emphasize the importance of sound effect in poetry: "Gerard Manley Hopkins, an outstanding searcher in the science of poetic language, defined verse as 'speech wholly or partially repeating the same figure of sound'" ("Linguistics and Poetics," 358–59).

25. Mei and Kao, "Tu Fu's 'Autumn Meditation,'" 47. Hereafter references to this work are given in parentheses in text.

26. Commenting on the effects of pseudoparalellism, Kao and Mei state, "The pseudo-parallel couplet is quite common, largely because the language of Recent Style poetry enjoys a considerable measure of license in the domain of form classes and grammatical con-structions, and the effects it produces-variety, dissonance, contrast—are more likely to be drowned out in the context of other parallelisms present in the couplet" ("Tu Fu's 'Autumn Meditation,'" 56).

27. Kao and Mei, "Syntax," 91. Hereafter references to this work are given in parentheses in text.

28. Fish, "What Is Stylistics?," 129.

29. Mei and Kao, "Tu Fu's 'Autumn Meditations,'" 45.

30. Wimsatt, *Verbal Icon*, 138.

31. Jakobson, "Linguistics and Poetics," 358.

32. Kao and Mei, "Meaning, Metaphor, and Allusion," 293. Hereafter references to this work are given in parentheses in text.

33. Kao and Mei, "Syntax," 91.

34. Mei and Kao, "Tu Fu's 'Autumn Meditations,'" 66.

35. Kao and Mei, "Syntax," 90.

36. Kao, "Zhongguo yuyan," 181–83.

37. Kao, "Xiaoling," 10. Hereafter references to this work are given in parentheses in text.

38. Kao, "Citi zhi meidian," 286.

39. Kao, "Xiaoling," 20.

40. Kao and Mei, "Syntax," 69.

41. Kao, "Zhongguo yuyan," 197.

42. For details, see Cai, "Danyin hanzi yu hanshi shiti zhi neilianxing."

43. Kao and Mei, "Syntax," 66, 69.

44. Cai, "Sound over Ideograph," 556.

45. Jakobson, "Linguistics and Poetics," 358.

46. Cai, *Matrix*, 556.

47. Cai, "Zaoqi wuyanshi xintan," 29.

48. Poem 133, "Chenfeng" 晨風 (Morning Wind), and poem 115, "Xishuai" 蟋蟀 (Crickets).

49. Cai, "Zaoqi wuyanshi xintan," 28–29.

50. Empson, *Seven Types of Ambiguity*.

51. Ibid., 21–24.

52. Cai, *Matrix*, 556–57. Hereafter references to this work are given in parentheses in text.

53. Cai, "Sound over Ideograph," 565.

54. Cai, "Zaoqi wuyanshi xintan," 37; Cai, *Matrix*, 78–82.

55. Cai, "Sound over Ideograph," 565.

56. Ibid., 565–66.

57. Cai, "Lingzi yu manci jiezou," 90.

58. For details of Cai's discussion, see Cai, "Lingzi yu manci jiezou," 84–85.

59. Ibid.

60. Ransom, "Criticism, Inc.," 588.

61. Cai, introduction, 6. Also see, Cai, "Danyin hanzi yu hanshi shiti zhi neilianxing," 326.

62. Cai, introduction, 6.

63. Ibid.
64. Cai, *Matrix*, especially chaps. 2 and 3 (21–94); Cai, "Zaoqi wuyanshi xintan," 39–52.
65. Cai, "Xiaoling," 51.
66. Cai, *Matrix*, 91–92.
67. Fang Dongshu, "Lun gushi shijiu shou" 論古詩十九首 (On the Nineteen Ancient-Style Poems), in Sui Shusen 隋樹森, *Gushi shijiushou jishi*, 3.74. Quoted in Cai, *Matrix*, 92.
68. Cai, *Matrix*, 92.
69. Empson, *Seven Types of Ambiguity*, 9.
70. Cai, *Matrix*, 91.
71. Ibid., 92.
72. Jakobson, "Linguistics and Poetics," 352.
73. Kao, "Wenxue yanjiu de lilun jichu," 16.
74. Ibid., 17.
75. Cai, "Danyin hanzi yu hanshi shiti zhi neilianxing," 315–16, 322; Cai, "Zaoqi wuyanshi xintan," 35.
76. Wimsatt, *Verbal Icon*, 72. John Crowe Ransom's thoughts on "universal" and "concrete" and Allen Tate's theory on "tension," which Wimsatt refers to here, can be found in Ransom, "Concrete Universal," and Tate, *Man of Letters in the Modern World*, 39.

References

Barry, B. *Beginning Theory: An Introduction to Literary and Cultural Theory*. Manchester: Manchester University Press, 1995.

Brooks, Cleanth, and Robert Penn Warren. *Understanding Poetry*. New York: Holt, 1938.

Cai, Zong-qi. "Danyin hanzi yu hanshi shiti zhi neilianxing" 單音漢字與漢詩詩體之內聯性 (Interconnection between Monosyllabic Chinese Language and the Poetic Forms of Chinese Poetry). *Lingnan xuebao* 嶺南學報 (Lingnan Journal of Chinese Studies) 5, no. 1 (2016): 277–326.

——. Introduction to *How to Read Chinese Poetry: A Guided Anthology*, edited by Zong-qi Cai, 1–9. New York: Columbia University Press, 2008.

——. "Lingzi yu manci jiezou, jufa, jiegou de chuangxin" 領字與慢詞節奏、句法、結構的創新 (The Lead Words and the Prosodic, Syntactic, and Structural Innovations in Manci Poems). *Beijing daxue xuebao (zhexue shehui kexue ban)* 北京大學學報（哲學社會科學版）(Journal of Peking University, Philosophy, and Social Sciences) 54, no. 4 (2017): 77–90.

——. *The Matrix of Lyric Transformation: Poetic Modes and Self-Presentation in Early Chinese Pentasyllabic Poetry*. Ann Arbor: Center for Chinese Studies, University of Michigan, 1996.

——. "Sound over Ideograph: The Basis of Chinese Poetic Art." *Journal of Chinese Literature and Culture* 2, no. 2 (2015): 545–72.

——. "Xiaoling cipai he jiezou yanjiu—cong yu jintishi guanxi de jiaodu zhankai" 小令詞牌和節奏研究—從與近體詩關係的角度展開 (Study of the Tunes and Rhythms of *Xiaoling*—from Its Relation to Recent-Style Poetry). *Wen shi zhe* 文史哲 (Journal of Chinese Humanities) 348, no. 3 (2015): 50–88.

——. "Zaoqi wuyanshi xintan—jiezou, jushi, jiegou, shijing" 早期五言詩新探—節奏、句式、結構、詩境 (A New Exploration of Early Pentasyllabic Poetry: Rhythm, Syntax,

Structure, and Vision). *Zhongguo wenzhe yanjiu jikan* 中國文哲研究集刊 (Collection of Chinese Literary and Philosophical Studies) 44 (2014): 1–56.

Eliot, T. S. "Tradition and the Individual Talent." In *Selected Essays, 1917–1932*, 3–11. New York: Harcourt, Brace, 1932.

Empson, William. *Seven Types of Ambiguity.* New York: New Directions, 1968.

Fish, Stanley. "What Is Stylistics and Why Are They Saying Such Terrible Things about It?—Part II." *Boundary* 2 8, no. 1 (1979): 129–46.

Frankel, Hans. "Fifteen Poems by Ts'ao Chih: An Attempt at a New Approach." *Journal of the American Oriental Society* 84, no. 1 (1964): 1–14.

Hightower, James R. "The Songwriter Liu Yung," pt. 1. *Harvard Journal of Asiatic Studies* 41 (1981): 323–76.

Hopkins, G. M. *The Journals and Papers.* Edited by Humphry House and Graham Storey. London: Oxford University Press, 1959.

Jakobson, Roman. "Linguistics and Poetics." In *Style in Language*, edited by Thomas A. Sebeok, 350–449. Cambridge: Technology Press of the Massachusetts Institute of Technology, 1960.

Kao, Yu-kung 高友工. "The Aesthetics of Regulated Verse." In *The Vitality of the Lyric Voice*, edited by Shuen-fu Lin and Stephen Owen, 332–85. Princeton, NJ: Princeton University Press, 1986.

———. "Citi zhi meidian" 詞體之美典 (The Aesthetics of the Ci). In *Meidian: Zhongguo wenxue yanjiu lunji* 美典：中國文學研究論集 (Aesthetics: Collected Essays on Studies in Chinese Literature), 284–90. Beijing: Sanlian shudian, 2008.

———. "Wenxue yanjiu de lilun jichu" 文學研究的理論基礎 (The Theoretical Basis for Literary Research). In *Meidian: Zhongguo wenxue yanjiu lunji* 美典：中國文學研究論集 (Aesthetics: Collected Essays on Studies in Chinese Literature), 1–18. Beijing: Sanlian shudian, 2008.

———. "Xiaoling zai shi chuantong zhong de diwei" 小令在詩傳統中的地位 (The Place of *Xiaoling* in the Tradition of Classical Chinese Poetry. In *Cixue* 詞學 (Study of Ci) 9 (1992), 1–21.

———. "Zhongguo yuyan wenzi dui shige de yingxiang" 中國語言文字對詩歌的影響 (The Influence of Chinese Language and Chinese Characters on Chinese Poetry). In *Meidian: Zhongguo wenxue yanjiu lunji* 美典：中國文學研究論集 (Aesthetics: Collected Essays on Studies in Chinese Literature), 179–216. Beijing: Sanlian shudian, 2008.

Kao, Yu-kung, and Mei Tsu-lin. "Meaning, Metaphor, and Allusion in T'ang Poetry." *Harvard Journal of Asiatic Studies* 38, no. 2 (1978): 281–356.

———. "Syntax, Diction, and Imagery in T'ang Poetry." *Harvard Journal of Asiatic Studies* 31 (1971): 49–136.

Liu Yong 柳永 (ca. 987–ca. 1053). "Gelianting" 隔簾聽 (Listening outside the Curtain). In *Quan Song Ci* 全宋詞 (Complete *Ci* Poetry of the Song), 5 vols., edited by Tang Guizhang 唐圭璋, 1:30–31. Beijing: Zhonghua shuju, 1965.

Mao shi zhengyi 毛詩正義 (The Mao Text of the Book of Poetry). In *Shisanjing zhushu* 十三經註疏 (Commentaries and Subcommentaries on the Thirteen Classics), compiled by Ruan Yuan 阮元 (1764–1849). 2 vols. Beijing: Zhonghua shuju, 1977.

Mei, Tsu-lin, and Yu-kung Kao. "Tu Fu's 'Autumn Meditations': An Exercise in Linguistic Criticism." *Harvard Journal of Asiatic Studies* 28 (1968): 44–80.

Owen, Stephen. "The Anxiety of Global Influence: What Is World Poetry?" *New Republic* 19 (1990): 28–32.

———. "Meaning the Words: The Genuine as Value in the Tradition of the Song Lyric." In *Voices of the Song Lyric in China*, edited by Pauline Yu, 30–69. Berkeley: University of California Press, 1994.

Quan Tang shi 全唐詩 (Complete *Shi* Poetry of the Tang), 25 vols. Beijing: Zhonghua shuju, 1960.

Ransom, John Crowe. "The Concrete Universal: Observations on the Understanding of Poetry." *Kenyon Review* 16, no. 4 (1954): 554–64.

———. "Criticism, Inc." *Virginia Quarterly Review*, no. 13 (1937): 586–603.

Richards, I. A. *Practical Criticism: A Study of Literary Judgment.* New York: Harcourt, Brace, 1929.

Smith, Barbara Herrnstein. "What Was 'Close Reading'? A Century of Method in Literary Studies." *Minnesota Review* 87 (2016): 57–75.

Sui Shusen 隋樹森, ed. *Gushi shijiushou jishi* 古詩十九首集釋 (Collected annotations on the Nineteen Ancient-Style Poems). Beijing: Zhonghua shuju, 1955.

Tate, Allen. *The Man of Letters in the Modern World: Selected Essays, 1928–1955.* New York: World, 1955.

Wimsatt, W. K. *The Verbal Icon: Studies in the Meaning of Poetry.* Lexington: University Press of Kentucky, 1954.

Decentering *Sinas*:
Poststructuralism and Sinology

LUCAS KLEIN

Abstract In *Of Grammatology* Jacques Derrida describes the "necessary decentering" that took place in Western philosophy following "the becoming-legible of non-Western scripts," when the European intellectual tradition was forced to confront its civilizational others. Derrida positions himself as contributing to this decentering, displacing the value-laden binary opposition central to structuralism. But as Derrida explained, the "first decentering limits itself" by "recenter[ing] itself upon" what he calls "the '*Chinese*' prejudice: all the philosophical projects of a universal script and of a universal language [which] encouraged seeing in the recently discovered Chinese script a model of the philosophical language thus removed from history." How has the approach to Chinese language and literature of that decentering known as poststructuralism limited itself or recentered itself, and how has sinology responded to the influence of poststructuralism? Insofar as the Chinese term for the *Sinae* (China) at the root of *sinology* is itself "middle" or "central" (中), how susceptible to decentering can sinology be? This article begins with a survey of poststructuralist writings about China by renowned post-structuralists, alongside responses to their work by sinologists and comparatists, arguing that poststructuralist writings tend to recenter themselves on a binary opposition between China and the West. The author then addresses the influence of poststructuralism on Chinese literary studies, to argue that the most successful poststructural decentering occurs in sinology when sinologists disseminate their decentering through a dissipated poststructuralism.

Keywords poststructuralism, sinology, literary theory, French theory

"China does not have any philosophy," explained Jacques Derrida, visiting China in 2001, "only thought" (transcribed as 中國沒有哲學，只有思想).[1] What could such a statement reveal about the odd role of poststructuralism in sinology, or

The Journal of Chinese Literature and Culture · 9:1 · April 2022
DOI 10.1215/23290048-9681163 · © 2022 by Duke University Press

what I'm defining for the purposes of this article as the study of Chinese literature in the West?

The reactions to Derrida's proclamation have been negative. His audience, a group of Chinese philosophers, were "stunned" 在座的人不禁愕然.[2] Bryan W. van Norden has said that Derrida's comments "are as condescending as talk of 'noble savages,' who are untainted by the corrupting influences of the West, but are for that very reason barred from participation in higher culture," and Carine Defoort and Ge Zhaoguang 葛兆光 state that Derrida's delimiting of the possibility of Chinese philosophy must remind "Chinese people of the denigrating statements made by . . . many Westerners . . . on the nonexistence or nonvalue of ancient Chinese philosophy."[3] Of course, Derrida did not mean to be disparaging. For him, *philosophy* is the name of a particular intellectual tradition that started in ancient Greece and has been dominant in the West nearly ever since—until recently, when it has undergone critique by the likes of Derrida for being logocentric (for believing in the epistemological supremacy of the *logos* [λόγος], whose translations include *word*, *speech*, and *reason*—and its ability to represent truth). To say that China has no philosophy, only thought, is to try to name something other to philosophy (I think of Derrida's contemporary Michel Foucault being named not professor of philosophy but Professor of the History of Systems of Thought at the Collège de France) and to say that Chinese thought—whatever its problems may be—does not have the particular problems of logocentrism that plague philosophy in the West.

Derrida is not the only notable recent French thinker to try to delimit philosophy or trace its limitations along lines of cultural specificity. "There is nothing to be done," Emmanuel Levinas said; "philosophy speaks Greek." By this he meant to lament having to "translate this non-Hellenism . . . into Hellenic terms"—the only terms in which he though we could "touch upon ultimate questions, assuming that there be ultimate questions."[4] Perhaps most famous for delimiting European philosophy against a Chinese other has been François Jullien, who has built a career on the expectation that, as Henry Y. H. Zhao has put it, "Chinese philosophy would throw into question all the 'great universals' of European thinking."[5] Jullien has written: "Because Chinese lies outside the great Indo-European language groups and uses another form of writing (ideographic, not phonetic), and because Chinese civilization . . . developed without any borrowings or influences from the European West for a long time, China presents a case study through which to contemplate Western thought from the outside—and, in this way, to bring us [Westerners] out of our atavism."[6] But such an attempt at treating China as "outside" has itself brought on critique. As Jean-François Billeter writes in *Contre François Jullien*, Jullien's "work is founded entirely on the myth of Chinese alterity" (son oeuvre est fondée tout entière sur le mythe de l'altérité de la Chine)—a myth whose "genesis" (la genèse du mythe) Billeter traces to the Jesuits.[7] And while Jullien almost always presents his othered Chinese thinkers "triumph[ing] through greater realism and economy," as Haun Saussy has pointed out, "there is no guarantee that the opposite conclusion will not be drawn, namely that Chinese culture is missing something important that the Europeans were lucky enough to find and develop."[8] Derrida's delimiting of philosophy against Chinese thought falls into the same trap.

Of all people, Derrida should have known better. The signature Derridean move is deconstruction, taking a concept and demonstrating that we understand it only in relation to what it is not, to its being in "binary opposition" to another concept, with one member of the binary opposition always valued or privileged over the other (light and dark, male and female, nature and culture, speech and writing, etc.). Deconstruction aims to decenter this division and destabilize its hierarchy, to show how the terms rely on each other and how the line between them on which their definitions rest is not as secure as we might think. To say that a certain culture has no philosophy, only thought, is to posit a textbook binary opposition, one term of which is clearly prioritized over the other. For Derrida that term may be *thought*, but for many of his interlocutors it is *philosophy*. Defoort and Ge, and van Norden are making the very Derridean move of deconstructing Derrida, decentering his postulation of the central difference between philosophy and thought, between China and the West. The hierarchy between philosophy and thought, and therefore the certainty and knowledge it underpins, is unstable.

This is not the first time that Derrida has made such a non-Derridean statement vis-à-vis China. In *Of Grammatology* (*De la grammatologie*, 1967), his most important book, at least as far as English-language literary theory is concerned, he writes that because China "remained structurally dominated by the ideogram," it provides "testimony of a powerful movement of civilization developing outside of all logocentrism."[9] How Derrida could write this in a book that begins by announcing his critique of "the *ethnocentrism* which, everywhere and always, had to control the concept of writing," and how China's developing outside all logocentrism squares with his statement elsewhere in the same book that there is no "outside the text" (il n'y a pas de hors-texte), is anyone's guess.[10] (I engage various sinologists' critiques of Derrida's statements about China and Chinese later in this article). This statement is all the more peculiar given that it comes at the end of his trenchant reading of how "Chinese writing," when it was first made known outside Asia, "functioned as a sort of European hallucination" of a "philosophical language . . . removed from history."[11] Was Derrida not hallucinating himself? Yet Derrida is not the only poststructuralist to have made perplexing remarks about China, even as poststructuralism has exerted real—

and, I think, good—influence on sinology. For that matter, many of the sinologists who have been most influenced by poststructuralism have themselves had perplexing attitudes about how to study Chinese literature and culture from and in relation to the West.

But how susceptible to decentering can sinology be, insofar as the Chinese term for the *Sinae* (China) at the root of *sinology* is itself "middle" or "central" (中)? To provide an overview of poststructuralist influence and its various intricacies and contradictions, this article proceeds in two parts: it begins with a brief survey of poststructuralist writings about China by some of the most renowned figures of poststructuralism or "French theory" (Michel Foucault, Julia Kristeva, Roland Barthes, and J. Hillis Miller), alongside significant responses to their work by sinologists and comparatists (Andrea Bachner, Rey Chow, Hilary Chung, Eric Hayot, Haun Saussy, and Zhang Longxi) to argue that poststructuralist writings have a tendency to recenter themselves on a binary opposition between China and the West. It then addresses the direct influence poststructuralism has had on Chinese literary studies or sinology, first by detailing how some scholarship has nevertheless reified the China-West binary (in Pauline Yu, Stephen Owen, Wai-lim Yip, and, differently, Ming Dong Gu) and then by offering examples of scholarship that has more successfully decentered the centrality of China and its self-other structures in sinology (by Zong-qi Cai, Jacob Edmond, Martin Svensson Ekström, Eugene Eoyang, Lydia H. Liu, Nicholas Morrow Williams, and Yurou Zhong). It concludes by arguing that the most successful poststructural decentering occurs in sinology when sinologists themselves decenter French theory and instead disseminate their decentering through a more dissipated poststructuralism.

Des Tours de la Chine

What follows is a quick tour through poststructuralist writings about or with mentions of China. Though sustained takes on Chinese literature by the luminaries of French theory are rare, the topic of China nevertheless comes up surprisingly often. Perhaps this is because China is already mentioned in the structuralism against which poststructuralism is defined.[12] In my definition of deconstruction above, the first part—that we understand a concept only in relation to what it is not—is structuralism: as Ferdinand de Saussure put it in his *Course in General Linguistics* (*Cours de linguistique générale*, 1916), "In language there are only differences" (it is the awareness that the terms such differences yield are hierarchized, and therefore centered on the kind of essentialism that structuralism purports to bypass, that defines the *post*structural outlook).[13] Relevantly, Saussure makes frequent mention of China to contrast it with the European languages more familiar to his students. He describes "only two systems of writing," one phonetic (which may be syllabic, alphabetic, etc.) and the other "an ideographic system," wherein

> each word is represented by a single sign that is unrelated to the sounds of the word itself. Each written sign stands for a whole word and, consequently, for the idea expressed by the word. The classical example of an ideographic system of writing is Chinese. . . . To a Chinese, an ideogram and a spoken word are both symbols of an idea; to him writing is a second language, and if two words that have the same sound are used in conversation, he may resort to writing in order to express his thought. But in Chinese the mental substitution of the written word for the spoken word does not have the annoying consequences that it has in a phonetic system, for the substitution is absolute; the same graphic symbol can stand for words from different Chinese dialects.[14]

With such an introduction to Chinese, where writing is claimed to be independent of speech and both speech and writing are understood to be equally symbolic of ideas, it should not be surprising that Derrida believed China could have developed "outside of all logocentrism."[15]

Sinologists could debate for a long time the extent to which the "ideograph" is related or unrelated to the sound of the Chinese word—suffice it to say, Chinese characters are not as independent of pronunciation as Saussure presents. But the accuracy of China as represented does not always matter to the poststructuralists. Michel Foucault, for instance, begins his *Order of Things* (*Les mots et les choses*, 1966) with China as imagined—if not mocked—by Argentinian writers Jorge Luis Borges:

> This book first arose out of a passage in Borges, out of the laughter that shattered, as I read the passage, all the familiar landmarks of my thought—*our* thought, the thought that bears the stamp of our age and our geography—breaking up all the ordered surfaces and all the places with which we are accustomed to tame the wild profusion of existing things, and continuing long afterwards to disturb and threaten with collapse our age-old distinction between the Same and the Other. This passage quotes a "certain Chinese encyclopaedia" in which it is written that "animals are divided into: (a) belonging to the Emperor, (b) embalmed, (c) tame, (d) sucking pigs, (e) sirens, (f) fabulous, (g) stray dogs, (h) included in the present classification, (i) frenzied, (j) innumerable, (k) drawn with a very fine camelhair brush, (l) *et cetera*, (m) having just broken the water pitcher, (n) that from a long way off look like flies." In the wonderment of this taxonomy, the thing we apprehend in one great leap, the thing that, by means of the fable, is demonstrated as the exotic charm of another system of thought, is the limitation of our own, the stark impossibility of thinking *that*.[16]

With a "great leap" (a loaded term!), the encyclopedia's ridiculous arrangement jolted Foucault awake to the arbitrariness and constructedness of any culture's sense of order, but it had nothing to do with China as a real place with real people constituting its real culture. As Zhang Longxi has noted, "Foucault does not give so much as a hint to suggest that the hilarious passage from that 'Chinese encyclopedia' may have been made up to represent a Western fantasy of the Other, and that the illogical way of sorting out animals in that passage can be as alien to the Chinese mind as it is to the Western."[17] And Andrea Bachner: "The 'Chinese' text becomes, in so many respects, a pretext, its cultural marker never more than a fabrication in the service of a philosophical machine of difference."[18]

Perhaps it was strategic of Foucault not to mention one way or another whether the Chinese encyclopedia was a fiction. For many Western intellectuals, the realities of China and their belief in fictions of it have proven hard to disentangle. This is already true of Saussure's description of Chinese as ideographic, but it was especially the case among intellectuals in France after World War II, where the Parti communiste français (PCF), directed by the Comintern in Moscow, had emerged as a leading political party yet suffered a loss of popularity by the fifties, particularly among intellectuals, for its support for the Soviet Union's invasion of Hungary in November of 1956 to quell the pro-democracy uprising there.[19] By the late 1960s, particularly after the PCF supported the workers' strikes but denounced the students during the May 1968 protests, some intellectuals in France were turning to China and Maoism in search of a purer, more radical, and less ethically tainted communism.[20] That China under Mao Zedong 毛澤東 was neither more ethically amenable than the USSR at that time nor purer or more interested in global revolution, particularly after Richard Nixon's visit in 1972, is a testament to how the realities and fictions of China got entangled for so many. This is the context for the 1974 visit to Cultural Revolution China by a small group of writers associated with the journal *Tel Quel*.[21] They took as true what they wanted to be true about China, even when they would otherwise scrutinize such truth claims.

The *Tel Quel* trip to China included Philippe Sollers, the editor of the journal, and probably the group's most devout Maoist; art critic and poet Marcelin Pleynet; Éditions du Seuil editor François Wahl; and the semioticians (there may not be a better word for it) Roland Barthes and Julia Kristeva, the latter married to Sollers. I look at Barthes's and Kristeva's takes on China, as they are the ones who have influenced literary criticism—including sinology—in English.[22] Barthes and Kristeva also present an interesting study in contrasts, as one liked China much more and wrote a lot about it, and the other was alienated by the visit and published very little.

Kristeva's *About Chinese Women* (*Des Chinoises*, 1974) is the only full-length study of China by any key poststructuralist. It is also one of the first books in any language to attempt a full women's history of China, from the Neolithic Banpo Village in Shaanxi, which she casts as matriarchal, through foot binding, to divorce laws in the People's Republic; she offers readings of *Honglou meng* 紅樓夢 (Dream of the Red Pavilion, 1791) and a poem by Li Qingzhao 李清照 (1084–1155). As Eric Hayot describes it, *About Chinese Women* attempts "to discover and describe an economy of gender and power wholly other to the Western psyche, one in which an original matriarchy and a feminine Taoism continue to produce people who cannot fit into the Western category of 'woman' or 'man.'"[23] For all its ambition, then, Kristeva's take falls back into the structuralism it is meant to surpass. As Rey Chow points out, by "othering and feminizing China," she is "repeating the metaphysics she wants to challenge."[24] Describing volleyball matches she happened to see in Beijing in 1974, for instance, Kristeva writes:

A match between Chinese and Iranian women: the Chinese women, with lithe, slender, athletic bodies, looking rather like skinny boys, silent, placid, precise, passing the ball or sending it over the net as if they were playing chess, but without the pained concentration . . . —a bit careless, a bit dreamy. The Iranian women, clearly more corpulent, hair in the wind, passionate, highly excited, hugging and kissing each other after each success, piercing the air with their shrill cries, which at first worried, then amused the Sunday crowd on the eve of May Day. In short, the Cartesians versus the Bacchantes. Needless to say, the Cartesians ran away with the game. . . . Needless as well to say that the Chinese boys—more frail, more adolescent—were beaten by the Iranian boys, real "machos," territorial lords. Certainly I tend to exaggerate the symbolic importance of this encounter, which I just happened to see because I was there are the moment and because the Chinese had decided to participate in the Olympics. But I can't help seeing a symptom there: the world of phallic supremacy, our Indo-European, monotheistic world, is still obviously in the lead. But if we take men and women together, here and in China, the co-efficient of ability, shrewdness—and, let us say—intelligence will be higher on the side of the Chinese. And this, because of Chinese women; because, after all, of the little "difference/resemblance" (as ancient Chinese logicians would say) between the two sexes in China.[25]

With this match, Kristeva "stages the contrast of nondifference versus difference," writes Saussy, as for her "Chineseness is the antithesis of antithesis itself."[26] Kristeva's take on China stumbles just where Derrida does, in imagining China to be "outside" the problems of the West.

Would it be better to imagine China as "inside" the problems of the West? Certainly the problems China faced in the mid-1970s were different from those facing France at the same time. An analysis of gender in China should not be subsumed into an analysis of gender in western Europe or North America: the political, economic, and even metaphysical predicaments of any part of the West at any given moment should not be normalized or naturalized to such an extent that they can pretend to explain the problems of other cultures. But it is the imagination that China represents a deconstruction of the male/female binary that signals its mental postulation, from the outside, as a solution to the problems Kristeva was trying to work through elsewhere. And by pinning this solution on the biological determinism of "the little 'difference/resemblance' . . . between the two sexes in China," she forecloses on the possibility that "our" "Indo-European, monotheistic world" could in fact ever learn from China.

To me, the best critical engagement with *About Chinese Women* is by Hilary Chung. While she criticizes Kristeva for her "tenuous extrapolations and speculations . . . without recourse to archival evidence, textual analysis or primary research" and "no mention of the state appropriation of feminism as a tool for the control and redefinition of femininity," she is nevertheless able to apply a Kristevan analysis to Republican-era Chinese literature by women: "If we are to talk about a feminine mode of expression we should do so in an anti-essentialist Kristevan sense: a disruptive mode of discourse expressive of marginality, subversion and dissidence. Thus, one could argue that early May Fourth writing as a whole writes *in the feminine* against the dominant literary discourse of Confucian patriarchy." Chung is not blind to the irony: "The problem in any application of [Kristeva's] analysis to Chinese literature is self-evident: although it opens up avenues for a fruitful anti-essentialist analysis of early May Fourth writing, how can such a project be viable when it is rooted in a seriously flawed construction of China?"[27] In fact, this friction is a central question behind Chinese literary studies' engagement with poststructuralism in light of its takes on China. But more on that later.

While Kristeva published perhaps too eagerly on China, Barthes, on the other hand, seemed to know that whereof one cannot speak, one must pass over in silence—or, near silence, anyway. Barthes's trip yielded only one published article, "Alors, la Chine" (1975), translated alternately as "Well, and China?" (1986) and "So, How Was China?" (2015). Barthes could not relate to the China he visited, yet he was reluctant to simply say he didn't like it there. China was illegible to him: leaving France for China, he said, "we leave behind us the turbulence of symbols and enter upon a very big, very old, very new country, where meaning [*signifiance*] is discreet to the point of rarity," and so coming back, he had "come home with—*nothing*." Not only did he find "Signifiers (the things that exceed meaning, cause it to overflow and to press on, towards desire) . . . rare," but "China presents very little to be read but its political Text," Maoist doctrine. Nor could he find any pleasure in that text: "To find Text . . . you have to go through an enormous swathe of repetitions." Practically the only thing he managed to read, in the semiotic sense, was "the current campaign against Confucius and Lin Piao," and describing it he sounds patronizing: "Its very name (in Chinese: *Pilin Pikong*) tinkles like a merry little bell, and the campaign divides into so many invented games." Only in his follow-up note, published the following year, does he say much of interest:

> On China, an immense object—and, for many, a hotly debated one—I tried to produce (this was where my truth lay) a discourse that was neither assertive, negative nor neutral. . . . By gently hallucinating China as an object located outside bright colours, strong flavours and stark meanings (all these things being not unconnected with the sempiternal parading of the phallus), I wanted to bind in a single movement the infinite feminine (maternal?) quality of the object itself. . . . This negative hallucination isn't gratuitous—it seeks to respond to the way many Westerners hallucinate the People's Republic of China in a dogmatic, violently affirmative/negative or falsely liberal way.[28]

He casts China as feminine, as Kristeva does, but without her pretentions of seeing China as genderless. Further, he is aware of his own masculinist cultural background and wants to find a way to transcend it. And though such transcendence is questionable, by acknowledging his own hallucination he both invokes and perhaps critiques Derrida's own discussion of Chinese in *Of Grammatology*. "Alors, la Chine" isn't very interesting, but his defense of it is.

Barthes's notebooks from his travels are also more interesting than the publication they produced. Translated into English too late to be of much influence to Chinese literature scholarship so far, *Travels in China* (*Carnets du voyage en Chine*, 2009) nevertheless offers a fuller read of Barthes's inability to read China.[29] As Saussy summarizes, Barthes "is repelled by his travelling companion Philippe Sollers, who is always trying to show off and debate Marxist theory with their Chinese guides and interlocutors."[30] In the face of figures such as Sollers and others, making "an intent and constant effort to speak about China from the point of view of China; a gaze coming from the inside," as well as those from the West who insist on the universality of their perspective, seeing "China *from the point of view* of the West," Barthes writes: "These two gazes are, for me, wrong. The right gaze is a *sideways gaze*."[31] Barthes fails at offering such a gaze in "Alors, la Chine," but I think the "sideways gaze" is without question the right way for sinologists to try to view China. This is how to avoid presenting as wholly outside the Western context or subsuming its analysis into those of western Europe or North America. The problem is, the sideways gaze is hard to achieve.

J. Hillis Miller, the next doyen of "French theory" under discussion, did not achieve the sideways gaze in his writings on China, for instance. Miller is a bit different from the others discussed here, as he was not French and did not write in French, yet as one of Yale's "Gang of Four" (with Harold Bloom, Paul de Man, and Geoffrey Hartman) responsible for popularizing or disseminating deconstruction and poststructuralism into the undergraduate English curriculum, his mentions of China deserve attention.[32] *An Innocent Abroad* (2015) collects fifteen lectures Miller gave in China in visits dating back to his first trip there in 1988. Where others went to China to fulfill an ideological need, Miller is clear-eyed about his utility: he was invited to lecture so often in China not because "Chinese academics want to become deconstructionists" but, rather, because

> I am seen as a person of some authority from the United States in language and literature study and in "theory" generally. This means that, in the view of Chinese academics, I can help them in their quite deliberate and self-conscious aim of creating up-to-date programs in the humanities and devising specifically Chinese forms of such disciplines as comparative literature or cultural studies or World Literature or even, paradoxically, Marxist aesthetics. They want to learn what we do, and then do it better and in a distinctively Chinese way.[33]

Can there be a "distinctively Chinese way" of studying literature? That is one of the themes of this article. Does such a proposal smack of positing China as "outside of all logocentrism," or does denying the idea rather demonstrate "the *ethnocentrism* which, everywhere and always, had to control the concept of writing"?[34] Miller addresses the question, implicitly, several times in his lectures. In "Effects of Globalization on Literary Study" (41–56), for example, he writes, "Literary study used to be organized chiefly as the separate study of national literatures. . . . Now such study is seen as a feature of imperialism. Each country . . . is seen as multicultural and multilingual, and therefore as falsified by the study of a single nation's literature."[35] Yet in "A Comparison of Literary Studies in the United States and China" (189–207), after a few pages addressing similarities, he announces differences gleaned from reading a feature on Chinese literature in the academic journal *MLQ*, such as, "Chinese scholars have relatively little overt interest in saying something new," engage in "a high level of abstraction in descriptive formulations about a given author or 'school,'" make "little stylistic or formal analysis," and seem to assume "that Chinese literature can be translated into English, and Western literature into Chinese, without important losses."[36] My culling makes Miller come off as meaner toward Chinese scholarship than he sounds in the lecture as a whole; he emphasizes that his generalizations come from reading one issue of one journal, and he reiterates that, "like all of my contrasts, these are tendencies, not absolute differences."[37] Nevertheless, there is a plain hierarchy in his opposition of "Chinese" and "Western" habits of writing about literature. The highlighting of the apparent belief in translation without loss is particularly important, as it echoes Miller's most paradigmatically poststructuralist presentation of China. From "The (Language) Crisis of Comparative Literature" (107–26):

> It is not even certain that it is right to call it "Chinese literature" or "poetry," since anything like an exact equivalent of those words does not exist, so I am told, in Chinese. The protocols for writing Chinese "poetry," and its uses over the centuries within Chinese culture, are different, to a considerable degree, from poetry and its uses in Euro-American culture. Our poetry is allusive and full of echoes of earlier poetry, echoes that an adept reader needs to recognize . . . , but nothing in our traditions quite matches the subtlety of echo in Chinese so-called poetry, at least so I am told. . . . To understand Chinese so-called poetry, you must learn how to read Chinese—a lengthy task.[38]

Miller is clear that his conclusions here come from second-hand information ("so I am told," "so I am told," "so I am told"), and perhaps he is trying to be polite—the impression he gives is that Chinese literature and poetry are not "literature" or "poetry" because they are something superior, richer—yet this pushes us into deeper problems than "China does not have any philosophy, only thought": if Chinese poetry is not poetry, what is it? Yes, there are differences between literature in Chinese and literature in any other language, but are these differences enough to decategorize literature and Chinese from each other? Whether Chinese literature is "literature" has nothing to do with writing in Chinese *an sich*, only with the narrowness or breadth of our working definition of literature. The other term in Miller's binary opposition is not even named, only posited as a hypothetical ineffable, an ineffable he says it would be almost impossible to understand ("a lengthy task"). By emphasizing translational loss and making his definitions of *literature* and *poetry* impossibly narrow, he idealizes Chinese literature nearly beyond existence, and certainly beyond accessibility via translation.

And so we have yet another poststructuralist who falls back on structuralism's central displacement of China and Chinese, undermining his deconstruction of binaries.

The First Decentering Limits Itself

If the overwhelming habit of poststructuralists signifying China has been to revert to structuralist differences with the West, why would sinologists want to be influenced by poststructuralism? Wasn't sinology doing fine with philology, and couldn't the handful of scholars who wanted to engage in more theoretical pursuits make do with structuralism proper?[39] Of course, some did decry the throwing open of "the portals of Chinese poetry studies to the gremlin progeny of Derrida's febrile brain," but poststructuralism has indeed proven influential in Chinese literary scholarship.[40] Why?

One answer is that Chinese literature is indeed literature, and one of the duties of scholars of any language's literature is to respond to the dominant or most compelling takes on literature in the environment of study. Within this, another answer is that, despite perplexing comments by its best-known practitioners, poststructuralism did in fact make structural room for attention to China. Derrida's *Of Grammatology* spends considerable time engaging in early modern European philosophers' curiosity about the Chinese script; he makes attention to China matter to the intellectual history of the West. From there, it is not far to make the case that "'the Western image of China'" is not "a subject entirely different from the present-day researcher's good-faith effort to understand the Chinese themselves."[41] Sinologists can have faith in the importance of our task of understanding China to the Euro-American intellectual project and then scrutinize that task at the same time as we scrutinize China.

But Derrida's narration of how China, or the understanding of Chinese, matters to European intellectual history is convoluted: describing a historical trajectory toward deconstruction, toward "the science of writing—*grammatology*—[which] shows signs of liberation all over the world," he centers on a moment in European intellectual history when something "shook up first and caused vacillation . . . in the transcendental authority and dominant category of the *epistémè*: being." That something was the "becoming-legible of non-Western scripts." Yet for all the epistemological wobbling it created, Derrida does not describe this moment as entirely positive: "The first decentering limits itself. It recenters itself upon . . . the '*Chinese*' prejudice: all the philosophical projects of a universal script and of a universal language . . . invoked by Descartes, outlined by Father Kircher, Wilkins, Leibniz, etc., encouraged seeing in the recently discovered Chinese script a model of the philosophical language [*langue*] thus removed from history." Derrida also calls this "'*Chinese*' prejudice" a "sort of European hallucination." The dream of a universal written language, a philosophical language that could transcend history, is just that—a dream. It is not something we should believe in—to say nothing of fantasizing that the Chinese written language could get us there—but it may have helped, says Derrida, make a crack in the authority of the reign of logocentric "being." And at the end of this, he said Chinese remains "a powerful movement of civilization developing outside of all logocentrism" because it is "structurally dominated by the ideo-gram."[42] The shaking and vacillation seem to have been intrinsic not only to Derrida's argument but also to his argumentation.

Shaking and vacillation are also evident in the reaction from theoretically minded sinologists. That is, they have been quite critical of Derrida here but mixed in how forgiving they want to be in the context of what else he is saying. Most recently, Andrea Bachner has argued that Derrida's "'Chinese' example is a symptom of a profound turn in thought: the reworking of signification under the sign of death."[43] Earlier, Rey Chow had argued that *Of Grammatology*, a "work that is radical, liberatory, antitraditional—an epochal intellectual intervention in every respect—is founded not only on a lack of information about and indif-ference to the workings of a language that provides the pivot of its critical turn but also on a continual stigmatization of that language, through the mechanical reproduction of it as mere graphicity, as 'ideographic' writing," so that the "inscrutable Chinese ideogram has led to a new scrutability, a new insight that remains Western and that becomes, thereafter, global."[44] John Cayley noted: "Derrida himself is hallucinating here. My own reading is that he is aware that he is doing so and regards it as a beneficial necessity."[45] To my knowledge, the first sinologist to critique Derrida for his claim that Chinese was "outside of all logocentrism" was Zhang Longxi, who wrote,

> The question that may be put to the contemporary effort to deconstruct the meta-physics of phonetic writing is whether such an effort has safely guarded itself against the same prejudice or hallucination. . . . A more fundamental question that necessarily follows is whether or not logocentrism is symptomatic only of Western metaphysics, that is, whether the metaphysics of Western thinking is really different from that of Eastern thinking and is not simply the way thinking is constituted and works. . . . In other words, if logocentrism is found present in the East as well as in the West, in nonphonetic as well as in phonetic writing, how is it possible for us to break away from, or through, its enclosure?[46]

Zhang sees himself to be pointing out the futility of any deconstruction, but for others his point would simply mean that Chinese literature can be decon-structed as well. Either way, whether the scholars in question were writing for Derrida or against him, the portals of Chinese literary studies had already been thrown open to the progeny of his brain.

The influence of poststructuralism on sinology more broadly could also be called a "first decentering" that limits itself by recentering on a kind of "'*Chinese*' prejudice." In response to both poststructuralism's critique of Western dualism and related comments by poststructuralist critics such as Paul de Man that literature "is the only form of language free from the fallacy of unmediated expression.... All literatures . . . have always designated themselves as existing in the mode of fiction," some sinologists asked, *All literatures?*[47] Stephen Owen wrote that, whereas for "the reader of Wordsworth, all is metaphor and fiction. . . . For Tu Fu's reader the poem is not a fiction: it is a unique, factual account of an experience in historical time, a human consciousness encountering, interpreting, and responding to the world."[48] Pauline Yu drew out the Western metaphysical reasons behind the idea that literature would be all metaphor and fiction, arguing that "mimesis is . . . predicated on a fundamental ontological dualism—the assumption that there is a truer reality transcendent to the concrete, historical realm in which we live, and that the relationship between the two is replicated in the creative act and the artifact," whereas "indigenous Chinese philosophical traditions agree on a fundamentally monistic view of the universe"; thus, "the Chinese poem was assumed to invoke a network of preexisting correspondences—between poet and world and among clusters of images."[49] They did not necessarily cite Derrida and others, but their generally poststructuralist approach made itself evident nonetheless.

At the time, Owen and Yu were considered the most poststructuralist of sinologists, whether that was a good thing or bad: Jonathan Chaves lambasts them for theorizing, while James J. Y. Liu said of Owen that "one has feelings of déjà vu, since many of the ideas appear to have been derived from such contemporary Western literary theorists and critics as Hans-Georg Gadamer, Wolfgang Iser, Stanley Fish, Harold Bloom, and Jacques Derrida, none of whom is mentioned by name."[50] Indeed, the idea that Chinese poetry is fundamentally nonfictional reads like a response to Derrida: whereas Derrida described the dream that Chinese was "a model of the philosophical language thus removed from history," Owen and Yu posited that Chinese could never be removed from history, according to the conceptualization of Chinese writing by the Chinese. Or, they frame the contrast between Chinese and Western poetries as "the contrast of nondifference versus difference," as Saussy wrote about Kristeva. This is also to say, then, that Owen and Yu are unresolved in their deconstructions (consider how similar they are in argument to works that position themselves against Derrida and poststructuralism)—or, rather, they simultaneously adhere to and dissent from poststructuralism, nodding to its critique of Western dualism and its shaping of literature while also carving a space outside of that dualism where literature could be something other than rhetoric and figuration.[51] The arguments also attempt to mediate between the Modern Language Association and the Association for Asian Studies or position the study of

Chinese literature between that of area studies and that of literature (also known as English).[52]

Other examples in line with Yu's and Owen's comparisons have followed. Wai-lim Yip's *Diffusion of Distances* (1993) comes to mind, critiquing the West's "epistemological world view developed from Platonic and Aristotelian metaphysics" while claiming that Chinese poets (and perhaps all speakers) "view things as things view themselves."[53] Though Owen and Yu have both been critical of Yip in print, the three are alike in critiquing poetry from the West for its cultural ideology while associating Chinese poetry with nature.[54] Poststructuralism has long been on the lookout for verbalizations of ideology, but if de Man was right that "what we call ideology is precisely the confusion of linguistic with natural reality," then Yip's statement about Chinese enabling the viewing of things as things view themselves is supremely ideological. Just when he thinks he is outside of ideology, we find him back in it.[55]

Mentioning ideology proper brings us to the curious case of Ming Dong Gu, particularly his book *Sinologism: An Alternative to Orientalism and Postcolonialism* (2013). He had earlier written "Mimetic Theory in Chinese Literary Thought," arguing against the Yu-Owen hypothesis and deconstructing the "dichotomous view" of a "Chinese emphasis on expression and the Western emphasis on imitation, the Chinese view of literature as spontaneous growth and the Western view of literature as conscious representation," which he says "is largely responsible for the nonmimetic view of Chinese literature and needs serious revision."[56] *Sinologism*, too, comes with a foreword by J. Hillis Miller, implying a poststructuralist approach from the arguments of the book as a whole. And yet another of his books is titled *Chinese Theories of Fiction: A Non-Western Narrative System*, implying a vision of Chinese theoretics as, again, not only outside Western ethnocentrism but outside a Western mindset *in toto*. As for *Sinologism*, its title names "the inner logic of the problems in China-West studies, which," he says, "is an ideological unconscious in China-West knowledge production." Gu spends the book critiquing the sinologistic expression of this ideological unconscious. But see the alternative he imagines in the conclusion:

> Once freed from the unconscious logic of Sinologism, cross-cultural studies will no longer rely on Western theories as universal paradigms, but use them as reference frameworks to study the historical conditions of non-Western cultures and societies, and there will appear truly scientific and objective approaches to non-Western materials, resulting in bias-free knowledge about non-Western cultures. In the field of China-West studies, so long as we become fully conscious of the logic of Sinologism and guard against its appearance in knowledge and scholarship, we will eventually be able to usher in a "golden age" when knowledge about China and other cultures is

pursued for its own sake, free from the interference of the political ideologies of colonialism, Western-centrism, ethno-centrism, and other political and ideological agendas.[57]

A scientific and objective approach to humanistic studies sounds terminally boring to me, but I suppose Gu's positing of bias-free knowledge on the other side of ideology is preferable to segregating Chinese and Western writing because of an assumed epistemological difference. Yet I note a utopianism in Gu reminiscent of Miller's postulation of a Chinese literature that transcends common definitions of literature, or of anyone's "effort to speak about China from the point of view of China," as Barthes described it. And poststructuralism, in my understanding, should be most suspicious of claims of transcendence, of objectivity and being free of bias—also known as subjectivity. With Gu's earlier search for finding a "nonwestern narrative system" in mind, his hopes here sound no less ideological, and no more poststructural, than Yip's dream of Chinese poets viewing things as things view themselves.

So, what can we say about sinological poststructuralism thus far? The first decentering limits itself, recentering on a "Chinese" prejudice: these critical projects of a Chinese correlative cosmology, invoked by Gu, outlined by Owen, Yu, Yip, etc., encouraged seeing in the recently discovered Chinese poem a model of the poetic language thus removed from rhetoric and ideology. For all that these scholars' arguments draw on poststructuralist analyses of the ideologies of Western rhetoric, their "intent and constant effort to speak about China from the point of view of China," in Barthes's words, is in fact no different from Derrida's positioning of Chinese as "outside of all logocentrism"—in which case, the pretense to offer the "gaze coming from the inside" is the same as looking at "China *from the point of view* of the West."[58] These scholars are not, in fact, demonstrating the strength of the sideways gaze.

A Dissipated Poststructuralism

Fortunately, other sinologists have adopted the sideways gaze of post-structuralist promise more successfully. The shaking and vacillating did yield, in some circles, a decentering of Chinese as outside in comparative sinology, or cross-cultural poetics. To the extent that there was a rupture (a dubious proposition, if a useful one), it was constituted with the work of Rey Chow and Haun Saussy. They have both exemplified the possibilities of poststructuralist sinology even as they have engaged in internal critique of the enterprise. In "Introduction: On Chineseness as a Theoretical Problem," Chow argued that, for scholars like Owen and Yu, "the practitioners of Chinese writing—or the Chinese practitioners of writing—are, in effect, read as ethnics, or natives, who are endowed with a certain *primitive logic*."[59] Saussy, meanwhile, focusing on the premodern where Chow focuses on the contemporary and modernity, deconstructed in his *Problem of a Chinese Aesthetic* (1993) the Chinese/West binary implicit in the Yu-Owen hypothesis first by tracing the question of Chinese rhetoric and metaphysics to the earliest European attempts to categorize Chinese language and culture (the Jesuit rites controversy in the seventeenth and eighteenth centuries over whether missionaries could make Christian converts in Chinese), and then by questioning assertions about the lack of Chinese allegory via readings of Xunzi's 荀子 (c. 310–c. 235 BCE) problematizations of "nature" (*xing* 性). Later, Saussy would write, in the context of reading poststructuralist presentations of China quoted above, that "deconstruction cannot be a list of authors, a belief system or a set of themes. It may articulate themes and present pictures of reality . . . but for the work of deconstruction to go forward these representations must be dispensable . . . it is entirely likely that the next things worth questioning with the methods of Derrida and de Man will prove have nothing in common with those on which junior deconstructors cut their teeth."[60] Saussy's forecasting about deconstruction was prescient (even as deconstruction lost its dominance among critical approaches to literary studies soon after those words were published). Other sinologists who strike me as particularly poststructuralist may not be citing Derrida or de Man as often as is the caricature of the deconstructive appeal to authority in many literature departments, but they have refused to see *Sinae* (China)—or the China/West distinction—as "central" (*zhong* 中), even as they engage in sinology.

In addition to Bachner, Chung, Hayot, and Zhang, already cited above (though Zhang would likely disavow poststructuralist influence, even as he has not been sinocentric in his comparative studies or sinology), some of the most influential sinologists who are to my mind most indebted to poststructuralism and devoted to getting past binaries are Zong-qi Cai, Eugene Eoyang, Xiaofan Amy Li, Lydia H. Liu, Yurou Zhong, Jacob Edmond, Nicholas Morrow Williams, and Martin Svensson Ekström. I briefly discuss them in pairings of scholars focusing on comparative poetics, on modern Chinese literature, and on classical philology—the last of which is often conceived of in opposition to theory. Much more could be said on all these works and others, but I offer these remarks so as not to leave the impression either that I only know how to be critical or that poststructuralism is no longer making an impact in the study of Chinese literature.

After Yu and Owen, Chinese and Western comparative poetics became one of the most available venues for deconstructive scholarship. Zong-qi Cai's *Configurations of Comparative Poetics* (2002) details Chinese and Western poetics as emerging from separate starting points but nevertheless involving many intersections and parallels, in large part due to the pluralities that define both traditions. Cai ends the book with an appeal to a transcultural perspective—which I see as roughly equivalent to the sideways gaze—which he says enables him "to discuss similarities as meaningful convergences between two equal traditions, rather than in terms of the conformity of a 'lesser' tradition to a 'superior' one."[61] In a manner not dissimilar, though less systematic, Eoyang's *Transparent Eye* (1993) makes the case that history "is not anal-retentive, but rather chaotic, disheveled, entropic, scatological if not eschato-logical" to argue against "authenticity" as a viable category either in translation or in cross-cultural poetics.[62] Xiaofan Amy Li's *Comparative Encounters between Artaud, Michaux, and the Zhuangzi* (2015) argues that the *Zhuangzi* 莊子 and writings by Antonin Artaud and Henri Michaux can be taken together to "point towards a nonnormative, relational and embodied ethics that values spontaneous action without subjective agency."[63] These books by Cai, Eoyang, and Li help destabilize the neat binary that defined Chinese/Western poetics in an earlier era.

In part because the earliest European attempts at categorizing Chinese language and culture, mentioned above, took place in early modernity, and the technologies that pushed modernity not only expanded such systematizing logic but also interpellated the whole world—not least of all China—into its sys-tematizations, the confluence of China and modernity has proven a fertile field for poststructuralist scholarship.[64] Lydia H. Liu's *Translingual Practice* (1995) reads Chinese literature "since its early exposure to English, modern Japanese, and other foreign languages" to see "whether one can still talk about change and transaction between East and West in twentieth-century China without privileging the West, modernity, progress, or other post-Enlightenment notions on the one hand and without holding on to a reified idea of indigenous China on the other."[65] Her *Clash of Empires* (2004) looks at the "hetero-cultural legacy of sovereign thinking [between China and Great Britain] in the nineteenth cen-tury," its most controversial argument also its most poststructuralist in terms of its discussion of the power of the word: she argues that "the translation of the written Chinese character *yi* [夷] at the time of the Opium War led to the invention of the super-sign *yi/barbarian* by the British, who believed that the use of the character was intended to insult the foreigner and thus sought to ban the word."[66] Yurou Zhong has also turned sinological poststructuralism into a positive science in her *Chinese Grammatology* (2019), looking at the "phono-centric turn of modern Chinese writing."[67] In treating contemporary poetry, meanwhile, Jacob Edmond has so thoroughly decentralized the China/West distinction that in analyzing poetry written in Chinese, Russian, and English he barely needs to address any binary. At any rate, the stakes have changed. *A Common Strangeness* (2012), which Eric Hayot on the back cover describes as "a long essay on the relation between the general and the particular after deconstruction," argues that "poets from China, Russia, and the United States . . . have shaped conceptions of the global," and Edmond's *Make It the Same* (2019) talks about what Liu calls "change and transaction between East and West . . . without privileging the West, modernity, progress, or other post-Enlightenment notions" by making the case that "copying and mimetic desire are not signs of non-Western derivativeness but qualities shared equally by non-Western and Western modernism."[68] These three scholars demonstrate that, in dealing with comparative studies of Chinese literature in modernity, a structural binary between Chinese and Western literature is no longer viable.

Classical philology has been the subfield of Chinese literary studies most resistant to literary theory—and not always for ideological reasons, but simply for the time it takes. Immediately after Paul W. Kroll states, for instance, that his "impossible ideal" for the scholar of Tang literature "is to be as conversant with all areas of Tang life and culture as an educated Tang scholar would have been," he adds, "Let me make clear that in saying this I am not directing a flank attack at 'theory.'"[69] Yet some philological scholars strike me as being particularly influenced by poststructuralism, against the odds. In *Imitations of the Self: Jiang Yan and Chinese Poetics* (2015), Nicholas Morrow Williams writes that "imitation poems" (*nishi* 擬詩)

> were the most self-conscious writing about intertextuality in the Six Dynasties [220–589 CE], since they were explicitly defined in terms of relations among preexisting literary works. . . . Roland Barthes has written that "the citations which go to make up a text are anonymous, untraceable, and yet *already read*: they are quotations without inverted commas."[70] Yet imitation poems make a virtue of necessity—finding poetic resonance in the double voice of poetry itself, as well as the gap between the fictional speaker and implied author.[71]

The passage resonates with many debates at the nexus of poststructuralism and Chinese literary studies, not just intertextuality but the relationships between author and speaker, fiction and textuality, and rhetoric and reality. Later, in "Sublimating Sorrow" (2019) Williams reads the "real ambiguity embedded in the text" of Qu Yuan's 屈原 (c. 340–278 BCE) long poem the "Li sao" 離騷 (Sublimating Sorrow), wherein "the character *li* 離 has at least two diametrically opposite significations: 'to depart' or 'to encounter.'" As "none of the tensions or contradictions is resolved in the 'Li sao' or in its reception history," he argues, the best tactic is to emphasize deconstructive undecidability: "In translating the poem the best option is to engage and to represent the contradictions themselves."[72] Similarly, Martin Svensson Ekström has written a series of articles that, not unlike Gu's deconstructions, question the denial of meta-phor in Chinese poetry.[73] But his clearest statement of poststructuralist alle-giance, to my knowledge, is in a passage touting the benefits of philological reading—which also happens to engage with the sinological debates I have traced out in this article. The sinologist, he writes, "is always and everywhere in danger of being misled or charmed by superficial similarities between Chinese and Western terms, concepts, and discourses. Conversely, he or she is to a similar degree in danger of exaggerating the division between Chinese cosmology and Western metaphysics, of experiencing the so-called cosmological gulf in every Platonic dialogue or in every saying attributed to Confucius." For instance, "If we translate *shi* 詩 as 'poetry,' we must take into consideration the differences that obtain between Graeco-Roman and Chinese conceptions of rhymed or metri-cally bound or ritualized language—what we instinctively would call 'poetry'— and compare what the ancient sources say about the origin, function, and formal qualities of *shi* and *poiēsis*, respectively." If comparative literature approaches these terms as ideas, he says, they will seem to have "geared the particular culture in specific directions. Thus *poiēsis* is often conceived of as abstract, contrived, metaphysical, metaphorical, in contrast to Chinese *shi* 詩, which is seen as concrete, spontaneous, cosmological." In contrast,

> a "philological" reading, as indicated, would not merely reverse the top-down model or insist that a more correct understanding of the linguistic, textual, or cultural unit in question lies in etymological or graphological analyses. (Indeed, such analyses have in the past been part and parcel of an incorrect dichotomization of China and the West.) It would insist, rather, on a constant awareness and revision of what we consider the "great ideas" that underpin, respectively, the Chinese and Western traditions to be in the light of readings that contextualize the "unit" in a far more rigorous manner than is usually seen, as well as taking etymology and graphology into account.[74]

Praising philology, Ekström winds up with deconstruction, with awareness and revision of the "great ideas" that underpin the Chinese and Western traditions in light of rigorously contextualizing readings. If Ekström shows that the opposi-tion between philology and deconstruction is not as stable as we might other-wise think, then perhaps deconstruction has been with us in sinology from the beginning, and this whole article should be rethought!

Be that as it may, these sinologists and comparatists demonstrate to me the place and pace of poststructuralism in sinology now. The aforementioned scholars are not part of a unified group—at times they have even gotten into debates with each other—but they are united in not centralizing their produc-tion of knowledge on a binary opposition of China and the West. They may not necessarily think of themselves as poststructuralists, but in this they represent a more dissipated poststructuralism, having absorbed its influences and seen around many of its blind spots. They show that poststructuralism does not have to be defined by statements about China being "outside" philosophy but, rather, can yield very successful sinology from its sideways gaze.

    LUCAS KLEIN   柯夏智
Arizona State University
Lucas.Klein@asu.edu

Notes

1. Du and Zhang, *Delida zai Zhongguo jiangyanlu*, 139.
2. Ibid.
3. Van Norden, *Taking Back Philosophy*, 25; Defoort and Ge, "Editors' Introduction," 3.
4. Levinas, *Of God Who Comes to Mind*, 85.
5. Zhao, "Contesting Confucius."
6. Jullien, *Detour and Access*, 9.
7. Billeter, *Contre François Jullien*, 9, 13. For context, see Zhao, "Contesting Confucius"; Botz-Bornstein, "Heated French Debate"; and Weber, "What about the Billeter-Jullien Debate?" On the history of European othering of China, see Hung, "Orientalist Knowledge and Social Theories."
8. Saussy, review of *La propension des choses*, 987.
9. Derrida, *Of Grammatology*, 98.
10. Ibid., 3, 177.
11. Ibid., 86, 82.
12. I mark here the caveat that the structuralism/poststructuralism split is largely an American categorization of postwar French thought. See Cusset, *French Theory*.
13. Saussure, *Course in General Linguistics*, 120.
14. Ibid., 25–26.
15. Another of Derrida's sources for his knowledge of Chinese was Marcel Granet, on whom see Saussy, *Ethnography of Rhythm*, 27–33.
16. Foucault, *Order of Things*, xvi. See Borges, "John Wilkins' Analytical Language," 231.
17. Zhang, "Myth of the Other," 110. But does Borges suggest that the Chinese encyclopedia is a joke? "In Borges's essay," Zhang notes, "The absurdities of the 'Chinese encyclopedia' are not recalled to represent an incomprehensibly alien mode of thinking," and Borges cites an actual German translator of Chinese fiction, Franz Kuhn (1884–1961)—though no one has ever found evidence of Kuhn having written up such a categorization, and as Zhang notes, "It is not at all uncommon for Borges in his writings to mix erudition with imagination, blending real names and titles with imaginary ones" (111).
18. Bachner, *Beyond Sinology*, 29.
19. The PCF had gained 47 seats in the National Assembly in the 1956 election, reaching 150 elected representatives, but it lost 140 seats in the elections of 1958. PCF opposition both to de-Stalinization and to Charles de Gaulle's foundation of the Fifth Republic likely contributed to these losses, as well.

20. Nikita Khrushchev's and Leonid Brezhnev's interests in détente with the United States also contributed to some intellectuals' loss of faith in the USSR as the spearhead for international revolution.

21. The *Tel Quel* group were not the only French intellectuals to travel to Maoist China. See Hughes, *France/China*, 33–66.

22. That said, for further readings of the trip and of China, esp. per Sollers, see Saussy, "Outside the Parenthesis"; Hayot, *Chinese Dreams*, 103–75; and Bachner, *Beyond Sinology*, 148–51.

23. Hayot, *Chinese Dreams*, 106.

24. Chow, *Woman and Chinese Modernity*, 7.

25. Kristeva, *About Chinese Women*, 195.

26. Saussy, "Outside the Parenthesis," 860–61. For criticisms from beyond the sinology realm, see Spivak, "French Feminism"; and Lowe, *Critical Terrains*, 136–89.

27. Chung, "Kristevan (Mis)Understandings," 74, 87, 88.

28. Barthes, "So, How Was China?," 98, 97, 99, 100, 101, 103–4.

29. For one engagement with Barthes's *Travels in China*, see Klein, "Dissonance of Discourses."

30. Saussy, review of *Travels in China*, 3.

31. Barthes, *Travels in China*, 177.

32. The name *Gang of Four* also implies a relationship to China, referencing the group that exerted control over much of the Chinese Communist Party during the last years of the Cultural Revolution.

33. Miller, *Innocent Abroad*, xxix.

34. Derrida, *Of Grammatology*, 3.

35. Miller, *Innocent Abroad*, 50.

36. Ibid., 195, 198, 199, 201.

37. Ibid., 195.

38. Ibid., 121.

39. I have in mind Mei and Kao, "Tu Fu's 'Autumn Meditations'"; Kao and Mei, "Syntax, Diction, and Imagery"; and Kao and Mei, "Meaning, Metaphor, and Allusion"; as well as Cheng, *Chinese Poetic Writing*. See Lian's and Varsano's contributions to this special issue.

40. Chaves, "Forum," 80.

41. Saussy, *Problem of a Chinese Aesthetic*, 3.

42. Derrida, *Of Grammatology*, 4, 100, 82, 82, 86, 98.

43. Bachner, *Beyond Sinology*, 26.

44. Chow, "How (the) Inscrutable Chinese Led to Globalized Theory," 70, 72.

45. Cayley and Yang, "Hallucination and Coherence," 775.

46. Zhang, "'Tao' and the 'Logos,'" 388–89.

47. De Man, "Crisis of Contemporary Criticism," 54.

48. Owen, *Traditional Chinese Poetry and Poetics*, 15.

49. Yu, *Reading of Imagery*, 5, 32, 36.

50. J. J. Y. Liu, review, 579. See Chaves, "Forum," 80.

51. For a representative work that positions itself against Derrida and poststructuralism with an argument similar to that that of Owen and Yu, see Sun, *Poetics of Repetition*.

52. Again, see Varsano's article on mediating between area studies and literature, or sinology and the disciplines, in her contribution to this special issue.

53. Yip, *Diffusion of Distances*, 48, 71.
54. See Owen, review; and Yu, "Hidden in Plain Sight?," 180–81.
55. De Man, "Resistance to Theory," 11.
56. Gu, "Mimetic Theory in Chinese Literary Thought," 421–22. See Gu, "Is Mimetic Theory in Literature and Art Universal?"
57. Gu, *Sinologism*, 5, 224–25.
58. Barthes, *Travels in China*, 177; Derrida, *Of Grammatology*, 98; Barthes, *Travels in China*, 177.
59. Chow, "Introduction," 15–16; see also Bowman, "Editor's Introduction."
60. Saussy, "Outside the Parenthesis," 856.
61. Cai, *Configurations of Comparative Poetics*, 254.
62. Eoyang, *Transparent Eye*, 22.
63. Li, *Comparative Encounters*, 4.
64. See Hayot, "Vanishing Horizons," 91–97.
65. L. H. Liu, *Translingual Practice*, xvi, 30.
66. L. H. Liu, *Clash of Empires*, 2.
67. Zhong, *Chinese Grammatology*, 3.
68. Edmond, *Common Strangeness*, 2–3; Edmond, *Make It the Same*, 11.
69. Kroll, "On the Study of Tang Literature," 6.
70. See Barthes, "From Work to Text," 160.
71. Williams, *Imitations of the Self*, 4.
72. Williams, "Sublimating Sorrow," 183.
73. See Ekström, "Illusion, Lie, and Metaphor"; Ekström, "One Lucky Bastard"; and Ekström, "Does the Metaphor Translate."
74. Ekström, "Sino-Methodologies, a Draft," 61–62.

References

Bachner, Andrea. *Beyond Sinology: Chinese Writing and the Scripts of Culture*. New York: Columbia University Press, 2014.

Barthes, Roland. "From Work to Text." In *Image, Music, Text*, translated by Stephen Heath, 155–64. London: Fotana/Collins, 1977.

———. "So, How Was China?" In *"The 'Scandal' of Marxism" and Other Writings on Politics: Essays and Interviews*, translated by Chris Turner, 94–104. London: Seagull Books, 2015.

———. *Travels in China*. Edited by Anne Herschberg-Pierrot. Translated by Andrew Brown. Cambridge: Polity, 2012.

———. "Well, and China?" Translated by Lee Hildreth. *Discourse* 8 (1986–87): 116–20.

Billeter, Jean-François. *Contre François Jullien*. Paris: Allia, 2006.

Borges, Jorge Luis. "John Wilkins' Analytical Language." In *Borges: Selected Non-Fictions*, edited and translated by Eliot Weinberger, 229–32. New York: Penguin, 2000.

Botz-Bornstein, Thorsten. "The Heated French Debate on Comparative Philosophy Continues: Philosophy versus Philology." *Philosophy East and West* 64, no. 1 (2014): 218–28.

Bowman, Paul. "Editor's Introduction." In *The Rey Chow Reader*, edited by Paul Bowman, ix–xxiii. New York: Columbia University Press, 2010.

Cai, Zong-qi. *Configurations of Comparative Poetics: Three Perspectives on Western and Chinese Literary Criticism*. Honolulu: University of Hawai'i Press, 2002.

Cayley, John, and Yang Lian 楊煉. "Hallucination and Coherence." *positions: east asia cultures critique* 10, no. 3 (2002): 773–84.

Chaves, Jonathan. "Forum: From the 1990 AAS Roundtable." *Chinese Literature: Essays, Articles, Reviews* 13 (1991): 77–82.

Cheng, François. *Chinese Poetic Writing: With an Anthology of T'ang Poetry*. Translated by Donald A. Riggs and J. P. Seaton. Bloomington: Indiana University Press, 1982.

Chow, Rey. "How (the) Inscrutable Chinese Led to Globalized Theory." *PMLA* 116, no. 1 (2001): 69–74.

———. "Introduction: On Chineseness as a Theoretical Problem." *Boundary 2* 25, no. 3 (1998): 1–24.

———. *Woman and Chinese Modernity: The Politics of Reading between West and East*. Minneapolis: University of Minnesota Press, 1991.

Chung, Hilary. "Kristevan (Mis)Understandings: Writing in the Feminine." In *Reading East Asian Writing: The Limits of Literary Theory*, edited by Michel Hockx and Ivo Smits, 72–91. London: RoutledgeCurzon, 2003.

Cusset, François. *French Theory: How Foucault, Derrida, Deleuze, and Co. Transformed the Intellectual Life of the United States*. Translated by Jeff Fort, Josephine Berganza, and Marlon Jones. Minneapolis: University of Minnesota Press, 2008.

Defoort, Carine, and Ge Zhaoguang 葛兆光. "Editors' Introduction." *Contemporary Chinese Thought* 37, no. 1 (2005): 3–10.

De Man, Paul. "The Crisis of Contemporary Criticism." *Arion: A Journal of Humanities and the Classics* 6, no. 1 (1967): 38–57.

———. "The Resistance to Theory." *Yale French Studies*, no. 63 (1982): 3–20.

Derrida, Jacques. *Of Grammatology*. Translated by Gayatri Chakravorty Spivak. 40th anniv. ed. Baltimore: Johns Hopkins University Press, 2016.

Du Xiaozhen 杜小真 and Zhang Ning 張寧, eds. *Delida zai Zhongguo jiangyanlu* 德里達中國講演錄 (Derrida's Lectures in China). Beijing: Zhongyang bianji chubanshe, 2003.

Edmond, Jacob. *A Common Strangeness: Contemporary Poetry, Cross-Cultural Encounter, Comparative Literature*. New York: Fordham University Press, 2012.

———. *Make It the Same: Poetry in the Age of Global Media*. New York: Columbia University Press, 2019.

Ekström, Martin Svensson. "Does the Metaphor Translate." In *Translating China for Western Readers: Reflective, Critical, and Practical Essays*, edited by Ming Dong Gu and Rainer Schulte, 277–99. Albany: SUNY Press, 2014.

———. "Illusion, Lie, and Metaphor: The Paradox of Divergence in Early Chinese Poetics." *Poetics Today* 23 (2002): 251–89.

———. "One Lucky Bastard: On the Hybrid Origins of Chinese 'Literature.'" In *Literary History: Towards a Global Perspective*, edited by Anders Pettersson, Gunilla Lindberg-Wada, Margareta Petersson, and Stefan Helgesson, 1:70–110. Berlin: De Gruyter, 2006.

———. "Sino-Methodologies, a Draft." *Verge: Studies in Global Asias* 1, no. 1 (2015): 59–65.

Eoyang, Eugene Chen. *The Transparent Eye: Reflections on Translation, Chinese Literature, and Comparative Poetics*. Honolulu: University of Hawai'i Press, 1993.

Foucault, Michel. *The Order of Things: An Archaeology of the Human Sciences*. Translator not credited. New York: Vintage Books, 1973.

Gu, Ming Dong. *Chinese Theories of Fiction: A Non-Western Narrative System*. Albany: SUNY Press, 2007.

———. "Is Mimetic Theory in Literature and Art Universal?" *Poetics Today* 26, no. 3 (2005): 459–98.

———. "Mimetic Theory in Chinese Literary Thought." *New Literary History* 36, no. 3 (2005): 403–24.

———. *Sinologism: An Alternative to Orientalism and Postcolonialism.* New York: Routledge, 2013.

Hayot, Eric. *Chinese Dreams: Pound, Brecht, Tel Quel.* Ann Arbor: University of Michigan Press, 2004.

———. "Vanishing Horizons: Problems in the Comparison of China and the West." In *A Companion to Comparative Literature*, edited by Ali Behdad and Dominic Richard David Thomas, 88–107. West Sussex: Wiley-Blackwell, 2011.

Hughes, Alex. *France/China: Intercultural Imaginings.* Oxford: Legenda, 2007.

Hung, Ho-Fung. "Orientalist Knowledge and Social Theories: China and the European Conceptions of East-West Differences from 1600 to 1900." *Sociological Theory* 21, no. 3 (2003): 254–80.

Jullien, François. *Detour and Access: Strategies of Meaning in China and Greece.* Translated by Sophie Hawkes. New York: Zone Books, 2004.

Kao, Yu-kung, and Tsu-Lin Mei. "Meaning, Metaphor, and Allusion in T'ang Poetry." *Harvard Journal of Asiatic Studies* 38, no. 2 (1978): 281–356.

———. "Syntax, Diction, and Imagery in T'ang Poetry." *Harvard Journal of Asiatic Studies* 31 (1971): 49–136.

Klein, Lucas. "A Dissonance of Discourses: Literary Theory, Ideology, and Translation in Mo Yan and Chinese Literary Studies." *Comparative Literature Studies* 53, no. 1 (2016): 170–97.

Kristeva, Julia. *About Chinese Women.* Translated by Anita Barrows. London: Marion Boyars, 1977.

Kroll, Paul W. "On the Study of Tang Literature." *T'ang Studies* 27 (2009): 3–18.

Levinas, Emmanuel. *Of God Who Comes to Mind.* Translated by Bettina Bergo. Stanford, CA: Stanford University Press, 1998.

Li, Xiaofan Amy. *Comparative Encounters between Artaud, Michaux, and the Zhuangzi: Rationality, Cosmology, and Ethics.* Oxford: Legenda, 2015.

Liu, James J. Y. Review of *Traditional Chinese Poetry and Poetics: Omen of the World*, by Stephen Owen. *Journal of Asian Studies* 45, no. 3 (1986): 579–80.

Liu, Lydia He. *The Clash of Empires: The Invention of China in Modern World Making.* Cambridge, MA: Harvard University Press, 2004.

———. *Translingual Practice: Literature, National Culture, and Translated Modernity—China, 1900–1937.* Stanford, CA: Stanford University Press, 1995.

Lowe, Lisa. *Critical Terrains: French and British Orientalisms.* Ithaca, NY: Cornell University Press, 1991.

Mei, Tsu-Lin, and Yu-kung Kao. "Tu Fu's 'Autumn Meditations': An Exercise in Linguistic Criticism." *Harvard Journal of Asiatic Studies* 28 (1968): 44–80.

Miller, J. Hillis. *An Innocent Abroad: Lectures in China.* Flashpoints. Evanston, IL: Northwestern University Press, 2015.

Owen, Stephen. Review of *Chinese Poetry: Major Modes and Genres*, by Wai-lim Yip. *Journal of Asian Studies* 37, no. 1 (1977): 100–102.

———. *Traditional Chinese Poetry and Poetics: Omen of the World.* Madison: University of Wisconsin Press, 1985.

Saussure, Ferdinand de. *Course in General Linguistics*. Edited by Perry Meisel and Haun Saussy. Translated by Wade Baskin. New York: Columbia University Press, 2011.

Saussy, Haun. *The Ethnography of Rhythm: Orality and Its Technologies*. New York: Fordham University Press, 2016.

———. "Outside the Parenthesis (Those People Were a Kind of Solution)." *MLN* 115, no. 5 (2000): 849–91.

———. *The Problem of a Chinese Aesthetic*. Stanford, CA: Stanford University Press, 1993.

———. Review of *La propension des choses: Pour une histoire de l'efficacité en Chine*, by François Jullien. *Journal of Asian Studies* 55, no. 4 (1996): 984–87.

———. Review of *Travels in China*, by Roland Barthes. *H-France Review* 13, no. 19 (2013). http://www.h-france.net/vol13reviews/vol13no19saussy.pdf.

Spivak, Gayatri Chakravorty. "French Feminism in an International Frame." *Yale French Studies*, no. 62 (1981): 154–84.

Sun, Cecile Chu-chin. *The Poetics of Repetition in English and Chinese Lyric Poetry*. Chicago: University of Chicago Press, 2011.

Van Norden, Bryan W. *Taking Back Philosophy: A Multicultural Manifesto*. New York: Columbia University Press, 2017.

Weber, Ralph. "What about the Billeter-Jullien Debate? And What Was It About? A Response to Thorsten Botz-Bornstein." *Philosophy East and West* 64, no. 1 (2014): 228–37.

Williams, Nicholas Morrow. *Imitations of the Self: Jiang Yan and Chinese Poetics*. Leiden: Brill, 2015.

———. "Sublimating Sorrow: How to Embrace Contradiction in Translating the 'Li Sao.'" In *Chinese Poetry and Translation: Rights and Wrongs*, edited by Maghiel van Crevel and Lucas Klein, 181–99. Amsterdam: Amsterdam University Press, 2019.

Yip, Wai-lim. *Diffusion of Distances: Dialogues between Chinese and Western Poetics*. Berkeley: University of California Press, 1993.

Yu, Pauline. "Hidden in Plain Sight? The Art of Hiding in Chinese Poetry." *Chinese Literature: Essays, Articles, Reviews* 30 (2008): 179–86.

———. *The Reading of Imagery in the Chinese Poetic Tradition*. Princeton, NJ: Princeton University Press, 1987.

Zhang, Longxi. "The Myth of the Other: China in the Eyes of the West." *Critical Inquiry* 15, no. 1 (1988): 108–31.

———. "The 'Tao' and the 'Logos': Notes on Derrida's Critique of Logocentrism." *Critical Inquiry* 11, no. 3 (1985): 385–98.

Zhao, Henry Y. H. "Contesting Confucius." *New Left Review* 44 (2007): 134–42.

Zhong, Yurou. *Chinese Grammatology: Script Revolution and Chinese Literary Modernity, 1916–1958*. New York: Columbia University Press, 2019.

Feminist Theories and Women Writers of Late Imperial China: Impact and Critique

GRACE S. FONG

Abstract *Feminism, feminist theory, feminist literary theory* were already highly contentious in what they represented to Euro-American critics and theorists in the 1980s, when scholars in Chinese literary studies began sustained research on women writers in late imperial China (ca. 1600–1911). Their research drew on developments in Western feminist theories while problematizing certain applications. In this article, I review major debates in 1980s and 1990s Western feminist literary theory, divided by the different approaches of Anglo-American and French feminist critics and gender studies, examining why specific arguments on women and language, genres studied, and theoretical underpinnings did not hold significant relevance to the study of similar issues when applied to women's writing in pre-twentieth-century China. Yet certain concepts were highly fruitful in critical analysis. Feminist theory was never monolithic, even when it was Eurocentric; theories were drawn from a plurality of different disciplines and schools. Concepts that came into currency—gender, gaze, voice, agency, subjectivity, authorship, and so on—from poststructuralist, postcolonial, cultural, and film studies proved to be useful tools in feminist literary studies. Some came to be deployed in scholarship on women's literature in historical China. In this context, I reflect on theoretical approaches in significant studies of women's writing of late imperial China and consider the impact or critique this subfield of Chinese literary studies posed to Western feminist theories and broader questions of the applicability of modern/postmodern feminist theories to literature of earlier periods and other cultures before the globalization of the twentieth and twenty-first centuries.

Keywords feminist theories, concepts and approaches, women's literature, Ming and Qing

Sinology and Feminism

This special issue on critical theory and Sinology provides an opportune venue to reflect on the confluence of feminist theory and criticism with developments

The Journal of Chinese Literature and Culture • 9:1 • April 2022
DOI 10.1215/23290048-9681176 • © 2022 by Duke University Press

in the field of Ming-Qing women's literary culture, particularly in the 1980s and 1990s.[1] Prior to the 1980s, studies of classical Chinese literature in the Western academy focused on a well-established tradition of canonical genres and authors from the period beginning with the Eastern Zhou dynasty (770–221 BCE) and ending with the Qing dynasty (1644–1911). The authoritative narrative written by eminent scholar Liu Dajie 劉大杰 (1904–1977), *Zhongguo wenxue fazhanshi* 中國文學發展史 (History of the Development of Chinese Literature), first published in the 1940s, remains a canonical work in Chinese literary history.[2] As pointedly noted by Maureen Robertson:

> In the 1,355 page edition of his history of premodern Chinese literature, a history that spans over 2,500 years, Liu Dajie mentions only five women who produced literary texts, none of them from periods later than the Song dynasty. Although we can safely assume that these women have not strayed into literary history because they were mistaken for men, it is clear that, given the extraordinary disproportion between the number of men and women represented, these five have been included as honorary men. They have, for literary and social reasons, been considered to have met criteria derived from and sustained by men's literary culture.[3]

In retrospect, the emergence of the field of women's writing and literary culture in the late imperial period in Chinese studies in North America was a propitious confluence of several signal events. First was the republication, in 1985, of an indispensable research tool: the comprehensive catalog *Lidai funü zhuzuo kao* 歷代婦女著作考 (Annotated Bibliography of Works by Women through the Ages) by Hu Wenkai 胡文楷 (ca. 1899–1988), originally published in 1957.[4] Hu's catalog records individual collections of writing by more than four thousand women. Of these, only 110 are from antiquity to the end of the Yuan dynasty (1279–1368); the rest are from the Ming and Qing periods. Consequently, Kang-i Sun Chang famously remarked, "No nation has produced more anthologies or collections of women's poetry than late imperial China."[5] Hu noted that many of these writings, recorded in local gazetteers and other sources, were lost or he had not personally seen them. Others were apparently still extant.[6] Most important, the publication of Hu's bibliography raised contemporary awareness of literary women in China's past as significant cultural producers and consumers; it identified surviving source materials and brought into view the possibility of doing research on them. Second was the accessibility given to foreign scholars during this period of opening up to locate and conduct research on women's extant writings that were kept in rare book archives in major libraries in China; women's voices suddenly became recoverable in these heretofore out-of-reach and unknown source materials. And third was the intersection of new literary research on Ming-Qing women writers with developments in feminist theory and criticism in the Western academy, the focus of this article. The first two circumstances together enabled the rediscovery of a significant number of collections of writing, especially poetry, the genre par excellence in which literary women wrote in the Ming and Qing periods. The third was the intersection with the vigorous theorization and analysis of women's literature during the second and third waves of feminism in the West (1960s–1980s, 1990s–2000s),[7] which energized if not always directly influenced research in this new terrain in Chinese literature.

While the "honorary men" included in Liu Dajie's literary history have been translated and studied, such as the Han woman scholar Ban Zhao (49–ca. 120) and especially the renowned *ci* 詞 (song lyric) poet Li Qingzhao 李清照 (1084–ca. 1145), and even a few other women poets in China's past outside of the canonical purview, such as Xi Peilan 席佩蘭 (1762–after 1829) and Wu Zao 吳藻 (ca. 1799–1862),[8] the very idea of women having a literary culture in the late imperial period was far from apparent. In 1988, Paul W. Kroll's condescending book review of Jeanne Larsen's translation of Tang courtesan Xue Tao's 薛濤 (768–831) poetry, *Brocade River Poems*, was published in the *Journal of the American Oriental Society*. In criticizing Larsen's translation and her overrepresentation of Xue Tao's talent and reputation, Kroll pointed to another "interesting element . . . relatively new on the sinological scene" that he found in this book:

> This is a concern with feminist issues, specifically with the retrieving of a distinct "women's literature" from the past. Worthy as this program may be, and notwithstanding the contributions recently made in this field by, for instance, scholars of medieval Western literature, there exists a major, undeniable obstacle with respect to reclaiming such a heritage from ancient and medieval China. To wit, there was no discernible Chinese tradition of literature written either by or for women. There is the occasional woman of whom has been preserved a limited number of poems (often only one), with no hint that these were produced for anything but a male audience. This fact, however, has not stopped some enthusiasts lately from discovering—or, rather inventing—such a tradition, presumably to show that sinology can be just as fashionable as other fields when it comes to "gender issues."[9]

Despite the sarcastic tone toward feminist and gender issues in relation to Sinology, Kroll's rejection of a "Chinese tradition of literature written either by or for women" in the early and medieval period is not without support from historical and textual evidence. Kroll's critique was made on the cusp of the momentous discovery of women's poetic culture in the Ming and Qing periods.[10]

A year later, a pioneering study of the phenomenon of women's literary culture and the subject of women's writing in late imperial China appeared in the journal *Late Imperial China*. In "The Epistolary World of Female Talent in Seventeenth-Century China," Ellen Widmer recovered a loose network of literary women based in the southeast region of Jiangnan whose letters and poems to each other were included in an epistolary collection compiled by male scholar-literati. Widmer showed that these women not only kept in touch with each other but also provided friendship and mutual support across temporal and geographical distances by exchanging letters and poetry. This revelation also questioned the May Fourth narrative of the oppressed "traditional" woman, pervasive through much of the twentieth century.[11] In conclusion, Widmer pointed to "these women's implicit challenge to traditional thinking about gender and creativity."[12] While Widmer did not reference any specific feminist theory or critical study, her statement indicates an effort to recuperate women's agency in late imperial China. Reflecting on this early intervention, Widmer reminisces on what led her to this research besides her discovery of these women's letters with this remark: "At the same time there was feminist theory making its way into my consciousness."[13] We may ask, which feminist theory made its way into Widmer's consciousness in the late 1980s and 1990s? Feminist theory was never singular; it was also far from focusing exclusively on literature. Feminist scholars engaged with and draw on a plurality of theories and frameworks from different disciplines, schools, and ideologies, from poststructuralism and deconstruction to psychoanalysis and Marxism, among many others. In random order, Widmer recalled: "Freudian theory, people like Judith Butler, Simone de Beauvoir. Gloria Steinem and Ms Magazine. Betty Friedan. Even politicians like Margaret Thatcher, Golda Meir. They opened up whole new ways of thinking about the world. That women are no less people than men. Their combined effect was to make me think why not use my training to look into what women were doing during the Ming and Qing?"[14] Feminism has retained its political and social activist roots from its beginning in the mid-nineteenth and early twentieth century, during the so-called first wave. Feminism's motivation for change, for the advancement and equality of women socially, politically, and intellectually broadly informs critical and theoretical elaborations in academic discourse. In Widmer's personal retrospective, we hear the impact of the inspirational and open-ended dynamism of feminism and feminist theories on a scholar of Chinese literature.

The difficulty with writing about the conjunction of feminism and Sinology is twofold: on the one hand is the pluralism of feminist theory; on the other, a certain resistance to Western theory in Sinology, especially since the rise of poststructuralism/postmodernism in the 1980s and 1990s.[15] In his 1989 book on theorizing the "subject" in the humanities, Paul Smith emphasizes feminism's multiplicity: "Feminism is constituted as a highly complex and widely diversified discourse, and one of its strengths is that it holds in tension and contradiction many different theoretical and practical propositions. Feminism is, in other words, an internally heterogeneous discourse, many aspects of which are concerned with questions of identity, subjectivity, and agency."[16] In this common concern for agency and a subject of change lies the potential for resistance to (patriarchal) hegemony. But the very diversity of feminist theories and critical approaches can and did become conflictual and fractured, resulting in dissenting and oppositional positions, discourses, and trajectories among feminist scholars, not to mention "attacks" and "backlash" from antagonistic male critics.[17] In the mid-1990s, Susan S. Friedman critiqued the monolithic focus on women and gender identity in American feminist criticism, which ignored the multidimensionality and intersectionality of identity formation and subject position in relation to race, ethnicity, sexuality, class, religion, nationality, and so on.[18] By the early 2000s, Rita Felski observed in *Literature after Feminism*: "The field of feminist criticism is ever more fragmented, many scholars focus on a specific genre, field, or subgroup of women, or alternatively spend their time deconstructing or endlessly qualifying the concept of woman. Judith Butler's wary statement, 'if one "is" a woman, that is surely not all one is,' pretty much sums up the tenor of much contemporary feminist work."[19]

The cool reception to poststructuralist theory in the Sinological field had several effects. There was a muted parting of the ways between those who "did" theory and those who did not. Feminist scholars deconstructed the monolithic concept of the traditional Chinese woman, engaging instead with women's multiple social roles and identities in critical analysis of their writing in a variety of literary genres.[20] Some scholars who adopted Western theoretical discourse assumed defensive positions. Maureen Robertson, in advance of or to fend off objections and criticism, stated explicitly her position in her groundbreaking analysis of gender representation in the dominant/male poetic tradition and women's entry into and reinscription of this tradition:

> Some recent models and concepts derived from cultural, feminist, and film theory outside the Chinese context can suggest alternative modes of reading and useful explanatory models for studying pre-modern poetries.... To the objection that critical concepts not derived from the Chinese tradition are in this context inappropriate, the answer must be that patriarchy and the gender arrangements that lead to a problematic relationship between women and their representation in language, and between women and writing, are not unique to the "West."[21]

These words and the venue in which they were uttered—*Late Imperial China* in 1992—marked a decisive new direction in Chinese literary studies and social history as the rediscovery of women's literary production in premodern China increased in scope and momentum. Women and gender difference began to drive sociohistorical research, textual analysis, ideological critique, and theoretical frameworks, generating new inquiries and innovative approaches and methodologies. Below I review several significant developments in Western feminist literary theory and criticism from the late 1970s to the early 2000s and show how they informed frameworks and approaches in the study of women's literary production in late imperial China, considering, on the one hand, questions of literary tradition and literary history, authorship, canon formation, and canonization in the context of women's writing, and, on the other, the deployment of transdisciplinary theories and concepts in critical analysis and de/constructive re/reading of gendered language and texts.[22]

A Literature of Their Own and a Female Literary Tradition

When sustained research took off on women writers in pre-twentieth century China, feminist critical theories and approaches were already contested ground among Euro-American scholars, critics, and theorists.[23] In her influential 1985 book *Sexual/Textual Politics: Feminist Literary Theory*, Toril Moi introduced, reviewed, and critiqued two main approaches in feminist literary theory and criticism. On one side was what Moi terms Anglo-American feminist criticism, represented by Elaine Showalter's *Literature of Their Own: British Women Novelists from Brontë to Lessing* (1977) and Sandra Gilbert and Susan Gubar's *Madwoman in the Attic: The Woman Writer and the Nineteenth-Century Literary Imagination* (1979). On the other side was French feminist theory, privileged by Moi and represented by the writings of Hélène Cixous, Luce Irigaray, and Julia Kristeva.[24] Briefly stated, the theoretical foundation of French feminist theory was Lacanian psychoanalysis, and reactions to it, in particular to Jacques Lacan's theory of male subject formation and phallocentrism, in which woman, without the phallus, is "lack" and the "other." In the form of *l'écriture féminine* (feminine writing), Cixous's and Irigaray's works celebrate the *jouissance* of the female body—idealized and, some would say, essentialized. Kristeva theorized the feminine "semiotic" language (fluid, even chaotic) exemplified in modernist avant-garde poetics, represented by the works of canonical male writers and poets such as Stéphane Mallarmé, James Joyce, and Antonin Artaud.[25] Given its orientation, French feminist theory had little theoretical or critical resonance for scholars engaging with the rediscovered writings of premodern women in classical Chinese genres.[26] Its relevance lay elsewhere.[27]

Elaine Showalter's *Literature of Their Own* was critiqued by Toril Moi for her unstated theoretical framework that "a text should reflect the writer's experience," which Moi considered a reflectionist or empiricist approach, essentializing by its biological determinism.[28] Indeed, Showalter describes her book as "an effort to describe the *female* literary tradition in the English novel from the generation of the Brontës to the present day,"[29] as though women's literature is a product of biological females rather than writing that is imbricated in socially constructed gender. Moi did praise Showalter's contribution to feminist criticism and literary history with her archival work and the rediscovery of minor, neglected, or forgotten women writers.[30] Showalter sought women writers' repeated themes, topics, patterns, and images and proposed a teleological literary history in three progressive phases, which she claimed was common to all literary subcultures. According to Showalter, for Victorian England there was first a feminine phase of "imitation" and "internalization" in which women wrote according to the ideas and values of the dominant culture— think Charlotte Brontë and George Eliot (1840–1880); then a feminist phase of "protest" in which women writers resisted these ideas and values and began to find their own, which included writers during the suffragette movement (1880– 1920); and last a female phase of "self-discovery" when they turned inward and searched for identity—think Katherine Mansfield and Virginia Woolf.[31] Despite Moi's critique, Showalter's women-centered and sociohistorical approach and her archival efforts to recover minor literature, here women's fiction, turned out to have broad impact on the literary field into the digital age—beyond print to digitization of archival materials and searchable databases of collections.[32]

A Literature of Their Own was followed two years later by what became another classic of Anglo-American feminist literary criticism: Sandra Gilbert and Susan Gubar's enormous 1979 work *The Madwoman in the Attic*. In their preface, the coauthors state that they "found what began to seem a distinctively female literary tradition" in their reading of women's writing from Jane Austin (1787–1809) to Sylvia Plath (1932–1963).[33] They locate recurring patterns of claustrophobic images, metaphors of confinement, and the figure of the "madwoman in the attic" (from *Jane Eyre*), which they read as a literary double that represents the rage and "anxiety of authorship" felt by the women authors living in a misogynistic world and writing in a male-dominated literary tradition.[34] Gilbert and Gubar refer to the work of Elaine Showalter and another early feminist critic Ellen Moers as having demonstrated "that nineteenth-century literary women *did* have both a literature and a culture of their own— that . . . there was a rich and clearly defined female literary subculture, a community in which women consciously read and related to each other's works."[35] Notwithstanding differences in language, genre, and subject matter, Anglo-

American feminist critics' discovery and their conceptualization of a women's literary tradition and subculture held appeal and offered ways to consider this phenomenon across time and space in other social and cultural contexts.

At a 1990 conference on *ci* poetry, literary scholar John Timothy Wixted delivered the essay "The Poetry of Li Ch'ing-chao: A Woman Author and Women's Authorship," published four years later in *Voices of the Song Lyric in China*, edited by Pauline Yu. Wixted engaged explicitly with the conceptualization of a "distinct female literary tradition" in Song China and the question of women's authorship raised by Gilbert and Gubar, only to disavow both. Wixted opens the essay with a series of questions:

> The poetry of Li Ch'ing-chao . . . prompts fundamental questions when viewed from Western perspectives, especially feminist ones. Is there a separate women's literary tradition in China? If so, what is her place in it? Has her corpus of writings been viewed as being specifically female, and has it been viewed differently by men and by women? Is there a distinct female consciousness operative in her writing as well as that of other women writers? In what sense, if any, might she be viewed as being a feminist? And finally, what light might analysis of her work shed on current Western theoretical debate about women's writing, which is often couched in universalist terms?[36]

Wixted should be recognized for his vanguard efforts among Sinologists to engage with Western feminist theory. But his choice of Li Qingzhao, one of the "honorary men" in Liu Dajie's literary history, and the near total loss of her writings make for an improbable subject for the inquiry. By the 1990s, his questions also rang essentialist and ahistorical. Wixted asked if Li Qingzhao referred to other women poets before or during her time, and if later women poets cited her or modeled their song lyrics on hers. Drawing evidence from meticulous and comprehensive sources on every mention of Li Qingzhao compiled by modern Chinese scholars, by the end of the essay Wixted answered the questions he posed in the negative and concluded that there was no "separate female consciousness" or a "separate female literary tradition." He admitted that perhaps these questions could be raised about women poets in the Ming and Qing, as scholars were beginning to identify, translate, and analyze them in their research. The changing tide in the recognition of later women lyricists in fact had already arrived on the scene in essays by Kang-i Sun Chang and Grace Fong, which turned to the issue of gender in relation to text and voice (discussed in the next section).[37]

Later in the same year, a colloquium was held titled "Poetry and Women's Culture in Late Imperial China," from which four papers were published in a special issue of *Late Imperial China* (1992)—two by historians Dorothy Ko and

Susan Mann and two by literary scholars Maureen Robertson and Ellen Widmer. While Robertson's groundbreaking article "Voicing the Feminine: Constructions of the Gendered Subject in Lyric Poetry of Medieval and Late Imperial China" engages with such concepts as subject, negotiation, and voice as central theoretical issues in her critical analysis, it is also concerned with the question of women's literary culture and tradition in premodern China. Robertson eloquently contends that,

> to account for the absence of women in standard Chinese literary histories, one must consider the naturalization and institutionalization of women's exclusion from all intellectual and literary activity, with rationales based upon a purported "natural order" that defines sexual difference in such a way as to empower patriarchy and allocate written language to the masculine, public sphere. Further, the consequent informality of women's education, the narrow construction by male writers of a feminine literary voice, and most of all the absence of mechanisms for the preservation of women's writings for most of the imperial period meant that until very late in this period no women's literary culture was visible, socially approved, and capable of giving rise to the concept of a tradition of women writing.[38]

Robertson explains the invisibility of women's literary tradition in most of Chinese history in terms of social, institutional, and material constraints imposed on their gender. Now the time has come, she argues, when a tradition of women's literature, or women's literary culture and authorship, in the Ming and Qing are conceivable and discernible.

Women Writers of Traditional China: An Anthology of Poetry and Criticism, edited by Kang-i Sun Chang and Haun Saussy, can be viewed as the first work to present a women's "literature of their own" in Sinological fashion, through translation and annotation of the selected poems. Insofar as canon formation was a much-debated topic and practice in feminist literary theory and criticism, implicating more broadly the humanities (questioning the Great Books) in the 1980s and 1990s, which was closely connected to issues of pedagogy and curricular change, and the "crisis of the humanities" writ large,[39] *Women Writers of Traditional China* can also be described as an effort to form a separate or alternative canon of Chinese literature in that anthologies function to select, present, and promulgate authors and texts and are instrumental in processes of canonization. With translations by a formidable team of some sixty scholars, selected poems by close to 150 women poets—most from the Ming and Qing—the anthology is organized chronologically, with each poet accompanied by a brief biographical account and notes on her poems. Also included are selected critical writings on women's poetry by both women (twenty-two total) and men (twenty-eight) from the Han to the end of the Qing dynasty in the section "Criticism." The editors' succinct introduction shows how poetry "[opened] up a women's tradition: a well-marked social function, a group of stylistic and personal models . . . , and contexts in which the display of talent was permissible and might eventually become truly public."[40] Published in 1999, the anthology literally put premodern women poets and writers on the map of China and Chinese studies, with maps of the southeast Jiangnan region where women poets flourished and of the distribution of women writers in counties of the Qing Empire, reproduced from the two new social histories of Ming and Qing women's literary culture by feminist historians Dorothy Ko and Susan Mann.[41] Pedagogically, *Women Writers of Traditional China*, serving as a much-needed textbook, enabled the entry of Chinese women writers into undergraduate curricula in the North American academy.

At the same time, *Women Writers of Traditional China* demonstrates a divergence from the theory and practice of gynocriticism advocated by Elaine Showalter and American feminist critics.[42] Characterized by Susan Friedman as "the historical study of women writers as a distinct literary tradition," gynocriticism is a women-centered and separatist approach based on sexual difference and the existence of patriarchy. But Friedman criticizes gynocriticism's privileging gender as the constituent of identity to the neglect of advances in other theories and discourses of identity and subjectivity, which emphasize their plurality and intersectionality.[43] While Chang and Saussy's anthology demonstrates an effort to "canonize" Chinese women poets, to give recognition to their writing,[44] the inclusion of male critics' writings on women poets and their lives and poetry is subtly informed by the concept of androgyny, the "ideal synthesis of male and female" in Western philosophy and aesthetics, as elaborated especially in Camille Paglia's *Sexual Personae: Art and Decadence from Nefertiti to Emily Dickinson* (1990) and referenced by Chang in her article "Ming-Qing Women Poets and Cultural Androgyny."[45] Chang uses cultural androgyny to characterize a complementary, rather than oppositional, aesthetic and literary culture shared by literati men and talented women in seventeenth-century late Ming society.[46] She describes an idealized picture of the feminine/feminized culture of marginalized male literati, who retreated to literature and the arts rather than engage in (or when they failed to succeed in) the public world of male pursuit in scholarship and politics. Conversely, literary women of talent created for themselves a world of scholarship and the arts parallel to that of the male scholars who often supported them. In Chang's optimistic view, "Ming-Qing women poets considered themselves part of the literati culture, in which men and women worked *together* to promote women's writing."[47] While there is an element of truth in this idealized literary culture of gender complementarity, in reality contending views expressing both support for and opposition to women's participation in learning and writing by both men and women persisted to the end of the imperial period.[48]

Research since the 1990s indeed demonstrates that women's literary culture in the Ming and Qing grew irreversibly to the end of the imperial period amid competing cultural currents and the vicissitudes of politics and history. Facilitated by the retrieval of material sources and feminist approaches, historians and literary scholars produced "histories" of writing women. In *The Red Brush: Writing Women in Imperial China* (2004), a massive 931-page tome, Wilt Idema and Beata Grant coauthored a "separate history" of women's literature consisting of translations of individual women's literary works contextualized by succinct biographical and historical material for the two-thousand-year imperial period. On the macrohistorical level, *The Red Brush* identifies two "high tides" of women's literature, first in the long seventeenth century that witnessed the rise of women's writing and publishing in the affluent society and innovative philosophical and artistic culture of the late Ming, and continuing to the turmoil of the Ming-Qing transition, followed by the consolidation of Manchu rule in the late seventeenth and early eighteenth century.[49] Contrary to expectation, Idema and Grant note during the prosperous period of the high Qing in the eighteenth century a "lull, . . . a temporary decline in the visibility of women's writing."[50] The authors do not provide comparative figures or possible causes for the "temporary decline" but point to the class dominance of gentry women writers in the second high tide beginning in the late eighteenth and through the nineteenth century.[51] They characterize the first high tide by the broad social classes of the women poets, who included prominent courtesans, gentry wives and daughters, and Chan Buddhist female masters and nuns; and the second high tide by the broader range of genres in which gentry women writers engaged, such as drama, *tanci* 彈詞 fiction, and prose in addition to the dominant genre of poetry.

In the publication of *The Cambridge History of Chinese Literature* (2010) edited by Kang-i Sun Chang and Stephen Owen, feminist and Sinological studies finally crossed paths after more than two decades of contact. This much lauded two-volume literary history covers three millennia from antiquity to 1375 and from 1375 to the present.[52] One innovative decision, in the editors' words, is "to move toward a more integrated historical approach, creating a cultural history or a history of literary culture" rather than a literary history with the customary practice of using genres and a strictly dynastic timeline as organizing principles.[53] From the perspective of women's literature, this reconceptualization of literary history effected the integration of gender issues and women's cultural production into the narrative at significant historical junctions in each chapter.[54] Giovanni Vitiello, in his review, notes the editors' interests in the "broader cultural and discursive contexts in which literary works have been produced" and, among issues for historical investigation, those "concerning the formation of identities, both in terms of ethnicity and gender."[55] In his glowing review, aptly titled "After Long Years," Paul Kroll now recognizes the "discernible Chinese tradition of literature written . . . by or for women" that he had categorically denied in early and medieval Chinese literature almost a quarter century before.[56] He praises the first chapter by Kang-i Sun Chang on "Literature of the early Ming to Mid-Ming (1375–1572)": "It is Chang's examination of women's writing that is of most moment. During this period, for the first time in Chinese history, women writers appear in numbers instead of as isolated and unusual figures. Not only do their own works call for notice, they also took the lead in rediscovering and reinterpreting the works of earlier women, such as Li Qingzhao."[57] Such recognition of women's place in the literary culture of late imperial China in both *The Cambridge History of Chinese Literature* and the book reviews bespeak the intervening literary and historical scholarship, which drew from feminist theories (among others), concepts, and critiques, that have brought Ming and Qing women writers into critical visibility. These efforts are the subject of the next section.

Critical and Theoretical Engagement

As indicated earlier, the 1990s marked the beginning of North American scholars' concerted engagement with the recovered literary writing by women of the Ming and Qing. To different degrees, implicitly or explicitly, concepts and theories drawn from or, rather, filtered through feminist critical practices were used as analytical tools to excavate the compositional and discursive significance of these writings and their cultural ecology over time. Terms such as *gaze, voice, subjectivity, authorship, agency,* and *self-representation* exemplify some of the salient theoretical concepts applied in feminist-oriented analysis by literary scholars. Many terms have maintained currency into the twenty-first century and become part of a shared critical vocabulary, while others grew into genres or even fields in feminist studies, in and out of Sinology.

In the early 1990s, several breakthrough literary studies characterized emergent trends inflected by feminist approaches in Sinological studies.[58] The authors of two studies explicitly introduced feminist theoretical concepts into their analysis. Maureen Robertson and Grace Fong took up the concepts of (male) gaze and (female) voice to investigate the gendered dimensions in the manipulation of image and rhetoric in the two foremost genres of poetry, *shi* and *ci*, in their respective articles "Voicing the Feminine" and "Engendering the Lyric."[59] The theory of the (male) gaze was developed by feminist film critic Laura Mulvey in her seminal 1976 article, "Visual Pleasure and Narrative

Cinema." Mulvey asserts that she appropriates Freudian and Lacanian psycho-analytic theory of male subject formation "as a political weapon" provided by patriarchy to deconstruct how classical Hollywood film is structured around the male gaze, which objectifies and stereotypes women through the looks of the camera, the male characters within the filmic diegesis, and through these, the male spectator, and exposes the underlying phallocentrism.[60] In this discursive context, Mulvey establishes viewing in classical Hollywood cinema as the pleasure of voyeuristic looking, that is to say, as scopophilia predicated on phallocentrism in which man (both as spectator and as male character) is the active "bearer of the look" and woman the passive "image" or eroticized object in the film.[61] She deconstructs the constructed visual pleasure in the sense that, as she puts it, "analyzing pleasure, or beauty, destroys it."[62] In Robertson's and Fong's studies, Mulvey's concept of the male gaze (minus its Freudian psycho-analytic implications of castration and lack) in classical Hollywood film seemingly finds an unproblematic application in the classic palace-style poetry (*gongti shi* 宮體詩) produced in the princely court and literary salon of Crown Prince Xiao Gang 蕭綱 (503–551) of the Liang dynasty (502–556). Xiao Gang commissioned the anthology *Yutai xinyong* 玉臺新詠 (New Songs from Jade Terrace), which came to exemplify palace-style verse in the later poetic tradition, castigated by Confucian-minded scholars but imitated by poets attracted to its incarnation of sensuous beauty and consummate skill necessary to capture it. A repertory of poems in *Yutai xinyong* depicts images of beautiful women for the consumption of male readers/spectators.[63] When the female persona speaks her feelings, Robertson argues, "these versions of a feminine voice and image" are "spoken by men and presented to a readership of men . . . ; they feature a non-referential, iconic image and projected voice, an empty signifier, into which the male author/reader may project his desire." She labels this feminine voice produced by male poets the "literati-feminine voice"[64] and illustrates her point with the poem "Cold Bedroom:"

> After you left, the spring pond
> was not the same; lotus gone,
> on the verge of freezing over.
> In my workbox, scissors feel icy,
> by the mirror, creams congeal.
> My slender waist is now so weak
> I fear it will give way
> under this cold dress.[65]

Robertson decodes the images spoken by the "literati-feminine voice" as follows: "The 'spring pond' (bed), 'lotus' (*he*, a pun for *he*, 'union'), and imagery of scissors, creams, waist, and what is 'under the dress' combine with the speaker's complaints about the 'cold' and her 'fear' to allow the poem to send the double message of helpless suffering and sexuality."[66] The poem plays on male desire and invites the reader into the imaginary space vacated by the absence of the lover.

As for Fong, although her study is on the *ci* genre, she also selects poems from *Yutai xinyong* to illustrate the "male gaze," rather than exemplary *ci*, such as the set written to the melody "Pusa man" 菩薩蠻 (Deva-like Barbarian), by the late Tang poet Wen Tingyun 溫庭筠 (ca. 812–ca. 870), frequently with lines depicting a lovelorn female persona that engage voyeurism:

> A feathered hairpin falls close to her face.
> She is lonely in the fragrance of her boudoir.
> Tears flow down her cheeks for one far away.
> The swallows fly off leaving spring to fade.[67]

The selected poem by Xiao Gang in *Yutai xinyong*, "On a Wife Taking a Nap during the Day," describes a female persona alone in her boudoir taking a nap by the window, hence affording an opening, a view into sensual close-ups of her body—face, hair, wrists, and perspiration:

> Smiling as she dreams, lovely dimples appear;
> sleeping on her chignon, crushed petals drop.
> Patterns of the bamboo mat impressed on jade wrists,
> fragrant perspiration soaks the red silk.

Fong follows with this reading: "The male gaze is blatantly implicated in the poem . . . and the reader with it, as the movement of a voyeur's eyes leads to a visual caressing of the female body."[68] Palace-style poetry is taken as analogous to classical Hollywood film, providing visual pleasure to male readers in verbal constructs. While analyzing poems in *Yutai xinyong* is made into an effective tool to deconstruct the gaze instituted in palace-style verse, if indeed analysis destroys pleasure as claimed by Mulvey, scholars may feel this analytic appropriation narrows the scope, variety, and influence on the formation of the visual poetics of palace-style poetry. Indeed, palace-style poetry grew out of developments of landscape poetry in the Six Dynasties, which focused on the descriptive mode, and its repertory was broader than the "literati-feminine" style—to use Robertson's term—represented in *Yutai xinyong*.[69] There, the focus on the description of elements of nature, the landscape, and the outside turned to objects and the interior, which included the objectification of women. Presented not as a direct critique of such recent appropriations of poems in the anthology but as a corrective to traditional misunderstanding of palace-style poetry in the broader context of Liang court culture, Xiaofei Tian reorients new developments in palace-style poetics, in particular its visual focus on objects and light, to the influence of Buddhism. She contends that the spread of Buddhism with its practices of meditative concentration and visualization prompted the development of a "new poetics of seeing" in the Liang court. With regard to palace-style poetry, Tian elaborates that "instead of a poetry 'about women and romantic love,' this poetry is about concentration, about new, focused ways of looking, and about the extraordinary, and yet often ignored, power of noticing."[70] Although one might agree with Tian that Liang palace-style poetry had a wider topical and thematic range than that evinced in the poems selected for inclusion in *Yutai xinyong*, from the perspective of gendered poetics in palace-style poetry the statement by Anne Birrell, who translated the complete *Yutai xinyong*, that the entire content of the anthology consists of 656 love poems would hold.[71] The poems in the *Yutai xinyong* suggest that court poets often took their fine-tuned sense of seeing and interest in describing scenes and objects to the boudoir and inner chambers rather than the meditation room or scholar's studio.

It is not surprising that voice would be a major issue of concern in early feminist interventions which has continued in recent scholarship. As Li Guo puts it so succinctly in the introduction to her 2015 monograph on the genre of women's *tanci* fiction in late imperial China: "My point of departure for this study is voice, a theme which I explore not merely as an affect of speaking established through women's textual maneuvers or constructed through patterns of oral narratives, but also as an act of acquiring social agency, of reinforcing one's subjectivity through speaking, of evoking the spirit of the past and embracing the present, and of finding empowerment and spiritual survival through one's own words."[72] Indeed, how did or could women, the "second sex" who occupied a subordinate position in patriarchal societies throughout history, articulate their subjectivities, speak their gendered selves in male-dominant cultural traditions? Economic, social, and cultural changes in the late Ming and Qing afforded opportunities to not a few women in scholar-literati and wealthy merchant families to study and acquire literacy and in many cases even cultivate their literary talents in the domestic setting because of both accommodating parents and their own desire and motivation. The unique nature, status, and function of poetry for self-expression and communication in Chinese culture and society facilitated women's entry into the dominant genre for writing the self.[73] How did women then inscribe their gendered selves in a poetic language that had been established by male poets for more than a millennium? In their early endeavors, Robertson and Fong approached this question by examining two different genres of poetry and set up the male appropriation of feminine voice and the objectification of the feminine image, discussed above, as a foil to their reading of historical women's poetic voice. Robertson showed women poets negotiating with the established poetic language using various strategies, such as assuming the gaze as the active viewer and giving a different meaning to conventional image codes in the context of the poem, recoding tropes from a gendered perspective, and rewriting the poetic context and response. Robertson aptly illustrates this with Pang Wan's 龐畹 (eighteenth century) poem "Things Whispered at the Window, Number One" 瑣窗雜事 (Suochuang zashi, yi), in which the poet "acknowledges the convention but recuperates the image [plum blossoms] in the voice of the married woman [a mother]."[74] In the process, Robertson suggests, women expanded the topical terrain of poetry to inscribe their gendered roles and experiences; she raises the potential ambiguity in women's language when they borrow the lover's discourse in writing about friendship as an area for exploration. In contrast, Fong, working with the *ci* genre, emphasizes the formation of the genre's feminine aesthetics and poetics in its origins in the entertainment quarters—the world of singing girls and courtesans in the late Tang. In her words, the *ci* genre "was primarily associated with the boudoir theme, with images of women in love, and, therefore, with the 'feminine' in language and sentiment." She then turns to examine how women poets negotiate the language of this "feminine" genre to voice feelings and emotions other than love longing, whether it is loneliness, joy, or sorrow, even though the topoi and diction of *ci* are marked by the male appropriation of the feminine.[75] In this early study, Fong also touches on the topic of women's homosociality, as illustrated by the *ci* of the prolific Manchu poet Gu Chun 顧春 (Gu Taiqing 顧太清, 1799–1877) and the voice of gender discontent and heroism in women's *ci*. The latter topics were later elaborated and deepened in the work of Xiaorong Li.[76]

Voice, especially in poetic realization, continues to occupy detailed critical attention in Wai-yee Li's monumental study *Women and National Trauma in Late Imperial Chinese Literature*,[77] which devotes almost two hundred pages (about one-third of the book) to close textual readings of cross-gender appropriations of voice in chapters 1 and 2, respectively titled in mirror-image fashion, "Male Voices Appropriating Feminine Diction" and "Female Voices Appropriating Masculine Diction." By the 2010s, explicit theorization was no longer felt to be necessary. Common theoretical terms, feminist or otherwise, had been assimilated into the critical vocabulary of Sinological scholarship.

In the twenty-first century, another noteworthy development was the sustained interest in gendered subjectivity and self-representation in premodern Chinese literature, which paralleled research directions and theoretical advances made in feminist scholarship on women's autobiographical writing in the West.[78] The titles of major sections in *Women, Autobiography, Theory: A Reader* compiled by Sidonie Smith and Julia Watson, such as "Experience and Agency," "Subjectivities," "Modes and Genres," "Histories," and "Voice and Memory," reflect the fundamental theoretical and interdisciplinary interests in this research domain. Already in the 1990s, the explicit focus on subject and subject positions was the second theoretical engagement by Robertson in her article "Changing the Subject." She examines women poets' subject position as author in their autobiographical prefaces written to the publication of their own poetry collections. She identifies a shift from a "discourse of women's virtue, in which women put forth modest excuses for engaging in writing, to a discourse of literature," in which they exhibit assertive confidence in their subject position as author in literary culture.[79] Robertson then draws on the concept of performance, made popular by feminist cultural critic Judith Butler in her book *Gender Trouble*, to examine women poets' self-representation in *shi* poetry. However, she restricts its application narrowly "to refer to instances in which women as writers assume authorial positions and interests that are gendered masculine and display their literary competence in reproducing text subjects modeled completely upon those originating in literati poetry."[80]

Abetted by a substantial corpus of rediscovered collections of writings authored by individual women in the hundreds made available by modern print and digital technology, scholars have been discovering wide-ranging forms and frameworks of self-writing or autobiographical writing by women in the Ming and Qing that invite investigation beyond local textual focus on tropes, metaphors, and rhetoric of the self to the forms and practices that women negotiated or appropriated from the dominant literary tradition or that they devised or invented to articulate their gendered self—their subjectivity and social agency—in writing their life experiences, thoughts, and emotions. Monographs by Beata Grant, Grace Fong, and Binbin Yang are examples that explore the rich autobiographical writings by women of different social statuses and genres of writing in addition to poetry, including Chan Buddhist discourse records (*yulu* 語錄), genealogical writing, letters, inscriptions on self-portraits, and travel journals.[81] Recent scholarship both draws inspiration as well as diverges from feminist theory and criticism. While Xiaorong Li reconceptualizes the feminine space of the boudoir as women poets textualized and resignified the social functions and aesthetic meanings of their lived space, Haihong Yang revisions the poetry and poetics produced and practiced by women as a dynamic "dialogic engagement."

Finally, also in Yang's book, we return to a contentious issue raised at the beginning of this article and at the beginning of research in the 1990s on women writers in Ming and Qing China: in chapter 2, "'To Blaze One's Own Path': Allusion and Renovated Subjectivity in Women's Poetry," Yang provides a clear case in the erudite woman historian-poet Wang Duan 汪端 (1793–1838), who "is consciously engaged in establishing a women's writing and cultural tradition,"[82] and the means by which Wang accomplishes this, according to Yang, is by alluding to women writers in the past and promoting the literary works and reputation of contemporary women poets in her own writings and publications.[83] By showing Wang Duan's aptitude in employing allusion, a pervasive Chinese literary device that requires broad erudition, as a discursive tool to produce revisionist readings of historical women's subjectivity, Yang's own scholarship has effectively put Sinological method to feminist ends.[84]

Conclusion

To conclude, we return to the iconic figure of the Chinese woman poet Li Qingzhao, here as outlined in Ronald Egan's recent magnum opus, *The Burden of Female Talent: The Poet Li Qingzhao and Her History in China* (2013). Egan enables us to recognize the constructive interaction of feminist theory and criticism and Sinological scholarship:

> The reconsideration of Li Qingzhao's life and works presented in this volume owes a substantial debt to feminist literary criticism and scholarship as it has developed in recent decades outside of Chinese studies. Discoveries about the meanings found in writings by women in Europe and America before the twentieth century, including well-known writers and those long neglected, have been valuable in clarifying gender dynamics and biases against women who write that are certainly not unique to China. Thus I have profited from reading studies by Rita Felski, Sarah Prescott, Paula Backscheider, and others. In addition, new insights developed during the past twenty-five years in the burgeoning fields of Chinese women's history and women's literary history, mostly focused on the Ming-Qing period, have also helped to shape my understanding of what questions to formulate and how to go about answering them.[85]

Ronald Egan's acknowledgment indicates the productive connection of Sinological scholarship with feminist literary criticism and theory in the more than two decades since the emergent research on women writers of the Ming and Qing. Reciprocal signs of recognition are also coming from the other direction as women writers of late imperial China will be participating in projects such as the Palgrave Encyclopedia of Early Modern Women's Writing (sixteenth–seventeenth century).

GRACE S. FONG   方秀潔
McGill University
grace.fong@mcgill.ca

Acknowledgment
I thank my colleague Miranda Hickman for her comments and questions when I was drafting the abstract for this article and the two anonymous readers for their suggestions.

Notes

1. I use the term *Sinology* in this article as it is in the title of the special issue and in the recent reclaimed meaning of Chinese or China studies broadly, rather than in its historically weighted meaning of the philological study of Chinese language and culture. Adrian Chan provides a simple, politically "neutral" definition: "The study of aspects of Chinese culture while reporting one's findings in a language other than Chinese" (*Orientalism in Sinology*, 1).

2. A detailed history of the numerous republications of Liu Dajie's magnum opus in the People's Republic of China is provided in the preface to the 2006 edition published by Fudan University Press (see https://www.fudanpress.com/news/showdetail.asp?bookid=3956). Numerous editions have also been published in Taiwan and Hong Kong.

3. Robertson, "Voicing the Feminine," 64. Li Qingzhao 李清照 (1084–ca. 1145) is the only woman poet whose name appears in Liu Dajie's table of contents as a *nü ciren* 女詞人 (woman song lyricist).

4. Hu and his wife, Wang Xiuqin 王秀琴 (ca. 1900–1934), conducted exhaustive research in the 1920s, and Hu continued the work after Wang's death. The first edition in 1957 was an untimely publication, coming at the beginning of the anti-intellectual Anti-Rightist campaign. The 1985 edition went out of print in the 1990s. Shanghai Guji Chubanshe printed an expanded edition in 2008, edited by Zhang Hongsheng, which includes 261 additional women writers; see Hu and Zhang, *Lidai funü*, 1136–83.

5. Chang, "Ming and Qing Anthologies," 147. Chang first made this eminently quotable pronouncement with slight variation in a lecture, titled "Ming-Qing Women Poets and Cultural Androgyny," delivered in 1995 and subsequently published in *Tamkang Review* (1999) and again in *Feminism/Femininity in Chinese Literature*, edited by Peng-hsiang Chen and Whitney Crothers Dilley (Brill, 2002).

6. Hu notes after the title of each item whether he had personally seen the work or not. Zhao Houjun 趙厚均, professor at East China Normal University and editorial team member of *Jiangnan nüxing bieji* 江南女性別集 (Literary Collections by Women in Jiangnan), vols. 1–5, edited by Hu Xiaoming and Peng Guozhong (Hefei: Huangshan Shushe, 2014–2019), estimates that approximately eight hundred to one thousand collections, roughly one-quarter of those identified in Hu Wenkai's catalog, are still extant. Pers. comm. with the author, 2015–16.

7. The "waves" of feminism are defined by their development as social and political movements rather than literary theories as such, although the currency of different critical theories may be associated with specific waves. See Dicker, *History of American Feminism*.

8.   See Swann, *Pan Chao*; Hawkes, "Xi Peilan"; and Wu Zao in Rexroth and Chung, *Orchid Boat*, 72–76.

9.   Kroll, ". . . Fair and Yet Not Found," 623.

10.   There was then also the customary Sinological disregard for the classical poetic tradition after the Song period. The enormous output of poetry by male scholar-literati in the Ming and Qing received little notice.

11.   Emma Teng reviews the development of "women's studies" within China studies in the Western academy in "Construction of the 'Traditional Chinese Woman'"; see especially her discussion of the May Fourth emphasis on the victimization of women in "traditional China" (116–17n4).

12.   Widmer, "Epistolary World," 34.

13.   Widmer, pers. comm., June 26, 2021.

14.   Ibid.

15.   Eugenia Lean provides a review of the resistance to theory among historians of China in "Reflections on Theory."

16.   Smith, *Discerning the Subject*, 138.

17.   Rita Felski cites vitriolic barbs against feminist scholars made by conservative male critics such as Harold Bloom and John Ellis in *Literature after Feminism*, 1–13.

18.   Friedman, "'Beyond' Gynocriticism and Gynesis."

19.   Felski, *Literature after Feminism*, 4.

20.   See Teng, "Construction of the 'Traditional Chinese Woman.'" As noted earlier, most commonly women wrote poetry in the major poetic genres of *shi* 詩 (poetry) and *ci* 詞 (song lyrics). They also wrote *tanci* 彈詞 fiction, variously translated as plucking rhymes, prosimetric narrative, or verse novel. See Idema and Grant, *Red Brush*, chap. 15, "Plucking Rhymes." The first prose fiction written by a woman, *Honglou meng ying* 紅樓夢影 (Shadows of the Dream of the Red Chamber), a sequel to the masterwork *Honglou meng* (Dream of the Red Chamber), was published in 1875. But Gu Taiqing 顧太清 (1799– 1877), the author of this work, wrote using a male-sounding penname, and her authorship was discovered only in the 1990s. See Widmer, "*Honglou meng ying.*"

21.   Robertson, "Voicing the Feminine," 66–67.

22.   Space and specialization limit this article to feminist-inspired research directly on women and the recuperation of their voices, experiences, and subjectivities inscribed in their poetry. I do not cover paradigm shifts in the study of gender and sexuality in other genres, notably fiction and drama, in works by literary scholars Maram Epstein, Keith McMahon, Tina Lu, and Giovanni Vitiello, among others, not to mention the field-changing contributions of such historians as Susan Mann, Dorothy Ko, Francesca Bray, and Janet Theiss, whose scholarship on women and gender have provided indispensable knowledge and contexts for understanding these women as social and historical subjects.

23.   Both phrases in the heading for this section are from Showalter, *Literature of Their Own* (title and p. 11).

24.   Moi, *Sexual/Textual Politics*, 11–13, 97–166. Their representative works discussed by Moi are Cixous's *Laugh of the Medusa*, Irigaray's *Speculum of the Other Woman*, and Kristeva's *Desire in Language: A Semiotic Approach to Literature and Art*.

25.   See the critique of *l'écriture feminine* and semiotic language in Jones, "Writing the Body."

26.   Kristeva's *About Chinese Women* (1974, English translation 1977) presented an ahistorical and idealized view. She mentioned Li Qingzhao (90–93) in the chapter titled "Confucius—

An Eater of Women." Written after her trip to China during the Cultural Revolution as a member of the leftist *Tel Quel* group of French intellectuals, the book had little, if any, impact on scholarship on Chinese literature.

27. In the 1990s, there was discernible interest in *l'écriture feminine* through translation among critics and women writers in China. It has been suggested that *l'écriture feminine* had an influence on body writing and private writing of Chinese women writers in 1990s, although some writers, such as Chen Ran and Lin Bai, deny any knowledge or influence of French feminine writing.

28. Moi, *Sexual/Textual Politics*, 4.

29. Showalter, *Literature of Their Own*, 11; emphasis added.

30. Moi, *Sexual/Textual Politics*, 55–56, 74–79. Showalter provides an impressive biographical index of two hundred Victorian women writers (1977 edition), many of whom had been forgotten in dusty corners of libraries.

31. Showalter, *Literature of Their Own*, 13.

32. See, e.g., the Orlando Project: Feminist Literary History and Digital Humanities (University of Alberta), https://www.artsrn.ualberta.ca/orlando/; Victorian Women Writers (Indiana University), webapp1.dlib.indiana.edu/vwwp/welcome.do; French Women Writers (University of Chicago), artfl-project.uchicago.edu/node/115; and, in the China field, Ming Qing Women's Writings, digital.library.mcgill.ca/mingqing/. See also Wernimont and Flanders, "Feminism in the Age of Digital Archives."

33. Gilbert and Gubar, *Madwoman in the Attic*, xi.

34. Surprisingly, Gilbert and Gubar's study of women's authorship draws on Harold Bloom's famous androcentric model in his 1973 *Anxiety of Influence: A Theory of Poetry*: "Our literary methodology has therefore been based on the Bloomian premise that literary history consists of strong action and inevitable reaction" (*Madwoman in the Attic*, xviii–xix).

35. Ibid., xii.

36. Wixted, "Poetry of Li Ch'ing-chao," 145. Wixted cites Western feminist literary theory in Vincent Leitch's *American Literary Criticism* (162n84) and addresses the mad woman figure in Gilbert and Gubar's volume (162n85). In another note he cites Kristeva's extensive musings on Li Qingzhao and sees a "quasi-parallel" for "female feminist writers in China" provided by Showalter's three phases in Anglo-American women's literary history (164–65n91).

37. Chang, "Liu Shih and Hsü Ts'an"; Fong, "Engendering the Lyric."

38. Robertson, "Voicing the Feminine," 64.

39. See the section "Canon" in Warhol and Herndl, *Feminisms*, and Guillory's sophisticated analysis in *Cultural Capital*, esp. chap. 1, "Canonical and Noncanonical."

40. Chang and Saussy, *Women Writers of Traditional China*, 5.

41. Ko, *Teachers of the Inner Chambers*; Mann, *Precious Records*. These three publications, complemented by the new theoretical and critical scholarship on women's literature, made it possible to offer courses on pre-twentieth-century women poets and writers in China for the first time in the late twentieth and early twenty-first century.

42. The term *gynocriticism* was coined by Showalter and first appeared in "Toward a Feminist Poetics" (1979).

43. Friedman, "'Beyond' Gynocriticism and Gynesis," 14.

44. For Chang's interest in canonization of women poets by male compilers of anthologies in the Ming and Qing, see Chang, "Gender and Canonicity."

45. Cited in Chang, "Ming-Qing Women Poets," 24n8.

46. Ibid., 24.

47. Ibid., 25.

48. Chang's "androgynous" literati culture bears similarity to what Charlotte Furth calls the "bohemian counterculture" of the late Ming and the high Qing, which rebelled against orthodox values yet remained dependent on elite wealth for economic and social support of their aesthetic pursuits. See Furth, "Patriarch's Legacy."

49. Idema and Grant, *Red Brush*, 6–7, 347–58. Ko, *Teachers of the Inner Chambers*, details these cultural developments and gentry women's roles in them.

50. Idema and Grant, *Red Brush*, 7.

51. Idema and Grant, *Red Brush*, 7, 567–77. With the recent digitization and reprints of collections of women's writings, it may be possible to answer the question of whether there was indeed a "lull" in the eighteenth century and the reasons for it. For a historian's treatment of writing women, see Susan Mann's history of women in the High Qing— "China's long eighteenth century"—in *Precious Records*, esp. chap. 4, "Writing."

52. See review essays by Kroll, "After Long Years"; Hegel, review; and Vitiello, review. The reviewers all questioned who the intended readership was, and they shared the complaint of the outrageous price of the two-volume set.

53. Chang and Owen, *Cambridge History of Chinese Literature*, xvi.

54. Not only in volume 2, where the reader would expect to encounter women writers in the Ming and Qing, but also in the earlier periods in volume 1, e.g., chap. 3, "From the Eastern Jin through the Early Tang (317–649)" by Xiaofei Tian, and chap. 4, "Cultural Tang," by Owen.

55. Vitiello, review, 56–57.

56. Kroll, in his review of Jeanne Larsen's book quoted above: ". . . Fair and Yet Not Found," 623.

57. Kroll, "After Long Years," 310.

58. In addition to the papers from two conferences held in 1990, published respectively in *Late Imperial China* 13, no. 1 (1992), and in the conference volume *Voices of the Song Lyric in China*, edited by Pauline Yu (1994), the landmark conference held at Yale in 1994, "Women and Literature in Ming-Qing China," organized by Kang-i Sun Chang and Ellen Widmer, led to the publication of selected papers in the volume edited by Widmer and Chang, *Writing Women in Late Imperial China*.

59. In this review of past scholarship, I refer to myself in the third person.

60. Mulvey, "Visual Pleasure," 6. Her approach has been critiqued by other feminist cultural critics for its neglect to theorize and examine female spectatorship and female pleasure. See essays in Pribram, *Female Spectators*. For a comprehensive study and formal analysis of classical Hollywood film from the 1920s to 1960s, see Bordwell, Staiger, and Thompson, *Classical Hollywood Cinema*.

61. Mulvey, "Visual Pleasure," 11.

62. Ibid., 8. She does this deconstruction to advocate for feminist, alternative cinema.

63. The gender of the anthology's intended readership is a debated issue. In his preface, the compiler Xu Ling 徐陵 (507–583) states that his anthology is intended for the beautiful palace ladies to enjoy and while away the time. Evidence of female readership could

provide theorizing on how female readers negotiated these texts. Birrell, *New Songs*, 337–41.

64. Robertson, "Voicing the Feminine," 69.

65. Ibid., 70.

66. Ibid., 70.

67. Fusek, *Among the Flowers*, lyric no. 8, second stanza, 39.

68. Fong, "Engendering the Lyric," 112.

69. I am grateful to one of the anonymous readers for calling my attention to this point. See the discussion of "descriptive verisimilitude" in Six Dynasties poetry by Chang, "Description of Landscape."

70. Tian, "Illusion and Illumination," 30. The poems in Tian's article are quoted from *Quan Liang shi* 全梁詩 (Complete Liang Poetry), making it difficult to tell whether or which poems are also included in *Yutai xinyong*.

71. Birrell, *New Songs*, 9. In reference to the new formal patterns, she also notes that most of the five hundred plus poems "dating from the fourth to the early sixth century follow a recognizably conventional pattern" in contrast to the more "flexible design" of the earlier poems (9).

72. Guo, *Women's Tanci Fiction*, 1.

73. See the seminal study by Stephen Owen on this aspect of Chinese poetry: "Self's Perfect Mirror."

74. Robertson, "Voicing the Feminine," 83.

75. Fong, "Engendering the Lyric," 108, 118–21, 123–24.

76. X. Li, "Engendering Heroism"; and X. Li, *Women Poets*, esp. chap. 3.

77. The book won the Joseph Levenson Prize for pre-1900 English-language, nonfiction scholarly books on China in 2016.

78. See Smith and Watson, *Women, Autobiography, Theory*; and Kadar, *Essays on Life Writing*. For an early study in the China field, see Fong, "Writing Self."

79. Roberston, "Changing the Subject," 183. For lack of access to original source materials in the 1990s, Robertson takes most of the prefaces from those reproduced in Hu, *Lidai funü*.

80. Ibid., 192. From a perspective of "cultural androgyny" in which literati men and women worked together to promote women's writing, Chang also noted that "these women writers were proud to model their works on great male masters such as Tao Qian, Wang Wei, and Du Fu" ("Ming-Qing Women Poets," 17).

81. See Grant, *Eminent Nuns*; Fong, *Herself an Author*; B. Yang, *Heroines of the Qing*; Waltner, "Life and Letters;" and Idema, "Biographical and the Autobiographical." Notable also is the strong autobiographical voice in the poetry of Manchu women in Idema, *Two Centuries*. Hu S., *Cainü cheye weimian*, contains a chapter on the autobiographical dimension in women's *tanci* fiction titled "Chuanxin yuwang" 傳心慾望 (Desire to Transmit the Heart/Mind), and Widmer suggests an autobiographical underpinning in Gu Taiqing's novel *Shadows of Dream of the Red Chamber* in "*Honglou meng ying*."

82. H. Yang, *Women's Poetry and Poetics in Late Imperial China*, 104.

83. Ibid., 104–17.

84. Many current publications on women's literary writings in the Ming and Qing are informed by feminist critical thinking but do not explicitly theorize, e.g., Yanning Wang's monograph *Reverie and Reality* on women's travel poetry and her publications in journals.

85. Egan, *Burden of Female Talent*, 8.

References

Birrell, Anne, trans. *New Songs from Jade Terrace*. Harmondsworth, UK: Penguin, 1986.

Bordwell, David, Janet Staiger, and Kristin Thompson. *The Classical Hollywood Cinema: Film Style and Mode of Production to 1960*. London: Routledge, 1988.

Chan, Adrian. *Orientalism in Sinology*. Palo Alto, CA: Academic Press, 2009.

Chang, Kang-i Sun. "Description of Landscape in Early Six Dynasties Poetry." In *The Vitality of the Lyric Voice: Shih Poetry from the Late Han to the T'ang*, edited by Shuen-fu Lin and Stephen Owen, 105–29. Princeton, NJ: Princeton University Press, 1986.

——. "Gender and Canonicity: Ming Qing Women Poets in the Eyes of the Male Literati." *Hsiang Lectures on Chinese Poetry* 1 (2001): 1–18.

——. "Liu Shih and Hsü Ts'an: Feminine or Feminist?" In *Voices of the Song Lyric in China*, edited by Pauline Yu, 169–87. Berkeley: University of California Press, 1994.

——. "Ming and Qing Anthologies of Women's Poetry and Their Selection Strategies." In *Writing Women in Late Imperial China*, edited by Ellen Widmer and Kang-i Sun Chang, 147–70. Stanford, CA: Stanford University Press, 1997.

——. "Ming-Qing Women Poets and Cultural Androgyny." *Tamkang Review* 30, no. 2 (1999): 11–25.

Chang, Kang-i Sun, and Stephen Owen, eds. *The Cambridge History of Chinese Literature*. 2 vols. Cambridge: Cambridge University Press, 2010.

Chang, Kang-i Sun, and Haun Saussy, eds. *Women Writers of Traditional China: An Anthology of Poetry and Criticism*. Stanford, CA: Stanford University Press, 1999.

Dicker, Rory C. *A History of American Feminism*. Berkeley, CA: Seal, 2008.

Egan, Ronald. *The Burden of Female Talent: The Poet Li Qingzhao and Her History in China*. Cambridge, MA: Harvard University Asia Center, 2013.

Felski, Rita. *Literature after Feminism*. Chicago: University of Chicago Press, 2003.

Fong, Grace S. "Engendering the Lyric: Her Image and Voice in Song." In *Voices of the Song Lyric in China*, edited by Pauline Yu, 107–44. Berkeley: University of California Press, 1994.

——. *Herself an Author: Gender, Agency, and Writing in Late Imperial China*. Honolulu: University of Hawaii Press, 2008.

——. "Writing Self and Writing Lives: Shen Shanbao's (1808–1802) Gendered Auto/Biographical Practices." *Nan Nü: Men, Women, and Gender in China* 2, no. 2 (2000): 259–303.

Friedman, Susan S. "'Beyond' Gynocriticism and Gynesis: The Geographics of Identity and the Future of Feminist Criticism." *Tulsa Studies in Women's Literature* 15, no. 1 (1996): 13–40.

Furth, Charlotte. "The Patriarch's Legacy: Household Instructions and the Transmission of Orthodox Values." In *Orthodoxy in Late Imperial China*, edited by Kwang-ching Liu, 187–211. Berkeley: University of California Press, 1990.

Fusek, Lois, trans. *Among the Flowers: The Hua-chien chi*. New York: Columbia University Press, 1982.

Gilbert, Sandra, and Susan Gubar. *The Madwoman in the Attic: The Woman Writer and the Nineteenth-Century Literary Imagination*. New Haven, CT: Yale University Press, 1979.

Grant, Beata. *Eminent Nuns: Women Chan Masters of Seventeenth-Century China*. Honolulu: University of Hawaii Press, 2008.

Guillory, John. *Cultural Capital: The Problem of Literary Canon Formation*. Chicago: University of Chicago Press, 1993.

Guo, Li. *Women's Tanci Fiction in Late Imperial and Early Twentieth-Century China*. West Lafayette, IN: Purdue University Press, 2015.

Hawkes, David. "Xi Peilan." *Asia Major*, n.s. 7, pts. 1–2 (1959): 113–21. https://doi.org/10.4324/9780203358818.

Hegel, Robert. Review of *The Cambridge History of Chinese Literature*, edited by Kang-i Sun Chang and Stephen Owen. *Chinese Literature: Essays, Articles, Reviews* 34 (2012): 162–75.

Hu Siao-chen 胡曉真. *Cainü cheye wei mian: jindai Zhongguo nüxing xushi wenxue de xingqi* 才女徹夜未眠：近代中國女性敘事文學的興起 (Burning the Midnight Oil: The Rise of Female Narrative in Early Modern China). Taipei: Maitian chubanshe, 2003.

Hu Wenkai 胡文楷, and Zhang Hongsheng 張宏生. *Lidai funü zhuzuo kao zengdingben* 歷代婦女著作考增訂本 (Annotated Bibliography of Works by Women through the Ages, Expanded Edition). Shanghai: Shanghai guji chubanshe, 2008.

Idema, Wilt L. "The Biographical and Autobiographical in Bo Shaojun's *One Hundred Poems Lamenting My Husband*." In *Beyond Exemplar Tales: Women's Biography in Chinese History*, edited by Joan Judge and Hu Ying, 230–45. Berkeley: University of California Press, 2011.

———, trans. *Two Centuries of Manchu Women Poets: An Anthology*. Seattle: University of Washington Press, 2017.

Idema, Wilt L., and Beata Grant, eds. *The Red Brush: Writing Women in Imperial China*. Cambridge, MA: Harvard University Asia Center, 2004.

Jones, Ann Rosalind. "Writing the Body: Towards an Understanding of *l'Ecriture Feminine*." *Feminist Studies* 7, no. 2 (1981): 247–63.

Kadar, Marlene, ed. *Essays on Life Writing: From Genre to Critical Practice*. Toronto: University of Toronto Press, 1992.

Ko, Dorothy. *Teachers of the Inner Chambers: Women and Culture in Seventeenth-Century China*. Stanford, CA: Stanford University Press, 1994.

Kroll, Paul W. "After Long Years: Reading *The Cambridge History of Chinese Literature*." *Journal of Chinese Studies* 55 (2012): 295–316.

———. ". . . Fair and Yet Not Fond." *Journal of the American Oriental Society* 108, no. 4 (1988): 621–26.

Lean, Eugenia. "Reflections on Theory, Gender, and the Psyche in the Study of Chinese History." *Research on Women in Modern Chinese History* 6 (1998): 141–73.

Li, Wai-yee. *Women and National Trauma in Late Imperial Chinese Literature*. Cambridge, MA: Harvard University Asia Center, 2014.

Li, Xiaorong. "Engendering Heroism: Women's Song Lyrics Written to the Tune *Man Jiang Hong*." *Nan Nü: Men, Women, and Gender in China* 7, no. 1 (2005): 1–39.

———. *Women Poets of Late Imperial China: Transforming the Inner Chambers*. Seattle: University of Washington Press, 2012.

Liu Dajie 劉大杰. *Zhongguo wenxue fazhanshi* 中國文學發展史 (History of the Development of Chinese Literature). Hong Kong: Hock Lum, 1979.

Mann, Susan. *Precious Records: Women in China's Long Eighteenth-Century*. Berkeley: University of California Press, 1997.

Moi, Toril. *Sexual/Textual Politics: Feminist Literary Theory*. London: Methuen, 1985.

Mulvey, Laura. "Visual Pleasure and Narrative Cinema." *Screen* 16, no. 3 (1976): 6–18.

Owen, Stephen. "The Self's Perfect Mirror: Poetry as Autobiography." In *The Vitality of the Lyric Voice: Shih Poetry from the Late Han to the T'ang*, edited by Shuen-fu Lin and Stephen Owen, 71–102. Princeton, NJ: Princeton University Press, 1986.

Pribram, E. Deidre, ed. *Female Spectators: Looking at Film and Television*. London: Verso, 1988.

Rexroth, Kenneth, and Ling Chung. *The Orchid Boat: Women Poets of China.* New York: McGraw Hill, 1972.

Robertson, Maureen. "Changing the Subject: Gender and Self-Inscription in Authors' Prefaces and *Shi* Poetry." In *Writing Women in Late Imperial China*, ed. Ellen Widmer and Kang-i Sun Chang, 171–217. Stanford, CA: Stanford University Press, 1997.

———. "Voicing the Feminine: Constructions of the Gendered Subject in Lyric Poetry by Women of Medieval and Late Imperial China." *Late Imperial China* 13, no. 1 (1992): 63–110.

Showalter, Elaine. *A Literature of Their Own: British Women Novelists from Brontë to Lessing.* Princeton, NJ: Princeton University Press, 1977.

———. "Toward a Feminist Poetics." In *Women Writing and Writing about Women*, edited by Mary Jacobus, 22–42. New York: Routledge, 1979.

Smith, Paul. *Discerning the Subject.* Minneapolis: University of Minnesota Press, 1988.

Smith, Sidonie, and Julia Watson, eds. *Women, Autobiography, Theory: A Reader.* Madison: University of Wisconsin Press, 1998.

Swann, Nancy Lee. *Pan Chao: Foremost Woman Scholar of China.* New York: Century, 1932.

Teng, Emma. "The Construction of the 'Traditional Chinese Woman' in the Western Academy: A Critical Review." *Signs: Journal of Women in Culture and Society* 22, no. 1 (1996): 115–51.

Tian, Xiaofei. "Illusion and Illumination: A New Poetics of Seeing in Liang Dynasty Court Literature." *Harvard Journal of Asiatic Studies* 65, no. 1 (2005): 7–56.

Vitiello, Giovanni. Review of *The Cambridge History of Chinese Literature*, edited by Kang-i Sun Chang and Stephen Owen. *China Review International* 20, no. 1/2 (2013): 54–60.

Waltner, Ann. "Life and Letters: Reflections on Tanyangzi." In *Beyond Exemplar Tales: Women's Biography in Chinese History*, edited by Joan Judge and Hu Ying, 212–29. Berkeley: University of California Press, 2011.

Wang, Yanning. *Reverie and Reality: Poetry on Travel by Late Imperial Chinese Women.* Lanham, MD: Lexington Books, 2014.

Warhol, Robyn R., and Diane Price Herndl. *Feminisms: An Anthology of Literary Theory and Criticism.* New Brunswick, NJ: Rutgers University Press, 1997.

Wernimont, Jacqueline, and Julia Flanders. "Feminism in the Age of Digital Archives: The Women Writers Project." *Tulsa Studies in Women's Literature* 29, no. 2 (2010): 425–35.

Widmer, Ellen. "The Epistolary World of Female Talent in Seventeenth-Century China." *Late Imperial China* 10, no. 2 (1989): 1–43.

———. "*Honglou meng ying* in Biographical and Literary Perspectives." In *The Beauty and the Book: Women and Fiction in Nineteenth-Century China*, 181–216. Cambridge, MA: Harvard University Asia Center, 2006.

Wixted, John Timothy. "The Poetry of Li Ch'ing-chao: A Woman Author and Women's Authorship." In *Voices of the Song Lyric in China*, edited by Pauline Yu, 145–68. Berkeley: University of California Press, 1994.

Yang, Binbin. *Heroines of the Qing: Exemplary Women Tell Their Stories.* Seattle: University of Washington Press, 2016.

Yang, Haihong. *Women's Poetry and Poetics in Late Imperial China: A Dialogic Engagement.* Lanham, MD: Lexington Books, 2017.

Cultural Memory and the Epic in Early Chinese Literature: The Case of Qu Yuan 屈原 and the *Lisao* 離騷

MARTIN KERN

Abstract The present essay combines the theory of Cultural Memory with ideas about textual repertoires, composite text, and distributed authorship that in recent years have been advanced in studies of early and medieval Chinese literature. In its first part, the essay introduces in detail the historical development and key features of Cultural Memory theory. In its second part, it applies this theory to the study of Qu Yuan 屈原 and the *Lisao* 離騷, the greatest poem of early China. Through detailed philological analysis, the *Lisao* is described not as a single text by a single author but as a composite, authorless artifact that participates in a larger Qu Yuan discourse distributed across multiple texts in both prose and poetry. This distributed "Qu Yuan Epic" is an anthology of distinct characteristics attributed to the quasi-mythological Qu Yuan persona—a persona that itself emerges as a composite textual configuration into which are inscribed the nostalgic ideals and shifting aspirations of Han imperial literati. This Han social *imaginaire* recollects the noble exemplar of the old Chu aristocracy; the dual prophecy of the fall of Chu to Qin and of Qin's subsequent collapse; the religious, historical, mythological, and literary traditions of Chu; the embodied paradigm of the ruler-minister relationship; and the gradual formation of the ideal of authorship through the transformation of poetic hero into heroic poet.

Keywords Cultural Memory theory, Qu Yuan, *Lisao*, composite text, textual repertoire

Introduction: Cultural Memory and Early Chinese Literature

The notion of Cultural Memory has become a powerful concept across all fields of the humanities and social sciences, in particular in continental European scholarship.[1] It was first introduced by the German Egyptologist Jan Assmann (University of Heidelberg) in his 1988 essay "Kollektives Gedächtnis und

The Journal of Chinese Literature and Culture • 9:1 • April 2022
DOI 10.1215/23290048-9681189 • © 2022 by Duke University Press

kulturelle Identität" (Collective Memory and Cultural Identity) and then fully developed in his 1992 *Das kulturelle Gedächtnis: Schrift, Erinnerung und politische Identität in frühen Hochkulturen* (The Cultural Memory: Writing, Remembrance, and Political Identity in Early High Cultures). Assmann's subsequent writings in English, as well as translations of his work on the topic, further popularized the theory.[2] Later in the 1990s, Aleida Assmann, a professor of English and literary studies at the University of Konstanz, began to publish her own extensive work on Cultural Memory; while Jan Assmann's work has been focused on antiquity—especially Egypt, Israel, and Greece—Aleida Assmann expanded the horizon all the way into the twentieth century and toward broader conceptual questions.[3]

Most likely because the Assmanns' principal studies did not become available in English until years after their original German publication, the concept of Cultural Memory was only slowly picked up in the study of Chinese literature.[4] There were, of course, earlier studies that reflected on acts of remembrance in Chinese literature, most notably Stephen Owen's *Remembrances: The Experience of the Past in Classical Chinese Literature* and Hans Frankel's "The Contemplation of the Past in T'ang Poetry,"[5] that predated the notion of Cultural Memory. Both studies, like a more recent one by David R. Knechtges,[6] were focused on medieval Chinese literature,[7] a field that would seem to invite much further work in which Cultural Memory could serve as an instructive device.[8]

Cultural Memory is a theoretical approach whose application illuminates a specific set of characteristics in social practices of appropriating the past. The perspective of Cultural Memory is a distinct subset of "memory studies" in general. The latter was since Roman antiquity devoted to the *ars memoria* (also as *memoria technica*), that is, memorization as a technical discipline (mnemonics).[9] It took its inspiration from a story about the Greek poet Simonides of Ceos (ca. 557–467 BCE). As told by Cicero (106–43 BCE), Simonides had famously improvised a mnemonic technique to recall the exact seating order at a banquet after the building had collapsed onto the participants; his reconstruction enabled each of the dead to be identified for proper burial. Following Aristotle's *On Memory and Reminiscence* (Latin: *De Memoria et Reminiscentia*), the anonymous *Rhetoric to Herennius* (*Rhetorica ad Herennium*, ca. 80 BCE), Cicero's *On the Orator* (*De Oratore*), and Quintilian's (55–100) *Institutes of Oratory* (*Institutio Oratoria*) all treat memorization as a rhetorical technique for the purposes of public speech, in particular using "places" (Greek *topoi*, Latin *loci*) to mentally "locate" ideas and expressions. Numerous medieval and early modern treatises expanded these early writings, as described by Frances Amelia Yates and Mary Carruthers.[10] In literary studies, Renate Lachmann has been instrumental in extending the notion of memory to the interpretation of intertextuality.[11] With varying degrees of depth, "memory" now also appears in the scholarship on early China.[12]

The present essay is not intended to review individual Sinological works relating to either "memory" in general or Cultural Memory in particular. Instead, I wish to lay out in clear terms what Cultural Memory actually is in the Assmanns' definition,[13] not least in order to provide some guidance against certain superficial invocations of the concept. I will not manage to capture every aspect of the Assmanns' work—lest I end up with a Borgesian world map—but will instead summarize its key theoretical premises.

In the second part of my essay, I put the concept to work in a new reflection on the Chinese arch-poet Qu Yuan 屈原 (trad. 340–278 BCE) and "his" poem *Lisao* 離騷 (Encountering Sorrow). In particular, I attempt to demonstrate how *only* the awareness of Cultural Memory, appropriately defined, can make sense of the many texts surrounding the Qu Yuan persona and poetry. In this context, I expand the Assmanns' notion further from my own perspectives on early Chinese literature—a literature with its own characteristics that enriches the notion of Cultural Memory with particular clarity—by addressing the closely interrelated phenomena of "textual repertoire" and "composite text."[14] As a result, I describe the Qu Yuan persona of the Han dynasty (202 BCE–220 CE) not as a historical person—let alone as the author of "his" texts—but as a composite textual configuration into which are inscribed the changing ideals of Han dynasty Cultural Memory. This social *imaginaire* recollects the exemplar of the old Chu aristocracy;[15] the prophesied fall of Chu to Qin together with the necessity of the subsequent collapse of Qin; the religious, historical, and mythological traditions of Chu; the embodied paradigm of the ruler-minister relationship; the literary heritage of Chu; the transformation of poetic hero into heroic poet; and the gradual formation of the ideal of authorship by Liu An 劉安 (179–122 BCE), Sima Qian 司馬遷 (ca. 145–ca. 85 BCE), Yang Xiong 揚雄 (53 BCE–18 CE), and Liu Xiang 劉向 (77–6 BCE).

What Is Cultural Memory?

All discussion of Cultural Memory as a form of "social" or "collective" memory goes back to the French sociologist Maurice Halbwachs (1877–1945), beginning with his *Les cadres sociaux de la mémoire* (The Social Frameworks of Memory), published in 1925, followed in 1942 by *La topographie légendaire des Évangiles en Terre Sainte: Étude de mémoire collective* (The Legendary Topography of the Gospels in the Holy Land: A Study of Collective Memory) and, posthumously published in 1950, *La mémoire collective* (The Collective Memory).[16] Halbwachs, born in Reims and educated in Paris and Göttingen, died in the German concentration camp of Buchenwald on March 16, 1945; much of his extended family was likewise murdered by the Nazis. Halbwachs is thus part of the very history that led to the first great wave of postwar memory studies, namely, in response to the Holocaust. The second wave followed in the 1990s after the disintegration of the Soviet Union. In both cases, the grand collective narratives of the past suddenly came undone, and the doors to suppressed identities and state-controlled archives came unlocked.

Following Halbwachs's insight that "no memory is possible outside of frameworks used by people living in society to determine and retrieve their recollections,"[17] the study of collective memory developed across numerous disciplines, with contributions from—in no particular order—history, art history, archaeology, literature, linguistics, philosophy, all area studies (including Sinology), sociology, media studies, anthropology, architecture, religion, biblical studies, political science, psychology, neuroscience, and others more.[18]

Halbwachs's "collective memory" theory inspired in particular two important debates: the first over the possible congruence of individual with collective memory and the second over the relation between memory and history.[19] If all human memory is neurologically based and therefore by definition individual, how can there be such a thing as "social" or "collective" memory? And how epistemologically useful as an approach to the past is "memory" versus "history," with its procedures of memorization versus those of historiography? What is the truth value of a "collective memory" that is thus doubly constructed, first as a psychological filter through which the past is perceived and second as an abstraction of such a filter that may not even exist outside the individual human mind? According to Erll, "There has been considerable confusion about the nature of the relationship between 'memory' and 'history.' Cultural memory is not the Other of history. Nor is it the opposite of individual remembering. Rather, it is the totality of the context within which such varied cultural phenomena originate."[20] And further:

> Despite the unavoidable heterogeneity of the terminology, there are two generally agreed-upon central characteristics of (conscious) remembering: its relationship to the present and its constructed nature. Memories are not objective images of past perceptions, even less of a past reality. They are subjective, highly selective reconstructions, dependent on the situation in which they are recalled. Re-membering is an act of assembling available data that takes place in the present. Versions of the past change with every recall, in accordance with the changed present situation. Individual and collective memories are never a mirror image of the past, but rather an expressive indication of the needs and interests of the person or group doing the remembering in the present. As a result, memory studies directs its interest not toward the shape of the remembered pasts, but rather toward the particular presents of the remembering.[21]

Thus, memory studies does not attempt some reconstruction and reification of events in the past but searches for the circumstances and procedures through which these events are called upon for the purposes and interests of a particular community in the present. This fundamental realignment in looking at the past diverges from both "history" and "tradition": it differs from history in that its stated focus of interest lies not in the past as such but in its successive retrospective configuration; and it differs from tradition in that it is not static or conservative, but—because of its responsiveness to an ever-evolving present—dynamic and innovative.

To cite a most recent example from the United States: on June 17, 2021, Juneteenth, that is, June 19, was named a federal holiday to commemorate the end of slavery in America, the first new federal holiday since the declaration of Martin Luther King Jr. Day in 1983. Nothing has changed about the historical events of June 19, 1865, in Galveston, Texas; what has changed, however, is how these events are now collectively commemorated by a nation trying to redefine its political identity from the perspective of the present and towards its future, in a celebration and renewal on every June 19 henceforth. Note the critical terms here: collective commemoration, nation, political identity, present and future, celebration, renewal. These are precisely the terms that mark Cultural Memory and distinguish it from "history." What matters from the perspective of Cultural Memory is under which circumstances, with which aspirations, and through which procedures the events of 1865 are now newly inscribed into the discourse of the nation.

Thus, the Cultural Memory of any society at any moment in time is not a stable entity, no matter the material carriers and symbols through which its durability is sought—be it inscribed buildings, statues, and other monuments;[22] it is an ongoing, ever-evolving process of renewed acts of both erasure and remembrance. For a while, the Cultural Memory of some place and community may seem firmly assured; but over time, it becomes destabilized, reconfigured, or expunged.[23] This process is always contested. Battles over "history" are not about "history" at all; they are about what to remember and how to remember it. This is immediately obvious in societies where different groups compete to advance different memories—for example, to tell different stories about the past or to tell the story of the past differently, as recently with the *New York Times*'s "1619 Project"[24]—but it is equally obvious in totalitarian states (as long ago described in George Orwell's *1984*) where all public memory is strictly monopolized and controlled and where only one version of the past—the one sanctioned by the state—is allowed to exist.[25]

To further define Cultural Memory, Jan Assmann distinguishes it from "communicative memory": the first can reach back thousands of years, while the second is within three or four generations, not exceeding about one hundred years.[26] In this model, the "communicative memory" includes "historical experiences in the framework of individual biographies," is "informal, without much form," "arising from interaction," connected to "living, organic memories, experiences, hearsay," and carried in nonspecific ways by "contemporary witnesses within a memory community." Cultural Memory, by contrast, comprises the "mythical history of origins" and "events in an absolute past"; it is "organized, extremely formal," and shaped in "ceremonial communication" and "festival"; it is expressed through "fixed objectifications, traditional symbolic classification and staging through words, pictures, dance, and so forth" and relies on "specialized tradition bearers."[27] Several notions in this definition of Cultural Memory require further clarification. First, it is important to take note of Jan Assmann's use of the word *myth*:

> Myths are also figures of memory, and here any distinction between myth and history is eliminated. What counts for cultural memory is not factual but remembered history. One might even say that cultural memory transforms factual into remembered history, thus turning it into myth. Myth is foundational history that is narrated in order to illuminate the present from the standpoint of its origins. The Exodus, for instance, regardless of any historical accuracy, is the myth behind the foundation of Israel; thus it is celebrated at Pesach and thus it is part of the cultural memory of the Israelites. Through memory, history becomes myth. This does not make it unreal—on the contrary, this is what makes it real, in the sense that it becomes a lasting, normative, and formative power.[28]

Next, Cultural Memory relies on *repeated acts of memorization*, that is, in the temporal structure of ritual:

> It is generally accepted that the poetic form has the mnemotechnical aim of capturing the unifying knowledge in a manner that will preserve it. Also familiar is the fact that this knowledge is customarily performed through multimedia staging in which the linguistic text is inseparable from voice, body, mime, gesture, dance, rhythm, and ritual action. . . . Through regular repetition, festivals and rituals ensure the communication and continuance of the knowledge that gives the group its identity. Ritual repetition also consolidates the coherence of the group in time and space.[29]

As the British anthropologist Paul Connerton has noted: "Rites have the capacity to give value and meaning to those who perform them. All rites are repetitive, and repetition automatically implies continuity with the past."[30] Consider in this context the specific phenomenon of the Chinese ancestral sacrifice: it is performed at regular intervals in a fixed spatial setting that organizes ancestral time by generations, with the remote founding ancestor at its center; it presents the current principal descendant not only as the filial offspring of the most recent ancestor but, through the descendant's enactment of filial piety, also as the model future ancestor who shall receive the same filial commemoration from his future descendants; and its language of hymns and inscriptions is highly formalized within a strictly limited, repetitive lexicon[31] that is rhythmically performed.[32] According to Wade T. Wheelock, ritual speech "is most often a fixed and known text repeated verbatim for each performance, and the constituents of the immediate ritual setting, to which the language of the liturgy will make frequent reference, are generally standardized and thus familiar to the participants, not needing any verbal explication. Therefore, practically every utterance of a ritual is superfluous from the perspective of ordinary conversational principles."[33] Most important, the ancestral ritual's tripartite structure as embodied in bronze inscriptions[34] is concerned with the past, the present, and the future, as expressed in a famous passage from the *Liji* 禮記 (Records of Ritual):

> In an inscription, one arranges and expounds the virtue and excellence of one's ancestors; one displays their achievements and brilliance, their efforts and toils, their honors and distinctions, and their fame and name to All under Heaven; and one deliberates all these in [inscribing] the sacrificial vessel. In doing so, one accomplishes one's own name by way of sacrificing to one's ancestors. One extols and glorifies the ancestors and thereby venerates filial piety.... Therefore, when a noble man looks at an inscription, he praises those who are commended there, and he praises the one who has made [the inscription].[35]
>
> 銘者，論譔其先祖之有德善，功烈勳勞慶賞聲名列於天下，而酌之祭器；自成其名焉，以祀其先祖者也。顯揚先祖，所以崇孝也 ⋯⋯ 是故君子之觀於銘也，既美其所稱，又美其所為。

Here, the dual figures of remembrance and "the rememberer remembered"[36] are in particular related to the act of writing, which for both Aleida and Jan Assmann is one of the defining features of Cultural Memory and related to text as canon.[37] It is easy to see the attraction of this idea, as it addresses both the durability of memory in script as well as the externalization of memory from the human mind into the written "storage" or "archive"[38] of "reusable texts" that can be actualized over long periods of time. It is also clear that writing was used in precisely this way as early as Western Zhou times (1046–771 BCE), for example, in the famous inscription of the water basin of Scribe Qiang (Shi Qiang-*pan* 史墙盤).[39] Moreover, as has often been noted, Western Zhou bronze inscriptions were only secondary texts based on primary writings originally on bamboo, versions of which must have been stored in the Western Zhou court archives.[40] And finally, one may view the formation of the Five Classics (*wu jing* 五經), sanctioned, shaped, and guarded by the early Chinese imperial state and its institutions of the imperial academy and library, as a particular realization of Cultural Memory.

Yet at the same time, complementary to the written archive, one might still consider the examples of long-lasting oral archives, whether in the early centuries of the Homeric epics or, even more dramatically, in the far larger and far more lasting Vedic textual repertoire—archives embedded and continuously reenacted in the formal structures of festivals and recitations. Likewise the ritual hymns of the *Shijing* 詩經 (Classic of Poetry) repeatedly express that the ritual practices themselves, not just a particular set of texts, present an extension of the remote past, often in rhetorical questions that are then answered with the recitation of past practice:

> Since times of old, what have we done?
> 自昔何為。[41]

> Truly—our sacrifices are like what?
> 誕我祀如何。[42]

> It is not [merely] here what we have here; / it is not
>   [merely] now what is now; / since ancient times,
>   it has been like this.
> 匪且有且，匪今斯今，振古如茲。[43]

Cultural Memory does not convey what is new; it repeats what is already known to all—not merely to recall the remote, "absolute past" (Aleida Assmann) but to re-present this past as the current moment. It is in this formalized, ceremonial gesture that the community of the present confirms its social/religious/political/cultural identity:

> The "remembered past" is therefore not to be equated with the objectively detached study of the past that we like to call "history." It is always mixed with projected identities, interpretations of the present, and the need for validation. That is why our study of memory has taken us into the depths of political motivation and the formation of national identity, for what we have here is all the raw material that goes to the making of identities, histories, and communities. The study of national memory is quite distinct from that of mnemotechnics and the art and capacity of memory; it deals with memory as a dynamic force that drives both action and self-interpretation.

> This force is part of what the French call *imaginaire*. We should not underestimate this form of imagination as a mere fiction. Such fictions or inventions underpin all cultural constructions.[44]

And further to the relationship between history and memory in the formation of identity, according to Aleida Assmann: "Abstract and generalized 'history' turns into re-embodied collective 'memory' when it is transformed into forms of shared knowledge and collective participation. In such cases, 'history in general' is reconfigured into a particular and emotionally charged version of 'our history' and absorbed as part of a collective identity."[45]

To summarize, Cultural Memory is defined as

- directed at foundational narratives and the mythical truth found within them;
- selectively reconstructing the past from the perspective of the present, in deliberate acts of remembrance and forgetting;
- collective and based on social interaction;
- shaped and guarded by institutional structures of power;
- defining, stabilizing, and perpetuating socially mediated identity;
- continuously actualized in textual and ritual repetition;
- dynamically responding to the needs of the present;
- normative, binding, obligatory, and canonical;
- preserved in durable media, particularly—but not only—writing.

To make the theory of Cultural Memory productive for individual analyses, one must consider the specific implications of these points. The particular power of Cultural Memory as a theory lies in its poststructuralist potential: Cultural Memory requires us to understand certain aspects of the past as reconstructed for present purposes and to reveal the function and meaning of such reconstruction for the identity-creating needs of the community that undertakes it. At its core, Cultural Memory is a theory of ideology criticism (*Ideologiekritik*) against the impulses of historical positivism. It clarifies the processes and practices by which meaning and identity are socially, institutionally, and materially constructed at particular times and places. It tries to explain how societies make sense of themselves by probing their foundational narratives, mythological commitments, and cultural procedures.

The "Qu Yuan Epic"

In the historical imagination ever since early Han times, Qu Yuan is the most important poet of early China, and the *Lisao* is the grandest poem of Chinese antiquity.[46] But far beyond being celebrated as China's arch-poet, the Qu Yuan persona embodies an entire set of identity-generating paradigms—first among them that of the high-minded, aristocratic, and loyal political advisor who ends in exile and suicide—that have sustained the ideals and aspirations of many a Chinese intellectual ever since. In the following, building on my earlier studies on aspects of the Qu Yuan persona, his authorship, and the *Lisao* poem,[47] I will expand my analysis from the perspective of "epic narrative." In the case of Qu Yuan, this epic is not a single poem but a cluster of texts in both prose and poetry, including the Qu Yuan biography in Sima Qian's *Shiji* 史記,[48] the *Lisao*, and other associated texts, some of which are found in the *Chuci* 楚辭 anthology,[49] others outside of it. Consider a standard definition of *epic*:

> An epic is a long narrative poem of heroic action: "narrative," in that it tells a story; "poem," in that it is written in verse rather than prose; "heroic action," while reinterpreted by each major epic poet, in that, broadly defined, it recounts deeds of great valor that bear consequence for the community to which the hero belongs. An epic plot is typically focused on the deeds of a single person or hero, mortal though exceptionally strong, intelligent, or brave, and often assisted or opposed by gods. Epic is set in a remote or legendary past represented as an age of greater heroism than the present. Its style is elevated and rhetorical.[50]

From a European perspective, an epic is considered a single, long narrative poem, but there is no reason why this should be the only definition of the genre. What counts is not that there is a single long text; what counts is what makes this long text an epic: it is narrative, poetic, and focused on the heroic action of a single protagonist who in both spirit and abilities stands high above the experiences of other mortals.

As a text distributed across multiple and diverse sources, the Qu Yuan story is an epic sui generis.[51] Compare, for example, Qu Yuan with the famous figure of Wu Zixu 伍子胥 (d. 484 BCE), another solitary hero and one far more widely known in early China.[52] Wu Zixu's multifaceted story, rich in historical detail and development, appears already extensively in pre-imperial texts; Qu Yuan's appears in none. Yet in pre-Qin or Han times, Wu Zixu's heroism is never told in poetry, let alone in pseudo-autobiographical poetry attributed to himself; he merely survives in stories and anecdotes. Qu Yuan, by contrast, is unique not only as China's first great poet but also in attracting an entire anthology of poetry centered on his paradigmatic experiences, not to mention the broader lore, written and oral, that clearly existed along and beyond what was selected and collected for transmission. Entirely unknown to the textual tradition before the Han, it was Qu Yuan alone who emerged as the exemplary figure of poet-hero and maligned royal advisor in whom Han intellectuals—and countless Chinese scholars since—were to recognize themselves. His complete absence to date in the numerous manuscript finds from pre-imperial Chu and even in Chu-area manuscripts from the early Western Han only further confirms how completely the "Qu Yuan Epic" was constructed by Western Han scholars who found their own identity in the mirror image of a true ancestor: an ancestor remote enough not to be known but only to be created in Cultural Memory and endowed with heroic powers not real but ideal, heroic failures not pathetic but tragic and transcendent.

Compare to the definition of the epic noted above the opening three stanzas of the *Lisao*, as they literally stage the protagonist as a mythological persona of divine ancestry who on an auspicious day "descends" into the world like a god and introduces himself in an intensely personal voice:

Stanza 1.

Distant descendant of the God Gao Yang am I,	帝高陽之苗裔兮
My august father's name was Bo Yong.	朕皇考曰伯庸
The *sheti* constellation pointed to the first month of the year,	攝提貞于孟陬兮
It was the cyclical day *gengyin* when I descended.	惟庚寅吾以降

Stanza 2.

The august one surveyed me and took my original measure,	皇覽揆余初度兮
Rising to bestow on me auspicious names:	肇錫余以嘉名
He named me "Correct Standard,"	名余曰正則兮
Styled me "Numinous Balance."	字余曰靈均

Stanza 3.

Lush am I, possessed of this inner beauty,	紛吾既有此內美兮
Further doubled in fine appearance:[53]	又重之以脩能
Shrouded in lovage and iris,	扈江離與辟芷兮
Weaving the autumn orchid as my girdle.	紉秋蘭以為佩

The "I" in this presentation, present in seven first-person pronouns, is the hero remembered; no ancient Chinese poet could have called himself a descendant of the gods. The performative nature of this impersonation is linguistically marked: "*this* inner beauty" (*ci neimei* 此內美), like deictic expressions in performance contexts in general, can only be understood as an actual gesture within the dramatic staging in front of an audience. The protagonist's "inner beauty" remains invisible except when represented through his lavish outward appearance. This does not necessarily mean that the *Lisao* as a whole was a text for public performance. It means that it contains elements of performance texts, just as it contains elements of other textual materials.

In my analysis the *Lisao* is best understood not as a single poem but as an anthology of modular fragments, a collection of expressions of different kinds and different origins. This analysis is centrally directed at four elements: first, different types of discourse, lexicon, and poetic register within the *Lisao*; second, blocks of texts that stand paratactically next to other blocks of texts, typically without transition; third, elements of intertextuality and repetition within the *Lisao*; and fourth, the intertextuality between the *Lisao* and certain other texts from the early layers of the *Chuci* anthology. In this, I treat the "Qu Yuan Epic" in general, and the *Lisao* in particular, as the manifestation of Cultural Memory in the form of a broader, authorless discourse that took shape over time before becoming fixed within the specific parts of the *Chuci* anthology, including in the discrete textual entities we now call *Lisao*, *Jiu ge* 九歌 (Nine Songs), *Jiu zhang* 九章 (Nine Manifestations), *Jiu bian* 九辯 (Nine Variations), and so on. This "Qu Yuan Epic" is a text both composed from diverse materials and distributed across several textual manifestations and thus a site of Cultural Memory par excellence. The version we see in the received anthology is merely the final, canonical version of the text, defined by the successive efforts and decisions of a series of commentators, including Liu An, Sima Qian, Liu Xiang, Ban Gu 班固 (32–92), Wang Yi 王逸 (89–158), and Hong Xingzu 洪興祖 (1090–1155) but also by the poetic responses and implicit interpretations of Jia Yi 賈誼 (200–169 BCE),[54] Wang Bao 王褒 (ca. 84–ca. 53 BCE),[55] Yang Xiong,[56] and others.

The Qu Yuan Biography
In the Western Han imagination, the story of Qu Yuan is directly tied to the destruction of the old eastern state of Chu 楚 by Qin 秦 in 223 BCE, two years before Qin's creation of the unified empire in 221 BCE. By the time of the fall of Chu, Qu Yuan (whose traditional dates are entirely dubious)[57] had long been dead, but according to the *Shiji*, he had already warned King Huai of Chu 楚懷王 (r. 328–299 BCE) that Qin was "a state of tigers and wolves that cannot be trusted" 秦虎狼之國，不可信也.[58] Both in the *Shiji* and elsewhere, this phrase is attributed to various other pre-Qin historical figures[59] while in the Qu Yuan biography, it is only spoken by him, who thus appears as the single prophet of Chu's demise: after Qu Yuan's death, "Chu was diminished by the day, until several dozen years later it was finally extinguished by Qin" 其後楚日以削，數十年竟為秦所滅.[60] Before Sima Qian, Qu Yuan must have been a figure of mythological significance in the territory of the former state of Chu, now a Western Han kingdom ruled by Liu An at Shouchun 壽春 (in modern Anhui), the last capital of pre-imperial Chu.

It was probably at Liu An's court that the first *Chuci* anthology was compiled and the persona of Qu Yuan defined.[61] But Qu Yuan was not only the prophet of the demise of Chu; his comment on Qin as being "the state of tigers and wolves" also presaged why Qin would ultimately fail, only to be replaced by a new dynasty, the Liu 劉 family's Han, that emerged from the former Chu territory.

This leads directly to the second way in which Qu Yuan represents Han concerns. In the Western Han view from Shouchun, Qu Yuan—descendant of one of the three royal lineages of the old state of Chu[62]—was an ancestor. The culture and history of Chu, now surviving at the old capital, was the culture and history of the Han imperial house.[63] The "Qu Yuan Epic" offered a view of both the former aristocratic Chu culture—now surviving with Liu An and his court— and of Chu history, mythology, and religion, distributed across different parts of the *Chuci* anthology.

The third way in which the Qu Yuan persona spoke to the intellectual and political needs of the early Han was that it exemplified and embodied the ruler-minister debate: the centrality of loyal and upright advisors for good rulership— a position of self-interest for Han intellectuals—together with the outcry over unjust punishment (as experienced by both Jia Yi and Sima Qian).[64] Jia Yi, just like Qu Yuan, ended exiled to the miasmic south; Sima Qian avoided Qu Yuan's fate of suicide only by submitting to castration. (By that time, Liu An had already been forced into suicide.) Thus, in their shared *Shiji* biography,[65] Qu Yuan and Jia Yi are mirrored and explained against each other—yet clearly from the perspective of Jia Yi as imagined by their Han biographer.

The fourth and final way in which the Qu Yuan persona responded to Han political and cultural imagination was his stature as the first heroic poet. Over the past twenty years or so, it has become common understanding in Western Sinology that the figure of the individual author had little purchase before the empire and is fundamentally an early Han construction at the hands of Liu An, Sima Qian, Liu Xiang, Yang Xiong, and others.[66] The urgency of this new idea is nowhere more clearly expressed than in Sima Qian's *Shiji*, where the historian presents himself as both the foremost reader and a new author in the image of those from the past whom he imagines as his intellectual and moral predecessors, first among them Confucius and Qu Yuan. Only twice does he claim to visualize the persona of the author just from reading; on Confucius, Sima Qian notes:

When reading the writings of Master Kong, I see him before me as the person he was. 余讀孔氏書，想見其爲人。[67]

Likewise, but now in much richer detail, on Qu Yuan:

> When reading *Lisao*, *Tian wen*, *Zhao hun*, and *Ai Ying*, I grieve over his resolve. Ever
> since I traveled to Changsha and saw where Qu Yuan drowned himself in the abyss, I
> never can help shedding tears, and I see him before me as the person he was.
> 余讀離騷、天問、招魂、哀郢，悲其志。適長沙，觀屈原所自沈淵，未嘗不垂涕，想見
> 其為人。[68]

As I commented in an earlier study on the Tang poet Du Fu 杜甫 (712–770),

> To Sima, the supreme reader and biographer, it is the text that leads us to the true
> nature of the person, where the author is finally known and understood. In this, the
> author becomes dependent on his reader: it is the latter who now imagines the former,
> and who rescues the text and with it the person. This, of course, is how Sima Qian not
> only remembers Qu Yuan and Confucius but also imagines himself, as he—another
> fated author—longs for his own posterity in the minds of later readers. The same is
> true for Du Fu. Like the ancient historian, the Tang poet seeks to create the pro-
> spective memory of himself. Qu Yuan as much as Confucius, and Sima Qian as much
> as Du Fu, is the noble person without power, the high-minded individual who insists
> on nothing but his moral excellence, and who creates a textual legacy that has no
> audience except in posterity.[69]

In sum, in the Western Han *imaginaire*, the Qu Yuan persona as a figure of
Cultural Memory was inscribed with a set of concepts supremely important to
the writers of the time, one that in this constellation had not existed before.

But how did this persona, and with it the "Qu Yuan Epic," come about? The
Lisao does not lend itself to a biographical reading; it mentions nothing about
the historical Qu Yuan. Its biographical (or autobiographical) reading depends
entirely on external material collected from a range of several other sources: the
biography in the *Shiji*; the two short pieces in the *Chuci* anthology—*Bu ju* 卜居
(Divining Where to Stay) and *Yufu* 漁父 (The Fisherman)[70]—that speak about
Qu Yuan in the third person but are nevertheless attributed to him; other Han
poems both within and outside the anthology; and various Han dynasty comments and entire commentaries, most fully Wang Yi's *Chuci zhangju* 楚辭章句
(Chapter and Verse Commentary to the *Chuci*), received through the *Chuci
buzhu* 楚辭補注 (Supplementary Annotations to the *Chuci*).[71] One cannot
reconstruct a Qu Yuan persona from the *Lisao* itself—in fact, nobody could have
connected the poem to the person were it not for the various external materials
that relate the person to the text.

It is futile to wonder whether the *Shiji* biography is indeed the work of Sima Qian himself. The text is an incoherent patchwork of multiple sources poorly stitched together that cannot even agree with itself on the name of its protagonist, Qu Yuan (identified as the author of *Huai sha* 懷沙 [Embracing Sand]) or Qu Ping 屈平 (identified as the author of the *Lisao*). It cannot agree with itself as to whether the *Lisao* was composed before or in response to its author's exile. Qu Yuan and Qu Ping—neither one mentioned in the *Lisao*—may well refer to the same historical person, but the biography does not harmonize them into one. Compiled from a range of different sources,[72] it opens a window on the rich and diverse nature of early Qu Yuan lore and its different traditions of mythological narrative and poetic performance. The biography reveals that literary material surrounding Qu Yuan existed in multiple parallel versions, none of which may be privileged as original or diminished as derivative. Thus, when we find direct textual parallels between the *Lisao* and Jia Yi's *Diao Qu Yuan* 吊屈原 (Mourning Qu Yuan)[73] or then again between *Xi shi* 惜誓 (Regretting the Oath; also attributed to Jia Yi),[74] *Diao Qu Yuan*, and other pieces in the *Chuci* anthology,[75] this does not suggest acts of "quotation" in the sense that one author cites the work of another, which would presume an early fixity of text for which there exists no other evidence. Instead, it suggests a shared body of expressions in the Han *imaginaire*.

While in pre-imperial times, Qu Yuan may have been a persona whose story was told in Chu, it is only in the Western Han that we see the full extent of his composite image as told in different parts of the *Shiji* biography: the political hero standing against the ruler, the minister wronged by his king, the aristocratic representative of a social order on the verge of collapse, and the autobiographic poet who laments his fate in verse. Particularly instructive is the passage that leads to the account of the composition of the *Lisao*:

Qu Ping was distressed that:	屈平疾
The king's listening was undiscerning,	王聽之不聰也
Slander and slur obscured insight,	讒諂之蔽明也
The twisted and the crooked harmed the common good,	邪曲之害公也
The square and the straight were no longer given a place.	方正之不容也
Thus, [he] worried and grieved in dark thoughts and made *Encountering Sorrow*.	故憂愁幽思而作離騷
	[*Shiji*, 84.2482]

The four rhymed lines in the middle,[76] all following the same syntactical and rhythmic structure, are a poetic fragment of unknown origin. This passage was almost certainly not invented by the historian himself; it must have come from some longer poetic account possibly understood as autobiographical, that is, in Qu Yuan's own voice. It is evidence for the existence of "Qu Yuan poetry" outside of the known anthology, poetry that may have circulated in smaller units and could be combined with other texts—in this case, the prose narrative of the biography. In such combinations, the figures of subject and object, of protagonist and autobiographical poet, could easily switch sides—just as the lines between biography and autobiography are blurred among the *Jiu zhang, Bu ju,* and *Yufu.*

This blurring occurs one more time in the *Shiji* biography.[77] Without being marked as such, the dialogical piece *Yufu,* otherwise included in the *Chuci* anthology and there attributed to Qu Yuan himself, appears as part of the biographical account. In it, a fisherman challenges Qu Yuan for being stubborn and unhappy because he cannot adapt to changing circumstances. Once again, it is not plausible that the biographer invented the stylized exchange for his narrative; he more likely incorporated it from an earlier literary version available to him. At the same time, compared to the anthology, the *Shiji* version does not include the full text of *Yufu.* It leaves out the fisherman's short song at the end that, as it happens, also appears independently in *Mengzi* 4A.8, where it has nothing to do with Qu Yuan (or a fisherman). Perhaps the *Shiji* author excluded the song; perhaps he did not know it. Either way, in the biography the story works better without it, giving Qu Yuan—now both hero and poet—the final word, highly emotional and personal: "I shall better throw myself into the everflowing stream and bury myself in the bowels of the river fish! How could I take my brilliant clarity and have it obscured by the confused blur of the world" 寧赴常流而葬乎江魚腹中耳，又安能以皓皓之白而蒙世俗之溫蠖乎! This is followed by a single sentence: "Then [he] made the poetic exposition of *Huai sha*" 乃作懷沙之賦. After the text of *Huai sha,* only one more thing is left to say: "Thereupon [he] embraced a stone and drowned himself to die in the Miluo River" 於是懷石遂自投汨羅以死.[78]

This is the moment when the dual nature of Qu Yuan as both poetic hero and heroic poet—as figure in the text and author of the text—breaks down: if Qu Yuan the hero is an archaic figure of noble solitude who acts decisively in the last moment of his life, Qu Yuan the poet, whose work survived his suicide, cannot just have "made" (*zuo* 作) his highly sophisticated poem impromptu nor could his creation have survived from such a moment. If Qu Yuan the hero, facing his fate, was alone when drowning himself in the Miluo river—with loneliness being a central motif of his legend—Qu Yuan the poet, responding to fate, was not alone when composing and reciting *Huaisha* moments earlier. Within the Han "Qu Yuan Epic," this contradiction did not matter: poet and hero could easily switch places.

Nearly a century later, Yang Xiong in his *Fan Sao* challenged Qu Yuan's decision: there was no reason for Qu Yuan to drown himself after having been slandered and exiled. He could have gone into hiding or he could have left Chu. But Yang Xiong aimed at a pre-imperial Qu Yuan persona: a man of other options. Sima Qian instead imagined Qu Yuan entirely under the conditions of the imperial state, which were Sima's own: a man facing his single ruler, and having nowhere to go but into demise. The dilemma and voice Sima Qian imagined for Qu Yuan was that of an imperial scholar-official: a voice not yet heard before the empire but a voice eminently meaningful to the Han Cultural Memory.

Repertoire and Authorship

In recent years, I developed a model of "repertoires and composite texts" to analyze *Shijing* poetry not as an assembly of discrete, individual poems but rather as an anthology of "repertoires": clusters of poems that are directly related to one another and are essentially a single poem in multiple variations.[79] This model downplays the notion of individual authorship. Instead, it assumes the existence of certain poetic themes that were associated with particular sets of poetic expression, and that could be flexibly actualized in ever new variations, written or oral. Such poetry is not stable at the level of the individual text, but it is largely stable at the level of the repertoire, or body of material from which any such individual text draws. The result is multiple interrelated poems that are similar but not identical, with the textual material mobilized in modular ways.

There is nothing unusual with such a model of ancient poetic composition. For the medieval European poetic traditions, its instability at the level of the poem has been called *mouvance* in Paul Zumthor's terminology[80] and *variance* in Bernard Cerquiglini's[81] with respect to both oral and written compositions, respectively. Importantly, the "author function"[82] does not exist as a controlling factor in the interpretation or stability of such texts. Any effort to retrospectively "reconstruct" or "discover" a particular author or specific historical moment of composition is conceptually misguided and artificially limiting for poems that come into being as ever-renewed instantiations from "poetic material" or "repertoires." Stephen Owen, in conceptualizing the intertextuality of early medieval Chinese poetry in these terms, speaks of "one poetry," that is, a textual corpus where the individual text is but "a single realization of many possible poems that might have been composed" within "a single continuum rather than as a corpus of texts either canonized or ignored. It has its recurrent themes, its relatively stable passages and line patterns, and its procedures."[83] To adopt the terminology from biology, the different phenotexts are all variations of the same underlying genotext.

This model of circumscribed poetic fluidity proves immensely productive in reconsidering the nature of ancient Chinese poetry across a wide range of genres. It relieves us of authorial attributions whose fictionality is blindingly obvious; it obviates the need to create chronologies, hierarchies, and linear directions of quotation; it accounts for the dense intertextual relations and modular textual "building blocks"[84] that move with ease between different textual instantiations across early Chinese writing; and it situates the poetic text in social practices of poetic exchange, performance, and variation. Finally—and pertinent to the present analysis—the distributed nature of poetic expression as found in the "Qu Yuan Epic" falls together with the collective dimension of Cultural Memory: the Western Han Qu Yuan is the result not of some individual textual construction but responds to the shared concerns of its time.

It is, however, necessary to be more specific about the notion of "inter-textuality" in the early Chinese context. Within the *Chuci* anthology, Heng Du—to some extent following David Hawkes and others before her—has distinguished between an early, interrelated core and a later set of imitation pieces; in her reading, they are separated by pieces that serve a paratextual function,[85] in particular *Bu ju* and *Yufu*, both of which name and define the Qu Yuan persona, mark his death, and hence close the canon attributed to him.[86] Reception, quotation, commentary, or imitation all become possible only after this textual closure. At least in some early recension of the *Chuci* anthology, the *Lisao* was regarded as the only work by Qu Yuan and a *jing* 經 (canon) followed by texts of *zhuan* 傳 (tradition);[87] as a remnant of this understanding, the title *Lisao jing* 離騷經 (The *Lisao* Canon) survived through Wang Yi's Eastern Han commentary yet was no longer understood.[88] While most scholars at a minimum still accept Qu Yuan's authorship for the *Lisao*—and hence the text as a single, discrete poem—my own analysis leads me to a more iconoclastic reading of the *Chuci* "core" in the poststructuralist tradition of Julia Kristeva, Roland Barthes, and Renate Lachmann (all going back to Mikhail Bakhtin).[89] In my model, the formation of the "Qu Yuan Epic" is the intertextuality of composite texts, textual repertoires, and Cultural Memory and at work both between the *Lisao* and other texts and within the *Lisao* itself.

It is, in fact, Wang Yi himself who offers the lead. For the *Jiu zhang* (including *Huai sha*), he notes that after Qu Yuan's death, "the people of Chu grieved and mourned him; generation after generation appraised his phrases and transmitted his verses from one to the next" 楚人惜而哀之，世論其詞，以相傳焉.[90] Likewise with *Tian wen*: "The people of Chu mourned and grieved over Qu Yuan; they collectively appraised and transmitted [the poem], and this is why it is said not to be in a meaningful order" 楚人哀惜屈原，因共論述，故其文義不次序云爾.[91] For *Yufu*, Wang Yi states that "the people of Chu longed and yearned for Qu Yuan and for this reason arranged his phrases so as to transmit them onward" 楚人思念屈原，因敘其詞以相傳焉.[92]

For Wang Yi, it is implausible that the pieces of *Jiu zhang* emerged from his suicide; *Yufu* talks about Qu Yuan in the third person; and *Tian wen* is too disorderly to be Qu Yuan's own final composition. Moreover, for the *Jiu ge*, Wang Yi sees Qu Yuan more as an editor than as an original author: because the southern religious songs which he encountered in exile were *bilou* 鄙陋 (vulgar and base), Qu Yuan remade them in order to give expression to his own vengeance and remonstrance. Thus, "their textual sense is incoherent, their stanzas and lines are mixed up, and they broadly diverge in their principal meaning" 故其文意不同，章句雜錯，而廣異義焉.[93]

Authorship in this sense is communal, composite, and distributed across the roles of compilers, editors, collators, and commentators. This would not have been lost on figures like Liu An, Liu Xiang, and Wang Yi as they engaged in their own successive efforts of reorganizing the *Chuci* anthology and of the Qu Yuan legend with it. But through their own poetic contributions to the anthology they also still created an authorial model for themselves, with Qu Yuan as their spiritual ancestor. As this new author came into view—likely first with Liu An—Western Han writers responded explicitly to it: Liu An with his *Lisao zhuan* (or *Lisao fu*), Sima Qian (or whoever else) with the *Shiji* biography, and in particular Liu Xiang with his *Jiu tan* where for the first time he mentions the *Jiu zhang* and attributes them to Qu Yuan. The *Jiu tan* are written precisely in the style of the *Jiu zhang*, down to structural devices such as proems and epilogues, and move freely between speaking about Qu Yuan in the third person and impersonating him in the first.[94] In their learned bookishness, the *Jiu tan* reflect Liu Xiang's stature at the imperial court where he organized the books in the imperial library and created a new system of inherited knowledge and intellectual and literary history.[95] Indeed, it appears that Liu Xiang's voice in the *Jiu tan*, more than any earlier one, defined the persona of Qu Yuan as that of the *Jiu zhang*.[96] Liu Xiang's Qu Yuan is a Qu Yuan in Liu Xiang's own image; and Liu Xiang's own voice is developed by way of defining Qu Yuan's.

I therefore propose to divide the anthology into three layers: first, an early layer that shows multiple instances of textual overlap (especially *Lisao*, *Jiu ge*, *Jiu zhang*, *Jiu bian*); second, a late layer that explicitly refers to these earlier texts (most prominently *Jiu tan*); and third, a layer whose texts seem to stand largely separate from both the earlier and the later layers (such as the "summons" poems, *Bu ju*, *Yufu*, and to some extent also *Tian wen*), but were at some point added to the anthology. What distinguishes the early (first) layer from the late (second) one is a much greater degree of horizontal, nonhierarchical intertextual fluidity within the textual repertoire before its canonization into discrete poems. These two layers thus represent two different modes of textual production: one modular and without emphasis on authorship, the other consciously authored in response and as such far more controlled, nonrepetitive, and self-contained. For example, the *Jiu ge* share sentences among themselves with considerable frequency, while Wang Yi's *Jiu si* 九思 (Nine Longings), the final addition to the anthology, never do.[97]

Jiu ge, *Jiu zhang*, and *Jiu bian* are themselves anthologies of distinct repertoires. While a few of their parts stand apart,[98] the clustering of the others in these series may reflect their original, mutual diffusion (consider, e.g., the proximity of *Xiang jun* 湘君 [Goddess of the Xiang River] and *Xiang furen* 湘夫人 [Lady of the Xiang River] within the *Jiu ge*). A particular expression of this fluidity is found in the *Jiu bian* whose individual sections are not even marked by separate titles. But for repertoires to work, it is not enough that their poems share ideas and expressions. They also must stand separate from the poems of other repertoires—as they clearly do, for example, between the *Jiu ge* and the *Jiu zhang*. Only one composite text finally unites these distinct repertoires in a single poem that for this very reason is then marked by an internal diversity of voice, perspective, and lexicon and by ruptures, repetitions, and sudden moments of discontinuity: the *Lisao*.

The "Qu Yuan Epic" as Poetic Intertext

Every Western Han and later source places the *Lisao* at the head of the *Chuci* corpus as its unquestionable origin and master text. But how does a poem of 373 lines[99] appear out of nowhere? How does it circulate through generations, especially during the tumultuous third century BCE and into the Han?

Since at least the Southern Song (1127–1279), scholars have noted the *Lisao*'s structure of discontinuous, nonlinear, mutually independent sections. One could, in fact, move some of these sections around without much consequence, especially as the text spirals forward with numerous repetitions. The many attempts to divide the text into two, three, four, five, eight, ten, twelve, thirteen, fourteen, or sixteen segments[100] all remain inconclusive for the same reason: while acknowledging the ruptures and repetitions, they still take the *Lisao* as a single poem by a single author, with a single voice and a single meaning.[101]

However, together with their own patterns of repetitions, the individual sections across the *Lisao* show very specific intertextual relations with other texts in the *Chuci* anthology, especially *Jiu ge*, *Jiu zhang*, and *Jiu bian* (and even *Tian wen*) that all carry their own themes, linguistic patterns, and lexicons. These differences create jarring effects on poetic voice, perspective of speech, and typology of imagery.[102] Thus, I propose that the *Lisao* is neither the composition by a single poet nor a single poem. It is an anthology of different elements of the "Qu Yuan Epic," just as the *Shiji* biography is a composite of different, mutually incongruous sources. In this reading, the *Lisao* does not precede the poetry of the *Jiu ge, Jiu zhang,* or *Tian wen.* Qu Yuan is not its author but the protagonist of his story that was told in a range of different sources. The *Lisao* is the canonical *jing* not as the first expression of that story but as its ambitious *summa*; the other works are secondary not in the sense that they follow the *Lisao* but that they are limited to specific contents and poetic registers. This reading does not claim a chronology for the received texts of *Jiu ge, Jiu zhang, Jiu bian,* or *Tian wen* relative to the *Lisao.* Instead, it suggests that their different registers and lexicons preceded all our anthologized versions, including that of the *Lisao,* before they all became separately organized into the anthology. Together, they represent particular aspects of the Cultural Memory of Chu as it was relevant to Han authors: its ancient religious practices (*Jiu ge*), its history and mythology (*Tian wen*), and the lament of the upright official (*Jiu zhang, Jiu bian*), the latter since Jia Yi identified with the figure of Qu Yuan.

The process of textual integration and compilation may have been accomplished by the literary scholars at Liu An's court, including Liu An himself, or may be the work of Liu Xiang. Note, however, how both *Lisao* and *Jiu zhang* still retain strongly performative elements, beginning with the presentation of the hero in the first three stanzas of the *Lisao.* Before its final textualization, the Qu Yuan story must have been told and retold, performed and reperformed, composed and recomposed over time in both oral and written forms. This is suggested not only by the performative elements, repetitions, and ruptures but also by the fact that certain sections of the *Lisao* are impossible to understand because they completely lack context—a context that must have existed in some earlier version or was provided externally, for example during performances, to the text of the *Lisao.*[103] Despite its length, the *Lisao* is not a self-contained text.

Traces of the textualization of the "Qu Yuan Epic" can be found everywhere: in the overlap of *Yufu* with the *Shiji* biography as well as in the poetic fragment within the latter, both noted above; extensive sharing of text both within the *Lisao* and between the *Lisao* and other poems; and sharing between texts outside of the *Lisao.* To cite just one example of the latter, consider the final ten lines (before the *luan* 亂 coda) of the *Jiu zhang* poem *Ai Ying* 哀郢 (Lamenting Ying),[104] a text that has no overlap with the *Lisao* at all.[105] These same ten lines also appear in the latter sections of *Jiu bian*—a text that otherwise shares multiple lines with the *Lisao*—but spliced apart and scattered across four passages.[106] While some scholars proceed simply on the traditional claim that *Ai Ying* was written by Qu Yuan and the *Jiu bian* afterwards by Song Yu 宋玉,[107] this would imply (a) the written stability and canonicity of *Ai Ying* at an early time and (b) a practice of "quotation" from that stable version for which there is little further evidence. It is at least as plausible that the compact ending of *Ai Ying* was at some point attached to the text, compiled from sentences somewhere[108] or that both *Ai Ying* and *Jiu bian* draw on shared material but use it in different ways. Interesting in this context is Okamura Shigeru's hypothesis that full-line parallels in the early layers of the *Chuci* were owed to the need for metric stability in recitation.[109] Okamura lists such parallels between *Jiu zhang*, *Jiu bian*, and *Lisao* but also fourteen lines (in twelve passages through all parts of the poem) that are fully or partially repeated within the *Lisao* itself.[110] Consider the following two stanzas:

> Stanza 47.
> At dawn I unlocked the cartwheels by the Azure   朝發軔於蒼梧兮
>   Parasol Tree,
> At dusk I arrived at the Hanging Gardens.   夕余至乎縣圃
> I wanted to linger a bit by these spirits' door-locks,   欲少留此靈瑣兮
> Yet the sun moved swiftly, approaching nightfall.   日忽忽其將暮
>
> Stanza 87.
> At dawn I unlocked the cartwheels by the Celestial   朝發軔於天津兮
>   Ford,
> At dusk I arrived at the Western Extremity.   夕余至乎西極
> The phoenix opened its wings to sustain my banner,   鳳皇翼其承旂兮
> Soaring and flapping on high, with wings balanced.   高翔翱之翼翼
>   [*Chuci buzhu*, 1.26–27, 44]

The paired place-names Azure Parasol Tree/Hanging Gardens versus Celestial Ford/Western Extremity are perfectly interchangeable,[111] the first as metonymies and the second as abstractions denoting east and west. For the structure "at dawn . . . at dusk" see also stanzas 4 and 17:

> Stanza 4.
> Swiftly I moved, as if I wouldn't be in time,   汩余若將不及兮
> I feared the years would not stay with me.   恐年歲之不吾與
> At dawn I plucked magnolias from the ridges,   朝搴阰之木蘭兮
> At dusk I pulled evergreens from the islets.   夕攬洲之宿莽
>
> Stanza 17.
> At dawn I drank the dew dropped from magnolias,   朝飲木蘭之墜露兮
> At dusk I ate the flowers fallen from autumn   夕餐秋菊之落英
>   chrysanthemums.

| If only my innate affects remain truly excellent and pure, | 苟余情其信姱以練要兮 |
| Though deprived and starving for long, how could this cause pain? | 長顑頷亦何傷 |

[*Chuci buzhu*, 1.6, 12]

Here, the generic locations "ridges"/ "islets" denote the cosmological opposition of mountain and water, while "magnolias" versus "evergreens"/"autumn chrysanthemums" once again signify east versus west.[112] All four stanzas create an opposition between the geographical ends of the world yet without ever describing the journey between them. All action is frozen in place with neither direction nor progress. Stanzas 4 and 47 together lament the passing of time, yet nothing is gained in the latter over the former. Stanza 57 as well includes the "at dawn . . . at dusk" formula, albeit in inverted sequence. This stanza shows the same combination of cosmological opposition and directionless action, now presumably by an elusive goddess:[113]

Stanza 57.

In tumultuous profusion, now separate, now in unison—	紛總總其離合兮
Suddenly she turned obstinate and hard to sway.	忽緯繣其難遷
At dusk she took refuge at Stone's End Mountain,	夕歸次於窮石兮
At dawn she washed her hair in Weiban Torrent.	朝濯髮於洧盤

[*Chuci buzhu*, 1.31–32]

Stanzas 4, 17, 47, and 87 could easily change places without any effect on the poem; stanza 57 is part of an abrupt and obscure pursuit of a female persona. Yet in addition to the repetitive pattern within the *Lisao*, the pursuit of the elusive goddess in conjunction with the "at dawn . . . at dusk" formula appears also in both *Xiang jun* and *Xiang furen* in the *Jiu ge*,[114] as does the profusion of plant imagery. The *Jiu ge* poems are largely consistent in their imagery and content and together form a single, self-contained unit of expression;[115] at certain passages in the *Lisao*, by contrast, their language surfaces as abruptly and without narrative contextualization as it then fades again, just as other semantic elements do, creating an overwhelming sense of discontinuity.

Such specific semantic elements are highly concentrated in certain parts of the poem while nearly absent elsewhere: the catalogues of ancient rulers, reminiscent of the *Tian wen*, are clustered in stanzas 37–41 and 72–74;[116] mythological places appear in stanzas 47–49, 54–55, 57, 59, and 86–89; plant imagery, while occasionally scattered individually, is concentrated in 3–4, 13,

17–18, 68–70, and 76–81. When they recur in random intervals of repetition, the same semantic elements are clustered together, forming identifiable textual units within the *Lisao*; and even more tellingly, different such elements do not overlap with one another in the same passages but seem mutually exclusive, thus revealing the composite nature of the *Lisao* as a whole.

Stanza 17, already discussed, is further relevant to the discussion of two separate structural features. First, consider the following four stanzas:

Stanza 14.

I hoped that the branches and leaves would grow lofty and lush,	冀枝葉之峻茂兮
Looked back and awaited my time to cut them.	願俟時乎吾將刈
Even if they wilted and broke, how could this cause pain?	雖萎絕其亦何傷兮
Yet I lament how the numerous fragrances are overgrown with weeds.	哀眾芳之蕪穢

Stanza 17.

At dawn I drank the dew dropped from magnolias,	朝飲木蘭之墜露兮
At dusk I ate the flowers fallen from autumn chrysanthemums.	夕餐秋菊之落英
If only my innate affects remain truly excellent and pure,	苟余情其信姱以練要兮
Though deprived and starving for long, how could this cause pain?	長顑頷亦何傷

Stanza 21.

Already cast off, I wore basil for my girdle,	既替余以蕙纕兮
And further extended it to fasten angelica.	又申之以攬茝
With what is cherished in my heart,	亦余心之所善兮
Even in ninefold death there will never be regret.	雖九死其猶未悔

Stanza 29.

I fashioned caltrop and lotus for my garb,	製芰荷以為衣兮
Collected hibiscus for my skirt.	集芙蓉以為裳
Not being known, this is indeed the end,	不吾知其亦已兮
If only my innate affects remain truly fragrant.	苟余情其信芳
	[*Chuci buzhu*,
	1.11, 12, 14, 17]

What makes these four stanzas identical in structure and hence freely interchangeable? In each of them, the first two lines offer a description of plants or some directionless action dedicated to them. And in each stanza, this is then followed by a couplet that has no description at all but is purely a statement of emotional conflict, each time with either *sui* 雖 ("even if") or *gou* 苟 ("if only"). In addition, note the verbatim parallels between stanzas 14 and 17, "how could this cause pain," and those between stanzas 17 ("if only my innate affects remain truly excellent") and 29 ("if only my innate affects remain truly fragrant"). If the descriptive plant imagery recalls the *Jiu ge*, the expression of emotion—dramatized by rhetorical questions, words like "pain," "truly," "heart," and "innate affects," and the intense use of first-person personal pronouns, in particular the emotive *yu* 余—evokes the voice of the *Jiu zhang*. In each stanza, the sequence is identical, and each time it is the plaintive *Jiu zhang* persona of the second couplet that drives the interpretation of the foregoing plant imagery. While the descriptive couplet may be put in past tense, the emotive one belongs to the present.

With this composite structure, no progress is seen between stanzas 14 and 29; all we have are variations on the exact same theme—variations, furthermore, that could further multiply without consequence. However, the structure just identified is almost unique to the first third of the text (it reappears only in reversal in stanzas 77 and 81); later in the poem, other repetitive structures dominate.

Stanzas 14 and 17 are further connected by way of their neighboring stanzas:

Stanza 13.

I watered the nine fields of orchids,	余既滋蘭之九畹兮
And further planted the hundred acres of basil.	又樹蕙之百畝
I arranged lingering blossoms and cart-halting flowers,	畦留夷與揭車兮
Mixed them with wild ginger and fragrant iris.	雜杜衡與芳芷

Stanza 18.

I fastened tree tendrils to tie the angelica,	攬木根以結茝兮
Threaded fallen pistils of creeping fit.	貫薜荔之落蕊
I reached up for cinnamon to string basil,	矯菌桂以紉蕙兮
Corded the winding vines of rope-creepers.	索胡繩之纚纚
	[*Chuci buzhu*, 1.10,12–13]

Whatever these two stanzas are meant to signify, they both differ from the ones just discussed in being entirely focused on the directionless action devoted to plants. There are no other stanzas of this kind in the entire *Lisao*, and nothing prepares the reader for their sudden, random, isolated appearance. Note, however, how they connect to stanzas 14 and 17: stanza 13 precedes stanza 14 that therefore continues the plant imagery for another couplet, but that logic does not apply to the sequence of stanzas 17 and 18. Either way, the protagonist keeps doing whatever he has done at some point before.

There are numerous other details to illustrate the composite, repetitive, nonlinear nature of the *Lisao* as a rich collage of distinct elements derived from distinct discourses that elsewhere in the *Chuci* anthology, sometime in the Han, became separately arranged in by and large coherent, self-contained textual series. What makes the *Lisao* polysemous and polyvocal is their combination within a single text. Much more must be said on

- the extensive parallels between *Lisao*, *Jiu zhang*, and *Jiu bian*;[117]
- those between *Jiu ge* and *Lisao* (and occasionally *Jiu zhang* and *Jiu bian*);[118]
- the series of identical phrases within the *Lisao* itself;
- the highly uneven distribution of the large number of first-person personal pronouns *yu* 余 and *wu* 吾 and their distinctly different uses in passages of emotive lament (mostly *yu*) versus those of a commanding sovereignty (mostly *wu*, e.g., in the formula *wu ling* 吾令, "I command," exclusively concentrated in stanzas 48, 51, 52, 56, 60);
- the clustering of emotive expressions, especially *kong* 恐 ("I fear"; stanzas 4, 5, 9, 61, 63, 75–76), *shang* 傷 ("pain"; 14, 17), *ai* 哀 ("I lament"; 14, 20, 45, 54), the emphatic *xin* 信 ("truly"; 17, 29, 58, 65), and the nouns *xin* 心 ("heart"; 15, 16, 21–22, 26, 32, 36, 61, 70, 85) and *qing* 情 ("innate affects"; 10, 17, 29, 35, 64, 73)—all of which appear predominantly in the first third of the poem and are seen with very high frequency in the *Jiu zhang* while being largely absent in the *Jiu ge*;
- syntactical structures such as *he* 何 ("how . . . ?"), *sui* 雖 ("even if"), and *gou* 苟 ("only if") that further emphasize emotion;
- the shifting voices, perspectives, and genders in the *Lisao* that resist any unified interpretation.[119]

For example, the complexities and uncertainties of intertextuality are on full display with stanzas 10–12:

Stanza 10.

I rushed forward in haste, front and behind,	忽奔走以先後兮
Reaching the footprints of the former kings.	及前王之踵武
Iris did not probe my loyal affection,[120]	荃不察余之中情兮
Instead trusting slander and exploding in rage.	反信讒而齌怒

Stanza 11.

I surely understood how being frank and forthright would bring disaster,	余固知謇謇之為患兮
Yet I endured it and could not let go.	忍而不能舍也
I pointed at Ninefold Heaven to be my witness,	指九天以為正兮
It was only for the cause of Spirit Perfected.	夫唯靈脩之故也
He said: When night falls, we shall meet—	曰黃昏以為期兮
Alas! He was halfway and then changed his path!	羌中道而改路

Stanza 12.

Earlier he had given me trustworthy words,[121]	初既與余成言兮
Later he regretted and fled, having some other.	後悔遁而有他
I did not make trouble for being left and separated,	余既不難夫離別兮
Yet was pained that Spirit Perfected so often changed.	傷靈脩之數化

[*Chuci buzhu*, 1.9–10]

Leaving aside questions of interpretation (Who is "Spirit Perfected"?), I focus on intertextuality. "Probe my loyal affection" (察余之中情兮; stanza 10, line 3) is repeated in stanza 35 but also in the *Jiu zhang* poem *Xi song* (where it is paired with another parallel from *Lisao* stanza 24).[122] "I pointed at Ninefold Heaven to be my witness" (指九天以為正; stanza 11, line 3) repeats in *Xi song* as "I pointed at Azure Heaven to be my witness" (指蒼天以為正).[123] Lines 5 and 6 of stanza 11 present a problem: they uniquely add to the four-line stanza structure but have no commentary by Wang Yi; thus, Hong Xingzu suspects that this couplet entered the text only later.[124] But how and why? Compare the following passage from the *Jiu zhang* poem *Chou si*:

In the past, the lord had given me trustworthy words,	昔君與我誠言兮
He said: When night falls, we shall meet.	曰黃昏以為期
Alas! He was halfway and then turned sideward,	羌中道而回畔兮
Instead, he now had this other intent.	反既有此他志

[*Chuci buzhu*, 4.137]

Obviously, we are reading two versions of the same passage, even with some minor changes and the lines in different order. Nothing makes us privilege the version of the *Lisao*; if anything, we should doubt the original presence of the two additional lines there. We cannot say when these lines entered the text;

perhaps they already existed in some Han version Wang Yi had not seen. Instead of engaging in futile efforts to determine a hierarchy of "copy" and "original" between these passages, I suggest we first of all acknowledge how easily lines from *Lisao* and *Jiu zhang* could converge and switch places—and may well have done so from the very beginning, when both were drawing on the same repertoire of the "Qu Yuan Epic."

Conclusion

The internal complexities of the *Lisao* itself and its relation to other early texts related to Qu Yuan are staggering and—as proven by the numerous different interpretations—not resolvable. This gives us several options. The worst possible choice would be to simply take one of the *Lisao*'s discursive layers and subjugate all others to it, reducing the text to a single meaning and purpose and sacrificing precisely the polysemous richness of its multiple, mutually incompatible but individually fascinating dimensions that distinguish the *Lisao* from all other early Chinese poetry. This choice, unfortunately, is that of the traditional interpretation where the *Lisao* ends up simply as a more chaotic *Jiu zhang*. A better choice would be to recognize and cherish the multiple ways in which the Qu Yuan story was imagined and told, perhaps starting in the late Warring States and then flourishing in the early Han when it answered to a considerable range of different ideological and cultural needs.

What changed from the early Han to Liu Xiang—and then even more forcefully with Wang Yi—were precisely these needs of the respective present for imagining a meaningful, identity-generating past. Liu An's Qu Yuan spoke to the nostalgic Chu *imaginaire* at Shouchun; Liu Xiang's Qu Yuan spoke to the identity of imperial scholar-officials and a new classicism that had space for Qu Yuan the suffering author and royal advisor but no more space for the seemingly bizarre world of Chu's religious, mythological, and erotic imagination. The Cultural Memory of the "Qu Yuan Epic" had changed to meet a new time.

    MARTIN KERN   柯马丁
Princeton University
mkern@princeton.edu

Notes

1. To identify "Cultural Memory" as a theoretical concept, it will be capitalized throughout. A catalog search in the Princeton University Library on June 16, 2021, returned 577 items with the phrase "cultural memory" in their titles; a search that included "cultural" and "memory" separately returned 2,638 items. These numbers refer just to English-language books.

2.   "Collective Memory and Cultural Identity" (1995), *Moses the Egyptian* (1997), *Religion and Cultural Memory* (2006), "Communicative and Cultural Memory" (2008), and *Cultural Memory and Early Civilization* (2011).

3.   In particular, *Erinnerungsräume* (1999); rewritten by the author in English as *Cultural Memory and Western Civilization* (2011).

4.   I first employed the concept in my 1996 German dissertation, *Die Hymnen der chinesischen Staatsopfer*, unaware of any earlier uses of Assmann's work in Sinology. The first sustained application of Cultural Memory to early Chinese literature was Kern, "*Shi jing* Songs as Performance Texts." For my pertinent more recent studies, see Kern, "'Harangues' (*Shi* 誓) in the *Shangshu*," and Kern, "Bronze Inscriptions, the *Shangshu*, and the *Shijing*." For some further engagement with Cultural Memory, see Davis, *Entombed Epigraphy and Commemorative Culture in Early Medieval China*; Swartz, "Intertextuality and Cultural Memory in Early Medieval China"; Nugent, "Structured Gaps"; Krijgsman, "Traveling Sayings"; and Khayutina, "Beginning of Cultural Memory Production." Furthermore, *Chinese Literature: Essays, Articles, Reviews* 27 (2005) collects four articles from a 2003 symposium, "Memory and Chinese Texts," at Indiana University, but only the introduction by Lynn Struve (Struve, "Introduction to the Symposium") refers to the Assmanns. Jan Assmann's *Cultural Memory and Ancient Civilization* has also appeared in Chinese translation as *Wenhua jiyi: Zaoqi gaoji wenhua zhong de wenzi, huiyi he zhengzhi shenfen*. By now, the new coinage *wenhua jiyi* 文化記憶 ("cultural memory") has gained circulation in Chinese scholarship.

5.   Expanded in Frankel, *Flowering Plum and the Palace Lady*, 104–43.

6.   Knechtges, "Ruin and Remembrance in Classical Chinese Literature." Knechtges does not refer to Cultural Memory.

7.   Owen's *Remembrances* further branches out into late imperial literature.

8.   Consider e.g., the early development of *yuefu* 樂府 (music bureau poetry) and *gu shi* 古詩 (ancient-style poetry), also including "imitation" (*ni* 擬, *dai* 代, etc.) poetry, as well as the *yong shi* 詠史 (Singing about History) section in chapter 21 of Xiao Tong's 蕭統 (501–531) *Wenxuan* 文選 (Selections of Refined Literature). In fact, Xiao Tong's entire anthology would deserve a dedicated study from the perspective of Cultural Memory.

9.   The English word derives from Greek *mnēmonikos*, "relating to memory." Mnēmosyne was the Greek goddess of memory, mother of the Muses.

10. Yates, *Art of Memory*; Carruthers, *Book of Memory*; Carruthers and Ziolkowski, *Medieval Craft of Memory*.

11. Lachmann, *Gedächtnis und Literatur*.

12. See e.g., Brashier, *Ancestral Memory in Early China*; Brashier, *Public Memory in Early China*, though without reference to Cultural Memory.

13. In addition to the Assmanns' own writings, an excellent introduction to the different theoretical models of "memory," including Cultural Memory, is Erll, *Memory in Culture*, 27–37. Erll provides a wealth of additional references to individual studies as well as to a series of handbooks, newly founded journals, and monograph series that have sprung up especially since the 1990s. See also *Cultural Memory Studies*, ed. Erll and Nünning. Seminal works that provide the principal points of reference—and that advance different positions especially regarding the perceived dichotomy of "memory" versus "history"—include Burke, "History as Social Memory"; Connerton, *How Societies Remember*; Hutton, *History as an Art of Memory*; Le Goff, *Storia e memoria* (*History and Memory*); Nora, *Les lieux de mémoire* (*The Places of Memory*); and Zerubavel, *Time Maps*.

14. For "composite text," see the seminal study by Boltz, "The Composite Nature of Early Chinese Texts." I use the word *composite* to denote literary production out of distinct, preexisting themes, expressions, or materials. For "repertoire," see Owen, *The Making of Early Chinese Classical Poetry*. For an earlier study conjoining the two concepts, see Kern, "'Xi shuai' and Its Consequences."

15. I am using the French sociological notion of the *imaginaire* to refer to the social and cultural image that Han scholars collectively created of and for themselves, similar to what Benedict Anderson has described in his *Imagined Communities*.

16. A new critical edition of this work in French was established by Gérard Namer in 1997. In English, Halbwachs's book first appeared as *The Collective Memory* (1980) and later as *On Collective Memory* (1992), further including the conclusion of *La topographie légendaire des Évangiles en Terre Sainte*.

17. Halbwachs, *On Collective Memory*, 43.

18. See "Short History of Memory Studies," in Erll, *Memory in Culture*, 13–37.

19. See the discussions in Burke, "History as Social Memory"; A. Assmann, "Transformations between History and Memory"; Erll, *Memory in Culture*, esp. 39–45, 96–101.

20. Erll, *Memory in Culture*, 7.

21. Ibid., 8. Halbwachs's insight that "a remembrance is in very large measure a reconstruction of the past achieved with data borrowed from the present, a reconstruction prepared, furthermore, by reconstructions of earlier periods wherein past images had already been altered" (*On Cultural Memory*, 68), according to Erll, "already points to what half a century later, within poststructuralist discussions, will be called 'the construction of reality'" (*Memory in Culture*, 17).

22. For early China, see Brashier, "Longevity Like Metal and Stone"; H. Wu, *Monumentality in Early Chinese Art and Architecture*; Kern, *Stele Inscriptions of Ch'in Shih-huang*.

23. See, e.g., Flower, *Art of Forgetting*.

24. "1619 Project," *New York Times*, August 14, 2019, https://www.nytimes.com/interactive /2019/08/14/magazine/1619-america-slavery.html.

25. Present examples are too obvious to need further reference here.

26. J. Assmann, *Cultural Memory and Early Civilization*, 36–41; see also Erll, *Memory in Culture*, 28–29.

27. See the table in J. Assmann, *Cultural Memory and Early Civilization*, 41, rephrased in Erll, *Memory in Culture*, 29.

28. J. Assmann, *Cultural Memory and Early Civilization*, 37–38.

29. Ibid., 41–42.

30. Connerton, *How Societies Remember*, 45.

31. Bloch's "Symbols, Song, Dance and Features of Articulation" characterizes ritual speech as "formalized" and "impoverished language," the "language of authority" where "many of the options at all levels of language are abandoned so that choice of form, of style, of words and of syntax is less than in ordinary language."

32. For detailed accounts of these elements, see Kern, "*Shi jing* Songs as Performance Texts"; Kern, "Bronze Inscriptions, the *Shangshu*, and the *Shijing*."

33. Wheelock, "Problem of Ritual Language."

34. See Falkenhausen, "Issues in Western Zhou Studies."

35. *Liji zhengyi*, 49.1590–91.

36. Owen, *Remembrances*, 16.

37. A. Assmann, *Cultural Memory and Western Civilization*, 169–206; J. Assmann, *Cultural Memory and Early Civilization*, 70–110.

38. A. Assmann, *Cultural Memory and Western Civilization*, 119–32, 327–94; see also Erll, *Memory in Culture*, 36–37. As noted by Erll, the Assmanns' notion of the archive extends the presence of Cultural Memory from the "modus of actuality" to the "modus of potentiality," while tradition only represents the former.

39. For a discussion of the interplay of written text, visuality, and orality in Scribe Qiang's inscription, see Kern, "Performance of Writing in Western Zhou China," 167–71.

40. For Western Zhou archives, see most recently Shaughnessy, "Possible Lost Classic."

41. *Mao shi* 209, "Chu ci" 楚茨 (Thorny Caltrop).

42. *Mao shi* 245, "Sheng min" 生民 (She Bore the Folk).

43. *Mao shi* 290, "Zai shan" 載芟 (Now Clearing Away).

44. A. Assmann, *Cultural Memory and Western Civilization*, 73.

45. A. Assmann, "Transformations Between History and Memory," 65.

46. The present essay should not be understood as a continuation of the twentieth-century debates of "the Qu Yuan Question" (*Qu Yuan wenti* 屈原問題) but as a new departure in discussing both Qu Yuan and "his" texts. Important critical voices in the earlier debate include Liao Jiping 廖季平 (1852–1932), Hu Shi 胡适 (1891–1962), He Tianxing 何天行 (1913–1986), Wei Juxian 衛聚賢 (1898–1990), and Zhu Dongrun 朱東潤 (1896–1988) in China, and Okamura Shigeru 岡村繁 (1922–2014), Suzuki Shūji 鈴木修次 (1923–1989), Shirakawa Shizuka 白川静 (1910–2006), Ishikawa Misao 石川三佐男, Misawa Reiji 三澤鈴尔, Inahata Kōichirō 稲畑耕一郎, and Taniguchi Mitsuru 谷口滿 in Japan. The earlier debates can be conveniently surveyed in Inahata, "Kutsu Gen hiteiron no keifu"; Huang Zhongmo, *Qu Yuan wenti lunzheng shigao*; Huang Zhongmo, *Yu Riben xuezhe taolun Qu Yuan wenti*; Huang Zhongmo, *Zhong-Ri xuezhe Qu Yuan wenti lunzheng ji*; Xu Zhixiao, *Riben Chuci yanjiu lungang*; Hightower, "Ch'ü Yüan Studies." While Republican period Chinese scholars often expressed doubts about Qu Yuan's historical existence or authorship, more recent Chinese scholarship has moved into the opposite direction.

47. Kern, "Du Fu's Long Gaze Back"; Kern, "*Shiji* li de 'zuozhe' gainian."

48. *Shiji*, 84.2481–91.

49. Hong, *Chuci buzhu*; see also Huang, *Chuci zhangju shuzheng*; Jin, Dong, and Gao, *Qu Yuan ji jiaozhu*; and for the *Lisao* in particular, see You, *Lisao zuanyi*.

50. *Princeton Encyclopedia of Poetry and Poetics*, 4th ed., edited by Ronald Greene and Stephen Cushman (Princeton, NJ: Princeton University Press, 2012), s.v. "Epic."

51. Earlier, Wang, *From Ritual to Allegory*, 73–114, had proposed to read a series of five poems on King Wen 文 in the "Da ya" 大雅 (Major Court Hymns) section of the *Shijing* as the epic of King Wen (in Wang's coinage, the "Weniad"). It should be noted, however, that in sheer scope, the poetic representation of King Wen is nowhere close to that of Qu Yuan nor does it develop the protagonist's interiority through his experiences of heroic struggle over time.

52. See Wu Enpei, *Wu Zixu shiliao xinbian*.

53. Reading—necessitated by the rhyme—*neng* 能 as *tai* 態.

54. Jia Yi's *Diao Qu Yuan* 吊屈原 (Mourning Qu Yuan) knows of Qu Yuan but does not mention him as a poet; see *Shiji*, 84.2492–96; the same is true for the poem *Ai shi ming* 哀時命 (Lamenting the Fate of One's Time), attributed to Yan 嚴 [i.e., Zhuang 莊] Ji 忌 (fl.

ca. 150 BCE) in *Chuci buzhu*, 14.259–67. The identified fragments of Liu An's *Lisao zhuan* 離騷傳 (Commentary on *Lisao*; possibly *Lisao fu* 離騷 [傅] 賦, Poetic Exposition on *Lisao*) refer to the text but not to the person; see *Chuci buzhu*, 1.1.

55. In *Chuci buzhu*, 15.268–80, Wang Bao is credited with the *Jiu huai* 九懷 (Nine Regrets).

56. For Yang Xiong's *Fan Sao* 反騷 (Contra [*Li*] *Sao*), see *Hanshu*, 87A.3515–21.

57. See Hawkes, *Songs of the South*, 60–61.

58. *Shiji*, 84.2484.

59. *Shiji*, 6.230, 7.313, 40.1728, 44.1857, 69.2254, 69.2261, 71.2308, 75.2354.

60. *Shiji*, 84.2491.

61. For summaries of the history of the *Chuci* anthology, see Hawkes, *Songs of the South*, 28–41; Walker, "Toward a Formal History of the *Chuci*"; Du, "Author's Two Bodies"; Chan, "*Jing/Zhuan* Structure of the *Chuci* Anthology."

62. *Shiji*, 84.2481.

63. See Li Zehou, *Mei de licheng*, 94.

64. See Schneider, *Madman of Ch'u*; Schimmelpfennig, "Quest for a Classic"; Waters, *Three Elegies of Ch'u*.

65. *Shiji*, 84.2481–504.

66. For some recent work see Lewis, *Writing and Authority in Early China*; Du, "Author's Two Bodies"; Li, "Concepts of Authorship"; Li, "Idea of Authority in the *Shih chi* (*Records of the Historian*)"; Kern, "Du Fu's Long Gaze Back"; Kern, "*Shiji* li de 'zuozhe' gainian"; Nylan, "Manuscript Culture in Late Western Han, and the Implications for Authors and Authority"; Zhang, *Authorship and Text-making in Early China*; Beecroft, *Authorship and Cultural Identity in Early Greece and China*; Walker, "Toward a Formal History," 22–87.

67. *Shiji*, 47.1947.

68. *Shiji*, 84.2503.

69. Kern, "Du Fu's Long Gaze Back," 168.

70. *Chuci buzhu*, 6.176–7.181.

71. For studies of the *Chuci zhangju*, see especially Schimmelpfennig, "Quest for a Classic"; Schimmelpfennig, "Qu Yuan's Transformation from Realized Man to True Poet"; Du, "Author's Two Bodies"; Chan, "*Jing/Zhuan* Structure."

72. Hawkes, *Songs of the South*, 51–61; Walker, "Toward a Formal History," 88–108.

73. Schimmelpfennig, "Quest for a Classic," 114–18.

74. *Chuci buzhu*, 11.327–31.

75. Hawkes, *Songs of the South*, 239; Walker, "Toward a Formal History," 165–67.

76. Line 2 rhymes in the *yang* 陽 category; the other three rhyme in *dong* 東. For their interrhyming in Han poetry, see Luo and Zhou, *Han Wei Jin nanbeichao yunbu yanbian yanjiu*, 179, 187–88.

77. The following four paragraphs follow closely Kern, "Du Fu's Long Gaze Back," 172–73.

78. *Shiji*, 84.2486, 2490.

79. Kern, "'Xi shuai' and Its Consequences"; Kern, "Formation of the *Classic of Poetry*."

80. Zumthor, *Toward a Medieval Poetics*.

81. Cerquiglini, *In Praise of the Variant*.

82. Foucault, "What Is an Author?"

83. Owen, *Making of Early Chinese Classical Poetry*, 73.

84. For "building blocks," see Boltz, "Composite Nature of Early Chinese Texts"; for "modularity," see Ledderose, *Ten Thousand Things*. I use both concepts in a slightly more expansive way than how they were originally presented by Boltz and Ledderose.

85. Du's use of "paratext" comes from Genette, *Paratexts*.

86. Du, "Author's Two Bodies."

87. Ibid., 281–83. For the full argument, see Chan, "*Jing/Zhuan* Structure," with an extensive review of earlier Chinese, Japanese, and English scholarship.

88. *Chuci buzhu*, 1.1–2.

89. Kristeva, "Word, Dialogue, and Novel"; Barthes, "Death of the Author"; Lachmann, *Gedächtnis und Literatur*. Recent scholarship in the digital humanities that examines large amounts of text through computer-assisted, corpus-based analysis has only further weakened previous claims on the sanctity of discrete authorship in traditional literature; see e.g., Moretti, *Distant Reading*, and Stallybrass, "Against Thinking."

90. *Chuci buzhu*, 4.120–21.

91. Ibid., 3.85.

92. Ibid., 7.179.

93. Ibid., 2.55.

94. Walker, "Toward a Formal History," 294–300, shows that Liu Xiang's rhymes deviate noticeably from those of the *Jiu zhang*, reflecting Western Han changes in phonology. Meanwhile, Wang Bao's *Jiu huai*, contemporaneous to the *Jiu tan*, show no awareness of the *Jiu zhang* but do rhyme according to their earlier phonology (ibid., 205–7, 290–92), possibly reflecting an archaizing mode of composition.

95. See Xu Jianwei, *Wenben geming*.

96. On Liu Xiang's role in the construction of Qu Yuan, see Chan, "*Jing/Zhuan* Structure."

97. Walker, "Toward a Formal History," 132, 175–78.

98. *Ju song* 橘頌 (Ode to the Orange Tree) in the *Jiu zhang*; *Guo shang* 國殤 (The Fallen of the State) and *Li hun* 禮魂 (Paying Tribute to the Souls) in the *Jiu ge*.

99. I count ninety-three stanzas, including the final *luan* 亂 (coda). Each stanza has 4 lines with end-rhymes on lines 2 and 4. The *luan* stanza I count as 5 lines, thus arriving at 373 lines. The additional 2 lines in stanza 11 (see below) I do not count.

100. For two recent summaries, see Shi and Zhou, "*Lisao* de fenduan yanjiu zongshu," 44–50; Zhou, "*Chuci* cengci jiegou yanjiu—yi *Lisao* wei li," 28–37.

101. For Jin, *Chuci jianghua*, 112–13, those who consider the *Lisao* chaotic do not understand it.

102. Yu, *Reading of Imagery in the Chinese Poetic Tradition*, 86–88, 99–100.

103. This is obvious from the numerous speculative and mutually exclusive interpretations of specific phrases and entire passages over the past two millennia; see the collected commentaries in You, *Lisao zuanyi*. Consider, for example, the sudden appearance of Nüxu 女嬃 in stanza 33 or of Fufei 虑妃 (or Mifei 宓妃) and Qianxiu 蹇修 in stanza 56.

104. *Chuci buzhu*, 4.136; Huang Linggeng, *Chuci zhangju shuzheng*, 5.1431–32.

105. See the discussion in Walker, "Toward a Formal History," 169–70.

106. See *Chuci buzhu*, 8.193–95, Huang Linggeng, *Chuci zhangju shuzheng*, 2.690, 693–94, 701–4, 725; Walker, "Toward a Formal History," 147–49.

107. E.g., Jin, Dong, and Gao, *Qu Yuan ji jiaozhu*, 504. Claims about the historically obscure Song Yu are a matter of belief, not evidence. I consider them irrelevant.

108. See Hawkes, *Songs of the South*, 163.

109. Okamura, "Soji to Kutsu Gen," 94.

110. Ibid., 97–98. The intra-*Lisao* correspondences listed by Okamura occur in the following stanzas: 10–35 (cf. also 67) 17–29, 31–54, 31–82, 39–58, 47–87 (two lines), 52–57, 53–63 (two lines), 55–84, 61–70, 68–76 (cf. also 9), 79–82 (cf. also 58).

111. See Huang Linggeng, *Chuci zhangju shuzheng*, 1.330, 1.514.

112. In Han dynasty *wuxing* 五行 (five phases) correlative cosmology, spring (the flowering season of the magnolia) is related to the east and autumn to the west.

113. For speculation about this persona, see the numerous opinions noted in You, *Lisao zuanyi*, 301–15.

114. *Chuci buzhu*, 2.63 (with *zhao* 朝 as *chao* 鼂) and 2.66.

115. See Hawkes, "Quest of the Goddess," 42–68.

116. Almost all rulers cataloged in stanzas 37–41 also appear in *Tian wen*.

117. Okamura, "Soji to Kutsu Gen," 92–93, lists twenty-six parallels between *Lisao* and *Jiu zhang*, twelve between *Lisao* and *Jiu bian*, and thirteen between *Jiu bian* and *Jiu zhang*. Note that *Lisao* and *Jiu bian*, while both having close relationships with *Jiu zhang*, correspond to them differently: *Jiu bian* shares sentences mostly with *Ai Ying*, while *Lisao* shares especially with *Xi song* 惜誦 (Regretful Recitation), *Si meiren* 思美人 (Longing for the Beautiful One), *Xi wang ri* 惜往日 (Regretting the Days Past), *Chou si* 抽思 (Unraveling My Longing), and *Bei huifeng* 悲回風 (Grieving Over the Whirling Wind); see the diagram in Okamura, "Soji to Kutsu Gen," 94.

118. For a list, see Walker, "Toward a Formal History," 224–27.

119. For present limits on space, I will explore these issues in a separate publication.

120. Reading *zhong* 中 as 忠.

121. Reading *cheng* 成 as 誠.

122. *Chuci buzhu*, 4.124.

123. Ibid., 4.121.

124. Ibid., 1.10.

References

Anderson, Benedict. *Imagined Communities*. London: Verso, 2006.

Assmann, Aleida. *Cultural Memory and Western Civilization: Functions, Media, Archives*. Cambridge: Cambridge University Press, 2011.

———. *Erinnerungsräume: Formen und Wandlungen des kulturellen Gedächtnisses* (Spaces of Memory: Forms and Transformations in Cultural Memory). Munich: Beck, 1999.

———. "Transformations between History and Memory." *Social Research* 75, no. 1 (2008): 49–72.

Assmann, Jan. "Collective Memory and Cultural Identity." Translated by John Czaplicka. *New German Critique* 65 (1995): 125–33.

———. "Communicative and Cultural Memory." In *Cultural Memory Studies: An International and Interdisciplinary Handbook*, edited by Astrid Erll and Ansgar Nünning, 109–18. Berlin: Walter de Gruyter, 2008.

———. *Cultural Memory and Early Civilization: Writing, Remembrance, and Political Imagination*. Cambridge: Cambridge University Press, 2011.

———. *Das kulturelle Gedächtnis: Schrift, Erinnerung und politische Identität in frühen Hochkulturen* (The Cultural Memory: Writing, Remembrance, and Political Identity in Early High Cultures). Munich: Beck, 1992.

———. "Kollektives Gedächtnis und kulturelle Identität" (Collective Memory and Cultural Identity). In *Kultur und Gedächtnis* (Culture and Memory), edited by Jan Assmann and Tonio Hölscher, 9–19. Frankfurt am Main: Suhrkamp, 1988.

———. *Moses the Egyptian: The Memory of Egypt in Western Monotheism*. Cambridge, MA: Harvard University Press, 1997.

———. *Religion and Cultural Memory: Ten Studies*. Translated by Rodney Livingstone. Stanford: Stanford University Press, 2006.

———. *Wenhua jiyi: Zaoqi gaoji wenhua zhong de wenzi, huiyi he zhengzhi shenfen* 文化記憶：早期高級文化中的文字、回憶和政治身份 (The Cultural Memory: Writing, Remembrance, and Political Identity in Early High Cultures). Beijing: Beijing daxue chubanshe, 2015.

Barthes, Roland. "The Death of the Author." In *Image—Music—Text*. Translated by Stephen Heath, 142–48. New York: Hill and Wang, 1978.

Beecroft, Alexander. *Authorship and Cultural Identity in Early Greece and China: Patterns of Literary Circulation*. Cambridge: University Press, 2010.

Bloch, Maurice. "Symbols, Song, Dance and Features of Articulation: Is Religion an Extreme Form of Traditional Authority?" *European Journal of Sociology* 15, no. 1 (1974): 55–81.

Boltz, William G. "The Composite Nature of Early Chinese Texts." In *Text and Ritual in Early China*, edited by Martin Kern, 50–78. Seattle: University of Washington Press, 2005.

Brashier, K. E. *Ancestral Memory in Early China*. Cambridge, MA: Harvard University Asia Center, 2011.

———. "Longevity Like Metal and Stone: The Role of the Mirror in Han Burials." *T'oung Pao* 81, no. 4–5 (1995): 201–29.

———. *Public Memory in Early China*. Cambridge, MA: Harvard University Asia Center, 2014.

Burke, Peter. "History as Social Memory." In *Memory: History, Culture and the Mind*, edited by Thomas Butler, 97–113. Oxford: Blackwell, 1989.

Carruthers, Mary. *The Book of Memory: A Study of Memory in Medieval Culture*. Cambridge: Cambridge University Press, 1993.

Carruthers, Mary, and Jan M. Ziolkowski. *The Medieval Craft of Memory: An Anthology of Texts and Pictures*. Philadelphia: University of Pennsylvania Press, 2002.

Cerquiglini, Bernard. *In Praise of the Variant: A Critical History of Philology*. Translated by Betsy Wing. Baltimore: Johns Hopkins University Press, 1999.

Chan, Timothy Wai-keung. "The *Jing/Zhuan* Structure of the *Chuci* Anthology: A New Approach to the Authorship of Some of the Poems." *T'oung Pao* 84, no. 5–6 (1998): 293–327.

Connerton, Paul. *How Societies Remember*. Cambridge: Cambridge University Press, 1989.

Davis, Timothy M. *Entombed Epigraphy and Commemorative Culture in Early Medieval China: A History of Early Muzhiming*. Leiden: Brill, 2015.

Du, Heng. "The Author's Two Bodies: The Death of Qu Yuan and the Birth of *Chuci zhangju* 楚辭章句." *T'oung Pao* 105, no. 3–4 (2019): 259–314.

Erll, Astrid. *Memory in Culture*. Translated by Sara B. Young. New York: Palgrave Macmillan, 2011.

Erll, Astrid, and Ansgar Nünning, eds. *Cultural Memory Studies: An International and Interdisciplinary Handbook*. Berlin: Walter de Gruyter, 2008.

Falkenhausen, Lothar von. "Issues in Western Zhou Studies: A Review Article." *Early China* 18 (1993): 139–226.

Flower, Harriet. *The Art of Forgetting: Disgrace and Oblivion in Roman Political Culture*. Chapel Hill: University of North Carolina Press, 2006.

Foucault, Michel. "What Is an Author?" In *Textual Strategies: Perspectives in Post-Structuralist Criticism*, edited and translated by Josué V. Harari, 141–60. Ithaca, NY: Cornell University Press, 1979.

Frankel, Hans. "The Contemplation of the Past in T'ang Poetry." In *Perspectives on the T'ang*, edited by Arthur F. Wright and Denis Twitchett, 345–65. New Haven: Yale University Press, 1973.

———. *The Flowering Plum and the Palace Lady: Interpretations of Chinese Poetry*. New Haven: Yale University Press, 1976.

Genette, Gérard. *Paratexts: Thresholds of Interpretation*. Translated by Jane E. Lewin. Cambridge: Cambridge University Press, 1997.

Halbwachs, Maurice. *Les cadres sociaux de la mémoire* (The Social Frameworks of Memory). Paris: Alcan, 1925.

———. *La mémoire collective* (The Collective Memory). Paris: Presses Universitaires de France, 1950.

———. *La topographie légendaire des Évangiles en Terre Sainte: Étude de mémoire collective* (The Legendary Topography of the Gospels in the Holy Land: A Study of Collective Memory). Paris: Presses Universitaires de France, 1942.

———. *On Collective Memory*. Translated by Lewis A. Coser. Chicago: University of Chicago Press, 1992.

Hanshu 漢書 (History of the Former Han). Beijing: Zhonghua shuju, 1962.

Hawkes, David. "The Quest of the Goddess." In *Studies in Chinese Literary Genres*, edited by Cyril Birch, 42–68. Berkeley: University of California Press, 1974.

———. *The Songs of the South: An Anthology of Ancient Chinese Poems by Qu Yuan and Other Poets*. Harmondsworth: Penguin Books, 1985.

Hightower, James Robert. "Ch'ü Yüan Studies." In *Silver Jubilee Volume of the Zinbun-Kagaku-Kenkyusyo*, edited by Kyōto daigaku jinbun kagaku kenkyūjo 京都大學人文科學研究所, 192–223. Kyoto: Kyōto University, 1954.

Hong Xingzu 洪興祖. *Chuci buzhu* 楚辭補注 (Supplementary Commentary to the *Chuci*). Beijing: Zhonghua shuju, 1983.

Huang Linggeng 黃靈庚. *Chuci zhangju shuzheng* 楚辭章句疏證 (*Chapter and Verse Commentary to the Chuci* with Explanations and Verifications). Beijing: Zhonghua shuju, 2007.

Huang Zhongmo 黃中模. *Qu Yuan wenti lunzheng shigao* 屈原問題論爭史稿 (A Draft History on the Debate over the Qu Yuan Question). Beijing: Beijing shiyue wenyi chubanshe, 1987.

———. *Yu Riben xuezhe taolun Qu Yuan wenti* 與日本學者討論屈原問題 (Discussing the Qu Yuan Question with Japanese Scholars). Wuchang: Huazhong ligong daxue chubanshe, 1990.

———. *Zhong-Ri xuezhe Qu Yuan wenti lunzheng ji* 中日學者屈原問題論爭集 (A Collection of Essays on the Debate over the Qu Yuan Question between Chinese and Japanese Scholars). Jinan: Shandong jiaoyu chubanshe, 1990.

Hutton, Patrick H. *History as an Art of Memory*. Hanover, NH: University Press of New England, 1993.

Inahata Kōichirō 稻畑耕一郎. "Kutsu Gen hiteiron no keifu" 屈原否定論の系譜 (The Genealogy of the Negation of Qu Yuan). *Chūgoku bungaku kenkyū* 中國文學研究 (Research on Chinese Literature), edited by *Waseda daigaku Chūgoku bungakukai* 稻田大學中國文學會 (Waseda University Society for the Study of Chinese Literature) 3 (1977): 18–35.

Jin Kaicheng 金開誠. *Chuci jianghua* 《楚辭》講話 (A Guide to the *Chuci*). Beijing: Beijing daxue chubanshe, 2010.

Jin Kaicheng 金開誠, Dong Hongli 董洪利, and Gao Luming 高路明. *Qu Yuan ji jiaozhu* 屈原集校注 (*The Anthology of Qu Yuan* with Collations and Commentary). Beijing: Zhonghua shuju, 1996.

Kern, Martin. "Bronze Inscriptions, the *Shangshu*, and the *Shijing*: The Evolution of the Ancestral Sacrifice during the Western Zhou." In *Early Chinese Religion, Part One: Shang through Han (1250 BC to 220 AD)*, edited by John Lagerwey and Marc Kalinowski, 143–200. Leiden: Brill, 2008.

——. *Die Hymnen der chinesischen Staatsopfer: Literatur und Ritual in der politischen Repräsentation von der Han-Zeit bis zu den Sechs Dynastien* (The Hymns of the Chinese State Sacrifices: Literature and Ritual in Political Representation from Han Times to the Six Dynasties). Stuttgart: Steiner, 1997.

——. "Du Fu's Long Gaze Back: Fate, History, Heroism, Authorship." In *Reading the Signs: Philology, History, Prognostication: Festschrift for Michael Lackner*, edited by Iwo Amelung and Joachim Kurtz, 153–73. Munich: Iudicium Verlag, 2018.

——. "The Formation of the *Classic of Poetry*." In *The Homeric Epics and the Chinese Book of Songs: Foundational Texts Compared*, edited by Fritz-Heiner Mutschler, 39–71. Newcastle upon Tyne: Cambridge Scholars, 2018.

——. "The 'Harangues' (Shi 誓) in the Shangshu." In *Origins of Chinese Political Philosophy: Studies in the Composition and Thought of the Shangshu (Classic of Documents)*, edited by Martin Kern and Dirk Meyer, 281–319. Leiden: Brill, 2017.

——. "*Shiji* li de 'zuozhe' gainian" 《史記》裡的 "作者" 概念 (The Notion of Authorship in the *Shiji*). In *Shiji xue yu shijie hanxue lunji xubian* 史記學與世界漢學論集續編 (Essays in *Shiji* Studies and World Sinology, Second Series), edited by Martin Kern and Lee Chihsiang 李紀祥, 23–61. Taipei: Tangshan chubanshe, 2016.

——. "*Shi jing* Songs as Performance Texts: A Case Study of 'Chu ci' ('Thorny Caltrop')." *Early China* 25 (2000): 49–111.

——. "The Performance of Writing in Western Zhou China." In *The Poetics of Grammar and the Metaphysics of Sound and Sign*, edited by Sergio La Porta and David Shulman, 109–76. Leiden: Brill, 2007.

——. *The Stele Inscriptions of Ch'in Shih-huang: Text and Ritual in Early Chinese Imperial Representation*. New Haven: American Oriental Society, 2000.

——. "'Xi shuai' and Its Consequences: Issues in Early Chinese Poetry and Manuscript Studies." *Early China* 42 (2019): 39–74.

Khayutina, Maria. "The Beginning of Cultural Memory Production in China and the Memory Policy of the Zhou Royal House During the Western Zhou Period." *Early China* 44 (2021): 19–108.

Knechtges, David R. "Ruin and Remembrance in Classical Chinese Literature: The 'Fu on the Ruined City' by Bao Zhao." In *Reading Medieval Chinese Poetry: Text, Context, and Culture*, edited by Paul W. Kroll, 55–89. Leiden: Brill, 2015.

Krijgsman, Rens. "Traveling Sayings as Carriers of Philosophical Debate: From the Intertextuality of the **Yucong* 語叢 to the Dynamics of Cultural Memory and Authorship in Early China." *Asiatische Studien/Études Asiatiques* 68, no. 1 (2014): 83–115.

Kristeva, Julia. "Word, Dialogue, and Novel." In *Desire in Language: A Semiotic Approach to Literature and Art*, translated by Thomas Gora et al., 64–91. New York: Columbia University Press, 1980.

Lachmann, Renate. *Gedächtnis und Literatur: Intertextualität in der russischen Moderne* (Memory and Literature: Intertextuality in Russian Modernism). Frankfurt am Main: Suhrkamp, 1990.

Le Goff, Jacques. *Storia e memoria* (History and Memory). Turin: Giulio Einaudi, 1977.

Ledderose, Lothar. *Ten Thousand Things: Module and Mass Production in Chinese Art.* Princeton, NJ: Princeton University Press, 2000.

Lewis, Mark Edward. *Writing and Authority in Early China.* Albany: State University of New York Press, 1999.

Li, Wai-yee. "Concepts of Authorship." In *The Oxford Handbook of Classical Chinese Literature (1000 BCE–900 CE)*, edited by Wiebke Denecke, Wai-yee Li, and Xiaofei Tian, 360–76. New York: Oxford University Press, 2017.

———. "The Idea of Authority in the *Shih chi* (*Records of the Historian*)." *Harvard Journal of Asiatic Studies* 54, no. 2 (1994): 345–405.

Liji zhengyi 禮記正義 (Corrected Meaning of the *Records of Ritual*), edited by *Shisan jing zhushu zhengli weiyuanhui* 十三經注疏整理委員會. Beijing: Beijing daxue chubanshe, 2000.

Li Zehou 李澤厚. *Mei de licheng* 美的歷程 (The Path of Beauty). Guilin: Guanxi shifan daxue chubanshe, 2000.

Luo Changpei 羅常培, and Zhou Zumo 周祖謨. *Han Wei Jin Nanbeichao yunbu yanbian yanjiu* 漢魏晉南北朝韻部演變研究 (A Study of the Evolution of Rhyme Categories during the Han, Wei, Jin, and Northern and Southern Dynasties). Beijing: Kexue chubanshe, 1958.

Moretti, Franco. *Distant Reading.* New York: Verso, 2013.

Nora, Pierre. *Les lieux de mémoire* (The Places of Memory). 3 vols. Paris: Gallimard, 1984–1992.

Nugent, Christopher M. "Structured Gaps: The *Qianzi wen* and Its Paratexts as Mnemotechnics." In *Memory in Medieval China: Text, Ritual, and Community*, edited by Wendy Swartz and Robert Ford Campany, 158–92. Leiden: Brill, 2018.

Nylan, Michael. "Manuscript Culture in Late Western Han, and the Implications for Authors and Authority." *Journal of Chinese Literature and Culture* 1, no. 1–2 (2014): 155–85.

Okamura Shigeru 岡村繁. "Soji to Kutsu Gen: Hīrō to sakka tono bunri ni suite" 楚辭と屈原——ヒーローと作家との分離について (*Chuci* and Qu Yuan: Separation of Hero and Author). *Nihon Chūgoku gakkai hō* 日本中國學會報 (Bulletin of the Sinological Society of Japan) 18 (1966): 86–101.

Owen, Stephen. *The Making of Early Chinese Classical Poetry.* Cambridge, MA: Harvard University Asia Center, 2006.

———. *Remembrances: The Experience of the Past in Classical Chinese Literature.* Cambridge, MA: Harvard University Press, 1986.

Schimmelpfennig, Michael. "The Quest for a Classic: Wang Yi and the Exegetical Prehistory of His Commentary to the *Songs of Chu*." *Early China* 29 (2004): 111–62.

———. "Qu Yuan's Transformation from Realized Man to True Poet: The Han-Dynasty Commentary of Wang Yi to the 'Lisao' and the Songs of Chu." PhD diss., University of Heidelberg, 1999.

Schneider, Laurence. *A Madman of Ch'u: The Myth of Loyalty and Dissent.* Berkeley: University of California Press, 1980.

Shaughnessy, Edward L. "A Possible Lost Classic: The *She ming*, or *Command to She*." *T'oung Pao* 106, no. 3–4 (2020): 290–307.

Shiji 史記 (Records of the Historian). Beijing: Zhonghua shuju, 1959.

Shi Zhongzhen 施仲貞, and Zhou Jianzhong 周建忠. "*Lisao* de fenduan yanjiu zongshu" 《離騷》的分段研究綜述 (Literature Review on Paragraphing the *Lisao*). *Nanjing shifan daxue wenxueyuan xuebao* 南京師範大學文學院學報 (Journal of the School of Chinese Literature, Nanjing Normal University) 4 (2010): 44–50.

Stallybrass, Peter. "Against Thinking." *PMLA* 122, no. 5 (2007): 1580–87.

Struve, Lynn. "Introduction to the Symposium: Memory and Chinese Texts." *Chinese Literature: Essays, Articles, Reviews* 27 (2005): 1–4.

Swartz, Wendy. "Intertextuality and Cultural Memory in Early Medieval China: Jiang Yan's Imitations of Nearly Lost and Lost Writers." In *Memory in Medieval China: Text, Ritual, and Community*, edited by Wendy Swartz and Robert Ford Campany, 36–62. Leiden: Brill, 2018.

Walker, Galal LeRoy. "Toward a Formal History of the *Chuci*." PhD diss., Cornell University, 1982.

Wang, C. H. *From Ritual to Allegory: Seven Essays in Early Chinese Poetry*. Hong Kong: Chinese University Press, 1987.

Waters, Geoffrey R. *Three Elegies of Ch'u: An Introduction to the Traditional Interpretation of the Ch'u Tz'u*. Madison: University of Wisconsin Press, 1985.

Wheelock, Wade T. "The Problem of Ritual Language: From Information to Situation." *Journal of the American Academy of Religion* 50, no. 1 (1982): 49–71.

Wu Enpei 吳恩培. *Wu Zixu shiliao xinbian* 伍子胥史料新編 (A New Compilation of Historical Materials about Wu Zixu). Yangzhou: Guangling shushe, 2007.

Wu, Hung. *Monumentality in Early Chinese Art and Architecture*. Stanford: Stanford University Press, 1995.

Xu Jianwei 徐建委. *Wenben geming: Liu Xiang, "Hanshu yiwenzhi" yu zaoqi wenben yanjiu* 文本革命：劉向、《漢書·藝文志》與早期文本研究 (A Textual Revolution: Liu Xiang, "Hanshu yiwenzhi," and the Study of Early Texts). Beijing: Shehui kexue chubanshe, 2017.

Xu Zhixiao 徐志嘯. *Riben Chuci yanjiu lungang* 日本楚辭研究論綱 (Outline of Japanese Research on the *Chuci*). Beijing: Xueyuan chubanshe, 2004.

Yates, Frances. *The Art of Memory*. London: Routledge and Kegan Paul, 1966.

You Guo'en 游國恩. *Lisao zuanyi* 離騷纂義 (Collected Annotations on the *Lisao*). Beijing: Zhonghua shuju, 1982.

Yu, Pauline. *The Reading of Imagery in the Chinese Poetic Tradition*. Princeton, NJ: Princeton University Press, 1987.

Zerubavel, Eviatar. *Time Maps: Collective Memory and the Social Shape of the Past*. Chicago: University of Chicago Press, 2003.

Zhang Hanmo. *Authorship and Text-making in Early China*. Boston: De Gruyter Mouton, 2018.

Zhou Jianzhong 周建忠. "*Chuci* cengci jiegou yanjiu—yi *Lisao* wei li" 《楚辭》層次結構研究——以《離騷》為例 (A Study of the Arrangement and Structure of the *Chuci*: Taking the *Lisao* as an Example). *Yunmeng xuekan* 雲夢學刊 (Journal of Yunmeng) 26, no. 2 (2005): 28–37.

Zumthor, Paul. *Toward a Medieval Poetics*. Translated by Philip Bennett. Minneapolis: University of Minnesota Press, 1992.

Mouvance in Medieval Chinese Textual Culture: *Lunyu* 論語 in a Dunhuang Florilegium

CHRISTOPHER M. B. NUGENT

Abstract This essay applies the approaches of the "new medievalism," *mouvance* or "mutability" in particular, to medieval textual materials purporting to contain parts of the classics, focusing on *Lunyu* 論語 (Analects), *Shangshu* 尚書 (Documents), and *Xiaojing* 孝經 (Classic of Filial Piety). Using Dunhuang manuscripts of the florilegium titled *Xinji wenci jiujing chao* 新集文詞九經抄 (New Compilation of Phrases Excerpted from the Nine Classics), the essay shows that the texts of these classics presented by such compilations differed substantially from the "official" texts of the time as represented by the versions carved in stone during the Kaicheng reign period (836–841). The essay further argues that such florilegia as *Xinji wenci jiujing chao* were likely widely used, implying that many readers in the period may have had a different conception of the contents of the classics from what we might assume they had. This has implications for our understanding of intertextuality in literary works from the period.

Keywords *Xinji wenci jiujing chao*, *Lunyu*, Dunhuang manuscripts, *mouvance*, intertextuality

Introduction

The curriculum for my daughter's seventh grade social studies class concentrated primarily on the ancient world. The quality of the materials was impressively high, and most of the year was focused on regions other than Europe (in distinct contrast to my own educational experiences at that age). Unsurprisingly, I paid particularly close attention when the class turned to China, and alas, one day my daughter brought home a set of quotations from Confucius that included a number of sayings unlikely to have any connection with the Master

The Journal of Chinese Literature and Culture • 9:1 • April 2022
DOI 10.1215/23290048-9681202 • © 2022 by Duke University Press

and his *Analects* (e.g., "Give a bowl of rice to a man and you will feed him for a day. Teach him how to grow his own rice and you will save his life"). I guessed that these came not from a published translation of *Lunyu* 論語 but rather from a Google search for "quotes from Confucius" or something of the sort.[1]

This is not, however, a simple case of "don't believe what you read online"; the situation is far more complex. The corpus of texts on the internet attributed to Confucius is diverse. On one end of the spectrum are the carefully produced, searchable texts of *Lunyu* found on sites like the Chinese Text Project or Scripta Sinica 漢籍全文資料庫.[2] One can also access a range of excellent translations into multiple languages, some accompanied by the Chinese original. Indeed, never in the history of humanity has the standard text of *Lunyu* been so widely accessible to such a broad range of readers. At the other end of the spectrum, there are innumerable sites, like those accessed by my daughter's teacher, that attach the name Confucius to a range of pithy sayings. The site that was one of the top hits when I searched for "quotes from Confucius" included some of the following:[3]

> "Choose a job you love, and you will never have to work a day in your life."
> "If you are the smartest person in the room, then you are in the wrong room."
> "When it is obvious that the goals cannot be reached, don't adjust the goals, adjust the action steps."
> "Anyone can find the switch after the lights are on."

These are mixed with quotes actually from *Laozi* 老子 ("The journey with 1000 miles begins with one step" 千里之行，始於足下)[4] and many quotes that are indeed from *Lunyu*, or at least very close:

> "Worry not that no one knows you; seek to be worth knowing."
> "When you see a good person, think of becoming like her/him. When you see someone not so good, reflect on your own weak points."
> "Never contract friendship with a man that is not better than thyself."
> "Only the wisest and stupidest of men never change."

Many of the inaccurate quotations are found on multiple sites; they most likely build off of each other. The result is a new Confucius who bears some resemblance to the one known by, for example, literate people in the Tang 唐 (618–907) period but who differs in multiple ways.

It is no revelation that the internet is not the most reliable source for information about early Chinese texts. What I would like to suggest in this essay, however, is that the textual environment of the late medieval period in China was not as different as we might expect from the situation I describe above. In the Tang period there was also a standardized, "official" *Lunyu* text, as exemplified by the *Kaicheng shijing* 開成石經 (Kaicheng Era Stone Classics) version carved on stone during the Kaicheng 開成 reign period (836–841) and still largely extant today at the Beilin 碑林 (Forest of Steles) in modern Xi'an. *Lunyu* circulated in other forms during the medieval period as well, including hand-copied manuscripts produced with vastly differing degrees of care, and even the memorized texts in the minds of the many (most often) men who set all or part of it to memory as part of their early education and, in some cases, as part of preparation for the *jinshi* 進士 (presented scholar) and *mingjing* 明經 (illuminate the classics) civil service examinations. Those "texts" of *Lunyu* were no doubt quite fluid, as memories fade and change much faster than does stone. Finally, *Lunyu* circulated not only as a full work but as parts excerpted by other works, including such imperially sponsored compilations as *Yiwen leiju* 藝文類聚 (Classified Extracts from Literature) and *Chuxue ji* 初學記 (Record of Early Learning) and many smaller-scale florilegia such as my focus here, *Xinji wenci jiujing chao* 新集文詞九經抄 (New Compilation of Phrases Excerpted from the Nine Classics), a work that has survived to the present only among the documents discovered at Dunhuang (but in multiple copies there). I argue that by shifting our gaze away from the classics as they functioned in the context of official educational culture and the exam system in the Tang, we not only get a different perspective on the classics; we may, to a meaningful extent, get different classics.

My approach in this essay is inspired by the recent scholarship on medieval European literature that has come to be called the "new medievalism." As Stephen G. Nichols explains, rather than designating a specific methodological approach in the manner of the New Historicism, the new medievalism points instead to "a predisposition to interrogate and reformulate assumptions about the discipline of medieval studies broadly conceived."[5] Much of the work done by scholars under this broad rubric is indebted, directly or indirectly, to critical theoretical approaches developed by such scholars as Michel Foucault, Jacques Derrida, and Julia Kristeva.[6] In particular, the insights of these writers on systems of authority have proven generative of new approaches towards medieval textual authority specifically. Elizabeth Bryan, who finds Derridean approaches transfer fruitfully to her study of medieval literature, writes as follows: "If we wish to understand attitudes about textual authority in a different system—like medieval scribal culture—we must acknowledge that a different system may lack the assumptions that textual authority resides in a single author and that only one version, the first or the last one, could be authoritative."[7] I take a similar approach in this essay. Note, however, that I am not arguing that medieval

Chinese literary culture lacked the notion that authority resided in one version of a work. Indeed, in the case of the classics, that notion was clearly present and indeed dominant—but only in certain contexts. In other contexts, it is not so much that *Lunyu*, for example, lacked authority, but rather that there were different *Lunyu* in different contexts.

At the heart of this approach is the idea of textual *mouvance* or "mutability," as articulated by the medievalist Paul Zumthor in his work on medieval poetic cultures. Scholars of classical and medieval European literature (like scholars of classical and medieval Chinese literature) had long recognized that texts change through the course of transmission in any textual culture based on orality and hand-copied manuscripts.[8] For much of the history of European textual scholarship, these alterations had typically been viewed as adulterations of the originally pristine, author-ized text; they were defects that had to be identified and cured, with doing so being the primary aim of the textual scholar. For Zumthor and the new medievalism, however, this fluidity is the very essence of medieval textual culture, something to be embraced rather than fixed. It is evidence that the concept of a "text" and a literary "work" was different in the medieval period. As Zumthor writes, "These very conditions of transmission, producing minor variants in words and odd phrases of the written text; more important variants, by which considerable stretches of text may be added, suppressed, modified, or transposed; and major variants in the number and order of structural elements of the text, could not but conspire to prevent the early formation of the idea of the work as something complete in itself."[9] Variance, on scales large and small, defines the world of medieval textuality, and scholars of medieval literature must understand how it functions. Bernard Cerquiglini argues that within the medieval manuscript context, "the work copied by hand, manipulated, always open and as good as unfinished, invited intervention, annotation, and commentary."[10] Because of this, the new medievalism regards with suspicion the critical text that claims to represent some ideal original version of a work. Rather than bringing us closer to medieval literature, such artificial constructs increase our distance from it.

The orientations and arguments of the new medievalism are applicable to any manuscript culture, and those of different periods in China are no exception. Scholars of early China have been at the forefront of confronting the reality of textual variation in the materials they study. Works by Martin Kern, Matthias L. Richter, and Dirk Meyer in particular have led the way here.[11] The motivating force for this work on early China is the increasing number of archaeological discoveries that include written materials. Texts that were thought to be stable have proven to have been fundamentally fluid, with copious variation opening up new vistas for understanding how they functioned in their original contexts.

Scholars of medieval Chinese literature face a different set of material challenges. The received tradition is massive, but the volume of manuscripts that have survived from the period, especially for works of "secular" literature is small in comparison, being mostly limited to the finds at Dunhuang. These limitations notwithstanding, scholars have begun to grapple with the issues brought forth by a recognition of *mouvance* as a fundamental characteristic of medieval Chinese literary culture. Stephen Owen and Xiaofei Tian have used evidence from the surviving print materials to investigate the formation of early classical poetry and the oeuvre of Tao Yuanming 陶淵明 (365–427) respectively.[12] Sarah M. Allen has addressed *mouvance* in Tang period narratives, and I have written on variation in poetic manuscripts found at Dunhuang (including manuscript copies of one of Li Bai's 李白 [701–762] best known poems).[13] Scholars in China and Japan have done foundational work identifying and cataloging variation in texts found in Dunhuang, though overall they have not tended to focus on the implications of variance for criticism in the way the new medievalists have.

The present essay takes Zumthor's idea of *mouvance* and looks at how "stretches of text may be added, suppressed, modified, or transposed" in the specific case of a small number of classical texts, focusing on *Lunyu* in particular, as they existed in a particular context: medieval florilegia discovered at Dunhuang. Florilegia, compilations of textual excerpts from a wide array of longer sources, were one way that readers in both medieval Europe and China dealt with the limited availability of written materials in a period in which every copy of every written work was created by hand. Writing of medieval Europe, Ann Blair notes that they "likely first originated as personal notes of items worthy of memory taken on the occasion of access to a text and then shared with others who would not otherwise have access to it."[14] Writing of the Liang period, Xiaofei Tian describes the similar practice of "producing an epitome" (*chaoshu* 抄書) as "not to copy out the entire book but parts of it—parts, no doubt, deemed important."[15] Such works would later be classified by bibliographers in the Song 宋 (960–1279) period as *leishu* 類書 (writings arranged by category). Full copies of most classical works, to say nothing of the longer histories of the Han 漢 (206 BCE–220 CE) and later periods, were hard to come by for anyone in the Tang who did not have access to the imperial library. Florilegia were thus an important source for many readers. Such compilations are numerous among the finds from Dunhuang. A limited list includes such works as *Zachao* 雜抄 (Miscellaneous Excerpts [also known by other titles]), *Tuyuan cefu* 兔園冊府 (Repository of Rabbit Garden Questions), *Wenci jiaolin* 文詞教林 (Forest of Phrases for Instruction), and the focus of the current essay, *Xinji wenci jiujing chao.*

Xinji wenci jiujing chao (hereafter *Jiujing chao*) itself consists of short excerpts from almost ninety earlier works and promises to provide its readers with the essentials of the written tradition. Though entirely unknown in the later bibliographic tradition, it appears to have enjoyed some popularity in its day, surviving in at least sixteen partial copies from Dunhuang, three of which can be combined to constitute what is likely a full text of the work.[16] Its author is unknown, as is the original date of composition. The scholar Zheng Acai 鄭阿財 gives a likely range of 755 to 883, with the latter being the year given for copying in the colophon of one of the manuscripts.[17]

While the title speaks of the "nine classics"—presumably indicating such works as the *Yi* 易 (Changes), *Shangshu* 尚書 (Documents), *Shi* 詩 (Poems), *San li* 三禮 (Three Ritual Texts), *Chunqiu* 春秋 (Spring and Autumn Annals), *Zuo zhuan* 左傳 (Zuo Tradition), *Gongyang zhuan* 公羊傳 (Gongyang Tradition), *Guliang zhuan* 穀梁傳 (Guliang Tradition), *Lunyu*, and the *Xiaojing* 孝經 (Classic of Filial Piety)[18]—the full set of works from which *Jiujing chao* excerpts is much broader, including histories, early philosophical works, Han apocrypha, and others.[19] Just as one thirteenth-century European florilegium claimed that "here you have at your fingertips briefly and in summary all that you could find in many bookchests full of large volumes,"[20] the preface to *Jiujing chao* boasts:

> It incorporates the nine classics; encompasses the esoteric and exoteric; fully elucidates the three histories: of these essentials nothing is neglected. The contemporary and ancient are carefully examined, ritual and ceremony comprehensively provided. 包括九經。羅含內外。通闡三史。是要無遺。今古參詳。禮儀咸備。[21]

This idea returns near the end of the preface, where it claims that "abridging complicated writings, fully elucidating what is within and without, drawing on the present and citing the past, of these essentials nothing is neglected" 刪節繁文。通闡內外。援今引古。是要無遺. The fact that the title refers to this being a "new" compilation implies that it may be based on earlier similar works. Zheng Acai argues for its indebtedness to *Wenci jiaolin* in particular.[22] This possibility that many of these compilations built on each other, rather than returning to the actual sources they cite (a practice followed by the compilers of *Chuxue ji*, who based their work heavily on *Yiwen leiju* and, of course, by the creators of the internet lists of quotes from Confucius noted above), is an issue to which I will return below.

In what follows I focus primarily on excerpts attributed to *Lunyu*, with some limited discussion of attributions to *Shangshu* and *Xiaojing*. *Lunyu* in particular is an appealing object of study in this context. Along with *Xiaojing*, it is the work most frequently cited as being memorized, often at a young age, by literate men. It formed the core of the "memorization corpus" with which exam candidates were expected to be thoroughly familiar. Moreover, as a source for quotations, Confucius dominates *Jiujing chao* overall. Of the approximately 435 separate entries,[23] 98 are attributed directly to Confucius or *Lunyu* (there are a dozen or so additional entries attributed to his various disciples). With 36 attributions, *Lunyu* itself is the second most cited textual source after *Shangshu* with 42 (*Xiaojing* has 10). Because my interest here is on how classical works circulated as parts of florilegia, I look only at the attributions to *Lunyu* specifically, rather than to Confucius as a general author figure.

The texts of *Lunyu* and other classics found in *Jiujing chao* are meaningfully different from the official text as represented by the *Kaicheng shijing* version. These differences are not found merely on the level of individual words; larger sections of text are rearranged or come from sources other than *Lunyu*. These differences are especially striking given *Lunyu*'s status as a frequently memorized work. What we find in *Jiujing chao* implies that the textual scope of *Lunyu* for Tang readers may have been quite different from what we typically think of it as being. Moreover, because different florilegia and *leishu* built on each other, the spread of this "alternative" *Lunyu* textual material could be broad.[24] Finally, because of the important role of *Lunyu* as a basic work most literate people would be expected to know, this has implications for how we think about intertextuality in medieval literary culture.

Lunyu in *Xinji wenci jiujing chao*

Jiujing chao includes thirty-six entries that it explicitly attributes to *Lunyu*, indicating this by introducing them with either *Lunyu yun* 論語云 or, in a number of examples in P.3621, *Yu yue* 語曰.[25] Of these entries, only eleven (30 percent) are identical or near identical to passages in the official *Lunyu* as represented by the *Kaicheng shijing* text. As noted, even many of these entries exhibit variation on a level that would be meaningful for a full textual critical comparison of the two texts. For example, entry 183 reads:

> The *Analects* says, "That which you do not desire, do not impose it on others. In your family, you will have none. In your state you will have no resentment."
> 語曰。己所不欲。勿施於人。在家無。在邦無怨。[26]

The *Lunyu* text reads:

> That which you do not desire, do not impose it on others. In your state you will have no resentment; in your family, you will have no resentment.
> 己所不欲。勿施於人。在邦無怨。在家無怨。[27]

There are two instances of variation here. The *Jiujing chao* text lacks a word after the first *wu* 無, presumably due to scribal error at some point in the chain of transmission, and *bang* 邦 and *jia* 家 appear in reversed positions. These are meaningful variations, and variations of this sort are ubiquitous in any manuscript culture, but they are of a smaller scale than the sort of *mouvance* that is my focus here, and I thus count passages with such limited variation as accurately replicating text from *Lunyu*.

Shifting to slightly more consequential variation, we find a number of instances in which *Jiujing chao* entries present an accurate quotation from *Lunyu* but add additional text to it at the end. A simple example is found in entry 98:

> The *Analects* says, "Kind but not wasteful, laboring but not resentful, desirous but not covetous, august but not proud, awesome but not ruthless. These are called the five excellences."
> 論語云。惠而不費。勞而不怨。欲而不貪。泰而不驕。威而不猛。謂之五美。

Other than the last phrase, this passage is found in identical form in the official *Lunyu* text, where it is a description of the "gentleman" (*junzi* 君子).[28] The final phrase, though not in *Lunyu*, merely caps the list and attaches a number and label to it. Indeed, *Lunyu* has a similar phrase preceding this passage, where the disciple Zi Zhang 子張 asks: "What are called the 'five excellences'?" 何謂五美. Though I do count this as departing from the *Lunyu* text because it adds a full additional phrase, the meaning of the original is preserved.

Another entry in *Jiujing chao* drawing on this same section of *Lunyu* adds more explanatory text and includes more meaningful variation. Entry 345 and a portion of a passage found in *Lunyu* 20.2, from which it likely derives, read as follows:

> The *Analects* says, "To not, but then to punish is called cruel. To not properly instruct but to execute is called brutal. As for these two misfortunes, those men who are worthy do not cause them."
> 論語云。不而罰謂之虐。不教而煞謂之暴。此二患。人賢不為。

> To not properly instruct but to execute is called cruel; to not admonish but to demand success is called brutal.
> 不教而殺謂之虐。不戒視成謂之暴。[29]

The similarities of both structure and content here are clear, but the degree of variance is substantial. That the *Jiujing chao* text lacks a verb following the first negating particle *bu* 不 may be ascribed to scribal error and would likely be recognized as such even by a reader not familiar with the original passage from *Lunyu*; the remaining variation results instead in language that is comprehensible but different. Where *Lunyu* connects execution (*sha* 殺) with being cruel (*nüe* 虐), *Jiujing chao* describes punishment (*fa* 罰) this way. Likewise, the *Jiujing chao* text declares execution when the victim had not received proper (moral) instruction as brutal (*bao* 暴), while the original *Lunyu* passage says this of demanding success without admonishment. In semantic terms, the adjectives used here vary little, but the situations they describe are not the same. The framing context is different as well. The original *Lunyu* passage gives these two situations as part of a list of the "four detestables" (*si e* 四惡). The version in *Jiujing chao* adds a phrase that changes the number to two and labels the situations as "misfortunes" (*huan* 患), rather than detestables. It further describes them as things that worthy men do not cause. While it is reasonable to see this particular *Lunyu* passage as the ultimate source of the *Jiujing chao* entry, the variation here changes the meaning and context of the original in a way that goes beyond what might be ascribed to simple scribal error.

Additions to the original *Lunyu* text are common in *Jiujing chao* entries. These typically fit well in thematic terms with the excerpt to which they are added. For example, entry 318 reads:

> The *Analects* says: "Even when suffering a year of famine, one's parents should not realize it. When one's parents are alive, do not travel far. When traveling, one must have a set direction."
> 雖遭凶年。父母不知。父母在。不遠遊。遊必有方。

The well-known admonition from *Lunyu* 4.19 against distant travel when one's parents are still alive is accurately excerpted here.[30] The claim that one should shield their parents from even the awareness of facing a famine, presumably by keeping them well-fed by surreptitiously forgoing food oneself, is not found anywhere in the official *Lunyu* text. The match, however, is a seamless one in thematic terms.

While the *Jiujing chao* preface provides no explanation for such changes (indeed, it gives no indication that its entries are anything but accurate quotations from their various sources), many of these additions seem to provide context and flesh out statements that are quite terse in *Lunyu* itself. For example, entry 42 reads:

> The *Analects* says, "The gentleman is composed and magnanimous. The lesser man is always worried. As he is not malevolent towards others, there is nothing that troubles him."
> 論語云。君子坦蕩蕩。小人長戚戚。不惡於人。無所憂懼。

The first two phrases here are an exact match for *Lunyu* 7.37.[31] While the last two phrases do not appear anywhere in the official text, they provide an explanation for what precedes them. The reason the gentleman is composed and magnanimous is that he does no evil towards his fellow man. He thus has no cause for worry. The Zheng Xuan 鄭玄 (127–200) commentary on this passage explains the term *qiqi* 戚戚 as "having many troubles" 多憂懼.[32] Though the additions in this *Jiujing chao* entry do not appear to be taken verbatim from a known commentary, they serve a similar purpose in making the main text more comprehensible to the reader.

In fact, there are a number of instances in which it appears that *Jiujing chao* entries excerpt not from main text of a given classic but from a commentary on it. As I will discuss briefly below, this is especially prominent in *Jiujing chao* entries attributed to the *Shangshu*, in which the "Kong Commentary" 孔傳 (Kong zhuan) ostensibly by Kong Anguo 孔安國 (d. ca. 100 BCE) is integrated into many of the entries. A similar example (entry 90) with an excerpt attributed to *Lunyu* reads as follows:

> The *Analects* says, "Heaven's numen is called the 'earth god'; earth's numen is called 'spirit.' If it is not one's ancestor yet one sacrifices to it, this is called 'obsequious.'"
> 論語云。天神曰祇。地神曰鬼。非其祖考而祭之曰諂。

This passage reads oddly, with its surprising identification of "Heaven's numen" (*tianshen* 天神) with a term typically used for the earth god. The most likely explanation is scribal error at some point for the orthographically similar *si* 祀, meaning "sacrifice." The phrase 天神曰祀 is found in commentaries to *Shangshu* and *Zuozhuan*. None of the text in entry 90 appears to come directly from *Lunyu* itself. The closest parallel is the first half of 2.24, which reads "If it is not one's ancestral spirit yet one sacrifices to it, this is obsequiousness." 非其鬼而祭之。諂也. While this is indeed similar to the last part of the *Jiujing chao* entry, the latter more likely derives from the Zheng Xuan commentary to 2.24: "If it is not one's ancestor yet one sacrifices to it, this is obsequiously seeking good fortune" 非其祖考而祭之者是諂求福.[33] Rather than being a quote from *Lunyu*, the entry is thus instead a mix of different commentarial material attached to *Lunyu* (and likely other classical works).

In many cases a *Jiujing chao* entry accurately conveys the meaning of a passage from *Lunyu* but substantially changes the wording. A particularly striking example of this is found in entry 186. It reads:

> The *Analects* says: "If you want to pursue success for yourself, first help others succeed. If you want to establish yourself, first establish others."
> 語曰。己欲求達。先達人。己欲立。先立人。

This clearly is based on the well-known passage from *Lunyu* 6.30 describing the "method of humaneness" 仁之方:

> Now as for the humane, wanting themselves to be established, they establish others; wanting themselves to succeed, they help others succeed.
> 夫仁者。己欲立而立人。己欲達而達人。[34]

There can be little doubt that the *Jiujing chao* line is connected to these lines from *Lunyu* 6.30; the meaning of each is essentially identical. At the same time, the wording differs substantially. While we have no evidence of the specific sources the compiler of *Jiujing chao* used, examples such as this at least suggest that some of the entries could have written based on his own memory of passages from *Lunyu*. This entry preserves structural features of the *Lunyu* passage as well as captures its basic meaning. It may well have been memorized by the compiler and then recalled inexactly. This is not surprising, as "memorization" in medieval European literary cultures often functioned in a similar way.[35] One might almost consider this a paraphrase; the compiler's memory for the meaning and rhetorical structure of the original *Lunyu* passage is accurate, but he has also put it into "his own words" through rearrangement and the addition of words, such as *xian* 先 ("first, prior, to put first"), that are only implied in the original *Lunyu* text. Of course, it is also possible that the compiler is simply basing his text, whether by memory or by having a written exemplar in front of him, on another source that similarly differs from the "official" *Lunyu* text. It may well be the case that this is a good representation of how much of *Lunyu* and other classical works existed in the minds and on the lips of many members of the literate elite.

In other cases, rearrangements and partial omissions can change the meaning of a passage more substantially, even conveying a meaning that is the opposite of the original. *Lunyu* 8.11 argues that innate abilities should not be the sole basis for judgements of moral worth. It reads:

> Supposing someone had talents as fine as those of Duke of Zhou; if they are arrogant and stingy, their remaining aspects are not worth looking at.
> 如有周公之才之美。使驕且吝。其餘不足觀也已。[36]

Jiujing chao's entry 307 reads:

> The *Analects* says, "Even if someone has the talents of Zhou or Confucius, their remaining aspects are not worth looking at."
> 語曰。雖有周孔之才。其餘不足觀。

The *Jiujing chao* text reads awkwardly, as *sui* 雖 typically precedes a concessive clause to contrast with the main point. This term can, in some contexts, function similarly to *wei* 唯 with the restrictive meaning of "only," resulting in something like "If only someone has the talents of Zhou or Confucius, their remaining aspects are not worth looking at." In any case, the omission of the middle phrase from the original *Lunyu* passage results in the impression that having the innate abilities of Zhou or Confucius is sufficiently impressive in and of itself that one need not consider the person's other qualities. This is the opposite of the meaning of the *Lunyu* passage, which sees such innate talents as meaningless if the person in question has other personality deficiencies.

Given the similarities in wording, it seems likely that the *Jiujing chao* entry here is based on the *Lunyu* passage. There are, however, indications that this particular passage had become even more unmoored from its original source. *Jiujing chao* entry 63 is identical to entry 307 in its wording, but it is there attributed not to *Lunyu* but instead to Taigong 太公. A similar entry in the *Wenci jiaolin* florilegium reads:

> Yan Shu says, "Even if someone has the talents of Zhou or Confucius and the cleverness of Yan Ying [ ] are not worth looking at."
> 顏舒曰。雖有周孔之才。晏嬰之機。□□不足觀也。[37]

Damage to the text notwithstanding, the similarities to the *Lunyu* passage and the *Jiujing chao* entry are clear. We also see substantial fluidity in terms of both attribution and content. The attribution to Yan Shu in *Wenci jiaolin* is particularly odd. If this is meant to be the Tang figure with that name, it would be the only attribution to a Tang figure in all of *Wenci jiaolin*. If it is another figure, their identity is unclear. The addition of the phrase about the cleverness of Yan Ying, the famous sixth-century BCE rhetorician from the state of Qi 齊, is a clear departure from both *Lunyu* and *Jiujing chao*, suggesting the possibility that this passage was subject to alteration on multiple levels. While the basic structure owes a clear debt to the *Lunyu* passage, it appears to have taken on a life of its own in later contexts.

Some entries in *Jiujing chao* combine near-direct quotations from *Lunyu* with vaguer paraphrases of themes from that work, with wording that may have come from later texts. Entry 310 reads:

> The *Analects* says, "If he himself is proper, his will will be carried out without issuing commands. If he himself is not proper, even if he commands it, people will not obey. Those above transform those below like the wind blowing down grass."
> 論語云。其身政。不令而行。其身不政。雖令不從。上之化下。猶風之靡草。

The first four phrases here are a near exact match with *Lunyu* 13.6.[38] The last two phrases do not appear anywhere in the official *Lunyu* text. They do, however, capture the meaning of a well-known passage from 12.19: "The moral power of the gentleman is the wind; the moral power of the lesser man is the grass. When the wind is on the grass it will surely bend" 君子之德風。小人之德草。草上之風。必偃.[39] The previous part of 12.19, like 13.6, focuses on how the proper behavior and moral attitude of those in power can guide those below without the need for punitive regulations. The *Jiujing chao* entry thus gives the impression of coherence and thematic fit with *Lunyu*, though it adds additional text not found in that work.

Though the final two phrases do indeed fit with *Lunyu* and match the basic sentiment of one of its best-known passages, their textual source is likely found elsewhere. In a discussion of the dangers of rulers emphasizing gain (*li* 利) over moral power (that is clearly indebted to *Mengzi* 孟子), a passage in *Shuoyuan* 說苑 (Garden of Persuasions) sets up a chain of moral influence in which gain-seeking rulers lead to covetous (*tan* 貪) feudal lords, who in turn create vulgar (*bi* 鄙) grand ministers, resulting in thieving commoners. The passage concludes: "Those above transform those below like the wind blowing down grass" 上之變下。猶風之靡草也.[40] Other than the synonymous *bian* 變 for *Jiujing chao*'s *hua* 化, the phrases are identical. A perfect match for the *Jiujing chao* phrase also appears in a thematically similar context in *Xinyu* 新語 (New Discourses).[41] While we cannot know the actual sources the *Jiujing chao* compiler used, the thematic coherence he achieves again gives the reader the sense that the full passage *could* indeed be from *Lunyu*, even if it is not.

Though *Jiujing chao* often mixes together text from *Lunyu* with thematically similar material drawn from elsewhere, in many entries with excerpts attributed to *Lunyu* it instead takes passages from multiple different sections of *Lunyu* and combines them into what it presents as a single passage. Entry 425 reads:

> The *Analects* says, "Zi You was serving as steward of a city. He asked about the sounds of strings and singing. The Master smiled faintly and laughed, saying, 'When killing a chicken, why use a blade for an ox?'"
>
> 論語云。子游為城宰。問弦歌之聲。夫子莞爾笑曰。割雞焉用牛刀。

Rather than coming from a single passage in *Lunyu*, this appears to be a combination of two. *Lunyu* 6.14 begins "Zi You was serving as steward of Wucheng" 子游為武城宰.[42] The rest of the passage has no connection with the *Jiujing chao* entry. However, *Lunyu* 17.4 is clearly the source of the rest of the entry. The first part reads "When the Master went to Wucheng, he heard the sounds of strings and singing. He smiled faintly and laughed, saying, 'When killing a chicken, why use an ox blade?'" 子之武城。聞弦歌之聲。夫子莞爾而笑曰。割雞焉用牛刀。[43] If this conjoining of two separate passages was done by accident, the cause for confusion on the part of the compiler (or the creator of an earlier source) is clear. The openings of these two *Lunyu* passages are indeed quite similar. At the same time, the way they are conjoined here results in an entry that reads differently from either of the original passages. In *Lunyu* it is Confucius who comes to Wucheng and hears elegant music. In *Jiujing chao*, Confucius's disciple Zi You asks about the music when serving as steward of the city. In *Lunyu* Confucius amusingly comments on Zi You's governance.[44] The *Jiujing chao* passage cannot be read this way. The textual differences are slight, but the result is a meaningfully different passage.

In other *Jiujing chao* entries that combine different *Lunyu* passages, the stitching together is less fluid. Entry 340 reads:

> The *Analects* says, "Not dutiful but rich, to me this is like floating clouds. It is not that I do not have them, but if they are not obtained with the proper Way, I do not esteem them."
> 論語云。不義而富。於我如浮雲。非己之不有。不以其道得之。不貴。

The first two phrases are derived from *Lunyu* 7.16, which reads in part, "Not dutiful but rich and esteemed, to me this is like floating clouds" 不義而富且貴。於我如浮雲.[45] The penultimate phrase appears in a similar passage found in *Lunyu* 4.5: "Wealth and esteem are what people desire. But if they are not obtained with the proper Way, do not hold onto them" 富與貴是人之所欲也。不以其道得之。不處也.[46] While both these sections can clearly be traced to *Lunyu*, the middle phrase does not appear anywhere in that work and seems particularly out of place. The general meaning of the entry is clear: one should only seek wealth and status through proper moral means. The different phrases, however, fit awkwardly in the entry and lack the fluidity of their source material.

Entry 204, one of the longest in all of *Jiujing chao*, is also the fullest example of this practice of conjoining disparate passages from *Lunyu* into a single entry. The full entry reads:

> The *Analects* says, "If you are magnanimous, then you will treat the masses with moral power. If you are diligent, then you will have accomplishments. If one in a high position is not magnanimous, is not respectful towards those below, and is not sorrowful when overseeing mourning rituals, how could I look upon them? If one is respectful but lacks ritual, then one will be troublesome. If one is compliant but lacks ritual, one will be timid. If one is brave but lacks ritual, one will be chaotic. If one is

upright but lacks ritual, then one will be constricting. Do not worry that others do not know of you, worry that that you do not go to others. Do not worry that you lack a position, worry about yourself not being established."

語曰。寬則德眾。敏則有功。居上不寬。為下不敬。臨喪不哀。吾何以觀之哉。恭而無礼則勞。順而無礼則葸。勇而無礼則乱。直而無礼則絞。不患人之不己知。患己不之人。不患無位。患己不立。

I have translated the text here as written, rather than correct what might seem like obvious errors. Some small variations notwithstanding, all of the text in this entry is indeed from *Lunyu*. Careful examination, however, shows the entry to be made up of small parts from five completely separate passages in that work. The entry is worth examining in detail because it shows how the compiler excerpts and stitches together parts of *Lunyu* to create an entry that, while entirely new as a single passage, reads smoothly and coherently (or at least as smoothly and coherently as its source). In what follows I discuss each passage and how it appears in *Lunyu*.

> 寬則德眾。敏則有功。
>
> ("If you are magnanimous, then you will treat the masses with moral power. If you are diligent, then you will have accomplishments.")

These phrases are taken from *Lunyu* 17.6, though they are not contiguous in that passage itself. The full quotation in which they appear reads as follows:

> Reverence, magnanimity, trustworthiness, diligence, and kindness. If you are reverent, then you will have no regrets. If you are magnanimous, then you will gain the masses. If you are trustworthy, then your people will put their trust in you. If you are diligent, then you will have accomplishments. If you are kind, then this will be enough to employ the people.
>
> 恭。寬。信。敏。惠。恭則不侮。寬則得眾。信則人任焉。敏則有功。惠則足以使人。[47]

The only difference between the *Jiujing chao* text and the excerpted phrases is the use of *de* 德 rather than *de* 得 in *Jiujing chao*. It is not clear why the compiler picked out only these two phrases from the rest. However, the following excerpt continues the theme of magnanimity.

> 居上不寬。為下不敬。臨喪不哀。吾何以觀之哉。
>
> ("If one in a high position is not magnanimous, is not respectful towards those below, and is not sorrowful when overseeing mourning rituals, how could I look upon them?")

This passage is nearly the same as the whole of *Lunyu* 3.26, with the only variation appearing in the second character of the second phrase where *Lunyu* has *li* 禮 (ritual) rather than *xia* 下 (below).[48] That phrase would thus be read as "is not respectful when conducting rituals" rather than "is not respectful towards those below." This passage is nowhere near the previous one in *Lunyu* itself but as noted, also addresses the importance of the ruler being magnanimous.

> 恭而無礼則勞。順而無礼則葸。勇而無礼則乱。直而無礼則絞。
>
> ("If one is respectful but lacks ritual, then one will be troublesome. If one is compliant but lacks ritual, one will be timid. If one is brave but lacks ritual, one will be chaotic. If one is upright but lacks ritual, then one will be constricting.")

This excerpt almost perfectly matches the first four phrases in *Lunyu* 8.2, with the only difference being where it has *shun* (Middle Chinese *zywinH*) 順 (compliant), *Lunyu* instead has the orthographically and phonologically similar *shen* (Middle Chinese *dzyinH*) 慎 (cautious).[49]

> 不患人之不己知。患己不之人。
>
> ("Do not worry that others do not know of you, worry that that you do not go to others.")

This passage is a near match for *Lunyu* 1.16. Where *Jiujing chao* has *zhi* 之 (go to) in the penultimate character position, this is surely an error for the homophonous *zhi* 知 (to know) that appears in the *Lunyu* passage in that position (both Middle Chinese *tsyi*).[50]

> 不患無位。患己不立。
>
> ("Do not worry that you lack a position, worry about yourself not being established.")

While structurally similar to the previous passage, this excerpt is instead from *Lunyu* 4.14. The second phrase in *Lunyu* has a slightly different wording and meaning, reading "worry about the means by which you establish yourself" 患所以立, rather than "worry about yourself not being established."[51]

Entry 204 may be an extreme example, but it is also an impressive one. The passage flows smoothly from one topic to another, making use of similar structures and thematic commonalities to join the different excerpts. The connection created by joining two passages that deal with magnanimity, noted above, is one example. There are also interesting connections here for readers who do know the original contexts of the excerpts. The third excerpt begins with the word *gong* 恭 (reverence). Though this word does not appear in the first excerpt, it is a key part of the original *Lunyu* passage from which it came. Rhetorical structures such as "if X (or not X), then Y," or "do not X, instead do Y" run throughout the entry. Though the final two excerpts do not come from the same passage in *Lunyu*, they do have a connection: the final excerpt is followed in *Lunyu* by phrases that are very similar to the excerpt just before it: "Do not worry that no one knows you; seek to do something worth knowing about" 不患莫己知。求為可知也. In short, though the parts of this entry were not together in *Lunyu*, they give the reader the impression they surely could have been.

To close this discussion of *Lunyu* in *Jiujing chao* it is important to note that of thirty-six entries attributed to *Lunyu*, there are five that do not appear in any form in the official version of that work. These are not paraphrases or rearrangements; they are closer to the spurious quotes from Confucius on the internet. Some of these have an aphoristic quality, such as entry 288:

> The *Analects* says, "If your speech does not accord with principle, it would be better not to speak. When medicine does not ward off illness, it can instead do harm to one's life. When speech does not accord with principle, it can instead do harm to one's person."
> 語曰。言不中理。不如不言。藥不當病。反傷其命。言不中理。反害其身。

No part of this entry appears in *Lunyu*, though it would not be out of place in that work.

Other examples are not from *Lunyu* itself but can be found in other works. Entry 159 reads "In cultivating oneself nothing is better than respectfulness; to avoid the powerful, nothing is better than compliance" 修身莫若敬。避強莫如順. This same passage appears in the *Hou Han shu*'s 後漢書 (History of the Former Han) "lie nü zhuan" 列女傳 (Biographies of Women);[52] it also forms part of a longer entry in *Wenci jiaolin*, where it is attributed to Taigong.[53] Similarly, *Jiujing chao* entry 158 reads:

> The *Analects* says, "It you wish that people don't know about something, it is best not to do it. If you wish that people don't hear something, it's best not to say it."
> 語曰。欲人勿知。不如勿為。欲人勿聞。不如勿言。

As with 288, this is an aphoristic saying that would not be out of place in *Lunyu*. It appears with slightly different wording (*mo* 莫 instead of *ru* 如) in both *Shuoyuan* and *Han shu* 漢書 (History of the Han). It is also included in *Wenci jiaolin* (with some slight variation) where it is also attributed incorrectly to *Lunyu*.

Shangshu **and** Xiaojing

While my focus here is on *Lunyu*, it is worth noting that we find similar patterns with other classics excerpted in *Jiujing chao*. As noted above, the classic most often cited in *Jiujing chao* is *Shangshu*, with forty-two attributions. Of these I found that only eighteen (43 percent) match the text found in the *Kaicheng shijing* text, following the same basic criteria used to categorize *Lunyu* passages. We find many of the same patterns as well. In some cases, part of the entry will be an accurate quotation from *Shangshu*, and part will be from another text entirely. In others the content will all be from *Shangshu* but from entirely different passages (which is especially jarring in the case of *Shangshu* as, unlike *Lunyu*, it does not consist primarily of short passages that can be easily combined).

There is one important pattern that we find in the *Shangshu* attributions that is different from what we see with *Lunyu*: of the twenty-four entries with excerpts that do not match the official *Shangshu* text, fifteen of them include text that is actually from the Kong Anguo commentary. Some entries are made up entirely of text from the commentary while others are a mix of main text and commentary. Interestingly, in many of these latter cases the commentary is actually from a different passage from the one with which it is combined in the *Jiujing chao* entry. Entry 51 is an example of this. It reads:

> The *Eminent Documents* says, "In his doing good, the fine man finds the day is not enough. In his doing evil, the fell man also finds the day is not enough. When evil continues and so will fill all, heaven must execute him. If it does not execute him, Heaven will instead be transgressing with him."
> 尚書云。吉人為善。惟日不足。凶人為不善。亦惟日不足惡貫已滿。天必誅之。若不誅之。天可與同過。

The first four phrases here are found in this exact form in the "August Oath" 泰誓 (tai shi) chapter of *Shangshu*.[54] The rest of the entry, however, is a paraphrase of the Kong commentary, not to that passage, but to an earlier one in this same chapter.[55] Moreover, text very similar to this entry is found in both an entry in *Wenci jiaolin* and in an entry in the untitled, fragmentary florilegium found in Dunhuang manuscript P.3368.[56]

A similar situation is found with *Jiujing chao* entry 190, though in this case the entire entry consists of commentary rather than main text. It reads:

> The *Documents* says, "If the ruler has moral power, his subjects find success. If the ruler lacks moral power, his subjects fall into error. If he uses moral power, there is order. If he does not use moral power, there is disarray."
> 書云。君之有德。惟臣成之。君子無德。惟臣誤之。以德則理。不以德則亂。

The first four phrases are from the Kong commentary to the "Charge to Jiong" 囧命 (Jiong ming),[57] while the last two are instead from the Kong commentary to the "Tai Jia" 太甲 chapter.[58] Perhaps the most interesting aspect of this is that this entry is identical to entry 210 in *Wenci jiaolin*.[59] Both this example and the previous one give strong support to the idea that florilegia such as these are building on other florilegia, rather than going back to the source texts from which they claim to excerpt. The odds that these same unusual joinings of text from separate sections of the classics in question would occur independently are many indeed. This also supports speculation that excerpts of this sort likely enjoyed far broader textual spread than our limited sample captures.

As a final example beyond *Lunyu* we turn to *Xiaojing*. While there are only ten entries attributed to it in *Jiujing chao*, it is an interesting case in that it is the shortest by far of the classics and the one most likely to have been memorized in full by the educated class. In spite of this, only three of the entries citing it in *Jiujing chao* contain excerpts that basically match the *Kaicheng shijing* text. The other seven entries have text that is either not in *Xiaojing* at all or is a mix of text from *Xiaojing* and other works, often stitched together smoothly. Entry 327 is of this sort and reads:

> The *Classic of Filial Piety* says, "In caring for them, have the utmost respect. When they are sick, have the utmost concern. When mourning them, have the utmost sorrow. In sacrificing to them, have the utmost gravity. When they are alive, serve knowingly through ritual. When they pass away, bury them with the proper ritual. Sacrifice to them with proper ritual; sacrifice to their spirits as if their spirits were present. Then their spirits will enjoy it."
>
> 孝經云。養則致其敬。病則致其憂。喪則致其哀。祭則致其嚴。生事知以禮。死葬之以禮。祭之以禮。祭神如神在。故鬼享之。

The first four phrases are taken from the tenth chapter of *Xiaojing* with some minor changes in wording (my translation follows the text as it appears in P.2598).[60] The next three phrases are near exact excerpts from *Lunyu* 2.5.[61] The penultimate phrase is from *Lunyu* 3.12, and the final phrase appears in two places in *Xiaojing*, though not from the same chapter as the first part of the entry.[62] As we have seen with similar combination of passages attributed to *Lunyu*, the entry is thematically coherent and the phrases fit together well. The portions that are not from *Xiaojing* give the impression that they could be. The result is a plausible *Xiaojing* but a different one nevertheless.

Conclusion

Writing of "the endless rewriting to which medieval textuality is subjected, the joyful appropriation of which it is the object," Bernard Cerquiglini asserts that "medieval writing does not produce variants; it *is* variance."[63] While our sources are limited, there is every indication that Cerquiglini's notion holds as true for the textual world of medieval China as it does for that of medieval Europe. This is clearly true on the level of the individual word, but it is also the case with larger textual blocks that were rearranged, paraphrased, reattributed, and invented. Moreover, this mutability is found not only in less "official" works composed and circulated in the medieval period itself but also with earlier textual materials that had a much more established cultural and even political role in literate society, such as the classics.

The available sources show a broad range of textual relationships to the classics among the literate elite. On one end, that which is most clearly defined is the institutional desire for exactitude and uniformity. This is the impetus behind inscribing definitive texts of the classics on stone and promulgating them as the "official" versions. Connected to this are testing mechanisms such as the *tiejing* 貼經 (pasting over the classic), which demand perfect memorization demonstrated by exact replication of portions of the official texts. Such mechanisms both depend on and support the concept of a stable and unchanging text. On the other end, in *Jiujing chao*, *Wenci jiaolin*, and similar florilegia, we see a very different relationship with the texts of the classics. They were clearly still revered, but the precise wording and, in many cases, even accuracy of attribution, were not the primary values of compilers of these works and their readers. Moreover, it may well be the case that this relationship with the classics was much more common than the precisely defined one represented by the exam and the stone inscriptions. Most literate people in the Tang would never take the *jinshi* or *mingjing* exams. All of them would have been expected to know something of some of the classics.

Thinking of *Lunyu* in particular, we can postulate an essentially endless array of *Lunyu*: the official text found in the *Kaicheng shijing* that would serve as the basis for exams; the multiple copies that circulated and exhibited the typical variation we find in any manuscript culture (it makes sense to think of these latter *Lunyu* as different texts and documents of a single work); and the *Lunyu* textual material that circulated in compilations such as *Jiujing chao* and others. Though these were incomplete and included substantial material that was not part of the official *Lunyu* text, they likely enjoyed a substantial audience. One might go as far as to argue that a composite *Lunyu* made up of such material would constitute not just a different text of the work *Lunyu* but even a different work, also called "*Lunyu*." The risk of falling into a version of the sorites paradox notwithstanding, there may be a point at which "*Lunyu*" is no longer *Lunyu*.

In terms of our approach to medieval Chinese literature broadly conceived, this textual reality and the "new medievalists'" approach to it potentially impacts, among other aspects, our understanding of intertextuality. Roland Barthes builds his notion of intertextuality with the word "text" (in both French and English), calling up its original associations of a tissue woven together. His idea of a text as "woven entirely with citations, references, echoes, cultural languages . . . antecedent or contemporary"[64] fits medieval Chinese literary production on multiple levels. As those in the field know well, the search for citations, references, and echoes makes up a substantial percentage of scholarship. But Barthes warns us that this search may be misguided, arguing that "the intertextual . . . itself being the text-between of another text, is not to be confused with some origin of the text: to try to find the 'sources,' the 'influences' of a work is to fall in with the myth of filiation."[65] The fluidity of *Lunyu* textual material in the medieval period (and likely all others) brings the problematic aspect of this search for origins into sharp relief. The *Lunyu*, for medieval readers and writers, whether on paper or in their minds (and on their lips), may well have been meaningfully different from the *Lunyu* we imagine.

There are many potential explanations for the extent of variation we find in these different *Lunyu* texts. When textual fidelity was important, it was achievable (within limits). Though "official" texts of *Lunyu* display some variety, it has typically been on the level of the individual word, not added or rearranged passages. Maintaining this high level of textual fidelity, however, was not important for many, perhaps even most, readers and learners. If not preparing for the exam, they needed only to be familiar with the general contents of *Lunyu*: well-known passages and basic moral lessons. Verbatim memorization was not required. Mary Carruthers describes a similar situation in the quotation of important texts in medieval Europe, writing: "But many writers gave paraphrases of texts, even when manuscripts containing the complete text were available to them. The reason is not far to seek. They are quoting from memory 'sententialiter,' according to the matter or *res*, rather than word-for-word. . . . One finds even the poetry of the *Aeneid* sometimes quoted approximately."[66] It is likely that the compiler of *Jiujing chao* could have accessed a full text of something closely approximating *Lunyu*; there is no indication it was anywhere near as difficult to find in the late medieval period as were copies of longer histories such as *Shiji* 史記 (Historical Records) or *Han shu*. However, he had also likely set many parts of *Lunyu* to memory, at least on the *sententialiter* level. Moreover, he clearly had access to other florilegia. Based on the title of his own compilation and striking similarities with *Wenci jiaolin*, it seems he borrowed from them substantially. *Jiujing chao* is thus likely a mix of general recollections and other sources at multiple removes from any original classical texts themselves. Compiling a florilegium in such a manner was easier and good enough for the purpose it was intended to serve.

Returning to the issue of intertextuality, the works that resulted from this process are themselves fundamentally intertextual, as they explicitly consist of parts of other texts. At the same time, they are new texts that were, perhaps, more widely and frequently encountered and consulted by many readers. As such, they were themselves the sources for the "citations, references, and echoes" found in literary works created by those readers. This reality requires us to alter, at least slightly, our approach to understanding allusions and references in medieval literature. We cannot assume that writers had necessarily fully learned the individual works to which we trace back their allusions. There is still a multitude of fabrics woven together, but their threads may have been reused in ways we are only beginning to understand.

 CHRISTOPHER M. B. NUGENT   倪健
Williams College
cnugent@williams.edu

Notes

1. The quotations were compiled by a student teacher; both she and the head teacher were most welcoming of an alternative set of quotes and commentary that I provided. My point, as will be clear below, is not to criticize them.
2. See Chinese Text Project, accessed July 7, 2021; ctext.org and Scripta Sinica, accessed July 7, 2021, hanchi.ihp.sinica.edu.tw/ihp/hanji.htm.
3. See Finn, "100 Confucius Quotes," Quote Ambition, accessed June 16, 2021, https://www.quoteambition.com/confucius-quotes/.
4. *Laozi* 老子, 64.260.
5. Nichols, "New Medievalism," 1.
6. For an excellent introduction to some of this work in an early stage, see Finke and Shichtman, *Medieval Texts and Contemporary Readers*.
7. Bryan, *Collaborative Meaning*, 7.
8. See Cherniack, "Book Culture," and Nugent, *Manifest in Words*, 4–18.
9. Zumthor, *Toward a Medieval Poetics*, 46.
10. Cerquiglini, *In Praise of the Variant*, 34–35.
11. See, for example, Kern, "Methodological Reflections"; Richter, *Embodied Text*; and Meyer, *Philosophy on Bamboo*.
12. Owen, *Making of Early Chinese Classical Poetry*; Tian, *Tao Yuanming and Manuscript Culture*.
13. Nugent, *Manifest in Words* and "Putting His Materials to Use"; Allen, *Shifting Stories*.
14. Blair, *Too Much to Know*, 35.
15. Tian, *Beacon Fire and Shooting Star*, 82.
16. These being P.2557, P.3621, and P.2598, where "P" stands for *Pelliot chinois*. All manuscripts were accessed digitally through Gallica (gallica.bnf.fr). P.3612 and P.2598 appear to have originally been part of the same document. Beyond the work of Zheng Acai, there is very little scholarship on *Jiujing chao*. See Zheng, *Dunhuang xiejuan* and Wang S., *Dunhuang leishu*, 89–98.

17. P.2598, the only manuscript with a date. For full discussion, see Zheng, *Dunhuang xiejuan*, 40–44.

18. For a list of various groupings from the period see Zheng, *Dunhuang xiejuan*, 24. For a fuller description of the evolution of the numerical designations for the classical canon, see Wilkinson, *Chinese History*, 401–2.

19. For a full list see Zheng, *Dunhuang xiejuan*, 28–30.

20. From the *Flores paradysi* (Flowers of Paradise), quoted in Blair, *Too Much to Know*, 36.

21. As is typical for such texts, there is no punctuation in the original. The punctuation I provide here is based on that in Zheng Acai's transcription.

22. Zheng, *Dunhuang xiejuan*, 39, 47–53.

23. A separate entry is designated as one beginning with a specific attribution for the text that follows. Note that the total number of entries varies slightly depending on the specific manuscript being used.

24. While his focus is different, I would note Michael Hunter's *Confucius beyond the Analects* as influencing my interest in this topic.

25. As noted earlier, there are many other entries in *Jiujing chao* that include text from *Lunyu* without mentioning that work specifically, instead attributing the passage to Confucius (or, in a few cases, to one of his disciples). As I am here interested in the presentation of *Lunyu* as a specific work, I do not address that material here.

26. Entry numbers are those used in Zheng, *Dunhuang xiejuan*.

27. *Lunyu*, 12.2; *KCSJ*, 6.2636–37. For every passage from *Lunyu* I give the standard book and passage number. I also give the location in *Jingkan Tang Kaicheng shijing* 景刊唐開成石經, hereafter abbreviated as *KCSJ*.

28. *Lunyu*, 20.2; *KCSJ*, 10.2672.

29. *Lunyu*, 20.2; *KCSJ*, 10.2672–73.

30. *KCSJ*, 2.2608.

31. Ibid., 4.2621.

32. Ruan, *Lunyu zhushu*, 7.62.

33. Ibid., 2.20.

34. *KCSJ*, 3.2617.

35. See further discussion in the conclusion.

36. *KCSJ*, 4.2613.

37. Zheng, *Dunhuang xiejuan*, 86. Two characters are unreadable due to physical damage to the document.

38. The only difference being that the official text has 正 rather than 政. See *KCSJ*, 7.2641.

39. *KCSJ*, 6.2638.

40. Liu, *Shuoyuan*, 5.111.

41. Wang L., *Xinyu jiaozhu*, 67.

42. *KCSJ*, 3.2615.

43. Ibid., 9.2660.

44. See *Confucius: Analects*, 200–201 for different interpretations of the meaning of Confucius's comment.

45. *KCSJ*, 4.2619.

46. Ibid., 2.2607.

47. Ibid., 9.2661.

48. Ibid., 2.2606.

49. Ibid., 4.2621–22.
50. Ibid., 1.2600.
51. Ibid., 2.2608.
52. Fan, *Hou Han shu*, 84.2788–89.
53. Zheng, *Dunhuang xiejuan*, 74.
54. Ruan, *Shangshu zhushu*, 11.154.
55. Ibid., 11.153.
56. See Zheng, *Dunhuang xiejuan*, 56, 300.
57. Ruan, *Shangshu zhushu*, 19.294.
58. Ibid., 8.119.
59. Zheng, *Dunhuang xiejuan*, 88.
60. *KCSJ*, 2591.
61. Ibid., 1.2601.
62. Ibid., 2.2605; 2590.
63. Cerquiglini, *In Praise of the Variant*, 77.
64. Barthes, *Image, Music, Text*, 160.
65. Ibid., 160.
66. Carruthers, *Book of Memory*, 87.

References

Allen, Sarah M. *Shifting Stories: History, Gossip, and Lore in Narratives from Tang Dynasty China*. Cambridge, MA: Harvard University Asia Center, 2014.

Barthes, Roland. *Image, Music, Text*. Translated by Stephen Heath. New York: Hill and Wang, 1977.

Blair, Ann M. *Too Much to Know: Managing Scholarly Information Before the Modern Age*. New Haven: Yale University Press, 2010.

Bryan, Elizabeth J. *Collaborative Meaning in Medieval Scribal Culture: The* Otho Laȝamon. Ann Arbor: University of Michigan Press, 1999.

Carruthers, Mary. *The Book of Memory: A Study of Memory in Medieval Culture*. Cambridge: Cambridge University Press, 1990.

Cerquiglini, Bernard. *In Praise of the Variant*. Translated by Betsy Wing. Baltimore: Johns Hopkins University Press, 1999.

Cherniack, Susan. "Book Culture and Textual Transmission in Sung China." *Harvard Journal of Asiatic Studies* 54, no. 1 (1994): 5–125.

Chinese Text Project. Accessed July 7, 2021. ctext.org.

Confucius: Analects. Translated by Edward Slingerland. Indianapolis: Hackett, 2003.

Fan Ye 范曄 (398–445). *Hou Han shu* 後漢書 (History of the Former Han). Taipei: Dingwen shuju, 1981.

Finke, Laurie A., and Martin B. Shichtman, eds. *Medieval Texts and Contemporary Readers*. Ithaca: Cornell University Press, 1987.

Finn, Amy. "100 Confucius Quotes." Quote Ambition. Accessed June 16, 2021. https://www .quoteambition.com/confucius-quotes/.

Hunter, Michael. *Confucius beyond the Analects*. Leiden: Brill, 2017.

Jingkan Tang Kaicheng shijing 景刊唐開成石經 (The Jing Cutting of the Tang Kaicheng Period Stone Classics). 4 vols. Beijing: Zhonghua shuju, 1997.

Kern, Martin. "Methodological Reflections on the Analysis of Textual Variants and the Modes of Manuscript Production in Early China." *Journal of East Asian Archaeology* 4 (2002): 143–81.

Laozi 老子. Beijing: Zhonghua shuju, 1984.

Liu Xiang 劉向 (77 BCE–6 BCE). *Shuoyuan jiaozheng* 說苑校證 (Garden of Persuasions, Collated and Corrected). Edited by Xiang Zonglu 向宗魯. Beijing: Zhonghua shuju, 1987.

Meyer, Dirk. *Philosophy on Bamboo: Text and the Production of Meaning in Early China*. Leiden: Brill, 2012.

Nichols, Stephen G. "The New Medievalism: Tradition and Discontinuity in Medieval Culture." In *The New Medievalism*, edited by Marina S. Brownlee, Kevin Brownlee, and Stephen G. Nichols, 1–26. Baltimore: Johns Hopkins University Press, 1991.

Nugent, Christopher M. B. *Manifest in Words, Written on Paper: Producing and Circulating Poetry in Tang Dynasty China*. Cambridge, MA: Harvard University Asia Center, 2010.

Nugent, Christopher M. B. "Putting His Materials to Use: Experiencing a Li Bai *Yuefu* in Manuscript and Early Print Documents." *East Asian Publishing and Society* 5 (2015): 32–73.

Owen, Stephen. *The Making of Early Chinese Classical Poetry*. Cambridge, MA: Harvard Asia Center, 2006.

Richter, Matthias L. *The Embodied Text: Establishing Textual Identity in Early Chinese Manuscripts*. Leiden: Brill, 2013.

Ruan Yuan 阮元 (1764–1849), ed. *Lunyu zhushu jiejing* 論語注疏解經 (*Analects* with Commentaries and Subcommentaries Explaining the Classic). In *Shisan jing zhushu fu jiaokan ji* 十三經注疏附校勘記 (Thirteen Classics with Commentaries and Appended Collation Notes). Taipei: Yiwen yinshuguan, 1965.

Ruan Yuan 阮元 (1764–1849), ed. *Shangshu zhushu fu jiaokan ji* 尚書注疏附校勘記 (*Documents* with Commentaries and Appended Collation Notes). In *Shisan jing zhushu fu jiaokan ji* 十三經注疏附校勘記. Taipei: Yiwen yinshuguan, 1965.

Scripta Sinica (*Hanji dianzi wenxian ziliao ku* 漢籍電子文獻資料庫). Accessed July 7, 2021. hanchi.ihp.sinica.edu.tw/.

Tian, Xiaofei. *Beacon Fire and Shooting Star: The Literary Culture of the Liang (502–557)*. Cambridge, MA: Harvard University Asia Center, 2007.

———. *Tao Yuanming and Manuscript Culture: The Record of a Dusty Table*. Seattle: University of Washington Press, 2005.

Wang Liqi 王利器, ed. *Xinyu jiaoju* 新語校注 (*New Discourses* with Annotations and Commentaries). Beijing: Zhonghua shuju, 1986.

Wang Sanqing 王三慶. *Dunhuang leishu* 敦煌類書 (Dunhuang Encyclopedias). Kaoxiung: Liwen wenhua shiye gongsi, 1993.

Wilkinson, Endymion. *Chinese History: A New Manual*. 5th ed. Cambridge, MA: Distributed by Harvard Asia Center, 2018.

Zheng Acai 鄭阿財. *Dunhuang xiejuan xinji wenci jiujing chao yanjiu* 敦煌寫卷新集文詞九經抄研究 (Research on Dunhuang Manuscripts of *New Compilation of Phrases Excerpted from the Nine Classics*). Taipei: Wenshizhe chubanshe, 1989.

Zumthor, Paul. *Toward a Medieval Poetics*. Translated by Philip Bennett. Minneapolis: University of Minnesota Press, 1992.

Theories of Spatiality and the Study of Medieval China

MANLING LUO

Abstract Space is a ubiquitous and essential dimension of human existence, so much so that it is often taken for granted. In what has been dubbed the "spatial turn," Western scholars in geography, philosophy, history, literature, and other disciplines have tried to reorient critical perspectives in order to account for the importance of space to humanity. Meanwhile, space/place has been a fairly prominent subject in the study of medieval China. This essay contrasts Western general and local theories and Sinological studies to show their divergent and overlapping concerns. The juxtaposition illustrates how Western theories of spatiality can help open up new possibilities for Sinological studies of medieval China. Meanwhile, such engagements can also enhance the relevance of Sinological studies of medieval China to the developments in broader academia and beyond.

Keywords spatiality, space/place, Western general and local theories, Sinological local theories, medieval China

Space is a ubiquitous and essential dimension of human existence. This essay, however, is not a current state-of-the-field review that provides a comprehensive account and assessment of existing scholarship on spatiality but a personal contemplation on "critical theory and Sinology," the theme of the special issue for the *Journal of Chinese Literature and Culture*, using spatiality as an anchoring point. Specifically, I am interested in thinking through issues related to the question of whether Western theories of spatiality that emerged from roughly the 1960s onward are relevant to the study of medieval China. Such theories have been influential, transforming how scholars in the West think about spatiality. They also led to what has been dubbed the "spatial turn" across

The Journal of Chinese Literature and Culture • 9:1 • April 2022
DOI 10.1215/23290048-9681215 • © 2022 by Duke University Press

disciplines, with manifestations including the opening of new spatial questions and the widespread use of Geographic Information Systems (GIS). To be sure, spatiality has already been an important subject in China studies. Regarding premodern China, there are numerous monographs and articles devoted to related issues in every historical period. I choose to focus, however, only on the medieval period (often taken to be from the third century to the tenth century) because of my own research interest. This choice in no way suggests that spatiality in the periods before or after is less important or interesting. By juxtaposing select examples of both Western theories of spatiality and studies of medieval China, I use the divergences and connections to reflect on a Sinologist's relationship with theory.

But what is theory? In the general sense of "theory" meaning "a hypothesis or set of ideas about something,"[1] human conceptions of space are probably as ancient as the species itself, embodied in how we live our lives and understand our world. "Theory" can also mean "abstract knowledge or principle, as opposed to practical experience or activity."[2] To avoid confusion of the two meanings, I use "conceptions of spatiality" to refer to people's understandings of their own space-related practices and imaginings in life and "theories of spatiality" to refer to critical ideas that modern scholars propose to explain the historical and contemporary human relations with space/place. Although these modern scholars might have drawn from their personal conceptions of spatiality, their ideas are theoretical in nature, aiming for broader validity than their personal experience and open to modifications and challenges as hypotheses.

For the sake of discussion below, I further distinguish between "general theories of spatiality," which are universal in orientation, and "local theories of spatiality," which are drawn from case studies of historically and spatially anchored human groups and do not extend their conclusions to others. The distinction is not meant to be hard and fast. While some studies may fit a single category, others straddle the two. In addition, people may not agree whether a specific work should be called a "general" or a "local" theory. The distinction is useful, however, for recognizing researchers' own stance as well as common perceptions of their works' scope and relevance. The employment of this distinction also reflects my belief that, contrary to what is often assumed, general theories are not superior to concrete case studies, and the latter produces particular knowledge that is also theoretically productive.

In what follows, I first identify issues that stand out in some Western general theories of spatiality that have been cited extensively, contrasting them with a few Western local theories to show their features. I then use select local theories on medieval Chinese cities, literary genres, famous mountains, and geographical writings to illustrate different and overlapping concerns of Sinologists. The last part is devoted to reflections on challenges and new possibilities.

My approach here can be said to be "spatial," which is thematic in focus and narrow in scope. Given the limitations of space, I will discuss only the English-language scholarship. Moreover, rather than a diachronic account of how scholarly trends have developed over time, I provide only select examples for a few identified themes to illustrate different approaches. Some scholars have explicitly identified how their predecessors' ideas on spatiality inform their thinking, whereas others do not. I duly note the sources of influence in the former case and do not assume direct connections among scholarly works in the latter. Regardless of whether I can specify the influences, I treat each scholar as a distinctive contributor to a general discourse on the theoretical and concrete challenges presented by issues of spatiality. My discussion of Western scholars and Sinologists is certainly incomplete and does not cover the range and complexities on both sides. I usually reference only one work of a scholar and focus only on its main points (or just the relevant aspect in some cases) without exhausting its rich insights. This is because I do not seek comprehensiveness but use examples as entry points for discussion. Among them, the works of Michel Foucault, Henri Lefebvre, Edward Soja receive more attention than others because I consider such details necessary for us to understand why they are cited the most. Meanwhile, there are many important works that I fail to cite here—the omissions, due to the limitations of space or of my reading, in no way undercut their great significance and should never be taken as a slight to their authors.

The Rediscovery and Re-examination of Spatiality in the West

Western studies of and reflections on spatiality go back a long way. Geography, for instance, analyzes the features of the different parts of the earth's surface and their relationship with human societies and is one of the oldest disciplines. In contrast, Euclidean geometry explores space in abstract terms and pertains to spatial properties including position, distance, shape, and size. Philosophy of space and time explores the issues of their character, existence, relation with human knowledge, and so on. What these different approaches have in common is that spatiality is very much taken as a fact of human life and the world. It has been roughly from the 1960s–1970s onward that scholars in humanistic geography, philosophy, history, literature, and other disciplines have begun to reorient critical perspectives in order to account for the importance and implications of space to humanity. These trends coalesced into a highly visible, intellectual movement often referred to as the "spatial turn." Some of the most oft-cited general theories are foundational to the development, illustrating the central, shared concerns of scholars in the humanities and social sciences.

The distinction between "space" and "place" is crucial in opening up critical perspectives on spatiality, even though discussions related to the spatial turn are divergent and employ different terms. Scholars of humanistic geography, as summarized by Tim Cresswell, have foregrounded the concept of "place," defining it as "a meaningful location" created from "space," geometric dimensions of areas and volumes.[3] In the words of Yi-Fu Tuan, "The ideas of 'space' and 'place' require each other for definition. From the security and stability of place we are aware of the openness, freedom, and threat of space, and vice versa. Furthermore, if we think of space as that which allows movement, then place is pause; each pause in movement makes it possible for location to be transformed into place."[4] Place can take different forms and scales. "At one extreme a favorite armchair is a place, at the other extreme the whole earth."[5] Because "place is also a way of seeing, knowing, and understanding the world,"[6] the perspective of place represents a range of possibilities.

For one thing, place epitomizes an existential condition of humanity that is irreducible and rich with significance, which is what philosophers try to expound on. Martin Heidegger, for example, argues that "dwelling" (*dasein*), or "Being-in-the-world," is the essence of human existence. He presents an apparently timeless farmhouse in the Black Forest as the idealized site where the natural and the human worlds fuse, where "the self-sufficiency of the power to let earth and heaven, divinities and mortals enter *in simple oneness* into things, ordered the house."[7] Meanwhile, Gaston Bachelard speaks of an "oneiric house" that is presumably within each of us.[8] As he puts it, "We are unable to relive duration that has been destroyed. . . . Memories are motionless, and the more securely they are fixed in space, the sounder they are."[9] While Bachelard underscores that human memory is spatial in nature, other philosophers have taken one step further to argue for the primacy of place in the formation of society altogether. J. E. Malpas, for instance, states, "Indeed the social does not exist prior to place nor is it given expression except in and through place—and through spatialised, temporalised ordering. . . . It is within the structure of place that the very possibility of the social arises."[10] In other words, spatiality as a fact of human life does not mean that it can be taken for granted but rather that we should recognize the primary function of place and accord it the corresponding prominence in critical analysis. These philosophers, however, do not elaborate on what concrete approaches can be adopted for this kind of new spatial analysis.

The differentiation between "space" as a raw material and "place" as a product brings forth the issue of "place-making," namely, how space is turned into place. Some scholars have highlighted the crucial role of individuals. In David Seamon's view, for example, a person's habitual movements, such as going to work, grocery shopping, and picking up kids from school, constitute "time-space" routines of their life. These routines surrounding a location give rise to a "place-ballet" that accounts for the formation of a strong "sense of place" at the heart of individual and collective identity.[11] By contrast, Michel de Certeau underscores the tension between the individual's agency in their spatial practice and the structural constraints they have to negotiate. The fixed grid of city streets, for example, is like the grammar of language, which determines the limits of one's spatial movements in daily life. Meanwhile, pedestrians have "walking rhetorics," which, as speech acts, allows them to appropriate the place and create their own space according to their desires.[12] We should note that de Certeau inverts the received definitions of "place" and "space" in humanistic geography as seen above. Regardless, such discussions foreground individuals' practices, experiences, and agency in the dynamic process of place-making.

Meanwhile, other theorists have directed their attention to the role of the social in place-making. However, these theorists, including Michel Foucault, Henri Lefebvre, and Edward Soja, do not distinguish between "space" and "place." Rather, they use "space" as an all-encompassing term, covering senses of raw material, product, and medium. Although Foucault is perhaps better known for his ideas on power and knowledge, he admits the importance of spatiality to him: "Geography must indeed necessarily lie at the heart of my concerns."[13] To him, "a mechanism of power reduced to its ideal form," for instance, is the Panopticon, "a pure architectural and optical system."[14] His concentrated theoretical discussion of space can be found in his lecture notes, which were prepared in 1967 but not published until 1984 (English version in 1986). Here Foucault makes clear that he is not concerned with "internal space" as explored by Bachelard, but the "external space" of human life. He asserts its centrality in human existence, pointing out that "we live inside a set of relations that delineates sites which are irreducible to one another and absolutely not superimposable on one another."[15] The failure to recognize this human condition is due to the predominance of historicism: "The great obsession of the nineteenth century was, as we know, history: with its themes of development and of suspension, of crisis and cycle, themes of the ever-accumulating past, with its great preponderance of dead men and the menacing glaciation of the world."[16] In such historicism, space is no more than a background or stage, immobile and transparent.

Consistent with his interest in peripheries, Foucault elaborates on what he calls "heterotopias," or "other spaces." He defines heterotopia as "real places—places that do exist and that are formed in the very founding of society—which are something like counter-sites, a kind of effectively enacted utopia in which the real sites, all the other real sites that can be found within the culture, are simultaneously represented, contested, and inverted."[17] Examples of heterotopias include mirrors, cemeteries, oriental gardens, museums, festivals, and boats. Foucault tries to present a systematic description of heterotopias by summing up six principles: (1) heterotopias are universal; (2) the same heterotopia can have shifting functions at different historical points of a society; (3) a heterotopia can juxtapose several spaces, even contradictory ones; (4) heterotopias are often linked to "slices in time"; (5) heterotopias have "a system of opening and closing"; and (6) heterotopias function "in relation to all the space that remains."[18] In other words, heterotopias embody the features of peculiar or marginal spaces vis-à-vis mainstream ones. They also illustrate how social space is heterogeneous and the sites therein are both distinctive and related to each other in complex ways.

Henri Lefebvre's seminal work is widely credited by scholars to be their source of inspiration. Although *The Production of Space* (1984, English 1991) does not follow conventional systematic exposition, Lefebvre's many statements are thought-provoking. He criticizes the longstanding approach of philosophers, mathematicians, and others who treat space as an abstract, mental thing, detached from concrete spaces as experienced by individuals. By contrast, he proposes a conceptual triad, "spatial practice," "representations of space," and "representational spaces." Spatial practice "embraces production and reproduction, and the particular locations and spatial sets characteristic of each social formation." Representations of space are tied "to knowledge, to signs, to codes, and to 'frontal' relations." Representational spaces embody "complex symbolisms," "linked to the clandestine or underground side of social life, as also to art."[19] Lefebvre also refers to the tripartite division as "the perceived-conceived-lived triad," the interconnected realms that allow the individual member of society to move from one to another through the corresponding functions of their body.[20]

To Lefebvre, what brings the different kinds of space together is their nature of being socially produced and as such, their immanence to social reality. In his words, "(social) space is a (social) product," which is both "a means of production" and "a means of control, and hence of domination, of power."[21] Social space can be consumed as a commodity (like tourism); it also underpins the social relations of reproduction and production (such as family and labor) and serves as a political instrument (including the state's control of cities and towns), albeit with "an outward appearance of neutrality" and even "emptiness."[22] This points to the very spatial nature of social reality. In the words of Lefebvre, "the social relations of production have a social existence to the extent that they have a spatial existence; they project themselves into a space, becoming inscribed there, and in the process producing the space itself. Failing this, these relations would remain in the realm of 'pure' abstraction—that is to say, in the realm of representations and hence of ideology: the realm of verbalism, verbiage and empty words."[23] Lefebvre's arguments enable us to recognize and move beyond the neutrality and transparency of space as a façade.

The social production of space is a process with historical dimensions, which entails both change and new possibilities. To Lefebvre, different societies in different times have distinctive ways of producing space. In his words, "Indeed each new form of the state, each new form of political power, introduces its own particular way of partitioning space, its own particular administrative classification of discourses about space and about things and people in space."[24] In particular, Lefebvre is keen to analyze the production of space under the capitalist system, exposing its inherent spatial contradictions and envisioning new alternatives. He opines, "On the horizon, then, at the furthest edge of the possible, it is a matter of producing the space of the human species—the collective (generic) work of the species—on the model of what used to be called 'art.'"[25] That is, he is optimistic about the future of creating a more egalitarian space for humanity.

Edward Soja elucidates and expands on Lefebvre's ideas, pointing out new directions. Although he also draws from Foucault, bell hooks, and many others, he identifies Lefebvre as his main source of inspiration, calling *The Production of Space* "arguably the most important book ever written about the social and historical significance of human spatiality and the particular powers of the spatial imagination."[26] To Soja, there has been a longstanding omission of space and an emphasis only on history and social life, and the most important contribution of Lefebvre lies in his injection of spatiality to create a dynamic trialectics. That is, "spatiality," "historicality" (or temporality), and "sociality" constitute "an *ontological trialectic*," and the "trialectics of being" "apply at all levels of knowledge formation."[27] The trialectics break open the link between history and society, a previously "all-inclusive ontological and epistemological dyad," and make it possible to move beyond the "binary reductionism or totalization" in interpreting human existence.[28] In addition, Soja also renames Lefebvre's conceptual triad as Firstspace (the real, physical space), Secondspace (the imagined, mental space), and Thirdspace (the real-and-imagined space), which constitute "the trialectics of spatiality."[29]

Soja argues that Thirdspace represents an innovative strategy in critical thinking, which he calls "thirding-as-Othering." He uses the term Thirdspace in two senses: it "is both a space that is distinguishable from other spaces (physical and mental, or First and Second) and a transcending composite of all spaces."[30] In the latter sense, it also refers to the injected spatiality vis-à-vis historicality (or temporality) and sociality in the trialectics of being. To Soja, the value of Thirdspace lies in its new epistemological possibilities. Binary categories, such as subject-object, center-margin, abstract-concrete, and material-mental, have long histories and are often taken for granted as ways of thinking in many disciplines. For Soja, however, binarism represents "a closed either/or opposition," and the addition of a third Other can crack it open by transforming it into the "dialectically open logic of both/ and also . . . ."[31] Thirding "does not derive simply from an additive combination of its binary antecedents but rather from a disordering, deconstruction, and tentative reconstitution of their presumed totalization producing an open alternative that is both similar and strikingly different."[32] For instance, in contrast to Firstspace and Secondspace counterparts, Thirdspace epistemologies "aris[e] from the sympathetic deconstruction and heuristic reconstitution of the Firstspace-Secondspace duality," taking the form of "an endless series of theoretical and practical approximations, a critical and inquisitive nomadism in which the journeying to new ground never ceases."[33] Likewise, the injection of spatiality into the historicality-sociality link does not invalidate it but opens up "a socio-spatial dialectic that by definition is also intrinsically historical" and a similar "spatio-temporal structuration of sociality."[34] This produces a trialectics that is filled with dynamic possibilities unimaginable in the original binarism.

Although these general theories of spatiality are universal in orientation, it does not mean that they are completely detached from culturally-historically specific cases. Lefebvre, for instance, evokes many concrete examples, such as the emergence of the perimeter of the Mediterranean as leisure destinations for industrialized Europe.[35] Soja provides in-depth empirical case studies, comparing urbanism of Greater Los Angeles and that of Amsterdam.[36] From these specific cases, however, they are concerned with drawing conclusions that are fixated upon the nexus between humans and space/place.

Scholars have tried to complicate such general theoretical models by developing local theories of spatiality based on concrete case studies and revealing specific factors at work. Take gender for instance. Barbara Hooper examines the philosophical and political roots of modern planning doctrine in the United States to expose its exclusion of feminist thought and practice. Although women played important roles in the early development of settlement housing and reforms, they were gradually pushed out of the sphere when planning became professionalized by 1910s. Meanwhile, planning theory and the construction of its history came to embrace scientific and objective standards grounded in the white male, bourgeois perspective. Unfortunately, the radical revisions to the history of planning in the 1980s by those such as Soja and John Friedmann repeat the same fatal flaw of the "exclusionary tradition of modernist/patriarchal/phallocentric thought."[37] What this exclusionary tradition obscures can be seen in Dolores Hayden's in-depth study of the lost tradition of feminist designs for American homes, neighborhoods, and cities. From the end of the Civil War to the beginning of the Great Depression, generations of feminists advocated a domestic revolution that recognized women's work and "linked all other aspects of feminist agitation into one continuous economic and spatial struggle undertaken at every scale from the home to the nation."[38]

In addition to gender, the issues of race and colonialism are also important factors. Reflecting on the experiences of herself and her African American community, bell hooks, for example, foregrounds the reality of spatialized racial hierarchy with the stark image of a small Kentucky town divided by the railroad tracks into two separate worlds.[39] She advocates "the politics of location," which "calls those of us who would participate in the formation of counter-hegemonic cultural practice to identify the places where we begin the process of re-vision."[40] To her, the marginal position to which African Americans are relegated spatially and socially is precisely this kind of potent political location, for marginality is a "space of radical openness."[41] Meanwhile, Edward Said offers one of the most influential critiques of colonialism. He demonstrates how British, French, and American imperialist agendas have constructed and engendered a complex reality of the Islamic Orient. Orientalism is more than an imaginative geography; it also encompasses academic institutions for the teaching and research of the Orient, a general "style of thought based upon an ontological and epistemological distinction made between 'the Orient' and (most of the time) 'the Occident,'" and a corporate institution "for dominating, restructuring, and having authority over the Orient."[42] Said is not concerned with a simple West-East dichotomy, in which Western colonial powers are victimizers and the Eastern peoples the victims. He points out how images and doctrines of Orientalism are accepted and reinforced by modernizing countries: "the modern Orient, in short, participates in its own Orientalizing."[43] Based on his analysis, he further envisions the possibilities of challenging and moving beyond "the worldwide hegemony of Orientalism."[44]

Moreover, scholars have also demonstrated that spatiality is inextricable from many other crucial dimensions in human life, including language, culture, and religion. Keith Basso, for example, presents a sophisticated ethnographic study of how the stories that Western Apache people tell about what happened in particular sites reveal a keen, robust, and deeply ethical sense of place. Articulated in concise, vivid place-names, the physical reality of landscape is imbued with an interior "landscape of moral imagination,"[45] which transmits historical knowledge and ancestral wisdom, allows individuals to develop their sense of self, and binds them into a community firmly anchored in place. While Basso evokes a number of philosophers, poets, and others whose works inspired him, Heidegger's concept of "dwelling" is important for him to reflect on how people sensing places dwell "on aspects of dwelling" as well as "on aspects of themselves, on sides and corners of their evolving identities."[46] Through the case of the Western Apache culture, Basso calls for ethnographers to do more on this front, for "sense of place is a universal genre of experience" that "may be found to exhibit transcultural qualities."[47] In parallel, Toni Huber's ethnohistorical reconstruction centers on the Tibetan pilgrimage tradition around Pure Crystal Mountain in Tsari during the 1940s and 1950s. He demonstrates that ritual literature shaped how the landscape was interpreted and navigated by practitioners, and both the physical and the imagined landscape in turn defined the ritual institutions established there. In addition, he also points out the working of gender in these institutions, as women were excluded from certain areas. His discussion also extends to the lives of local people, who helped to sustain the cult. In providing a comprehensive account of the Tibetan esoteric and popular traditions of ritual at Pure Crystal Mountain, Huber notes that although his work is informed by Victor Turner's ritual theory, he, like many others, has "found little to support his [i.e., Turner's] general thesis in relation to Tibetan pilgrimages."[48]

The list of local theories of spatiality is literally endless, but the few examples above suffice to illustrate several important points. The enterprise of local theories is to excavate, examine, and explain the conceptions of spatiality by particular groups of people. They demonstrate that many factors can be bound up with spatiality or, put another way, that spatiality is immanent in different dimensions of social life and has concrete, powerful impacts on how societies function. We also see that scholars of local theories of spatiality are not necessarily interested in making connections to general theories or generalizing their conclusions for broader claims. Those who do evoke general theories often do not stop at accepting their universal validity. Basso, for instance, breaks down Heidegger's concept of "dwelling" to elaborate on what it specifically entails, whereas Huber points out that Turner's model of pilgrimage and ritual is wanting in multiple ways. Whether they deal with historical or contemporary cases, some scholars of local theories share the same political concerns as those of general theories, hoping to use their insights to make interventions in today's human-space relationship for a better, progressive future.

Local Sinological Theories: Spatiality in Medieval China

Spatiality was also central in many different aspects of medieval China, and it is a subject that has attracted many studies. Introduced to China around the second century, Buddhism, for instance, started to gain a solid foothold during the medieval period. It brought a whole foreign system of cosmology, including visions of paradises and hells as well as new monastic practices of building construction and spatial usages.[49] Chinese monks who journeyed to India to study and retrieve authoritative teachings produced records that have been seen as early examples of travel writing.[50] Meanwhile, religious Daoism promoted their practitioners' specialty in accessing transcendental worlds, innovated and expanded their ideas of the cosmos, and developed their own monastic tradition.[51] In popular imagination, supernatural geography, where demonic, ghostly, or divine beings thrived and occult events happened as envisioned and explored in anomaly accounts, encompassed not just otherworldly realms but also the spaces of the mundane world, including the domestic sphere.[52] Moreover, geographic writings by individual writers were produced in great numbers, and governments tried to compile maps and geographic information for areas under their jurisdiction, although their efforts were not necessarily sustained due to a variety of factors. These practices laid the foundation for the systematic productions of local and empire-wide gazetteers in the Song 宋 (960–1279) and later periods.[53] There were also other important space-related trends examined by scholars in art history, archaeology, architecture, and other fields.[54]

Because of limitations of space, I offer just four groups of examples that center around major cities, literary genres, famous mountains, and geographic writings, respectively. These topics bring together studies from multiple disciplines and illustrate clusters of debates about issues on spatiality that Sinologists consider important. Regardless of their specific topics, these Chinese case studies adopt a common historical method, trying to excavate and analyze medieval Chinese conceptions of spatiality. Although the scholars discussed here may have intended to capture or reconstruct relevant historical "truths," I treat their analyses as local theories for two reasons. First, they deal with particular groups of people and their spatial practices and understandings. Second, as hermeneutic interpretations, they are subject to challenges and modifications. As we shall see below, these local, Sinological theories on spatiality are diverse and diffuse. The contrasts and connections of their arguments and approaches to those of Western general and local theories allow us to think more broadly about new possibilities.

The Sui-Tang Capital Chang'an 長安: *Comprehensive and Selective Views*
Chang'an (present-day Xi'an) was the capital of the Sui 隋 (581–618), when it was referred to as Daxing City 大興城, and of the Tang 唐 (618–907) dynasties and was one of the largest metropolises in the world at the time. It housed more than one million people at its height and was the most important political, economic, and cultural center of the empire. As the eastern terminus of the famous Silk Route, it was also instrumental to exchanges between Eurasia and

the Chinese empire in particular and East Asia in general. With the instability that befell and eventually brought down the Tang in the late ninth and early tenth centuries, however, the city was ruined and abandoned. Embodying the glory of the period, the city loomed large in later cultural imaginations and has been a prominent subject of interest among modern scholars.

There are those who have tried to provide comprehensive views of the city. A history of Chinese imperial capitals has to take the Sui-Tang Chang'an into account. Nancy Shatzman Steinhardt, for instance, presents a succinct overview of the city in her survey of the Chinese history of imperial city planning, also noting the influences of Chang'an's plan in other parts of East Asia.[55] For Chye Kiang Heng, the Sui-Tang Chang'an was a closed city with walls protecting compartmentalized city spaces, which represented aristocratic power, in stark contrast to the Song capitals Dongjing 東京 (present-day Kaifeng) and Lin'an 臨安 (present-day Hangzhou), open cities that accommodated the interests of a new gentry of bureaucrats and other members of their social world.[56]

The most detailed reconstruction of Chang'an's urban and socioeconomic development is by Victor Cunrui Xiong.[57] He draws from traditional historians' works, unofficial histories, encyclopedias, anthologies, and so on but uses archaeological findings to verify and correct their lack of precision. After tracing Chang'an's earlier history in the Han 漢 period (206 BCE–220 CE), Xiong shows that the Sui-Tang constructions were based on two paradigms, the canonical and the geomantic. He then discusses the Palace City, the Imperial City that housed the central government, ritual centers in the suburbs, the business sector both inside and outside the East Market and the West Market, and the residential ward system. He also describes the rise and fall of monastic communities in the city, covering not just Daoist and Buddhist but also Zoro-astrian, Manichaean, and Nestorian. In addition to the detailed picture of Chang'an's spatial structure and its historical changes, he emphasizes what he calls the "morphology" of the city, offering insights into the rationales behind constructions as well as the institutions associated with sites.

In contrast to this kind of comprehensive views of Chang'an constructed by historians, literary scholars seem more interested in selective views, focusing on issues such as specific human experiences of the urban space. The 2011 special issue of the *Tang Studies* on Sui and Tang cities is a case in point.[58] In his introduction to the issue, Jack Chen argues against the use of the modern city as the yardstick and the assumption of it as the destiny for the premodern coun-terpart. He states, "A better account of the medieval city, then, should proceed from an understanding of the city as it was experienced by its denizens, and not in terms of historical teleology."[59] To him, literary and historical sources provide the avenues for accessing those experiences. Chen's own article in the same issue analyzes texts on figures or events associated with Anyi Ward 安邑坊, a residential ward in Chang'an that bordered the East Market to the south. These texts, including anecdotes from gazetteers and miscellaneous collections, accounts of anomaly, and poetry, are drastically different from each other, and Chen argues that they show "how the histories of particular sites within the city constitute discontinuous experiences of space through time."[60] By contrast, Alexei Ditter focuses on the "Record of Monasteries and Stupas," a memoir by the writer Duan Chengshi 段成式 (ca. 803–863) of his visits with two friends to seventeen monasteries in 843. Ditter argues that Duan portrayed monastic spaces "as locations occupying set coordinates on Chang'an's urban grid, as settings for notable past occurrences, as sites of visual spectacle and public display, and as retreats to which visitors fled to escape the stresses of urban life."[61] Duan's account was also a "memorial" of personal friendship as well as "a public memory of the city and its people."[62]

While Linda Rui Feng's essay in this special issue examines Chang'an residents' appropriations of the vertical dimension of space as represented in Tang poems and tales,[63] I focus on her monograph here. This is because the monograph deals more extensively with the experience of Chang'an and elaborates more systematically on theoretical framing. She identifies Lefebvre's tripartite distinctions of "perceived space, conceived space, and lived space," de Certeau's "itinerary view," and Victor Turner's concept of "the liminal" as her "theoretical models."[64] Her discussion focuses on accounts of examination candidates whose pursuit of an official career required them to travel to and sojourn in Chang'an and engendered a distinct examination culture. To her, these narratives foreground the liminality of candidates' identity with regard to officialdom and explore their complex experiences as urban neophytes. In Feng's words, "Chang'an was megalopolis, political launch pad, and perhaps most importantly, cultural paradigm," serving as "the site and mechanism of transformations central to literati identity in the latter half of the Tang."[65] While Feng's analysis of the experience of space centers specifically upon a subgroup of literati in the pre-degree stage of their career, she also considers such experience at the collective level as part of literati identity.

Literary Genres and Poeticized Place

Spatiality was a prominent subject of medieval Chinese literature in the sense that its various poeticized manifestations defined important literary expressions in and across subgenres. The so-called *shanshui shi* 山水詩 (landscape poetry), for instance, is characterized by the poet's descriptions of his perception and experience of mountains and waters, or landscape.[66] In the *tianyuan shi* 田園詩 (farmstead poetry), the poet's focus is on his life in the countryside.[67]

Meanwhile, mobility is an important topic of travel writing in poetic or prose forms.[68] Travels, however, need not be physical, as the poet can also portray an imaginary journey to the otherworldly lands in the *youxian shi* 遊仙詩 (poetry on roaming as an immortal).[69] Specific works, nonetheless, do not necessarily fit squarely into categories, as they often incorporate different images and motifs. In addition, geographical locales, such as Jiangnan 江南 (the Southland), also became persisting images or themes that bridge diverse literary sub-genres.[70] These studies are often genre-centered, focusing on a genre's development, representative writers, and individual works. Because spatiality is an inherent part of the object of discussion, it is often taken for granted rather than treated as a problematic.

Among the various aspects of spatiality, the medieval author's sophisticated literary strategies for poeticizing place have received much attention. While examples are numerous, Wendy Swartz's article on the famous landscape poet and Buddhist layman Xie Lingyun's 謝靈運 (385–433) "Rhapsody on Dwelling in the Mountains" is illustrative. Swartz notes that Xie describes in detail what his immense estate contains, including peaks, valleys, streams, fields, parks, animals, plants, and architecture; he also charts the topography in light of "more distant geographical locations in all four directions," in effect "situating his home at the center of the cosmos."[71] That there is nothing wanting at his massive estate enables him to turn inward and reject external stimuli in order to reach the Buddhist way of emptiness. The physical space of his dwelling becomes a foil and a bridge to an inner, mental space of transcendence.

The meanings of such poeticized place are open to debate, albeit usually tied to literati identities and ideals. Swartz argues that to Xie Lingyun, the mountain dwelling constitutes a retreat removed from the court for "his reclusion and quest for Buddhist enlightenment."[72] By contrast, Harrison Huang believes that Xie's portrayals of his excursion in nature and appreciation of landscape should be seen in the traditions of *youlan* 遊覽 (viewing excursion), such that they constitute a literary performance of impersonating a ruler touring and surveying the lands.[73] To Stephen Owen, mid-Tang poets' writings on their ponds, gardens, and other spaces reveal a construction of the "private sphere."[74] In contrast to the earlier motif of reclusion as a rejection of the court life, this private sphere is compatible with officialdom; it can be enjoyed during the poet's "time off" from his public duties and enables a witty, self-conscious staging of his pleasure as a natural man for his readers in an enclosed, controlled space. Xiaoshan Yang further demonstrates that such an interest in the private sphere was shared widely and developed over time by literati in their efforts to search for alternatives to conventional values.[75]

Challenging the implicit assumption that the landscape portrayed by the poet was what he saw in nature, some scholars have explored the issue of textuality as an important dimension of spatiality in literary representations. Paul Kroll, for example, calls attention to the differences between the mentality of the medieval poet and that of present-day readers in his essay. He argues that the medieval poet did not simply describe the nature as it was but took for granted "the primacy of the word" and "the religious potency of the living world."[76] The primacy of the word, in particular, entails three levels of meaning: "the world as text" to be deciphered, "the world seen through words" by hyperliterate writers, and the compositions of these writers "being conditioned and stimulated, to varying degrees, by the verbalized visions of previous writers."[77] The indebtedness of a writer to his predecessors brings to the fore the issue of intertextuality. Owen offers, for instance, a diachronic analysis of *huaigu* 懷古 (meditation on the past) poems devoted to Jinling 金陵 (present-day Nanjing). The works by writers from the medieval period to the twentieth century demonstrate "an overlay of sites, images, and phrases that shaped the way the city was seen."[78] He identifies key moments in the development, when themes of impermanence, loss, and contrast were first set, when famous poems "took possession of the site," and when writers had to struggle with the "the trap of repetition" at different levels.[79]

Apart from textuality, other scholars have turned to the issue of visuality. Paula Varsano, for example, argues that previous scholars have overemphasized textuality in landscape poetry. Drawing from ideas about "the interface of visuality,"[80] she uses medieval writers' poetic theory and their poems on climbing high to show that they considered actual perceptive experience no less important than textual knowledge. In her words, "the writer's responses to textual and visual stimuli are conceived as functioning psychologically on a continuum, rather than as qualitatively distinct processes."[81] By contrast, Ao Wang foregrounds what he calls "spatial imaginaries," imaginations and representations of space by mid-Tang writers in their poems and essays. On one hand, he adopts "space" as the encompassing term in the way of Lefebvre but still finds it "helpful to maintain a certain distinction between space and place" as made by scholars like Tuan and Cresswell.[82] On the other hand, he evokes W. J. T. Mitchell's theory on images, pointing out that spatial imaginaries are in effect images produced by the mind's eye.[83] To him, mid-Tang cartographic advancements went hand in hand with the invention of spatial imaginaries in literature because multitalented literati were at the heart of both.

Famous Mountains and a Multidisciplinary Lens

Mountains occupied a prominent place in medieval Chinese sacred geography in particular and cultural imagination in general. The state maintained a classification system of mountains and the imperially designated Wuyue 五嶽 (Five Marchmounts), five sacred peaks corresponding to the five cardinal directions (east, south, west, north, and center), were held in the highest regard and believed to protect the imperium. The court offered their deities lofty titles and dispatched messengers to make regular offerings at those sacred peaks. Associated with the divine, the Five Marchmounts and other famous mountains attracted religious practitioners and other visitors and were the sites of pilgrimage, cultivation, inscription, sightseeing, and other activities. Studies of famous medieval mountains often explore their literary, artistic, historical, and religious facets through a multidisciplinary lens. The literary aspect overlaps with what we have discussed in the previous subsection on literary genres, as ascending mountains figures conspicuously in landscape literature and travel writing.[84] The following examples provide some additional perspectives on medieval mountains.

Robert Harrist examines stone inscriptions on mountains from the first through the eighth centuries as visual culture and public art. Referencing Tuan, he points out that the acts of carving texts into rocks and cliffs entailed "a transformation of space into place."[85] In addition, he evokes Lawrence Keppie's study of stone inscriptions from the Roman world and notes a fundamental difference: Chinese inscriptions were made on the surface of the earth rather than on a man-made structure. He thus argues for taking into full account the landscape context. In examining stone inscriptions commemorating public works, transfiguring landscape into paradise, displaying Buddhist sutras and deity names, and serving as a monarch's autographic monument, he demonstrates how social, familial, religious, and political forces shaped the tradition and the meanings of such public, artistic writing.

In addition, Edward Schafer's study of Mount Mao 茅山 illustrates the approach of trying to offer a comprehensive history of a mountain during the medieval period.[86] Drawing from poetry, collections of miscellaneous accounts, Daoist scriptures, and other sources, he covers the topics of regional geography, landscape and natural history, buildings, secular life and industries, and spiritual life. To him, Mount Mao is what brings together the diverse materials, and he seems to assume a consistency of the physical mountain with the various representations of it across different genres.

Whereas Schafer treats Mount Mao's connection with the Highest Clarity school of Daoism as one of its many dimensions, other scholars have focused in particular on mountains' religious associations. Franciscus Verellen, for instance, examines Daoist conceptions of *dongtian* 洞天 (grotto-heavens), mountain caves leading into subterranean paradises inhabited by immortals.[87] Such ideas, which can be traced to texts in the Highest Clarity school from the fifth to sixth centuries, were systematized in the Tang as a crucial part of Daoist sacred geography in addition to the Five Marchmounts. Exemplified by the series of ten great ones and thirty-six lesser ones, grotto-heavens presumably exist beneath mountains, constituting a complex system linked by secret passageways. They can be accessed through Daoist rituals, including those performed at a mountain site to send supplications directly to immortals, in a private oratory through liturgical procedures, and in mental space through visualization.

Like their Daoist counterparts, medieval Buddhists were also active in making claims to sacred mountains or creating new sacred sites, although existing studies often gravitate toward later periods.[88] Raoul Birnbaum, for example, looks into how Mount Wutai's 五臺山 caves were appropriated to create Buddhist sacred geography. He argues that there are four types of caves on Mount Wutai: "dwelling caves," "paradise caves of the mountain lords," "manifestation caves," and "a cave of initiatory rebirth."[89] Part of human practices in general, dwelling caves, for instance, were employed by Buddhist ascetics and referenced in scriptures. Meanwhile, Daoist ideas of "grotto-heavens" were adopted and modified to promote Buddhist paradise. Except for the last type, which seems to be of later origin, the other three were built on diverse themes from medieval and earlier sources. Bernard Faure shows that although Mount Song 嵩山, the Zhongyue 中嶽 (Central Marchmount), used to be associated with prominent Highest Clarity school Daoists and some literati recluses, it attracted monks of the Chan Buddhist school after a connection between Bodhidharma 菩提達摩 (d. 535), the so-called First Patriarch of Chan, and the Shaolin Monastery 少林寺 was established. By the mid-Tang most of the temples on the mountain were of the Chan school, in particular of the Northern Chan lineage. In contrast, the Southern Chan lineage enshrined the flesh body and other relics of the Sixth Patriarch Huineng 慧能 (638–713) and turned Caoxi 曹溪 (in today's Qujiang, Guangdong), a previously obscure locale, into a cultic center.[90]

The Buddhist takeover of a mountain is only one of many possible scenarios, and James Robson's monograph on Mount Heng 衡山, the Nanyue 南嶽 (Southern Marchmount), demonstrates that different religions could coexist at the same site. Robson's work is an in-depth study with well-defined theoretical positions. He distinguishes his project clearly from earlier approaches in the study of Chinese religion: he does not focus on exemplary religious figures and doctrines, neither does he adopt a sectarian approach. He states instead that his "methodological underpinnings" are "situated at the intersection of a number of nested disciplines and recent theoretical concerns within the humanities: place studies, sacred geography, and local or micro-history."[91] The Western scholars he references in his methodological discussion include Edward Casey,

Lefebvre, Mircea Eliade, Jonathan Z. Smith, and many others. Evoking Lefebvre's tripartite distinctions of space as adapted by David Harvey, for instance, Robson emphasizes that he employs all three vantage points of "the physical, the mental, and the cultural" in his analysis.[92] With an eclectic approach based on different methodologies, he demonstrates the multidimensional nature of the religious history of Nanyue. An important part of mountain classification systems central to the cults of the state, Nanyue referred to different mountains over time, and its physical and mythical landscapes were envisioned in historical and literary sources. As a result of Nanyue's perceived natural and numinous qualities, both Daoists and Buddhists laid claims to the mountain, and the traditions coexisted in amicable as well as contentious ways.

Geographical Writings: Worldviews and Power Dynamics
As mentioned earlier, the medieval period saw the production of a large number of geographical writings, which compiled information on areas at the local, regional, or even imperial level. The majority of them, however, only have a title or some fragments preserved. The few complete works and the extant fragments have often been regarded as historical sources, valued for the historical information they contained, whereas their narrative components, including biographies and anecdotes, have attracted the attention of literary scholars. Recent studies have also critically analyzed geographic writings as distinctive works, with an emphasis on revealing their hidden politics as products of their time.

Andrew Chittick, for instance, traces the formation of the geographical writing tradition in the early medieval period, shedding light on its political, social, and intellectual milieu. He coins the term "local writing" to refer to those early medieval compilations that "deal with the people, customs, history, and/or natural features of a clearly delimited geographical area."[93] Although such local writings were diverse in form and content, Chittick points out that they can be divided into two main groups, the biographically or the geographically oriented. The former celebrates the lives of eminent men associated with specific locales and tries to claim for them the prestige of human achievements. In contrast, the latter often provides snippets of information on aspects of a region and develops "locality stories," which define "that location's enduring moral and cultural 'character,' written into the *qi* energy of the location, and affecting all who lived there."[94] Chittick argues that local writing "was not generally antagonistic to imperial culture," even as it highlighted "the idea of *feng*, the spirit or energy of a local place."[95]

In contrast to Chittick, D. Jonathan Felt sees a more contentious relationship between the worldviews conveyed in early medieval geographical writings and the established imperial counterpart. As his theoretical framework,

Felt uses "metageography," a term defined by Martin Lewis and Kären Wigen as "the set of spatial structures through which people order their knowledge of the world."[96] Felt also points out that "metageographies are one type of representation of space," the second of Lefebvre's famous conceptual triad.[97] He argues that the collapse of the Han empire and the ensuring political fragmentation in the early medieval period gave rise to four new metageographies, distinct from the imperial counterpart, which asserted the centrality of the court in Sinitic civilization as well as the centrality of Sinitic civilization in the world as a whole. The "metageography of ecumenical regionalism" refers to local writings that highlighted the distinctiveness of regions and the roles of local elites. The "metageography of northern and southern dynasties" concerns the competing claims of regimes dominating northern and southern China at the time. The "metageography of the hydrocultural landscape" focuses on natural river systems as the structure of the natural and human landscape. The "metageography of the Indo-Sinitic bipolar worldview" denotes the perspective that emerged after the introduction of Buddhism; it envisions the world as eastern and western halves, each with its own linguistically, politically, and culturally defined center. These new alternatives challenged the traditional imperial metageography and had enduring influences in later history.

Focusing on a specific collection, one of my own articles explores different kinds of power dynamics regarding city residents' engagements with space and the textual representations of those engagements. A memoir of the ruined capital city of the Northern Wei dynasty 北魏 (386–534) compiled by Yang Xuanzhi 楊衒之 in roughly 547 CE, the *Luoyang qielan ji* 洛陽伽藍記 (Records of Buddhist monasteries in Luoyang) has been seen as a representative of the *duyi zhi* 都邑志 (records of cities). Although I evoke theorists including Lefebvre, Foucault, and Soja, I specifically adopt the concept of "place" from humanistic geography and use "place-making" as an overarching framework. I argue that Yang Xuanzhi actually portrays three modes of place-making, "architectural (staking ownership of physical space by creating new structures, modifying existing ones, or changing the nature of their usages), literary (writing about particular spaces), and hermeneutic (identifying and interpreting the histories of specific structures or sites)."[98] The politics of place-making occurred at two interrelated levels. Within Yang's memoir, we see his representations of the different modes of historical place-making in Luoyang as being open to people of diverse sociopolitical statuses, carrying distinctive powers, and entailing competition and even violence. In the larger context of Yang's contemporaneous environment, his memoir engaged in both the literary and hermeneutic place-making of Northern Wei Luoyang, a project that was in effect pitted against the architectural place-making of usurpers at court who abandoned Luoyang, created a new capital, and eventually founded their own dynasty. The analysis of the complex spatial politics in Northern Wei also contributes to the theorization of place-making by identifying its different modes and probing their dynamic relationships.

Reflections

Compared to the Western general and local theories discussed in the first section of this article, the examples of local Sinological theories cited above are more diverse and dispersed, linked loosely by their thematic foci. Many Sinological studies appear to have been developed independent of Western theories, with the exceptions of the more recent ones, which in particular engage with general theories by Lefebvre, Tuan, and others. Since these general theories are often seen as ushering in a "spatial turn" in the humanities and social sciences, it is worth asking whether a similar movement is happening in the field of medieval China studies. There are perhaps still too few studies to be called a trend, but it is my hope that more Sinologists will take up work along these lines. I argue that Western theories hold great promise in helping us develop new understandings of spatiality in medieval China. This does not mean, however, that we can simply graft Western theories to medieval Chinese materials. Rather, we need to carefully contemplate the relevance, terms, and implications of engagement so that we can be rooted in what we do while reaching out to participate in more extensive intellectual conversations and make greater impact beyond our field.

From the fact that spatiality is a fundamental human condition, it follows that general and local theories of spatiality outside our field are relevant. There are certainly scholars who believe in general theories as the ultimate authority, whereas those on the opposite end dismiss them as irrelevant to concrete case studies. To me, however, neither general nor local theories are superior, and they are complementary to and connected with each other. In terms of theoretical orientation, they represent "zoom-out" and "zoom-in" perspectives, respectively. The former tries to find and elucidate fundamental patterns of spatiality in a perceived universalistic context, whereas the latter reveals its complex manifestations in specific cultural-historical contexts. Nonetheless, general theories are not detached from concrete cases, as we have seen above in Lefebvre's discussion of Mediterranean vacation resorts and Soja's comparison of Greater Los Angeles and Amsterdam. Meanwhile, the concerns and conclusions of local theories have implicit or explicit connections with general theories. Although Xiong does not evoke any general theory on spatiality, his comprehensive reconstruction of Sui-Tang Chang'an sheds light on premodern people's spatial engagements, an issue part and parcel of general theories' concern with human relationships with space/place. While Basso provides a solid ethnographic study of how Western Apache people understand their local sites, he also discusses "sense of place" as a universal phenomenon and the relevant paradigm of analysis. Both the "zoom-in" and the "zoom-out" perspectives are indispensable and beneficial for our research. In the study of spatiality in medieval China, if zooming in means careful, grounded analysis of our source materials, zooming out entails engaging with theories outside the field. More specifically, general theories outside the field can facilitate a broader contextualization of Chinese cases, which calls attention to their underlying fundamental mechanisms, whereas local theories outside the field enable a comparative perspective, which often brings distinctive features into sharper relief.

Meanwhile, we also have to be mindful of the historical and cultural gaps between medieval Chinese materials and modern theories of spatiality. Michael Baxandall's concept of the "period eye," for instance, reminds us of the dangers of simple, mechanical imposition of modern values on premodern cases. In his words, the fifteenth-century Italian people, "painters and public, attended to visual experience in distinctively Quattrocento ways" and "the quality of this attention became a part of their pictorial style."[99] Likewise, spatiality is not only universal but also historically and culturally conditioned. How medieval Chinese people understood and engaged with space would be different from their counterparts in other societies of other times and places. As a goal of research, however, the time-and-place-specific period eye remains an ideal because we can never fully understand a historical phenomenon in its original contexts as people of the time understood it. This is in part due to the limitations of source materials and in part due to our own historical embeddedness. We are, after all, not persons of the past but the present. It is in this sense that our interpretations of medieval Chinese spatiality must remain theoretical, that is, what we think of how medieval Chinese people understood and engaged with space retains an abstract and hypothetical quality no matter how specific our research may strive to be.

Such a recognition does not nullify the meaning of our work but rather affirms its value and openness. Although we do not have direct, full access to the period eye, we have the advantage of hindsight afforded by historical distance, which enables new critical assessments. Our historical interpretations entail these two kinds of perspective—our sources' historical view and our own, contemporary view—simultaneously, which are not contradictory but complementary. The period eye demands full respect for historical materials and sets parameters for scholars, impeding the free imposition of later values, whereas hindsight makes it possible for them to uncover and critique what people of the time took for granted and to develop new perspectives. Moreover, what we bring to bear on historical materials have to do with how we understand our own conditions: what we see is determined by what we can see. Each generation of scholars can thus provide unique insights, making possible scholarly development and innovation. Even though surviving historical materials tend to be limited, the possibilities of revealing and exploring their rich complexities are infinite.

In this sense, our keenness to apprehend spatiality in medieval China can be enhanced by engagements with both general and local theories of spatiality outside the field, at levels such as specific arguments, methodologies, and ways of thinking. At the level of specific arguments, Western general theories of spatiality seem more transplantable than their local counterparts because of their claims of generality. Lefebvre's argument that space is socially produced, for instance, strikes a universal resonance—a main reason for the popularity of his work. By contrast, Basso's conclusion on the systematic formation of an interior moral landscape through oral storytelling among Western Apache people would be hard for Sinologists to borrow directly because there was not any parallel tradition in medieval China.

At the methodology level, both Western general and local theories can be very useful. Lefebvre's tripartite distinctions of space, for instance, have often been evoked, for they help to differentiate various types of space for more nuanced analysis. Although Basso's ethnographic methodology of interviewing people is not feasible for the study of medieval China, his skillful ways of teasing out how narratives represent Western Apache people's "sense of place" and instill socio-moral visions are inspiring to me. Such approaches can help us rethink the relationship between narrative and spatiality in the medieval Chinese context.

Behind the specific arguments and methodologies of Western theories in the "spatial turn" are new ways of thinking. As mentioned above, it is new understandings of the centrality of spatiality in human existence that characterize the turn. The local Sinological theories that developed independently from Western theories also focus on the issues of space/place and can be said to indicate Sinologists' recognitions of the centrality of spatiality as well. In these local theories, however, space/place is often treated as an end product of human action and conception. The Sui-Tang capital Chang'an as reconstructed by Xiong, for instance, is shown to be a massive, complex cityscape, whereas the poeticized place studied by literary scholars is what writers of the time imagined and represented, whether or not its connections to the physical world were strong. By contrast, a central idea underlying the "spatial turn" is that space/place is a medium or means for the human creation of reality. An argument like Lefebvre's that space is socially produced foregrounds the imbrication of space in all aspects of human society: as a medium of power, it is the very means through which social relations acquire their existence. Although Xiong's analysis of how Chang'an embodied imperial and geomantic ideals is certainly relevant, what Lefebvre points to is much broader and more far-reaching, that is, a reorientation of perspective by using spatiality as a critical lens for examining social phenomena.

While the new possibilities that Western theories of spatiality can offer are wide open, as Sinologists' recent engagements with them have suggested, I find a few directions particularly intriguing. First, Lefebvre's theory of space as "a means of production" and "a means of control" can be very useful for understanding the hierarchical nature of medieval China. In addition to the design and construction of the capital, how were the social relations of the time produced and reproduced in various forms of what I call "architectural place-making"? In what ways did non-architectural modes of spatial production, including literary ones, contribute to these processes? Second, Lefebvre's tripartite distinctions call attention to different manifestations of space, whereas Soja's formulation of Thirdspace as an innovative mode of critical thinking is thought-provoking in ways that move beyond spatial typologies. What terms and categories should we create or excavate to account for the complexities of space in the medieval Chinese context? How would Thirdspace as an antidote to conventional binary categories help us better understand spatiality in medieval China? Third, Soja's concept of the "trialectics of being," consisting of spatiality, historicality (or temporality), and sociality is modeled on Lefebvre's tripartite distinctions of space and expanded from Foucault's critique of the longstanding domination of historicism. What does it mean to treat space, history (or time), and society on an equal footing? How can we develop concrete hermeneutic approaches that would embody a more open and dynamic epistemological ideal? Fourth, class, gender, ethnicity, and other dimensions have been shown to be integral parts of how spatiality functions. How can we take them into consideration and expand our analytical paradigms to illuminate the complexities of spatiality in medieval China?

These questions indicate that the rich potentials of Western theories of spatiality for Sinological research lie less in their specific arguments or transposable methodologies that we may borrow but more in their new ways of thinking that can inspire our own innovations. Such innovations would be soundly built upon medieval Chinese source materials and anchored in the medieval Chinese context on the one hand and engage in productive dialogues with theories outside the field on the other. Western theories of spatiality, for instance, inevitably take for granted certain ways of seeing the world. Even general theories that aim for universal claims have their limitations, such as overabstraction. They can and should be expanded, modified, or challenged with the insights drawn from Sinological studies. Textuality, for example, is an area that has received little attention in general theories but is rich with theorizing potential. The diversity and complexities of medieval Chinese textual representations of spatiality, as we have seen in the examples above, offer opportunities for thinking about the distinctive roles of writing in the social production of space in civilizations with a writing tradition. In addition, since written texts constitute important sources for understanding spatiality in medieval China, they can also prompt us to reflect on the epistemic issues of textual mediation and historical studies of spatiality. To be clear, my point is not that developing general theories should be the ultimate goal of Sinologists but rather that our engagements with theories outside the field should be not a one-way but a two-way street.

Only through such productive engagements can we become part of the broader intellectual dialogues beyond our field. As abundant evidence demonstrates, multidisciplinary and interdisciplinary perspectives enable cross-fertilization of ideas. While active engagements with general and local theories outside the field will be good for the advancement of studies of medieval China, such engagements can make our research accessible to broader audiences and enhance the visibility of the field. Traditionally, medieval studies was only about the European Middle Ages. Although initiatives such as the "Global Middle Ages" are encouraging trends that try to expand the narrow confines of medieval studies,[100] we can also be more proactive on our end to change the reality of Sinology's invisibility within the academy's topography and to push through the barriers of Western-centrism. By reaching out to broader audiences, our work can also have greater relevance beyond academia, as a more sophisticated understanding of China's history and culture can serve as a crucial antidote to stereotyping.

    MANLING LUO
Indiana University
luom@iu.edu

Acknowledgments

I would like to thank Heather Blair, Sarah Van der Laan, Michelle Moyd, and Anya Peterson Royce for reading through different versions of this essay. Participants at the *Journal of Chinese Literature and Culture* Symposium held in July 2021 gave me useful suggestions, and the insightful comments from the two anonymous reviewers were particularly helpful. I also benefited from James M. Hargett's and Robert E. Hegel's careful reading of the final version.

Notes

1. For the entry on "theory" in the *Oxford English Dictionary*, accessed August 1, 2021, see https://www-oed-com/view/Entry/200431?redirectedFrom=theory#eid.
2. "Theory," *Oxford English Dictionary*, accessed August 1, 2021, https://www-oed-com/view /Entry/200431?redirectedFrom=theory#eid.
3. Cresswell, *Place*, 7, 8.
4. Tuan, *Space and Place*, 6.
5. Ibid., 149.
6. Cresswell, *Place*, 11.
7. Heidegger, "Building Dwelling Thinking," 160.
8. Bachelard, *Poetics of Space*, 8.
9. Ibid., 15–16.
10. Malpas, *Place and Experience*, 35–36.
11. Seamon, "Body-Subject, Time-Space Routines, and Place-Ballets."
12. de Certeau, *Practice of Everyday Life*, 91–110.
13. Foucault, "Questions on Geography," 77.
14. Foucault, *Discipline and Punish*, 206.
15. Foucault, "Of Other Spaces," 23.
16. Ibid., 22.
17. Ibid., 24.
18. Ibid., 24–27.
19. Lefebvre, *Production of Space*, 33.
20. Ibid., 39–41.
21. Ibid., 26.
22. Ibid., 348–49.
23. Ibid., 129.
24. Ibid., 281.
25. Ibid., 422.
26. Soja, *Thirdspace*, 8.
27. Ibid., 70–71.
28. Ibid., 72.
29. Ibid., 64–69, 73–74.
30. Ibid., 62.
31. Ibid., 60.
32. Ibid., 61.
33. Ibid., 81–82.
34. Ibid., 72.
35. Lefebvre, *Production of Space*, 58–59.
36. Soja, *Thirdspace*, 186–320.
37. Hooper, "'Split at the Roots,'" 50.
38. Hayden, *Grand Domestic Revolution*, 5.
39. hooks, *Feminist Theory*, xvi.
40. hooks, *Yearning*, 145.
41. Ibid., 149.
42. Said, *Orientalism*, 2–3.
43. Ibid., 325.

44.   Ibid., 328.
45.   Basso, *Wisdom Sits in Places*, 146.
46.   Ibid., 107.
47.   Ibid., 148.
48.   Huber, *Cult of Pure Crystal Mountain*, 8.
49.   For example, see Sadakata, *Buddhist Cosmology*; Prip-Møller, *Chinese Buddhist Monasteries*.
50.   Boulton, "Early Chinese Buddhist Travel Records as a Literary Genre."
51.   Z. Wang, *Daoism Excavated*; Schafer, *Pacing the Void*; Bokemkamp, *Ancestors and Anxiety*; Kohn, *Monastic Life in Medieval Daoism*.
52.   Campany, *Strange Writing*.
53.   Hargett, "Song Dynasty Local Gazetteers and Their Place in the History of *Difangzhi* Writing."
54.   For a few examples, see E. Y. Wang, *Shaping the Lotus Sutra*; Eckfeld, *Imperial Tombs in Tang China*; Steinhardt, *Chinese Architecture*.
55.   Steinhardt, *Chinese Imperial City Planning*, 93–96, 101–21.
56.   Heng, *Cities of Aristocrats and Bureaucrats*.
57.   Xiong, *Sui-Tang Chang'an*.
58.   One of the featured articles is Victor Cunrui Xiong's study of Luoyang, the so-called Eastern Capital of the Tang. I do not discuss it here because he adopts an approach similar to that of his monograph on Sui-Tang Chang'an. See Xiong, "*Miscellaneous Record of the Reign of the Great Enterprise* and Sui Luoyang," 6–26.
59.   Chen, "On Sui and Tang Cities," 2.
60.   Chen, "Social Networks, Court Factions, Ghosts, and Killer Snakes," 61.
61.   Ditter, "Conceptions of Urban Space in Duan Chengshi's 'Record of Monasteries and Stupas,'" 81–82.
62.   Ibid., 82.
63.   Feng, "Negotiating Vertical Space."
64.   Feng, *City of Marvel and Transformation*, 9–11.
65.   Ibid., 1.
66.   There are many studies of landscape poetry. For origins of the genre, see Holzman, *Landscape Appreciation in Ancient and Early Medieval China*.
67.   Kwong, "Rural World of Chinese 'Farmstead Poetry' (*Tianyuan Shi*)."
68.   For a survey of travel writing from the Six Dynasties through the Tang, see Hargett, *Jade Mountains and Cinnabar Pools*, 18–89.
69.   For a discussion of early works that can be considered fountainheads of the subgenre, see Chan, "Jade Flower and the Motif of Mystic Excursion in Early Religious Daoist Poetry."
70.   See Wang and Williams, *Southern Identity and Southern Estrangement in Medieval Chinese Poetry*.
71.   Swartz, "There's No Place Like Home," 29.
72.   Ibid., 36.
73.   Huang, "Excursion, Estates, and the Kingly Gaze."
74.   Owen, "Wit and the Private Life."
75.   Yang, *Metamorphosis of the Private Sphere*.
76.   Kroll, "Lexical Landscapes and Textual Mountains in the High T'ang," 65.
77.   Ibid., 88–90.

78.   Owen, "Place," 417.
79.   Ibid., 434, 453.
80.   Varsano, "Do You See What I See?," 34.
81.   Ibid., 36.
82.   A. Wang, *Spatial Imaginaries in Mid-Tang China*, 11–12.
83.   Ibid., 8–10.
84.   For example, Kroll, "Verses from on High."
85.   Harrist, *Landscape of Words*, 18.
86.   Schafer, *Mao Shan in T'ang Times*.
87.   Verellen, "Beyond Within."
88.   In fact, studies of Buddhist mountains often focus on post-Tang periods. For example, Hargett, *Stairway to Heaven*.
89.   Birnbaum, "Secret Halls of the Mountain Lords."
90.   Faure, "Relics and Flesh Bodies."
91.   Robson, *Power of Place*, 6.
92.   Ibid., 7–8.
93.   Chittick, "Development of Local Writing in Early Medieval China," 36–37.
94.   Ibid., 52.
95.   Ibid., 69.
96.   Lewis and Wigen, *Myth of Continents*, ix.
97.   Felt, *Structures of the Earth*, 4.
98.   Luo, "Politics of Place-Making," 48.
99.   Baxandall, *Painting and Experience in Fifteenth-Century Italy*, 27.
100. See the program's website at http://globalmiddleages.org.

References

Bachelard, Gaston. *The Poetics of Space*. New York: Orion, 1964.

Basso, Keith H. *Wisdom Sits in Places: Landscape and Language among the Western Apache*. Albuquerque: University of New Mexico Press, 1996.

Baxandall, Michael. *Painting and Experience in Fifteenth-Century Italy: A Primer in the Social History of Pictorial Style*. Oxford: Oxford University Press, 1974.

Birnbaum, Raoul. "Secret Halls of the Mountain Lords: The Caves of Wu-t'ai shan." *Cahiers d'Extrême Asie* 5 (1989): 115–40.

Bokemkamp, Stephen R. *Ancestors and Anxiety: Daoism and the Birth of Rebirth in China*. Berkeley: University of California Press, 2007.

Boulton, Nancy E. "Early Chinese Buddhist Travel Records as a Literary Genre." PhD diss., Georgetown University, 1982.

Campany, Robert Ford. *Strange Writing: Anomaly Accounts in Early Medieval China*. Albany: State University of New York Press, 1996.

Chan, Timothy Wai-Keung. "Jade Flower and the Motif of Mystic Excursion in Early Religious Daoist Poetry." In *Interpretation and Literature in Early Medieval China*, edited by Alan K. L. Chan and Yuet-Keung Lo, 165–88. Albany: SUNY Press, 2010.

Chen, Jack W. "On Sui and Tang Cities: An Introduction." *Tang Studies* 29 (2011): 2–5.

———. "Social Networks, Court Factions, Ghosts, and Killer Snakes: Reading Anyi Ward." *Tang Studies* 29 (2011): 45–61.

Chittick, Andrew. "The Development of Local Writing in Early Medieval China." *Early Medieval China* 9 (2003): 35–70.

Cresswell, Tim. *Place: A Short Introduction*. Oxford: Blackwell, 2004.

de Certeau, Michel. *The Practice of Everyday Life*. Translated by Steven Rendall. Berkeley and Los Angeles: University of California Press, 1985.

Ditter, Alexei. "Conceptions of Urban Space in Duan Chengshi's 'Record of Monasteries and Stupas.'" *Tang Studies* 29 (2011): 62–83.

Eckfeld, Tonia. *Imperial Tombs in Tang China, 618–907: The Politics of Paradise*. London: Routledge Curzon, 2005.

Faure, Bernard. "Relics and Flesh Bodies: The Creation of Ch'an Pilgrimage Sites." In *Pilgrims and Sacred Sites in China*, edited by Susan Naquin and Chün-fang Yü, 150–89. Berkeley: University of California Press, 1992.

Felt, D. Jonathan. *Structures of the Earth: Metageographies of Early Medieval China*. Cambridge, MA: Harvard University Asia Center, 2021.

Feng, Linda Rui. *City of Marvel and Transformation: Chang'an and Narratives of Experience in Tang Dynasty China*. Honolulu: University of Hawaii Press, 2015.

———. "Negotiating Vertical Space: Walls, Vistas, and the Topographical Imagination." *Tang Studies* 29 (2011): 27–44.

Foucault, Michel. *Discipline and Punish: The Birth of the Prison*. Translated by Alan Sheridan. New York: Vintage Books, 1977.

———. "Of Other Spaces." Translated by Jay Miskowiec. *Diacritics* 16, no. 1 (1986): 22–27.

———. "Questions on Geography." In *Power/Knowledge: Selected Interviews and Other Writings*, edited and translated by Colin Gordon, 63–77. New York: Pantheon Books, 1980.

Global Middle Ages. http://globalmiddleages.org (accessed August 1, 2021).

Hargett, James M. *Jade Mountains and Cinnabar Pools: The History of Travel Literature in Imperial China*. Seattle: University of Washington Press, 2018.

———. "Song Dynasty Local Gazetteers and Their Place in the History of *Difangzhi* Writing." *Harvard Journal of Asiatic Studies* 56, no. 2 (1996): 405–12.

———. *Stairway to Heaven: A Journey to the Summit of Mount Emei*. Albany: SUNY Press, 2006.

Harrist, Robert E., Jr., *The Landscape of Words: Stone Inscriptions from Early and Medieval China*. Seattle: University of Washington Press, 2008.

Hayden, Dolores. *The Grand Domestic Revolution: A History of Feminist Designs for American Homes, Neighborhoods, and Cities*. Cambridge, MA: MIT Press, 1981.

Heidegger, Martin. "Building Dwelling Thinking." In *Poetry, Language, Thought*, translated by Albert Hofstadter, 145–61. New York: Harper and Row, 1971.

Heng, Chye Kiang. *Cities of Aristocrats and Bureaucrats: The Development of Medieval Chinese Cityscapes*. Honolulu: University of Hawaii Press, 1999.

Holzman, Donald. *Landscape Appreciation in Ancient and Early Medieval China: The Birth of Landscape Poetry*. Hsin-chu: National Tsing Hua University, 1996.

hooks, bell. *Feminist Theory: From Margin to Center*. 2nd edition. Cambridge, MA: South End, 2000.

———. *Yearning: Race, Gender, and Cultural Politics*. Boston: South End, 1990.

Hooper, Barbara. "'Split at the Roots': A Critique of the Philosophical and Political Sources of Modern Planning Doctrine." *Frontiers: A Journal of Women Studies* 13, no. 1 (1992): 45–80.

Huang, Harrison. "Excursion, Estates, and the Kingly Gaze: The Landscape Poetry of Xie Lingyun." PhD diss., University of California, Berkeley, 2010.

Huber, Toni. *The Cult of Pure Crystal Mountain: Popular Pilgrimage and Visionary Landscape in Southeast Tibet*. Oxford: Oxford University Press, 1999.

Kohn, Livia. *Monastic Life in Medieval Daoism: A Cross-Cultural Perspective*. Honolulu: University of Hawaii Press, 2003.

Kroll, Paul W. "Lexical Landscapes and Textual Mountains in the High T'ang." *T'oung Pao: International Journal of Chinese Studies* 84, no. 1 (1998): 62–101.

———. "Verses from on High: The Ascent of T'ai Shan." *T'oung-Pao* 69 (1983): 223–60.

Kwong, Charles. "The Rural World of Chinese 'Farmstead Poetry' (*Tianyuan Shi*): How Far Is It Pastoral?" *Chinese Literature: Essays, Articles, Reviews* 15 (1993): 57–84.

Lefebvre, Henri. *The Production of Space*. Translated by Donald Nicholson-Smith. Oxford: Blackwell, 1991.

Lewis, Martin W., and Kären E. Wigen. *The Myth of Continents: A Critique of Metageography*. Berkeley: University of California Press, 1997.

Luo, Manling. "The Politics of Place-Making in the *Records of Buddhist Monasteries in Luoyang*." *T'oung Pao* 105 (2019): 43–75.

Malpas, J. E. *Place and Experience: A Philosophical Topography*. Cambridge: Cambridge University Press, 1999.

Owen, Stephen. "Place: Meditation on the Past at Chin-ling." *Harvard Journal of Asiatic Studies* 50, no. 2 (1990): 417–57.

———. "Wit and the Private Life." In *The End of the Chinese 'Middle Ages,'* 83–106. Stanford: Stanford University Press, 1996.

Prip-Møller, J. *Chinese Buddhist Monasteries: Their Plan and Its Function as a Setting for Buddhist Monastic Life*. Hong Kong: Hong Kong University Press, 1982.

Robson, James. *Power of Place: The Religious Landscape of the Southern Sacred Peak (Nanyue 南嶽) in Medieval China*. Cambridge, MA: Harvard University Asia Center, 2009.

Sadakata, Akira. *Buddhist Cosmology: Philosophy and Origins*. Translated by Gaynor Sekimori. Tokyo: Kōsei, 1997.

Said, Edward W. *Orientalism*. 25th anniversary ed. New York: Vintage Books, 1994.

Schafer, Edward H. *Mao Shan in T'ang Times*. 2nd ed. Boulder: Society for the Study of Chinese Religions, 1989.

———. *Pacing the Void: T'ang Approaches to the Stars*. Berkeley: University of California Press, 1977.

Seamon, David. "Body-Subject, Time-Space Routines, and Place-Ballets." In *The Human Experience of Space and Place*, edited by Anne Buttimer and David Seamon, 148–65. London: Croom Helm, 1980.

Soja, Edward W. *Thirdspace: Journeys to Los Angeles and Other Real-and-Imagined Places*. Cambridge, MA: Blackwell, 1996.

Steinhardt, Nancy Shatzman. *Chinese Architecture: A History*. Princeton: Princeton University Press, 2019.

———. *Chinese Imperial City Planning*. Honolulu: University of Hawaii Press, 1990.

Swartz, Wendy. "There's No Place Like Home: Xie Lingyun's Representation of His Estate in 'Rhapsody on Dwelling in the Mountains.'" *Early Medieval China* 21 (2015): 21–37.

Tuan, Yi-Fu. *Space and Place: The Perspective of Experience*. Minneapolis: University of Minnesota Press, 1977.

Varsano, Paula. "Do You See What I See? Visuality and the Formation of the Chinese Landscape." *Chinese Literature: Essays, Articles, Reviews* 35 (2013): 31–53.

Verellen, Franciscus. "The Beyond Within: Grotto-Heavens (*Dongtian* 洞天) in Taoist Ritual and Cosmology." *Cahiers d'Extrême-Asie* 8 (1995): 265–90.

Wang, Ao. *Spatial Imaginaries in Mid-Tang China: Geography, Cartography, and Literature.* Amherst: Cambria, 2018.

Wang, Eugene Y. *Shaping the Lotus Sutra: Buddhist Visual Culture in Medieval China.* Seattle: University of Washington Press, 2005.

Wang, Ping, and Nicholas Morrow Williams, eds. *Southern Identity and Southern Estrangement in Medieval Chinese Poetry.* Hong Kong: Hong Kong University Press, 2015.

Wang, Zhongjiang. *Daoism Excavated: Cosmos and Humanity in Early Manuscripts.* Translated by Livia Kohn. St. Petersburg, FL: Three Pines, 2015.

Xiong, Victor Cunrui. "The *Miscellaneous Record of the Reign of the Great Enterprise* and Sui Luoyang." *Tang Studies* 29 (2011): 6–26.

———. *Sui-Tang Chang'an: A Study in the Urban History of Medieval China.* Ann Arbor: Center for Chinese Studies, University of Michigan, 2000.

Yang, Xiaoshan. *Metamorphosis of the Private Sphere: Gardens and Objects in Tang-Song Poetry.* Cambridge, MA: Harvard University Asia Center, 2003.

Whither Theatricality? Toward Traditional Chinese Drama and Theater (*Xiqu* 戲曲) as World Theater

PATRICIA SIEBER

Abstract The essay provides a brief review of how certain approaches to theatricality evolved in response to particular theatrical archives or repertoires in non-Chinese contexts. It then considers a number of recent studies of Chinese drama and theater in light of the following issues: the nature of theatrical language, the emergence and uses of fictionality, and the reconstruction of performance aesthetics. In focusing on these particular areas, the essay seeks to show how such research can contribute toward countering entrenched characterizations of *xiqu* as "non-drama," "spectacle," or "pure heritage." The final section of the article proposes some future avenues of inquiry in order to deepen the dialogue between Sinology and theater studies while providing tools for sustaining the practice of *xiqu* and fostering broader appreciation of traditional Chinese theater in Anglophone, Chinese-speaking, and other contexts.

Keywords theatricality, traditional Chinese theater, theatrical language, fictionality, performance aesthetics

Introduction

In the 1960s, Peter Brook famously offered a minimalist definition of theater in order to home in on what he thought defined a theatrical experience: "I can take any empty space and call it a bare stage. A man walks across this empty space while someone else is watching him, and this all that is needed for an act of theatre to be engaged."[1] With the hindsight of over half a century, Brook's attempt to strip the theatrical act down to its base essentials can be seen to be clearly marked by certain spatial, ocular, and gendered assumptions, and as

The Journal of Chinese Literature and Culture · 9:1 · April 2022
DOI 10.1215/23290048-9681228 · © 2022 by Duke University Press

such, far from offering a universal definition, it instead points to the pitfalls of broad generalizations. At the same time, theater scholars and practitioners hunger for ways to make a subject intelligible, especially if they feel that it has been ignored, sidelined, misunderstood, or maligned. Traditional Chinese theater (*xiqu* 戲曲, song-drama or musical drama) is one such topic where the need to define it succinctly may be accompanied by a perhaps even greater urgency to position it as an object of more and more in-depth investigations in order to make it part of a broader scholarly conversation and sustain its practice and appreciation around the world.

Historically, drama and theater have been at the forefront of popularizing "China" in the West. The acculturation often bypassed the categories of "theater" and "theatricality" altogether in favor of assimilating Chinese theater to either the category of "drama" and attendant terms such as "tragedy" and "comedy"[2] or to the category of "opera" and its various musical instantiations (Peking Opera, Cantonese Opera, Yue Opera, Kun Opera, etc.).[3] Hence, one of the challenges before us is how to frame a performative form that showcases all manner of verbal arts but gives equal due to singing, choreographed dance, and other kinesthetic tools to realize the performative potential of playtexts. In its non-conformity with Western categories of performance genres (theater, opera, dance, musical theater), traditional Chinese theater—or what we now call *xiqu*[4]—threatens to be miscategorized, shortchanged, or ignored. We can bemoan these terminological quandaries; alternatively, we can delineate how Sinologists from a variety of disciplines have used Chinese theater as a heuristic device to unpack entrenched binaries such as opera versus theater, China versus West, antiquity versus modernity, thereby laying a foundation to rethink the history of theatricality more broadly.

In what follows, I will give a brief overview of some influential approaches to theatricality in other world theaters with a view toward engendering a dialogue that does not relegate Chinese theater to the status of a footnote. Second, I will provide a sampling of how contemporary Anglophone China scholars have approached notions of *xiqu* theatricality in innovative ways.[5] I will showcase work that seeks to elucidate the dynamic interplay between textual archive and performative repertoire.[6] Scholarly explorations of theatrical language, theatrical representation, and performance characteristics have the potential to unsettle cultural stereotypes that have coalesced around traditional Chinese musical theater in Western contexts on the one hand and to broaden comparative discussions of drama and theatricality on the other. Finally, I will sketch out some possible future avenues of inquiry that could contribute to a deprovincialized history of theatricality and potentially reach new audiences in Anglophone, Sinophone, and other contexts.

Toward a Multidisciplinary History of Theatricality

As theater scholars have noted, the notion of theatricality is not a robustly developed category of analysis. For one, in everyday language, the meanings of the term shade from neutral description to pejorative characterization.[7] Moreover, within the field of theater studies, theatricality is similarly beset by conflicting judgements on its desirability in actual theatrical contexts and on its heuristic value.[8] Part of the challenge rests in defining whether theatricality is primarily a function of the theater or whether it is independent of theatrical activities. Even if the discussion is limited to theater itself, scholars largely agree that theater is a type of social communication,[9] but they are not necessarily in agreement on what theater's primary medium is. Is it verbal communication? Is it bodily movement? Is it musical expression? In an attempt to wrestle with the typically multisensory nature of theatrical communication, scholars have mobilized the tools of social anthropology, history, and literary studies among others to come to grips with the complexity of the phenomenon of theater. In doing so, they have developed different approaches to theatricality that are often tied to the particular archive and/or repertoire that they have chosen to investigate.

One group of theater scholars has chosen to make use of the concepts of social anthropologists. Such a convergence between theater studies and anthropology was perhaps most famously elaborated by Victor Turner who, in an attempt to present an "anthropology of performance," noted that "the basic stuff of social life is performance" because "human beings" as a "species" are given to "dramatic modes of communication."[10] In keeping with this interest in defining the embedded and pervasive nature of "dramatic communication," theater scholar Joachim Fiebach argues that theater's primary specificity is "the ostentatious display of audiovisual movements" to denote "symbolic action."[11] In other words, in this view, the body takes precedence over other expressive means such as language, setting, or culturally specific definitions of the theatrical. Symbolic action can relate to otherwise invisible realities (belief systems, discourse, ideologies) and how it structures and potentially subverts social power (governance, social life, cultural forms). On the one hand, such a focus on embodiment seeks to elide an Aristotelian and potentially ethnocentric understanding of a text-centered form of theatricality and as such is suitable for non-Western contexts and societies based on orality; on the other hand, such a movement-oriented definition makes it hard to differentiate between theater and other kinds of kinetic arts such as dance, sports, and the like. In other words, since symbolic action encompasses a wide variety of activities, it may difficult to isolate a generic and fairly abstract idea of "performance" and the "dramatic" from specific instantiations of the "theatrical."

In another approach to theatricality, history becomes the preferred sister discipline with which to examine theatrical practices. This approach has been most influentially advanced by Shakespeare scholars such as Stephen Greenblatt, Peter Stallybrass, Jean Howard, and others, who pioneered the "New Historicism." Combining the study of print culture and a focus on the history of reading, such scholarship investigated playscripts and theatrical practices as they related to issues of power, ideology, and social relations in an updated take on the notion that "all the world is a stage" (*theatrum mundi*). Despite New Historicism becoming the dominant approach within early modern English drama studies, some scholars have cautioned against what they see as the potential blind spots of such an all-encompassing emphasis on state-society relations. In Thomas Postlewait's view, if all analysis of early modern English culture conforms to a "dramatistic paradigm of social life" characterized by "total theatricality," then the distinction between performance within the theater and the epitheatrical culture of self-fashioning threatens to be elided.[12] As Postlewait polemically puts it: "But if the idea of theatricality serves as the grand theory of everything, what can the concept tell us specifically about anything?"[13] As a suggestion for ways to go beyond this potential impasse, Henry S. Turner noted that perhaps a broadly conceived and sophisticated attention to "form" could address a fundamental question that had fallen out of favor in New Historicist approaches, namely, "what conventions allowed the theater to function as a specific kind of representation distinct from prose narrative, or poetry, or architecture or painting, even as it often drew on the imaginative and formal resources of these other modes?"[14]

Indeed, in a third approach to theatricality, the formal aspects of the artistic creation, transmission, and reception of playscripts are at the heart of scholarly inquiry into theatricality. In this view, theater is intimately related to the emergence of and cross-borrowing between well-defined but permeable and evolving literary genres. The study of ancient Greek and Roman tragedies and comedies has excelled in this area, partly because unlike the oral traditions examined by anthropologists (absence of playscripts) and the early modern European theater (continuity of language between then and now), these early classical traditions call for detailed linguistic examinations in order to become intelligible to modern readers. Thus in the copious and multilingual body of classicist scholarship on Greek comedy, for example, a subset of studies pays meticulous attention to question of dialect, register, pragmatic function, and modes of speech,[15] types of laughter embedded in texts,[16] and dramatic technique in order to explore to what extent "Athenian comedy was always metatheatrical, and found new ways of demonstrating its debts and awareness of other theatrical genres and the process of the theatre itself."[17] Insofar as Greek comedy is typically periodized as Old, Middle, and New Comedy, such studies also seek to tie questions of linguistic theatricality to changing concerns among playwrights and audiences alike,[18] thus showing that attention to form need not be blind to social contexts.

In a fourth approach, formal, temporary, and social consideration blend into a semiotic conception of theater as what theater scholar Marvin Carlson has most influentially termed a "memory machine." In his celebrated book, *The Haunted Stage*,[19] Carlson argued that theater is, at heart, not the sort of random encounter invoked in the initial quote by Peter Brook, but rather a kind of negotiated and evolving understanding between (professional) actors and a (paying) theatergoing audience centered around certain performance aesthetics. In his telling, the regularity and repetitive nature of the exchange between certain actors and regulars accounts for the power of the theater. In other words, it is not the one-time or one-off performance that theater scholars need to bring into focus but rather the unwritten contract between what actors offer and what audiences appreciate. Carlson terms this effect of shared memories of prior performances "ghosting." Specifically, as plays are recycled and adapted over and over as a part of an evolving repertoire, regulars would compare one performance of a given play against another one that they might have watched there or elsewhere. Similarly, as actors develop reputations and specialize in certain styles or parts, a particular performance by that actor might evoke overtones of a previous performance of that or another play. Far from simply disappearing into the role, the social body of the actor may very well open up additional layers of meaning. In addition, in theater, though in theory it could take place anywhere, typically, mature theatrical traditions demarcate certain sites as "theatrical space" either because of repeated use of the same space or because of reliance on conventionalized physical markers to transform an ordinary space into a "theatrical space." Thus, a given performance of a play by a certain actor could also trigger memories of prior performances in that same venue. Carlson's calibrated approach allows scholars to keep theater's dual identity as a collective and individual event in focus while inviting the investigation of cultural specificity in audience-performer relations.

Such methodological pluralism around approaches to "theatricality" in theater studies offers some advantages for the analysis of theatrical traditions that do not readily map onto Western or non-Western analogues. Social anthropology may have hogged the theoretical spotlight in the study of non-Western theaters, the new historicism may be dominant for early modern Anglophone drama, and literary approaches are richly represented in the study of ancient Greek theater. However, the remaining sources do not require us to favor one approach over another, given that Chinese theatrical history is long (at least dating back to the Song dynasty); features orally transmitted components of theater (e.g., the pedagogy of acting); abounds in rich and as of yet under-studied textual and visual documentation in manuscript, print, pictorial, and decorative media; has a continuously evolving and living performance tradition (dating back to the sixteenth century); and was represented at all levels of society in conjunction with many other forms of cultural display. We need not be compelled to explore Chinese theater from the vantage point of a ready-made theory to match a particular theatrical archive. On the contrary, we can look upon the complexity of the extant source materials and their ongoing trans-mission as an opportunity to "make historical distinctions."[20] As Fiebach notes, "an insightful and meaningful history of theater inevitably would have to be written as a specifically cultural history."[21] Precisely because the configuration of the theatrical archive in China is congruous neither with an oral non-Western society nor with a towering author like Shakespeare, neither with an Aristotelian schemata of tragedy and comedy nor with a clearly delineated genre distinction (opera vs. theater vs. dance), the writing of such a history also offers opportu-nities for new theories of the theater. Detailed studies can contribute to the writing of a new, genuinely global theater history that goes beyond the inclusion of China-specific encyclopedia entries,[22] tokenistic incorporation of the same handful of plays,[23] or grossly underresearched claims in current textbook his-tories of world theater.[24]

In what follows, I present recent work on a number of issues related to theatricality. Not all studies under review here necessarily foreground their approach to the theatrical in very explicit terms nor do they necessarily sub-scribe to a uniform understanding of theatricality. However, what they do share is a concern with "historical distinctions." In grouping these discussions around questions of theatrical language, representation, and performance characteris-tics, the essay seeks to highlight research that challenges orientalist and self-orientalizing legacies of previous public and academic circulations of Chinese theater.

The Varied Theatricality of Dramatic Language

When French Sinologist Stanislas Julien (1797–1873) translated *Huilan ji* 灰闌記 (The Chalk Circle) in its entirety in 1832, he noted that the arias were particularly hard to fathom on account of the plethora of conventionalized poetic expressions. Undaunted and ever keen on besting his missionary pre-decessors, Julien nevertheless tried his best to address the linguistic complexity of the text in absence of relevant lexicographic tools.[25] However, when we examine the popular reception of Chinese theater from the nineteenth century onward, European and American critics typically neglected the linguistic aspect of drama in favor of other elements of performances—dance, music, costumes, singing, acrobatics, among others. To be sure, such audiences had to contend with the language barrier, but what is perhaps most striking is the near-total absence of curiosity regarding the verbal building blocks of the theatrical presentations they encountered.[26] Hence, recent research that attends to the theatricality of the language of Chinese plays has the potential to dislodge the entrenched notion that Chinese theater is synonymous with spectacle.

Always alive to the imbrication of language registers, phrasing, and mood, Chinese theater critics from the Yuan dynasty onward commented on the peculiar texture of dramatic language. While some critics found drama too vulgar to count it among *wenzhang* 文章 (belles lettres) properly speaking,[27] others were entranced by drama's ability to bring very different modes of Chinese language into meaningful proximity with one another. The juxtaposition of high and low, Literary Sinitic and dialect, poetic arias and approximations of spoken registers among other binaries created many opportunities for a highly theatrical approach to language usage—that is, a self-conscious exploitation of the disparities of linguistic forms and their paralinguistic associations that were, in the words of Yuan song and drama critic-cum-anthologist Zhou Deqing 周德清 (1277–1365), designed to "startle" audiences.[28] Sinological work on Chinese plays has used different approaches to tease out the ways that playwrights and actors alike sought to make good on the demand for novelty. Equally and importantly, however, as the discussion below illustrates, what Chinese theater practitioners hoped to accomplish with dramatic language also substantially varied over time. In that regard, studies on specific plays stand to enrich our understanding of how Chinese theater pushed the development of new literary forms in China while also expanding our awareness of the possibilities inherent in theatrical modes of speech in comparative contexts.

In her research on Northern *zaju* 雜劇 (lit. "varied" or "wide ranging" plays), Patricia Sieber argues that the amalgamation of different rhetorical stances to create complex protagonists given to a wide range of emotional and moral stances constituted one of the signature achievements of early *zaju* theater.[29] In analyzing the fourteenth-century rendition of *Baiyueting* 拜月亭 (The Pavilion for Praying to the Moon, mid-fourteenth century), Sieber lists the following rhetorical modalities used by the main female lead: the language of filial tenderness, the language of filial counsel, the language of female decorum, the language of wifely care and worry, impassioned invective against the father, the language of wifely fidelity, the language of social satire, the poetic language of female longing, the invocation of Heaven, among others. Previously, these modes had appeared in isolation from one another in different written genres. In bringing them together in the space of four brief acts to characterize the main lead's aspirations, emotions, and situational adjustments, *Baiyueting* creates new complexity for the characterization of protagonists from all walks of life. Thus, far from being an incidental aspect of the play itself, linguistic variety created dynamic depth for the main lead, whoever that role happened to represent. In its capacity to give a nuanced voice to previously undervoiced characters such as maids, courtesans, widows, and young women in distress, *zaju* theater redrew the boundaries of public discourse.[30]

In a related vein, Regina S. Llamas's work on *nanxi* 南戲 (early Southern drama) has drawn attention to the linguistic facets of the theatrical. As she notes with regard to the earliest extant Southern play, *Zhang Xie zhuangyuan* 張協狀元 (Top Graduate Zhang Xie, 1408) "the verbal repertoire makes use of the ambiguity of language, puns, homophones, quips on the formation of characters, and the formality of rhyme, riddles, onomatopoeia, and incongruity, both in the form of absurd remarks and discordant replies."[31] Her discussion also highlights the metatheatrical aspect of "self-referential remarks to role-acting and costume."[32] In her view, "metatheater is employed throughout the play both as humor—perhaps intended as a parody of the object under consideration—and also to underscore the fictional nature of the theater."[33] For example, when the female lead Poorlass seeks out her newly graduated husband, the gatekeeper says, "Oh, it's just a fake female" in allusion to the fact that men could play female protagonists.[34] Furthermore, metatheatrical aspects also were sedimented in the dramatic structure of individual scenes. Specifically, the *mo* role interacts with the comic roles of the *jing* 淨 (comic) and the *chou* 丑 (clown), but rather than offering a punchline or an overarching assessment, he "conducts a contiguous commentary, not in dialogue with the comic, but directed away, to the audience or reader, making reference to commonly known stories . . . or restating the obvious."[35] As Llamas notes, such a role maintains a delicate balance between poking fun at human passions and excesses while also pointing to the importance of considered judgment and self-control. Thus in Llamas's telling, attention to language demonstrates that a traditional Chinese play can neither be reduced to a didactic exposé nor to gross farce as modern critics have charged but rather should be understood as a dynamic construct that makes use of a plurality of voices within a play to make the audience laugh and reflect at the same time. Insofar as the longstanding preoccupation with tragedy has overshadowed the recognition of the comic genius of Chinese drama, such a nuanced consideration of Chinese humor challenges longstanding clichés.[36]

In her analysis of the seminal piece of the *chuanqi* 傳奇 (mature Southern drama) tradition, Tang Xianzu's 湯顯祖 (1550–1616) *Mudanting* 牡丹亭 (Peony Pavilion, 1598), Sophie Volpp explores how the use of specific linguistic registers and literary allusions is designed to intervene in the literary and philosophical debates of the late Ming period (1550–1644). Specifically, she argues that the language usage by minor characters serves as a foil to romantic heroine Du Liniang 杜麗娘's richly textured, imaginative use of what has been variously called "vernacular," "plain Chinese," or "mixed-register" writing.[37] For example, the heroine's tutor, Chen Zuiliang 陳最良, not only embodies the stock figure of a pedant, but his mindless use of citations from the classic amounts to a "theatrical and thus inauthentic" speech mode that indexes how men of learning had instrumentalized the words of the ancients for the sake of careerism. In Volpp's view, insofar as Tang targets both antiquarian and nouveau riche pretensions to Confucian mastery, the exposé of such blind mouthing of classical platitudes amounts to an "anti-theatricalist" stance. At the same time, as Volpp points out, Tang Xianzu was at pains to implode the boundaries between different literary modes as evidenced by the famous persiflage of Sister Stone, a Daoist nun, who remained unmarried on account of her impenetrable "stone hymen." In Sister Stone's retelling of her sexual history in the form of one of the most well-known childhood primers, *Qianzi jing* 千字經 (The Thousand Character Classic), the lofty and the obscene shade seamlessly into one another. In such humorous passages, "the puns . . . juxtapose two parallel linguistic worlds, a refined register and a vulgar register that mirrors and mocks it, by playing on the different significances of an ideograph in classical and vernacular Chinese."[38] Thus, in contrast to other reformist writers of the time, Tang does not locate authenticity in the vernacular register per se but rather conceives of the vernacular as a parody of classical language practices.[39]

Similarly, in her discussion of critic and playwright Wang Jide's 王驥德 (d. 1623) lesser-known *zaju Nan wanghou* 男王后 (The Male Queen, before 1623), Volpp shows that verbal skills and rhetorical ingenuity rather than simple visual illusion are central to the protagonist"s cross-gender performance.[40] Meanwhile, Kong Shangren's 孔尚任 (1648–1718) *Taohuashan* 桃花扇 (Peach Blossom Fan, 1699) revisited the distinction between elite and vernacular registers in new ways. In Volpp's reading, the play shows how the storyteller Liu Jingting 柳敬亭 (1587–1670), a highly educated performer, who was much in demand among elite circles, brought a seasoned eye to bear on the pretensions of the scholarly elite while being able to express himself in popular as well as elite registers. Yet in Kong's prefaces to his play, he complained about the routine bowdlerization of fine plays by actors. Thus, in Volpp's telling, Kong's use of different language registers suggests that *Peach Blossom Fan* is construed as a training ground for readers to acquire the ability to fully immerse themselves in a play world while being simultaneously aware of its illusory nature.[41]

Hence, if we just look at these three examples drawn from *zaju*, *nanxi*, and *chuanqi* theater respectively, it becomes obvious that playwrights used the theatrical juxtaposition of rhetorical devices for different ends. If *zaju*'s mixing of registers served to highlight depth of characterization and *nanxi*'s to balance entertainment with reflection, then *chuanqi* could be understood as a literary experiment in exploding stable boundaries between registers. Even within the *chuanqi* tradition, different playwrights deploy the contrast between high and low registers for different ends. If Tang was keen on drawing on the vernacular to parody standard classical usage, Kong foregrounded versatility across registers as a defining attribute of theatrically versed practitioners. In other words, within the Chinese theatrical tradition, the theatricality of language did not serve a singular purpose, but depending on genre, period, playwright and other factors, it could be mobilized for very different effects. At the same time, such differing approaches to language also point to another related issue, namely questions regarding the epistemological ground upon which dramatic writing and theatrical performance rested.

The Contested Nature of the Theatrical Imagination

In eighteenth- and nineteenth-century Western discourses on Chinese theater, critics tended to concentrate on plot rather than rhetoric; moreover, plot was often pressed in the service of illustrating a Chinese custom or recounting an event in Chinese history.[42] What came to be one of Western literature's most prized features—its imaginative powers—was either largely overlooked or actively denied in translations or descriptions of Chinese theater. However, from a contemporary academic vantage point, it is noteworthy that Chinese theater was a relative latecomer to an already extremely rich and diverse literary and textual culture and as such has the potential for scholars to revisit the question of the importance of the imagination in the production, circulation, and consumption of Chinese literature anew. More specifically, theater can help us intervene not only in the question of how historical materials were adapted on the Chinese stage but also how theater engaged with different forms of fictionality. As Henry Turner observed in a comparative context, "the very large question of just how 'fiction' worked onstage has received less critical attention than it should and . . . seems . . . to mark an exciting horizon for new work."[43]

The most ambitious effort to reconstruct the emergence of fictionality in Chinese theater is Lin Hong Lam's *The Spatiality of Emotion in Early Modern China*. As Hu Ying notes, Lam's is that rare book in Chinese Studies that is equally at home in the density of its source materials and in its theoretical engagement with principally French and German theorists.[44] Lam's research maps out a tripartite structure of how audiences related to theatrical productions in China over the course of the late medieval to the early modern period. In reading a set of literary sources drawn from many different genres, Lam identifies three main modes of audience response, namely what he terms "weather," "dream," and "face-off." The book insists that only one of these, namely the so-called face-off (*sheshen chudi* 設身處地), qualifies as an instantiation of "theatricality" as originally defined by literary critic William Egginton in an early modern European context.[45] In this mode, audiences do not connect with their emotions either by being "naturally swayed" (weather) (Han period onward) or being "infinitely released" (dreaming) (Song/Yuan period), but instead, their feelings are only accessible through external mediation as readers (print) or through spectatorship (theater) (late Ming period).[46] In this scheme, a clear epistemological boundary between fiction and reality in the audience's mind did not take hold until the late sixteenth century when Tang Xianzu's *Peony Pavilion* appeared (1598), long after the first heyday of full-blown Chinese theater in the Yuan dynasty.

Lam's claims with regard to the dramatic and song literature of the Song-Yuan period have not gone unchallenged. In a recent essay, Casey Schoenberger argues for the existence of spectator-accessible fictional worlds within the corpus of Yuan and early Ming plays as a byproduct of urbanization.[47] Schoenberger draws on "text world theory" to argue that we can distinguish between different epistemic layers within these plays: text worlds (playscripts), theater world (the theatrical apparatus), and a fictional world that distinguishes between spectator-accessible and character-accessible subworlds.[48] Within that fictional world, Schoenberger draws on Wilt Idema's observation that Yuan plays often feature an asymmetric relationship between a star and a subsidiary role designed to aid the audience to enter the fictional world.[49] Rather than indicating a seamless movement between different dream states in the manner of Lam, such dramatic configurations constitute an innovative way to delineate "deictic fields," that is, particular perspectives within the fictional subworld that the spectator is meant to access and shift between. In his close reading of *Huolang dan* 貨郎旦 (The Street Vendor in the Female Role), Schoenberger identifies two simultaneous, character-accessible subworlds where each protagonist puts on an act. The simultaneous pretense of each character for the benefit of the other necessitates suspension of disbelief on the part of an omniscient viewer, who must be, in what may be an early case of dramatic irony, aware of the fakery involved in order for the play to make sense.[50]

If in some cases, theatrical juxtaposition between different "acts within plays" served primarily comic effects, in other textual examples of this period, the implied pairing of theatricalized characters with textual or real-life avatars constituted a form of remonstration with the powers that be. In a detailed analysis of Sui Jingchen's 睢景臣 (ca. 1257–ca. 1320) famous song suite "Gaozu huan xiang" 高祖還鄉 ("Han Gaozu Returns to His Home Village"), Karin

Myhre shows that, compared with relevant descriptions in the *Shiji* 史記 (Records of the Historian), the theatrical treatment of the encounter between the emperor and the villagers encodes a world that is distinct from historical precedent and from contemporary imperial practice. Not only is the reader given cues that the emperor in the song is presented as a protagonist on a stage, but the unhappy villager, a seemingly uncomprehending interlocutor, can be similarly understood as an actor. As Myhre observes, "Through selective use and inversion of historical models coupled with a shift of mode from a narrative to a performance, Sui has put into play the stability of normative frames and identities, as well as the boundaries between author, character, and player and reader and spectator."[51] In this view, theatricality is not aligned with ritual reenactment or moralizing self-expression, but instead, its linguistic habitus—the quotidian language, the excess of meanings, and the clash of storylines—gestures toward an erosion of the kind of interpretive authority encoded in the classics and in historiography.

In an essay on the Southern adaptation of *The Orphan of Zhao*, another *zaju* play with roots in the *Records of the Historian* and earlier historical traditions, Yuming He similarly highlights revisionist aspects of the theatrical imagination. If the Northern *zaju* had remained loyal to a small cast of aristocratic characters and their heroic retainers, the Southern *chuanqi* play cycle commonly known under the title *Ba yi ji* 八義記 (Tale of Eight Heroes) expanded the setting to become "a complex urban space of commercial exchange, social envy, and intrigue," populated by a whole, newly invented cast of urban characters where "any concern for historical verisimilitude [has been thrown] to the winds."[52] Instead, as He documents, the printed playtexts as well as the accompanying illustrations draw together characters from different social strata—ordinary impoverished orphans, female wine shop owners, ambitious upstarts from the commoner classes—and place them into the world of the city streets. Importantly, as He argues, in contrast to the *zaju* version, the city space itself occasions the progression of the play more so than any single character. In other words, rather than making the transmission of official historiography the basis for a play,[53] the play is suffused by "public spectacle and gossip"[54] but also turns questions of identity on its head. Far from being a true orphan, the eponymous orphan of the play is in fact reunited with his parents thanks to the sacrifice of another orphan, who died in lieu of the orphan's father. Moreover, rather than focusing on the orphan and his kin, the play's focus rests on Tu'an Gu, the restless commoner with a surfeit of social ambition. Thus the *chuanqi* drama plays with the father-son bond as it is "replete with mistakes about parentage, of sons not knowing their fathers and of would-be fathers who fall victim to those they took for sons,"[55] a theme underscored by different kinds of themed comic routines that recontextualize canonical texts for comic effect. As He cautions us, just because the newly invented features of plays are claimed to be part of "antiquity,"[56] it should not deceive us into thinking that Chinese theater is slavishly beholden to "history." History, in this view, is always contested terrain that could be restaged in alternative guises.

In some cases, theatrical renditions of historical events not only experimented with fictional alternative but superseded the authority of historiographic accounts. In her recent book, *Feeling the Past in Seventeenth-Century China*, Xiaoqiao Ling revisits the divide between "history" and "theater" in her discussion of Kong Shangren's *Peach Blossom Fan*.[57] Rather than getting entangled in the question of whether the play is an accurate, historically based account of major figures active during the Ming/Qing transition or a fictional recreation, Ling instead approaches the play and assorted paratextual materials from the point of view of memory studies. In particular, she analyzes the famous section of "sources" that precede the play known as "Investigations" ("Kaoju" 考劇) as a "memorial archive" to argue that the list of twenty sources contained therein strives "to document a contested memorial landscape of the Southern Ming among a close-knit community of writers."[58] Specifically, Kong deployed dramatic tension to resolve conflicting accounts and created a network of solidarity of figures aligned against the archvillain Ruan Dacheng, himself an accomplished dramatist and troupe-owner.[59] At the same time, the particular array of texts cited from many different genres underscores the "*acquired* nature of the historical events dramatized" in the play.[60] As the play makes use of "two temporal sequences" as framing devices, Ling suggests that these frames call for different "modes of remembrance."[61] The first frame, instantiated by the Old Keeper of Rites as well as a fisherman (the storyteller Liu Jingting) and the woodcutter (music master Su Kunsheng), is construed as "emotionally invested mourners of the fallen Ming."[62] These figures model the remembrance of the past as an affective, identity-forming process in keeping with Kong's overall aesthetic design for the play as a vehicle for cultural continuity and collective remembrance in the face of the traumatic experience of the fall of the Ming. At the same time, through an elaborate and unprecedented structure of character casting, Kong's play also immerses the audience in the lives of the protagonists as they unfold in order to "actually *feel*"[63] their emotions. Thus in the shuttling back and forth between different forms of remembrance, theatricality is neither externalized nor purely internal but mediates between different affective modalities.[64] In its emphasis on recuperative feeling, Ling's project points to another aspect that has vexed discussions of Chinese theater, namely irrespective of whether audiences believed what they read or watched was fiction or history, how were they thought to emotionally process theatrical texts and performances?

A Multimodal History of Performance Aesthetics

If Chinese theater has had any presence in comparative theater studies, it is via German playwright Bertolt Brecht's (1898–1956) interaction with Mei Lan-fang's (1894–1961) theatrical performances. How much Chinese theater aesthetics contributed to Brecht's influential theory of "Verfremdungseffekt" (alienation effect)—the desire to impel audiences to take revolutionary action offstage through an unmasking of the brutal nature of reality on stage—is a point of dispute among scholars. Even when the mediating aspect of Chinese theater for Brecht's formulation is granted, there is no consensus on whether Brecht fundamentally misunderstood the nature of the Chinese theatrical tradition or whether he apprehended something of substance.[65] For instance, Min Tian argued that, contrary to Brecht's idea that Chinese *xiqu* conventions made the familiar strange to its Chinese audiences, the success of *xiqu* aesthetics in fact depended on the audience's familiarity with and appreciation of such performance skills.[66] Meanwhile, in Siyuan Liu's view, while Brecht may have misapprehended the fundamentals of audience/performer relations in Chinese theater, his understanding of "gestus" (gesture, bodily comportment) as a "social(ized) gesticulation as opposed to psychologized facial expression [and] as contextualized and alterable comportment" nevertheless attested to Brecht's insight into what Brecht described as the "masterly use of gesture as seen in Chinese acting."[67]

In a nuanced reconceptualization of Brecht's concern with "theatricalized ethics," theater scholar Haiping Yan homed in on the communicative nature of audience/performer relations in producing *xiqu* aesthetics: "Fully cognizant of its [the performance's] suppositionality, the 'imaginatively knowing' and 'actively feeling' audience is constitutive of the drama's actualization through their decision-making process; their presence is integral to the acting process, and indispensable to the production of theatricality."[68] Expanding on Yan's formulation of the pact between audience and actor, theater scholar Megan Evans pointed to the actor's skill as a catalyst that makes ethically harrowing scenarios aesthetically thrilling and imaginatively actionable: "The embodied potency of extraordinary skill exhibited in a successful *xiqu* performance itself expands the boundaries of 'what there is to know' both in terms of how the actor feels about the character's situation and how the audience responds to the performance."[69] Thus, most importantly, perhaps, the legacy surrounding Brecht's intercultural theorizing foregrounds the importance of performance and more specifically, the actor and the audience, as a vital conduit for the realization of performance aesthetics. In this view, then, theatricality is not an abstracted universal, but a positively coded concept that revolves around identifying "the essential performance characteristics"[70] of particular theatrical styles.

This performative line of emphasis has had particular currency among China scholars who have been trained in theatre studies and in some cases actively direct Chinese-style productions themselves. In her contribution to a special *Asian Theatre Journal* issue (1994) on desirable future English-language studies on Chinese theatre, Elizabeth Wichman called for studies on modern *xiqu* culture that could positively impact "the status and creative authority of *xiqu* performers in China today" through sustained attention to "performance and performers, their training and creative work rather than on scripts, history or sociopolitical issues."[71] In the interim, new research on the changes within the modern *xiqu* repertoire shows that the creative agency of individual *xiqu* performers was ineluctably intertwined with script, performance, and sociopolitical issues. In his analysis of the PRC reform campaigns of the 1950s, Siyuan Liu demonstrates how what he terms "*xiqu*'s gestic theatricality" was systematically diminished through official and informal interventions in the play repertoire and in the performance techniques.[72] Meanwhile, scholars of dynastic *xiqu* have also expanded their scope of inquiry to include performative aspects, all the associated methodological quandaries notwithstanding. This body of work seeks to delineate the performance qualities of historical forms of Chinese theater while creatively working within the limitations of available sources. Among the different aspects of mise-en-scène relevant for theatrical performance, recent studies of stage directions (role types, exits and entrances, physical actions, emotional states, gestures, sound effects), costume, and voice techniques elucidate both continuities and ruptures in the long durée of Chinese *xiqu* performance and of related song traditions. A hallmark of such work is its intrinsically multidisciplinary nature.

Building on earlier work on stage directions in Yuan *zaju* and in Ming *chuanqi*,[73] Judith T. Zeitlin's *The Phantom Heroine: Ghost and Gender in Seventeenth-Century Chinese Literature* examines the figure of the female ghost, or what she calls the "phantom heroine," in the context of the theatrical culture in late sixteenth- and seventeenth-century China.[74] Attending to the female ghost both as a literary artefact and as a theatrical event, Zeitlin notes that tremendous theatrical potential inheres in the figure of the ghost. The staging of a ghost made visible what ordinarily was not visible as ghosts hovered on the threshold of the here and there, or as Alice Rayner put it, [theatrical] "ghosts wait for the secrets to be released into time."[75] Moreover, typically the same actor or actress embodied humans and their ghostly counterparts. Such a pairing of human and ghostly guises called for acting virtuosity (different forms of gestic embodiment)[76] while also providing a window onto how the actor, the role, and the character were thought to relate to one another (metatheatrical doubling).[77] In order to identify the theatrical differentiation between female humans (*dan*

旦) and female ghosts (*hun dan* 魂旦), Zeitlin draws on a multidisciplinary archive of sources to reconstruct a "semiotic code of ghosts in drama" through special attention to stage practices (e.g., stage business, sound effects) and acting conventions (e.g., special gestures, dance movements, costume and accessories, formulaic lyrics).[78] Key among the source materials are stage directions in relevant plays, the particular arias sung by the actress in both of her guises, woodblock-printed illustrations of ghost scenes, associated paintings, as well as photographs of modern stage conventions.[79] Stage directions proliferated as plays became part of a flourishing late Ming print culture.[80] While they cannot be naively taken at face value, it is also true that many *chuanqi* playwrights were known to be intimately familiar with staging conventions, and thus, in Zeitlin's view, such notations most likely were in dialogue with actual stage practices. Importantly, in contrast to early modern European stage directions found in print sources, printed Chinese stage directions utilized a specialized perfor-mance language, suggesting that "the imaginative reading process for Chinese drama may have always retained" an "indissoluble link to the stage."[81]

Stage directions as well as woodblock illustrations and paintings also figure prominently in Guojun Wang's exploration of how attire in historical and per-formative contexts entered into complex negotiations in his *Staging Personhood: Costuming in Early Qing Drama*. The new Qing rulers instituted strict regula-tions regarding attire among Manchu, Mongolian, and Han peoples alike. Importantly, they required the defeated Han majority to adopt the hairstyle of a queue and new forms of dress. Ming-dynasty state attire, by contrast, was rel-egated to the realm of theatrical costuming, while Manchu clothing was offi-cially banned from performances in all settings, and the Manchus themselves were forbidden from attending theatrical performances in playhouses in order for strict segregation to be maintained between the ruling minority and the populace at large, even if such bans were unevenly enforced. The exception were the Manchu rulers themselves who recruited eunuchs and professional per-formers to enact plays in Ming-dynasty costume at court to relish the imagi-native spoils of their military victory. However, for Chinese male Qing-dynasty subjects, the appearance of Ming dynasty clothing on stage might resonate in entirely different ways. Literati expressed strong nostalgia for the fallen regime and the associated way of life. As Wang demonstrates in his close readings of several seventeenth-century plays, such policies invited playwrights to exploit the stage directions devoted to costuming as a site to explore intertwined questions of gender and ethnicity in a period rife with shifting allegiances and commemorations. In examining theatrical costuming as a contested site for Manchu/Chinese identities and social relations, Wang notes that in a global context, the Ming/Qing transition may be a rare case where ethnic tensions surfaced in theatrical costuming.[82]

A multimodal approach has also informed research on the reconstruction of another vital aspect of Chinese theatrical performance, that is, the world of sound. In its most focused dimensions, the landscape of theatrical sound concerns specific singing styles, the art of voice production, and the pedagogy of singing. Accordingly, musicologists and other scholars have analyzed the musical contours of particular tune choices and their aesthetic effects[83] while also seeking to reconstruct conceptions of singing and voicing,[84] traditions of voice pedagogy, and methods of actor-singer training.[85] In dynastic China, singing took place in many contexts, and given the importance of the audience/performer nexus noted above, song style, timing, and ambience all fed into the acoustic choices (singers) and the auditory experiences (audience). Hence, some scholars have insisted that the soundscape of singing performances cannot be divorced from the ambient site of the performance itself.[86] In "Courtesan vs. Literatus: Gendered Soundscapes and Aesthetics in Late-Ming Singing Culture," Peng Xu argues that theater scholars need to pay attention to a host of hitherto neglected questions: What was the sonic environment of singing performances? What was the audience's 'point of audition'? How did the specific place of the performance figure into the singing styles? What factors might have prompted the singer to make particular aesthetic decisions with regard to volume, vocal color, and ornamentation? Who were the singing teachers, and what pedagogies did they adopt? In plays, how was singing represented diegetically (e.g., characters, plot elements, settings) and extradiegetically (e.g., musical mode, tune pattern choice, prosody)? Through an examination of a range of late Ming textual and visual sources, Xu identifies two gendered singing styles associated with specific environments, that is, the feminine warbling of intimate banquet performances and the masculine whistling in mountainous nature settings. She goes on to suggest that certain *chuanqi* plays suggest that courtesan-actor-singers were expected to combine these styles. Xu's nuanced exploration of the allure of "pure singing" (*qingchang* 清唱, singing devoid of other facets of dramatic performance), though distinct from a full-blown theatrical realization of those same tunes, underscores the importance of the acoustic dimensions of the late Ming cult of feeling.[87] While sources are limited compared to the roughly contemporaneous development of Italian operatic bel canto singing, perhaps other methodologically inventive moves will further expand the exploration of the sonic aesthetics of dynastic Chinese plays and songs.

Conclusion: Future Research Horizons

The study, appreciation, and intercultural diffusion of traditional Chinese theater in European-language contexts have been a long and slow process. If Chinese drama was among the earliest forms of literature to catch the attention of European scholars in the 1730s, the US academy did not begin to embrace instruction on Chinese theater until the 1940s and 1950s.[88] In the interim, the last two decades have seen a steady growth of dissertations and books thanks to the pioneering efforts of a contingent of US-based faculty—Cyril Birch, J. I. Crump, Patrick Hanan, Robert E. Hegel, C. T. Hsia, Wilt L. Idema, David Johnson, David Todd Roy, Stephen H. West, and Elizabeth Wichman, among others—who trained cohorts of drama scholars at a number of research institutions. So what might be some exciting directions for the historiography of Chinese drama and theater adumbrated by the work that these new generations of scholars have undertaken?

Much *xiqu* research has a comparative angle, yet the findings of Sinologists about the history and practice of Chinese theater have yet to resonate more broadly among scholarly communities interested in world theater, world dance, or world music. Even general introductory surveys on world theater that address some facet of the *xiqu* tradition often describe Chinese theater in predictably formalistic terms.[89] Thus, it might be incumbent on the field of Chinese theater studies to ask: how can we contribute to a global history of theater? Or to put it more pointedly, if we venture beyond essentialist, nationalist, or preservationist claims about the unique qualities of Chinese *xiqu*,[90] how can we theorize the potentially distinctive aspects of this art form in a comparative context? Obviously, there are no definitive answers on how to approach Chinese theatricality as world theater, but I will sketch out some observations below.

In the area of the material aspects of drama, a global history of reading playtexts could be immeasurably enriched if we systematically worked through the rich corpus of published plays[91] while also teasing out the complex interactions between print and manuscript traditions.[92] We might work with the heuristic suspicion that reading drama in dynastic China was a different operation than reading drama in Shakespearean or other contexts. As noted above, stage directions figured in rather particular ways in the Chinese theatrical corpus, embedding theatrical modalities in the act of reading. In the realm of the structure of the text, perhaps further work can shed light on the complex operation of different kinds of language registers within the confines of a single play. Here, perhaps an analysis of the movement between different kinds of delivery (singing, declaiming, speaking) in combination with a consideration of the alternation of moods might shed new light on Chinese models of theatrical engagement. Furthermore, an in-depth consideration of the recoverable kinesthetic and musical elements in historical sources, as challenging as that might be, could provide a basis for better theorizing the nature of Chinese theater as a generically distinctive form that is a constantly evolving *Gesamtkunstwerk* that continues to eschew attempts to categorically or practically assimilate it to

Western-derived taxonomies of theatricality. At the same time, such a history also cannot be blind to the fact that modern *xiqu* has been continually engaged with various other theatrical traditions and as such cannot be reduced to the status of a "pure" heritage.[93] Instead, perhaps we might want to have recourse to what Maggie Green calls "literary time"[94]—that is, the remarkable tenacity of certain sociocultural and aesthetic configurations that resist "campaign time" or "dynastic time," all the variability and new inflections notwithstanding.

In terms of the social history of Chinese theater, three aspects may be particularly worthy of further investigation. First, in dynastic China, in contrast to the textual projects of official historiography and poetic self-expression, Chinese drama was at its heart a collective but institutionally pluralistic art form. Thus, conceptualizing Chinese theater in a frame of the "theatricality of power" is bound to fall short of the plural ways in which different communities generated their own forms of theatrical display and mobilized competing versions of ostensibly "identical stories." Even if these different theatrical sectors entered into complex arrangements with one another, theater, even in its most moral guises, could be mobilized to speak truth to power. One way to further investigate the importance of this remonstrative aspect of the Chinese theatrical tradition may be a more comprehensive investigation of the breadth and depth of the theatrical archive beyond the handful of iconic plays that have received the lion's share of scholarly attention.

Another avenue of inquiry might be to focus on the centrality of gender in the world of the theater relative to other forms of public discourse in dynastic China. Was China among the first world theaters to accord female actors the status of recognized artists? In light of the indentured nature of much theatrical labor and its embedment within an epitheatrical sexual economy,[95] we also have to honestly reckon with the precarious social underpinnings of female stardom.[96] By the same token, given the prominence of non-gender straight acting from the inception of the Chinese theatrical tradition to the present day,[97] perhaps a more comprehensive history of how the aesthetics of cross-gender and transgender impersonation shaped playwrighting, actor training, and audience interest may also yield unexpected results. Needless to say, such a history would also need to come to terms with culturally specific yet changing notions of gender, sexuality, and family organization.[98] And thirdly, while some work has been done to investigate audience/performer relations, we could push both archival work and our theorizing further in order to formulate compelling alternatives to Brecht's alienation effect that would allow us to explain the ubiquity of Chinese theater and its affective import among different social strata in dynastic China.

To facilitate broader diffusion of knowledge of and appreciation of Chinese drama among new audiences, different types of translations might be another worthwhile endeavor.[99] In the realm of *zaju*, Wilt L. Idema and Stephen H. West have translated dozens of plays from various textual strata of the Yuan corpus.[100] Their pioneering and indefatigable efforts have paved the way for the adoption of Chinese texts into the undergraduate curriculum. In the meantime, we have only scratched the surface of an immense and varied corpus of longish *chuanqi* plays. Moreover, in addition to translating for the textbook market, we might also consider a more self-consciously literary approach either as a solo effort or perhaps most fruitfully as a translatorial collaboration between people with different skill sets and literary orientations.[101] We might also think about producing "stage" or "performance translations" designed to be used in an actual production.[102] As Elizabeth Wichman and Megan Evans have suggested, such translations could take the form of texts that are singable in one of the current *xiqu* styles; alternatively, they could be structured in such a way as to allow for integration with *xiqu*-style theatrical principles. Not only could such translations inspire new intercultural afterlives for the plays in question, but the opportunity to act in a *xiqu* style performance, even in English translation, might give rise to new acting pedagogies.[103]

And finally, we might also want to harness the power of the digital humanities. Not only would open access sites build audiences for *xiqu* around the world, but with the right kind of design, such digital resources might also invite informed, appreciative, or creative responses from those selfsame users. As noted above, *xiqu* has been driven by stylistic variation, individual creativity, and institutional mandates. Curated documentation of the archive and the repertoire of *xiqu* theatricality offers a window not only to historical practices but can also broaden access to a repertoire of creative solutions and future possibilities for theater practitioners in the Chinese-speaking world and elsewhere. Moreover, different facets of *xiqu* have engaged with modern media— spoken drama, film, dance, and the visual arts to name the most obvious.[104] Thus such a digital future may also document the rich resonances and afterlives of historical and modern *xiqu* in the culture at large[105] while, in Emily Wilcox's words, contribute toward "decentering whiteness."[106] In that light, Brook's attempt to imagine a "bare stage," as the quintessential environment for "an act of theatre to be engaged" between two lone men, however fitting that might seem for *xiqu* at first glance, in all likelihood is impossibly solipsistic.[107] Perhaps our work on Chinese *xiqu* can show that the ostensibly "bare stage" is ghosted by other technologies, alternate social constellations, different mental and sensory operations, and distinctive performance aesthetics while being every inch as theatrical in its diverse ways to make sense of the world through theater.

PATRICIA SIEBER 夏頌
The Ohio State University
sieber.6@osu.edu

Acknowledgments

I want to express my thanks to the guest editor of this issue, Steve Roddy, for his persistent nurturing of this contribution through the COVID-19 global health emergency and the associated shadow pandemics. I am grateful for the incisive suggestions by the two peer reviewers. I am also indebted to my fellow contributors, particularly Martin Kern and Paola Varsano, for the observations and thought-provoking questions they raised during the symposium held for this special issue in summer 2021. I also want to acknowledge the inspiration derived from the comments of Wenbo Chang, Erxin Wang, and Mengling Wang about my presentation there. In different ways, these conversations prompted me to think about the notion of a global history of Chinese theater in more concrete terms. Finally, I thank Regina Llamas and Paize Keulemans for their thoughtful comments on an earlier draft.

Notes

1. Brook, *Empty Space*, 9.
2. Sieber, *Theaters of Desire*, 7–40. D. Chang, *Representing China on the Historical London Stage*, 52–96.
3. For a brief discussion on how the term *Chinese opera* gained currency in nineteenth-century usage in England, see Thorpe, *Performing China on the London Stage*, 10n3; on mid-nineteenth-century American English terminology for traditional Chinese theater, see Lei, *Operatic China*, 31–39. For an argument on its continued relevance, see Zeitlin, "Introduction," 16–17.
4. On the problems surrounding the term *xiqu*, see Kang, *Zhongguo xiju shi yanjiu rumen*, 1–20. My thanks to Paize Keulemans for bringing this study to my attention.
5. For a survey of key studies from the first major wave of Anglophone studies of classical Chinese drama, see Guo, "Overview of Research on Classical Chinese Drama in North America." My choice of studies to discuss is necessarily selective and has no pretensions to being exhaustive. For a synthetic account of a broader range of research on traditional Chinese theater, see Sieber and Llamas, "Introduction."
6. On these terms and their relationship, see Taylor, *Archive and the Repertoire*.
7. Fiebach, "Theatricality," 24; Carlson, "Resistance to Theatricality."
8. Postlewait and Davis, "Theatricality: An Introduction," 1–39.
9. See Nellhaus et al., *Theatre Histories*, for an attempt to write a global theater history with a communicative approach that is structured around different media (orality, manuscript culture, print culture, periodical print culture, electronic communication).
10. Quoted in Fiebach, "Theatricality," 20.
11. Ibid., 17. In the discussion to illustrate this definition across cultures from Africa to Asia, he points to Antje Budde's discussion that foregrounds the acrobatics in traditional Peking Opera and a "bodily skills"-centered etymology of a Chinese instantiation of such a body-centered definition of theater (19).
12. Postlewait, "Theatricality and Antitheatricality in Renaissance London," 118–19.

13. Ibid., 120.
14. Turner, "Toward a New Theatricality?," 29–35.
15. See, for example, Willi, "Language(s) of Comedy."
16. Halliwell, "Laughter."
17. Marshall, "Dramatic Technique and Athenian Comedy," 145.
18. See for example, Foley, "Performing Gender in Greek Old and New Comedy."
19. Carlson, *Haunted Stage*.
20. Postlewait, "Theatricality and Antitheatricality in Renaissance London," 122.
21. Fiebach, "Theatricality," 24.
22. See the short entries on Chinese playwrights and theatrical forms in Kennedy, *Oxford Encyclopedia of Theatre and Performance*, and the somewhat longer ones in Leiter, *Encyclopedia of Asian Theatre*; for medium-length entries on Chinese actors, theatrical styles, and institutions, see Williams, *Cambridge Encyclopedia of Stage Actors and Acting*.
23. See the inclusion of Guan Hanqing's 關漢卿 *The Injustice of Dou E* as the sole Chinese play in Gainor et al., *Norton Anthology of Drama*. Cf. Chun, "Introduction," 2.
24. The above mentioned Nellhouse et al., *Theatre Histories*, is riddled with errors when it comes to traditional Chinese theater. For a particularly egregious example, see the chapter entitled "Secular and Early Professional Theatre, 1250–1650," where the authors advance a set of patently false claims: "Print had a different impact in East Asia (China, Korea, and Japan). Even with movable type, printing was done by hand—a laborious and expensive process; perhaps that is why few plays were printed. To enjoy drama, Asian audiences needed to attend live performances" (151).
25. Julien, *Hoeï-lan-ki*, x–xxv. For the afterlife of such translations on the French stage, see Lo, *La Chine sur la scène française au XIXe siècle*.
26. In Dongshin Chang's terminology, in historical British theater, a "Chinaface style" represented China on a "visual, formal level as opposed to a textual, conceptual level" (D. Chang, *Representing China on the Historical London Stage*, 2–6). For similar ideations among non-Chinese audiences in nineteenth-century California toward what she terms "Chinese nondrama," see Lei, *Operatic China*, 43–50. On how contemporary New York audiences only spontaneously applauded for an acrobatic interlude in the 1998 performance of *Peony Pavilion* and the many visual stimulants in the performance more generally, see Rolston, "Tradition and Innovation in Chen Shi-Zheng's *Peony Pavilion*," 138, 140–41.
27. For a discussion of this debate in the Yuan dynasty, see Shih-pe Wang, "Plays within Songs."
28. On Zhou's language philosophy, see Sieber, "Flavor All Its Own," 209–10.
29. Sieber, "*Pavilion for Praying to the Moon* and *The Injustice to Dou E*."
30. In Western contexts, women did not become significant as actors or singers until the late sixteenth century. See Nellhaus et al., *Theatre Histories*, 169.
31. Llamas, *Top Graduate Zhang Xie*, 63.
32. Ibid., 63.
33. Ibid., 67.
34. Ibid., 274.
35. Ibid., 65.
36. Humor too was subject to historical change. For an exemplary study in the modern Chinese context, see Rea, *Age of Irreverence*.

37. Volpp, *Worldly Stage*, 89–128. The term *vernacular* was until recently the unchallenged standard term to refer to more colloquial registers of written Chinese. *Plain Chinese* was advanced as a back translation of *baihua* 白話 as a non-Eurocentric alternative in an influential article by Shang, "Writing and Speech." In order to bring out the literary richness and diversity of the *vernacular* or *plain Chinese* more clearly, Sieber proposed *mixed-register literature* as yet another way to describe this written form. See Sieber, "Flavor All Its Own," 226–27.

38. Volpp, *Worldly Stage*, 92.

39. Neither of the two 1998 *Peony Pavilion* productions referenced above, however, engaged with humor in this way. Sellars's cut the humorous scene altogether in the interest of time, and Chen simplified the translation and created involuntary humor. See Swatek, "Boundary Crossings," 149, 154. On Chen's increased use of slapstick, see Zeitlin, "My Year of Peonies," 128.

40. Volpp, *Worldly Stage*, 129–72. On this point, see also Tan, review, 433–34.

41. Volpp, *Worldly Stage*, 214–48.

42. D. Chang, *Representing China on the Historical London Stage.*

43. Turner, "Toward a New Theatricality?," 33.

44. Hu, review, 471–72.

45. Egginton, *How the World Became a Stage.*

46. As Curie Virág cautions, it is not clear why the discourse of an audience's emotions has to be stripped of all interiority, even if it might make sense to challenge the idea that emotions are exclusively interior events. See Virág, review.

47. Schoenberger, "Storytellers, Sermons, Sales Pitches, and Other Deceptive Features of City Life," 131–33.

48. Ibid., 140.

49. Idema, "Why You Have Never Read a Yuan *Zaju*," 783.

50. Schoenberger, "Storytellers, Sermons, Sales Pitches, and Other Deceptive Features of City Life," 152–56.

51. Myhre, "Performing the Emperor," 46, 47. For two other essays in the same issue that stress the theatrical dimensions of certain *sanqu* songs, see Idema, "Ultimate *Sanqu* Song," and W. Chang, "Performing the Role of the Playwright." For related plays, see Idema, "Founding of the Han Dynasty in Early Drama."

52. He, "Adopting *The Orphan*," 165–66.

53. The Yuan *zaju* also introduced some imaginative elements. Specifically, Ji Junxiang added the eponymous orphan's adoption by archvillain Tu'an Gu, thus heightening the dramatic conflict around which father to be loyal to. See Shih-pe Wang, "*Orphan of Zhao*."

54. He, "Adopting *The Orphan*," 169.

55. Ibid., 174.

56. Ibid., 181–82.

57. Ling, *Feeling the Past in Seventeenth-Century China.* For an alternative reading of the tensions in this play, see Li and Guo, "*Peach Blossom Fan* and *Palace of Everlasting Life*."

58. Ling, *Feeling the Past in Seventeenth-Century China*, 251.

59. On Ruan's place within the political and theatrical history of the period, see Zhang, "*Green Peony* and *The Swallow's Letter*."

60. Ling, *Feeling the Past in Seventeenth-Century China*, 251.

61. Ibid., 267.

62. Ibid., 268.

63. Ibid., 275.

64. Insofar as the fall of the Ming was the first major historical event that was dramatized across Eurasia, compelling possibilities of a comparative history of theatricality beckon. See Keulemans, "Tales of an Open World"; D. Chang, *Representing China on the Historical London Stage*, 15–51.

65. Yan, "Theatricality in Classical Chinese Drama."

66. Tian, "'Alienation Effect' for Whom?" For a summary of this debate, see also Evans, "Translating Bodies," 110–12.

67. Quoted in Liu, *Transforming Tradition*, 8. Brecht noted that "the actor has to find a sensibly perceptible outward expression for his characters, preferably some action that gives away what is going inside him. The emption in question must be brought out, must lose all its restrictions so that it can be treated on a big scale." Quoted in Liu, *Transforming Tradition*, 8–9. In a similarly sympathetic reinterpretation of Brecht, Haiping Yan observed that Brecht "astutely recognizes how subjunctive and suppositional performance could both inscribe a specific system of ethics and exceed the limits of the system, thereby activating transformative imaginations" ("Theatricality in Classical Chinese Drama," 75).

68. Yan, "Theatricality in Classical Chinese Drama," 86.

69. Evans, "Translating Bodies," 111. For a similar understanding of the "goal of theatricalization as the display of exceptional achievement," see Carlson, "Resistance to Theatricality," 249. On the pleasurable surplus of theater, see Postlewait and Davis, "Theatricality: An Introduction," 21.

70. Postlewait and Davis, "Theatricality: An Introduction," 21, 22.

71. Wichman, "*Xiqu* Research and Translation with the Artists in Mind," 99.

72. Liu, *Transforming Tradition*, 98–156. For the term "gestic theatricality," see 155. For other relevant studies, see Greene, *Resisting Spirits*; DeMare, *Mao's Cultural Army*; Fan, *Staging Revolution*; and some of the essays gathered in Mezur and Wilcox, *Corporeal Politics*, and in Chen, Chun, and Liu, *Rethinking Chinese Socialist Theaters of Reform*.

73. For a broad survey of theatrical techniques derived from Zang Maoxun's edition of Yuan *zaju*, see Crump, *Chinese Theater in the Days of Kublai Khan*, 67–175; for a masterful statistical survey across different editions of Yuan *zaju*, see Tian, "Stage Directions in the Performance of Yuan Drama." On Ming *chuanqi*, see Swatek, Peony Pavilion *Onstage*.

74. Zeitlin, *Phantom Heroine*, 131–80.

75. Rayner, *Ghosts*, x.

76. On acting virtuosity in Yuan *zaju* contexts, see Idema, "Traditional Dramatic Literature," 801; and Sieber, "*Pavilion for Praying to the Moon* and *Injustice to Dou E*," 80–83.

77. Zeitlin, *Phantom Heroine*, 134, 171–80.

78. Ibid., 140–71. In the late 1990s, a new subfield within theater studies arose, the so-called theater semiotics, which sought to reclaim theatricality as a positive concept (see Carlson, "Resistance to Theatricality," 242–43). It aimed to describe the various theatrical codes that constitute a performance. While many useful studies were written under its auspices, no definitive models could emerge because of the complexity and variability of the communicative processes involved (see Postlewait and Davis, "Theatricality: An Introduction," 22–25).

79. Zeitlin, *Phantom Heroine*, 140–71. For a detailed examination of a broad range of late Ming acting conventions through a comparison of visual sources from woodblock printed

books and modern stage photographs, see also Hsiao, *Eternal Present of the Past*, 87–174. For an analysis of text-image relations with regard to the stage and the reader's imagination, see Sieber and Zhang, "*Story of the Western Wing.*"

80. Zeitlin, *Phantom Heroine*, 141–42. As Zeitlin notes, the increase in stage directions was a byproduct of the transformation of playscripts into reading material.

81. Ibid., 142. On the prevalence of the phrases "ke" 科 or "jie" 介 (gestures/acting out) by themselves or in combination with other performative markers in Yuan and Ming editions of Yuan *zaju*, see Tian, "Stage Directions in the Performance of Yuan Drama," 407.

82. Wang, *Staging Personhood*, 42. For a discussion of stage directions in the context of various forms of Qing court theater, see Tan, "*Song of Dragon Well Tea* and Other Court Plays," 316–18.

83. Mark, "From Page to Stage"; Lam, "*Southern Story of the Western Wing.*"

84. Zeitlin, "Pleasures of Print"; Zeitlin, "From the Natural to the Instrumental."

85. Zeitlin, "'Notes of the Flesh' and the Courtesan's Art in Seventeenth-Century China"; Xu, "Music Teacher."

86. On the soundscape in communal settings, see Yung, "*Mulian Rescues His Mother.*"

87. On this point, see also Zeitlin, *Phantom Heroine*, 140.

88. Pang, "(Re)Cycling Culture," 375.

89. Westlake, *World Theatre*, 52–58.

90. On the nationalist essentialism, see Goldstein, *Drama Kings*.

91. On a possible methodological model, see He, *Home and the World*.

92. Goldman, "*Eight-Court Pearl*"; L. Chen, *Staging for the Emperors*.

93. For an exemplary study of the transcultural dynamics at play in Mei Lanfang's innovations in Beijing opera, see Yeh, "Mei Lanfang and Modern Dance."

94. Greene, *Resisting Spirits*, 16.

95. Stevenson, "One as Form and Shadow."

96. See for example, Bossler, "Sexuality, Status, and the Female Dancer"; Y. Chen, "'Queering' the Nation?'"

97. Kile, "Transgender Performance in Early Modern China"; Goldman, *Opera and the City*; Li R., *Soul of Beijing Opera*, 83–119; J. S. C. Lam, "Impulsive Scholars and Sentimental Heroes."

98. Bossler, *Courtesans, Concubines, and the Cult of Female Fidelity*; Guo, "Male *Dan* at the Turn of the Twenty-First Century."

99. For a history of early play translations in European languages, see Idema, "From Stage Scripts to Closet Dramas"; for French translations, see Li S., *Zhongguo xiqu zai Faguo de fanyi yu jieshou*.

100. Representative works include Wang Shifu, *Moon and the Zither*, and West and Idema, *Orphan of Zhao and Other Yuan Plays*.

101. For the literary results of a collaboration between scholars, students, and a poet, see Hsia, Li, and Kao, *Columbia Anthology of Yuan Drama*; for an example of self-consciously reflective translation practice in the context of the Yuan song tradition, see Sieber et al., "In Search of Pure Sound." When the Royal Shakespeare Company launched the China Classics project, they paired a literary translator with a playwright with Asian roots. In the case of the *Injustice to Dou*, well-known translator Gigi Chang (of *The Legend of the Condors* translation fame) retranslated the play to provide the point of departure for *Snow in Midsummer*, contemporary playwright Frances Ya-chu Cowhig's radically topical

reworking of the original story. For a performance review of Cowhig's play, see Swatek, "Performance Review."

102.   For the hallmarks of such texts, see Bassnett, "Theatre and Opera."

103.   Wichman, "*Xiqu* Research and Translation with the Artists in Mind." Evans lists the following *xiqu* principles as possible ways to create an embodied "replication" even without recourse to *xiqu*-specific gestures and vocal patterns: integration of music with onstage action, precisely scored rhythmic transitions, and clarity of emotional progression supported by precise physical score ("Translating Bodies," 120). On how *xiqu*-style training inflected American film actor training, see Pang, "(Re)Cycling Culture," 381–82.

104.   Feng, *Intercultural Aesthetics in Traditional Chinese Theatre*; Ferrari, *Transnational Chinese Theatres*.

105.   For relevant sites, see the TEXTCOURT Project (https://textcourt.web.ox.ac.uk/; accessed November 14, 2021), the Digital Library of Chinese Theatre (https://chinesetheatre.leeds .ac.uk/; accessed November 14, 2021), the Pioneers of Chinese Dance Digital Archive (https://quod.lib.umich.edu/d/dance1ic?page=index; accessed November 14, 2021), the Chinese Film Classics Project (https://chinesefilmclassics.org/; accessed November 14, 2021), and the Chinese Theater Collaborative (https://chinesetheatercollaborative.org; accessed November 14, 2021; under construction).

106.   Wilcox, "Introduction," 8–12.

107.   On the puritanical, antitheatrical overtones of a discursive preoccupation with the "bare stage," see Carlson, "Resistance to Theatricality," 248.

References

Bassnett, Susan. "Theatre and Opera." In *The Oxford Guide to Literature in English Translation*, edited by Peter France, 96–103. Oxford: Oxford University Press, 2000.

Bossler, Beverly. *Courtesans, Concubines, and the Cult of Female Fidelity: Gender and Social Change in China, 1000–1400*. Cambridge, MA: Harvard University Asia Center, 2013.

———. "Sexuality, Status, and the Female Dancer: Legacies of Imperial China." In *Corporeal Politics: Dancing East Asia*, edited by Katherine Mezur and Emily Wilcox, 25–43. Ann Arbor: University of Michigan Press, 2020.

Brook, Peter. *The Empty Space*. New York: Atheneum, 1968.

Carlson, Marvin. *The Haunted Stage: The Theatre as Memory Machine*. Ann Arbor: University of Michigan Press, 2003.

———. "The Resistance to Theatricality." *SubStance* 31, no. 2–3 (2002): 238–50.

Chang, Dongshin. *Representing China on the Historical London Stage: From Orientalism to Intercultural Performance*. New York: Routledge, 2015.

Chang, Wenbo. "Performing the Role of the Playwright: Jia Zhongming's *Sanqu* Songs in the Supplement to *The Register of Ghosts*." *Journal of Chinese Literature and Culture* 8, no. 1 (2021): 59–88.

Chen, Liana. *Staging for the Emperors: A History of Qing Court Theatre, 1683–1923*. Amherst, NY: Cambria, 2021.

Chen, Xiaomei, Tarryn Li-min Chun, and Siyuan Liu, eds. *Rethinking Socialist Theaters of Reform: Performance Practice and Debate in the Mao Era*. Ann Arbor: University of Michigan Press, 2021.

Chen, Yu-hsing Jasmine. "'Queering' the Nation? Gendered Chineseness, Cross-Dressing, and the Reception of *Love Eterne* in Taiwan." *Prism: Theory and Modern Chinese Literature* 18, no. 1 (2021): 49–88.

Chun, Tarryn Li-min. "Introduction: Chinese Socialist Theater: Between Revolution and Reform." In *Rethinking Chinese Socialist Theaters of Reform: Performance Practice and Debate in the Mao Era*, edited by Xiaomei Chen, Tarryn Li-Min Chun, and Siyuan Liu, 1–33. Ann Arbor: University of Michigan Press, 2021.

Cowhig, Frances Ya-chu. *Snow in Midsummer*. New York: Methuen, 2018.

Crump, J. I. *Chinese Theater in the Days of Kublai Khan*. Tucson: University of Arizona Press, 1980.

DeMare, Brian James. *Mao's Cultural Army: Drama Troupes in China's Rural Revolution*. Cambridge: Cambridge University Press, 2015.

Egginton, William. *How the World Became a Stage: Presence, Theatricality, and the Question of Modernity*. Albany: SUNY Press, 2003.

Evans, Megan. "Translating Bodies: Strategies for Exploiting Embodied Knowledge in the Translation and Adaptation of Chinese *Xiqu* Plays." In *Staging and Performing Translation: Text and Theatre Practice*, edited by Roger Baines, Cristina Marinetti, and Manuela Perteghella, 107–25. London: Palgrave Macmillan, 2011.

Fan, Xing. *Staging Revolution: Artistry and Aesthetics in Model Beijing Opera during the Cultural Revolution*. Hong Kong: Hong Kong University Press, 2018.

Feng, Wei. *Intercultural Aesthetics in Traditional Chinese Theatre: From 1978 to the Present*. New York: Palgrave Macmillan, 2020.

Ferrari, Rossaella. *Transnational Chinese Theatres: Intercultural Performance Networks in East Asia*. Cham: Palgrave Macmillan, 2020.

Fiebach, Joachim. "Theatricality: From Oral Traditions to Televised 'Realities.'" *SubStance* 31, no. 2–3 (2002): 17–41.

Foley, Helene P. "Performing Gender in Greek Old and New Comedy." In *The Cambridge Companion to Greek Comedy*, edited by Martin Reverman, 259–74. Cambridge: Cambridge University Press, 2014.

Gainor, Ellen J., Stanton B. Garner, and Martin Puchner, eds. *The Norton Anthology of Drama*. 3rd ed. New York: Norton, 2017.

Goldman, Andrea. "*The Eight-Court Pearl*: Performance Scripts and Political Culture." In Sieber and Llamas, *How to Read Chinese Drama*, 325–45.

———. *Opera and the City: The Politics of Culture in Beijing, 1770–1900*. Stanford: Stanford University Press, 2012.

Goldstein, Joshua. *Drama Kings: Players and Publics in the Re-creation of Peking Opera, 1870–1937*. Berkeley: University of California Press, 2007.

Greene, Maggie. *Resisting Spirits: Drama Reform and Cultural Transformation in the People's Republic of China*. Ann Arbor: University of Michigan Press, 2019.

Guo, Jie. "The Male *Dan* at the Turn of the Twenty-First Century: Wu Jiwen's *Fin-de-Siècle Boylove Reader*." *Prism: Theory and Modern Chinese Literature* 18, no. 1 (2021): 70–88.

Guo Yingde. "An Overview of Research on Classical Chinese Drama in North America (1998–2008)." *Asian Theatre Journal* 27, no. 1 (2010): 149–71.

Halliwell, Stephen. "Laughter." In *The Cambridge Companion to Greek Comedy*, edited by Martin Revermann, 189–205. Cambridge: Cambridge University Press, 2014.

He Yuming. "Adopting *The Orphan*: Theater and Urban Culture in Ming China." In *The Ming World*, edited by Kenneth M. Swope, 161–84. London: Routledge, 2020.

———. *Home and the World: Editing the "Glorious Ming" in Woodblock-Printed Books of the Sixteenth and Seventeenth Centuries*. Cambridge, MA: Harvard University Asia Center, 2013.

Hsia, C. T., Wai-yee Li, and George Kao, eds. *The Columbia Anthology of Yuan Drama*. New York: Columbia University Press, 2014.

Hsiao, Li-ling. *The Eternal Present of the Past: Illustration, Theater, and Reading in the Wanli Period, 1573–1619*. Leiden: Brill, 2007.

Hu Ying. Review of *The Spatiality of Emotion in Early Modern China: From Dreamscapes to Theatricality*, by Ling Hon Lam. *Critical Inquiry* 46, no. 2 (2020): 471–73.

Idema, Wilt L. "The Founding of the Han Dynasty in Early Drama: The Autocratic Suppression of Popular Debunking." In *Thought and Law in Qin China*, edited by Eric Zürcher, 183–207. Leiden: Brill, 1990.

———. "From Stage Scripts to Closet Drama: Editions of Early Chinese Drama and the Translation of Yuan *Zaju*." *Journal of Chinese Literature and Culture* 3, no. 1 (2016): 175–202.

———. "Traditional Dramatic Literature." In *The Columbia History of Chinese Literature*, edited by Victor H. Mair, 785–847. New York: Columbia University Press, 2001.

———. "The Ultimate *Sanqu* Song: Yao Shouzhong's 'The Complaint of the Ox' and Its Place in Tanaka Kenji's Scholarship on *Sanqu*." *Journal of Chinese Literature and Culture* 8, no. 1 (2021): 12–30.

———. "Why You Have Never Read a Yuan Drama: The Transformation of *Zaju* at the Ming Court." In *Studi in onore di Lanciello Lanciotti*, edited by S. M. Carletti, M. Sacchetti, P. Santangelo, 765–91. Naples: Istituto Universitario Orientale, Dipartimento di Studi Asiatici, 1996.

Julien, Stanislas, trans. *Hoeï-lan-ki, ou L'histoire de cercle de craie: dramae en prose et en vers*. London: Oriental Translation Fund, 1832.

Kang Baocheng 康保成. *Zhongguo xiju shi yanjiu rumen* 中國戲劇史入門 (An Introduction to the Study of the History of Chinese Drama). Shanghai: Fudan University Press, 2009.

Kennedy, Dennis, ed. *The Oxford Encyclopedia of Theatre and Performance*. Oxford: Oxford University Press, 2003.

Keulemans, Paize. "Tales of an Open World: The Fall of the Ming Dynasty as Dutch Tragedy, Chinese Gossip, and Global News." *Frontiers of Literary Study in China* 9, no. 2 (2015): 190–234.

Kile, Sarah. "Transgender Performance in Early Modern China." *differences: A Journal of Feminist Cultural Studies* 24, no. 2 (2015): 130–49.

Lam, Joseph S. C. "Impulsive Scholars and Sentimental Heroes: Contemporary Kunqu Discourses of Traditional Chinese Masculinities." In *Gender in Chinese Music*, edited by Rachel Harris, Rowan Pease, and Shzr Ee Tan, 87–106. Rochester, NY: University of Rochester Press, 2013.

———. "*The Southern Story of the Western Wing* (*Nan Xixiang*): Traditional Kunqu Composition, Interpretation and Performance." In Sieber and Llamas, *How to Read Chinese Drama*, 191–211.

Lam, Ling Hon. *The Spatiality of Emotion in Early Modern China: From Dreamscapes to Theatricality*. New York: Columbia University Press, 2018.

Lei, Daphne P. *Operatic China: Staging Chinese Identity Across the Pacific*. New York: Palgrave Macmillan, 2006.

Leiter, Samuel, ed. *Encyclopedia of Asian Theatre*. Westport, CT: Greenwood, 2007.

Li, Mengjun, and Guo Yingde. "*The Peach Blossom Fan* and *Palace of Everlasting Life*: History, Romance, and Performance." In Sieber and Llamas, *How to Read Chinese Drama*, 285–305.

Li, Ruru. *The Soul of Beijing Opera: Theatrical Creativity and Continuity in the Changing World.* Hong Kong: Hong Kong University Press, 2010.

Li Shengfeng 李聲鳳. *Zhongguo xiqu zai Faguo de fanyi yu jieshou* (1789–1870) 中國戲曲在法國的翻譯與接受 (1789–1870) (The Translation and Reception of Chinese Theater in France, 1789–1870). Beijing: Beijing daxue chubanshe, 2015.

Ling, Xiaoqiao. *Feeling the Past in Seventeenth-Century China.* Cambridge, MA: Harvard University Asia Center, 2019.

Liu, Siyuan. *Transforming Tradition: The Reform of Chinese Theater in the 1950s and Early 1960s.* Ann Arbor: University of Michigan Press, 2021.

Llamas, Regina S, trans. *Top Graduate Zhang Xie: The Earliest Extant Chinese Southern Play.* New York: Columbia University Press, 2021.

Lo, Shi-lung. *La Chine sur la scène française au XIXe siècle* (China on the French Stage in the Nineteenth Century). Rennes Cedex: Presses Universitaires de Rennes, 2015.

Nellhaus, Tobin, et al., eds. *Theatre Histories: An Introduction.* 3rd ed. London: Routledge, 2016.

Mark, Lindy Li. "From Page to Stage: Exploring Some Mysteries of *Kunqu* Music and Its Melodic Characteristics." *CHINOPERL* 32, no. 1 (2013): 1–29.

Marshall, C. W. "Dramatic Technique and Athenian Comedy." In *The Cambridge Companion to Greek Comedy*, edited by Martin Revermann, 131–46. Cambridge: Cambridge University Press, 2014.

Mezur, Katherine, and Emily Wilcox, eds. *Corporeal Politics: Dancing East Asia.* Ann Arbor: University of Michigan Press, 2020.

Myhre, Karin. "Performing the Emperor: Sui Jingchen's 'Han Gaozu Returns to His Home Village.'" *Journal of Chinese Literature and Culture* 8, no. 1 (2021): 31–58.

Pang, Cecilia J. "(Re)Cycling Culture: Chinese Opera in the United States." *Comparative Drama* 39, no. 3–4 (2005–6): 361–96.

Postlewait, Thomas. "Theatricality and Antitheatricality in Renaissance London." In *Theatricality*, edited by Tracy C. Davis and Thomas Postlewait, 90–126. Cambridge: Cambridge University Press, 2003.

Postlewait, Thomas, and Tracy C. Davis. "Theatricality: An Introduction." In *Theatricality*, edited by Tracy C. Davis and Thomas Postlewait, 1–39. Cambridge: Cambridge University Press, 2003.

Rayner, Alice. *Ghosts: Death's Double and the Phenomena of Theatre.* Minneapolis: University of Minnesota Press, 2006.

Rea, Christopher. *The Age of Irreverence: A New History of Laughter in China.* Berkeley: University of California Press, 2015.

Rolston, David. "Tradition and Innovation in Chen Shi-Zheng's *Peony Pavilion.*" *Asian Theatre Journal* 19, no. 1 (2002): 134–46.

Schoenberger, Casey. "Storytellers, Sermons, Sales Pitches, and Other Deceptive Features of City Life: A Cognitive Approach to Point of View in Chinese Plays." *CHINOPERL* 38, no. 2 (2019): 129–64.

Shang, Wei. "Writing and Speech: Rethinking the Issue of Vernaculars in Early Modern China." In *Rethinking East Asian Languages, Vernaculars, and Literacies, 1000–1900*, edited by Benjamin A. Elman, 254–303. Leiden: Brill, 2014.

Sieber, Patricia. "A Flavor All Its Own: Some Theoretical Considerations on *Sanqu* as Mixed-Register Literature." *Journal of Chinese Literature and Culture* 8, no. 1 (2021): 203–35.

———. "*The Pavilion for Praying to the Moon* and *The Injustice to Dou E*: The Innovation of the Female Lead." In Sieber and Llamas, *How to Read Chinese Drama*, 78–100.

————. *Theaters of Desire: Authors, Readers, and The Reproduction of Early Chinese Song-Drama (1300–2000)*. New York: Palgrave Macmillan, 2003.

Sieber, Patricia, et al. "In Search of Pure Sound: *Sanqu* Songs, Genre Aesthetics, and Translation Tactics." *Journal of Chinese Literature and Culture* 8, no. 1 (2021): 163–202.

Sieber, Patricia, and Regina S. Llamas, eds. *How to Read Chinese Drama: A Guided Anthology*. New York: Columbia University Press, 2022.

Sieber, Patricia, and Regina S. Llamas. "Introduction: The Culture Significance of Chinese Drama." In Sieber and Llamas, *How to Read Chinese Drama*, 1–27.

Sieber, Patricia, and Gillian Yanzhuang Zhang. "*The Story of the Western Wing*: Theater and the Printed Image." In Sieber and Llamas, *How to Read Chinese Drama*, 101–26.

Stevenson, Mark. "One as Form and Shadow: Theater as a Space of Sentimentality in Nineteenth-Century Beijing." *Frontiers of History in China* 9, no. 2 (2014): 225–46.

Swatek, Catherine C. "Boundary Crossings: Peter Sellars's Production of *Peony Pavilion*." *Asian Theatre Journal* 19, no. 1 (2002): 147–58.

————. *Peony Pavilion Onstage: Four Hundred Years in the Career of a Chinese Drama*. Ann Arbor, MI: Center for Chinese Studies, 2002.

————. "Performance Review: *Snow in Midsummer* by Frances Cowhig." *CHINOPERL* 37, no. 2 (2018): 161–70.

Tan, Tian Yuan. Review of *Worldly Stage: Theatricality in Seventeenth-Century China*, by Sophie Volpp. *Harvard Journal of Asiatic Studies* 72, no. 2 (2012): 430–37.

————. "*Song of Dragon Well Tea* and Other Court Plays: Stage Directions, Spectacle, and Panegyrics." In Sieber and Llamas, *How to Read Chinese Drama*, 309–24.

Taylor, Diana. *The Archive and the Repertoire: Performing Cultural Memory in the Americas*. Durham, NC: Duke University Press, 2003.

Thorpe, Ashley. *Performing China on the London Stage: Chinese Opera and Global Power, 1759–2008*. New York: Palgrave Macmillan, 2016.

Tian, Min. "'Alienation Effect' for Whom? Brecht's (Mis)interpretation of the Classical Chinese Theatre." *Asian Theatre Journal* 14, no. 2 (1997): 200–222.

————. "Stage Directions in the Performance of Yuan Drama." *Comparative Theatre* 39, no. 3–4 (2005–2006): 397–443.

Turner, Henry S. "Toward a New Theatricality?" *Renaissance Drama*, n.s. 40 (2012): 29–35.

Virág, Curie. Review of *The Spatiality of Emotion in Early Modern China: From Dreamscapes to Theatricality*, by Ling Hon Lam. *China Review International* 24, no. 1 (2017): 37–41.

Volpp, Sophie. *Worldly Stage: Theatricality in Seventeenth-Century China*. Cambridge, MA: Harvard University Asia Center, 2011.

Wang, Guojun. *Staging Personhood: Costuming in Early Qing Drama*. New York: Columbia University Press, 2020.

Wang Shifu 王實甫. *The Moon and the Zither: The Story of the Western Wing*. Edited and translated with an introduction by Stephen H. West and Wilt L. Idema. Berkeley: University of California Press, 1995.

Wang, Shih-pe. "*The Orphan of Zhao*: The Cost of Loyalty." In Sieber and Llamas, *How to Read Chinese Drama*, 127–50.

————. "Plays within Songs: *Sanqu* Songs from Literary Refinement (*ya*) to Popular Appeal (*su*)." *Journal of Chinese Literature and Culture* 8, no. 2 (2021): 307–40.

West, Stephen H., and Wilt L. Idema, ed. and trans. *The Orphan of Zhao and Other Yuan Plays: The Earliest Known Versions*. New York: Columbia University Press, 2014.

Westlake, E. J. *World Theatre: The Basics*. London: Routledge, 2017.

Wichman, Elizabeth. "*Xiqu* Research and Translation with the Artists in Mind." *Asian Theatre Journal* 11, no. 1 (1994): 97–100.

Wilcox, Emily. "Introduction: Toward a Critical East Asian Dance Studies." In *Corporeal Politics: Dancing East Asia*, edited by Katherine Mezur and Emily Wilcox, 1–21. Ann Arbor: University of Michigan Press, 2020.

Willi, Andreas. "The Language(s) of Comedy." In *The Cambridge Companion to Greek Comedy*, edited by Martin Revermann, 168–85. Cambridge: Cambridge University Press, 2014.

Williams, Simon, ed. *The Cambridge Encyclopedia of Stage Actors and Acting*. Cambridge: Cambridge University Press, 2015.

Xu, Peng. "Courtesan vs. Literatus: Gendered Soundscapes and Aesthetics in Late-Ming Singing Culture." *T'oung Pao* 100, no. 4–5 (2014): 404–59.

———. "The Music Teacher: The Professionalization of Singing and the Development of Erotic Vocal Style during Late Ming China." *Harvard Journal of Asiatic Studies* 75, no. 2 (2015): 259–97.

Yan, Haiping. "Theatricality in Classical Chinese Drama." In *Theatricality*, edited by Tracy C. Davis and Thomas Postlewait, 65–89. Cambridge: Cambridge University Press, 2003.

Yeh, Catherine. "Mei Lanfang and Modern Dance: Transcultural Innovation in Peking Opera, 1910s–1920s." In *Corporeal Politics: Dancing East Asia*, edited by Katherine Mezur and Emily Wilcox, 44–59. Ann Arbor: University of Michigan Press, 2020.

Yung, Sai-shing. "*Mulian Rescues His Mother*: Play Structure, Ritual, and Soundscapes." In Sieber and Llamas, *How to Read Chinese Drama*, 349–66.

Zeitlin, Judith T. "From the Natural to the Instrumental: Chinese Theories of the Sounding Voice before the Modern Era." In *The Voice as Something More: Essays toward Materiality*, edited by Martha Feldman and Judith T. Zeitlin, 54–76. Chicago: University of Chicago Press, 2019.

———. "Introduction: Toward a Visual Culture of Chinese Opera." In *Performing Images: Opera in Chinese Visual Culture*, edited by Judith T. Zeitlin and Yuhang Li, 14–29. Chicago: Smart Museum, University of Chicago, 2014.

———. "My Year of Peonies." *Asian Theatre Journal* 19, no. 1 (2002): 124–33.

———. "'Notes of the Flesh' and the Courtesan's Art in Seventeenth-Century China." In *The Courtesan's Arts: Cross-Cultural Perspectives*, edited by Marta Feldman, 75–99. Oxford: Oxford University Press, 2006.

———. *The Phantom Heroine: Ghosts and Gender in Seventeenth-Century Chinese Literature*. Honolulu: University of Hawai'i Press, 2007.

———. "The Pleasures of Print: Illustrated Songbooks from the Late Ming Courtesan World." In *Gender in Chinese Music*, edited by Rachel Harris, Rowan Pease and Shzr Ee Tan, 41–65. Rochester, NY: University of Rochester Press, 2013.

Zhang, Ying. "*The Green Peony* and *The Swallow's Letter*: Drama and Politics." In Sieber and Llamas, *How to Read Chinese Drama*, 235–56.

Inward Turns, Then and Now

ALEXANDER DES FORGES

Abstract The term *involution* has been used to characterize economic development and state formation in eighteenth- through twentieth-century China; more recently, it has seen unprecedented popularity in Chinese-language social media as a representation of the lived experience of individuals in the contemporary era. In each of these cases, the trope of involution implies a judgment on the productivity of labor and resources invested and is often tied to discourses of "Chinese uniqueness." In Sinological circles as in social media, however, the dynamics that involution claims to represent are better explained through Malthusian approaches to the problem of population increase and Marxist understandings of the relationship between capital and labor: the dynamics in question are not unique to China but typical of broader movements in the world system. I argue nonetheless that the rhetoric of involution deserves closer investigation, and focus particular attention on involution's origins in the field of aesthetics and the rise of involutionary parallelism in the Ming-Qing examination essay. It is here that the dynamics of cultural capital that dominate in the Ming and Qing anticipate the effects of surveillance capital in the twenty-first century. When a so-called eight-legged essay folds back into its own prose both literally and figuratively, can we simply dismiss the complex interiority that results? Or does it speak as well to our contemporary anxieties about individual identity in the age of algorithms?

Keywords involution, eight-legged essay, productivity, subjectivity, parallelism

The term *involution* (*neijuan* 內卷) has enjoyed a certain vogue for decades in Sinological circles as a characterization of economic development in early modern China and state formation in the twentieth century; more recently, it has seen unprecedented popularity in Chinese-language social media as a means to describe and explain the specific lived experience of individuals in the contemporary era. Whether this term is used to critique processes of agricultural development, the intensification of the modern bureaucratic state, the use of

The Journal of Chinese Literature and Culture • 9:1 • April 2022
DOI 10.1215/23290048-9681241 • © 2022 by Duke University Press

qualifying examinations that do not relate in substantive ways to the positions that individuals are being chosen for, or excessive focus on GPA as an indicator of intellectual ability, involution—*neijuan*—constitutes a judgment on the productivity of labor and resources invested, a critical assessment of the mismatch between ends aimed at and means chosen to achieve those ends. In the words of Clifford Geertz, who initiated use of the term "involution" in the anthropological context, it is an "ultimately self-defeating process."[1]

These uses of *involution* connect with a tradition of locating China outside the movement of world history that begins with Hegel, a tradition in which the state form itself is identified as a primary mode of production.[2] In more recent decades, scholars of Chinese political, social, and economic history have employed the trope of involution to ground a variety of discourses of difference, most notably in the controversy over a proposed "great divergence" between the market economies of Western Europe and China in the nineteenth century.[3] Similarly, the dramatic surge in online usage of *neijuan* over the course of the last year has often tied this term to discourses of "Chinese uniqueness" (*Zhongguo tese* 中國特色) or, at the very least, distinctiveness.[4] In Sinological circles as in social media, however, the dynamics that the trope of involution claims to represent can in fact be explained more parsimoniously and systematically through reference to Malthusian approaches to the problem of population increase and Marxist understandings of the relationship between capital and labor (substantiated in detail by Thomas Piketty in his *Capital in the Twenty-First Century*). Indeed, although involution is invoked primarily in discussions of China (and less often, Asia more broadly), the dynamics in question are not unique to China but typical of broader movements in the world system.

Although the concept of involution is of questionable analytic value in these cases, I argue nonetheless that the rhetoric of involution repays closer investigation and focus particular attention on involution's origins in the field of aesthetics. Given the image of state bureaucracy as a form that encourages involutionary development and the notable significance of involutionary parallelism as a defining characteristic of civil service examination essay style, the connection between China and involution may seem overdetermined. At the same time, taking involution primarily as an aesthetic concern allows us a better understanding of the productive dimensions also found in these inward turns and the ways in which the dynamics of cultural capital that dominate in the Ming and Qing anticipate the effects of surveillance capital in the twenty-first century. When a so-called eight-legged essay (*bagu wen* 八股文) folds back into its own prose both literally and figuratively, can we simply dismiss the complex interiority that results? Or does it speak as well to our contemporary anxieties about individual identity and the exploitation of our attention in the age of algorithms?

. . . . .

The scandal of involution is the failure of a specified indicator to grow in prescribed fashion; the precise indicator varies, but it is ordinarily one privileged
due to its significance to modernization narratives that take the Western
European experience as the standard of reference. So for Geertz, Philip Huang,
and Kenneth Pomeranz, involution refers to the per capita productivity of labor
failing to increase—a question of economics. Duara, who focuses on "state
involution," highlights instead the failure of state revenue increase to match or
outpace the increase in revenue flowing to informal brokers who mediate
between citizens and bureaucracy.[5] Ideally, for Geertz, the farmers in Java who
"[drive] their terraces, and in fact all their agricultural resources, harder by
working them more carefully" would produce more than they had in the past,
but in this case the increase in labor is applied to the same limited land area as
previously: under the involutionary regime, the per-unit yield of the land
increases but not that of the labor applied to that land.[6] For Duara, "state
making" is the ideal, defined as the state increasing its revenue and control over
the population's surplus production; involution occurs here when informal
brokers expand their revenue and their autonomy vis-à-vis the formal state
structure instead.

But is involution something measured only by the numbers? I have
remarked elsewhere on the fact that Geertz draws the concept of involution not
from the fields of political science, anthropology, sociology, or economics but
rather from Alexander Goldenweiser's discussion of decorative aesthetics in the
"primitive" work of art. Goldenweiser writes,

> But there are also instances where pattern merely sets a limit, a frame, as it were,
> within which further change is permitted if not invited. . . . The pattern precludes the
> use of another unit or units, but it is not inimical to play within the unit or units. The
> inevitable result is progressive complication, a variety within uniformity, virtuosity
> within monotony. This is *involution*. A parallel instance, in later periods of history, is
> provided by what is called ornateness in art, as in the late Gothic. The basic forms of
> art have reached finality, the structural features are fixed beyond variation, inventive
> originality is exhausted. Still, development goes on. Being hemmed in on all sides by a
> crystallized pattern, it takes the function of elaborateness.[7]

Let us pause for a moment to reflect on this curious fact: in their representation
of the material dynamics of Chinese society, theories of socioeconomic development in the early modern period, analyses of political power in the twentieth
century, and critiques of alienated labor in the current moment all rely on a

trope that originates in the aesthetic assessment of works of art. The genealogy of this concept begs interesting questions: can we in fact judge the degree of involution characteristic of different societies in terms that are not ultimately aesthetic in nature but quantitative? To what extent is involution necessarily constituted as a relation between an interior and an exterior? And finally, given its origin in aesthetics and its interest in "play" and "virtuosity," is involution not set to work as appropriately in inquiries into subjectivity as in the investigation of political, social, and economic processes?

As a written genre nearly unique to China, resulting from a state-centered mode of production, the "eight-legged" examination essay would seem to epitomize this type of stagnation in literary terms. Early twentieth-century reformers identified the examination essay as a feudal relic, grouping it together with foot-binding and opium addiction as practices that were understood to hold the nation back.[8] Even the very form of these essays seems to betray a bureaucratic mentality in its attention to balance and control. If for Hegel China's location "outside the World's History" is determined in part by its supposedly meritocratic process of bureaucratic recruitment, it might seem that the examination essay genre would bear witness to the world-historical futility of investing ever more labor in a field defined most narrowly.[9]

The term *eight-legged essay* itself is of course misleading. In the Ming and Qing (fifteenth–nineteenth centuries), when these essays were written, the term *shiwen* 時文 (modern prose essay) was more commonly used. There was never an official requirement that essays be written using parallel structures, and *eight-legged essay* originated as a term only in the late seventeenth century, at a moment when the genre had suddenly become the focus of critical attention; more often than not, it had a pejorative sense.[10] But although many essays did not have eight legs, and some were not even constructed in parallel form, this name for the essay does serve as a useful indicator of how important the trope of parallelism would become to general perceptions of the genre. The highly symmetrical parallelism seen in certain parts of the majority of essays was contrasted not only against vernacular prose (*baihua wenxue* 白話文學) but also against the classical or "archaic" prose (*guwen* 古文) popular in the Ming and Qing, which was thought to progress in one direction rather than doubling back, in order to make its point in straightforward and economical fashion.[11]

Even when viewed strictly from a formal perspective, however, these essays were more complicated than their reputation would suggest. The careful author could work to fold parallel lines back on themselves to yield a textual structure in which the question "is this section parallel?" has a different answer depending on which level is the reader's focus. There are sections of the text that seem not to be parallel, only to turn out to have a parallel later in the reading process; there are other sections that seem at first to be parallel, but themselves turn out not to have a parallel match when it would later be expected to appear. I refer to this inward folding and intensified complexity, this play of repetition and variation, as *involutionary parallelism*; it has a significance to the history of Chinese prose in the Ming and Qing that is akin to the introduction of counterpoint in Western music.[12]

Here I would like to give an example from an essay by Zhu Xie 諸燮 (1535 *jinshi*).[13] This essay, written on the topic "Ordinary men and women in their foolishness can share in knowing it, but in reaching its perfection, Sages too have that which they are unable [to do] in it," drawn from the *Zhongyong* 中庸 (Doctrine of the mean), is representative of a great many essays written in the sixteenth through nineteenth centuries in its nuanced take on parallel structure.[14] After a brief introductory section consisting of the *poti* 破題 (topic-breaker) and *chengti* 承題 (topic receiver), Zhu launches into an extended two-leaf (*liangshan* 兩扇) setup, which I quote here in full. To give a clearer sense of the different moments of parallelism that constitute the involutionary mode, I have indented the paragraphs differently according to the type of parallelism that they manifest.

Perceiving the Way of this world is possible through knowledge: ordinary men and women have knowledge and the Sage has knowledge. If we limit ourselves to talking about understanding, who would not say that the knowledge of the Sage is not that which the ordinary men and women have a part in? But as a thing in itself, innate moral knowledge (liangzhi 良知) *is not divided into wisdom and ignorance.*

> *In this ground where there is no need for thinking or worrying, one is endowed with the true principle of clear perception and does not rely on seeking outside [oneself];*
> *Amidst unrecognition and unknowing, one embodies the marvelous effect of clear comprehension that does not originate in external discipline.*

This is because the foolishness of ordinary men and women has nonetheless a part in knowledge, such that if we were to expand that which is known by ordinary men and women up to the point where nothing is not known, it seems as though they would understand as much as a Sage.

> *But the traces near and far differ, and the reach of eye and ear are sometimes limited by the non-comprehensiveness of vision and hearing;*
> *The times past and present differ, and the investigation of written records is sometimes troubled by the incompleteness of documentary evidence.*

So there is also that which cannot be known by the Sage.

> *That which is known by the ordinary people is the understanding each individual is endowed with;*

That which is not known by the Sage is wisdom in its entirety.
Only in their individually endowed [understanding] are the ordinary men and women similar to the Sage;
Only in its entirety is the Way not exhausted by the Sage.
If one's knowledge reaches the level of a Sage and still is not sufficient to exhaust the Way, then there is no complete knowledge in this world, and the wonder of this Way must have something that transcends knowledge and perception. The Way is expansive in its uses, could it be exhaustively known?
Embodying the Way of this world is possible through action: ordinary men and women take action and the Sage takes action. If we limit ourselves to talking about capability, who would not say that the ability of the Sage is not that which ordinary men and women have a part in? But in and of itself, moral ability does not initially admit distinction between things and myself.

Profitable use depends on income and expenditure, and although one may not have exhausted the subtleties, [it is possible that] one still does not lose sight of the constant of compliance;
Daily use is how one spends one's life, and although one may not have the ability to examine oneself, [it is possible that] one still does nothing that does not fit the virtue of Heaven's principle.
This is because the unworthiness of ordinary men and women has nonetheless a part in ability, such that if we were to expand that which ordinary men and women are capable of up to the point where there is nothing beyond their ability, it seems as though they would be as capable as a Sage.

But sometimes one's assignment is restricted, so even though one has virtue appropriate to receive orders, ultimately one has no way to complete meritorious actions that would accord with Heaven;
One's power may have that which obstructs it, so even though one has a mind to save everyone, ultimately one has no way to fully distribute one's assistance.
So there is also that which the Sage is not capable of.

That which the ordinary people are capable of is what is shared at the origin;
That which the Sage is not capable of is the great purpose in its completeness.
Only what is shared can be demanded of ordinary men and women;
Only completeness cannot be demanded of the Sage.
If one's actions reach the level of a Sage and still are not sufficient to exhaust the Way, then there is no complete ability in this world, and the magic of this Way must have something that goes beyond the surface of material things. The Way is expansive in its uses, could it be exhausted through actions?

彼見天下之道存乎知：夫婦有知，聖人亦有知也，自局於明者觀之，孰不曰聖
人之知非夫婦所與知也，然而良知之本體，則無分於聖愚焉。

    何思何慮之地，具明覺之真機而不假外求；

    不識不知之中，涵明通之妙用而非由於外鍊。

蓋夫婦之愚有可與知者矣，乃若充夫婦之所知以至於無所不知，宜若聖人之易
事也。然而

    遠近異迹，而耳目所逮或限於聞見之未周；

    古今異時，而載籍所稽或苦於文獻之未備。

則聖人亦有所不知焉。是則

      夫婦之所知者，各具之明也；

      聖人之所不知者，全體之智也。

    惟其各具也，夫婦之所以同於聖人；

    惟其全體也，道之所以不盡於聖人也。

知至聖人而猶不足以盡道，則天下無全知，而斯道之妙，蓋有超乎知識之外者
矣。道之費也，而可以知盡哉？

體天下之道存乎行：夫婦有行，聖人亦有行也，自限於力者觀之，孰不曰聖人
之能非夫婦所與能也，然而良能之本體，初無間於物我焉。

    利用以出入者，雖精微之未究而不失順應之常；

    日用以終身者，雖習察之未能而無適非天理之懿。

蓋夫婦之不肖有可與能者矣，乃若充夫婦之所能以至於無所不能，宜若聖人之
能事也。然或

    分有所制，則雖有受命之德而終無以成格天之功；

    勢有所阻，則雖有兼濟之心而終無以弘博施之澤。

則聖人亦有所不能焉。是則

      夫婦之所能者，本原之同也；

      聖人之所不能者，大用之備也。

    惟其同也，可以責道於夫婦；

    惟其備也，不可以責備於聖人也。

行至聖人而猶不足以盡道，則天下無全能，而斯道之神，蓋有出於形器之表者
矣。道之費也，而可以行盡哉？

Given the time frame in which this essay was composed, the immediately striking feature is its explicit endorsement of Wang Yangming's 王陽明 (1472–1529) emphasis on *liangzhi* 良知 (innate moral knowledge, moral intuition): it is notable that this early in the sixteenth century, Zhu Xie—who would eventually place third in the metropolitan examination of 1535—would make a point of centering his argument on this controversial concept that is nowhere hinted at in the original *Zhongyong* passage.[15] We will return to this point later; here I would like to focus on the structure of the text.

When we begin reading this essay, the portion that is not indented in this formatting seems at first to be straight classical prose, not particularly parallel at all. On encountering the lines beginning "In this ground where there is no need for thinking and worrying" and "Amidst unrecognition and unknowing," it seems that we have found our first parallel section, so I have indented these lines. We return briefly to a bridge section in straightforward prose (not indented), followed by another parallel set of lines, which I have again indented. The process is then repeated a second time, and we seem to be drawing to a conclusion, but it turns out there is much text to be read.

Indeed, as soon as the reader hits the clause "Embodying the Way of this world is possible through action," it starts to become clear that everything that previously seemed to lack a parallel, to be simply straightforward prose, does in fact have a double; it just took a while to get around to it. Conversely, those sections of the first half of the essay that we originally identified as parallel sets in and of themselves (those beginning "In this ground where there is no need" and "But the traces near and far differ") will turn out in contrast *not* to have perfectly corresponding matches in the second half of the essay: the sections beginning "Profitable use depends on income and expenditure" and "But sometimes one's assignment is restricted" do not constitute parallel matches to their counterparts in the first half.

The final flourish comes with the line "That which the ordinary people are capable of is shared at the origin" when we realize that the two sections that are twice-indented above are parallel in and of themselves and *also*—counter to our newly formed expectation—parallel between the two wings of the essay. It is clear that this involution aims to make active use of stylistic norms to challenge the reader rather than lulling him or her to sleep. Given that parallelism was a first resort for readers required to make sense of an unpunctuated essay that they were encountering for the first time, any complexity or unexpected turns introduced by the author would make the task of the reader that much more difficult.

Goldenweiser's relatively neutral characterization of involution in terms of elaboration would seem to apply quite nicely to Zhu Xie's essay. More specifically, Stanley Tambiah writes of "administrative involution" in government defined in part by "a principle of bipartition and duplication of similar units, so that not only are 'departments' balanced against one another, duplicating functions, but also within departments there occurs bipartition into parallel, virtually redundant units."[16] There are also clear formal similarities between the dissatisfactions expressed by critics of involution, which often make use of tropes of problematic subdivision and doubling, and criticisms of the eight-legged essay genre in general. Geertz writes of the repeated division of rice paddies in increasingly granular fashion; for Duara the issue is a class of brokers whose (illegitimate) development mirrors that of the bureaucracy that depends on them. The duplication that some found suspect in the examination essays was of lines of argument: Wei Xi 魏禧 (1624–1681) protests that "when you are finished with your argument, you then have to force yourself to create another argument to balance it."[17] Other more practical writers focused instead on the technical means by which this duplication could be achieved: dividing one argument into two layers, overturning the initial argument to yield a second layer, supplementing one layer with a second layer, and so on.[18]

This interest in *how* to construct a parallel text leads us to an important point, which is particularly salient in the case of involutionary essays like Zhu Xie's. Parallelism in the essay genre is not so much an inherent quality of a text as it is a product of writers' and readers' labor; a product of the temporally situated reading process and point of view in time—what is or is not parallel in the essay depends where you are in the essay when you are asked. To consider only one's judgment after having finished the essay without taking into account the provisional assessments formed, held for a period of time, and then possibly discarded along the way would be to fall into the same mistake that de Certeau critiques in analyses of pedestrian routes in the city that "transform action into legibility, but in doing so [cause] a way of being in the world to be forgotten."[19]

The labor invested is significant—clearly it is hard work to write and read such an essay. My choice of *involution* as a trope for this mode of essay production refers not only to the concrete arrangement of the words on the page, but also to the broader social paradigm proposed to explain the dynamics of labor and economic change across a wide span of the early modern world. At the level of social practice, the trope of involution—in Geertz's sense as well is in the usage of contemporary critics online—seems particularly appropriate to candidates who work harder, for more years, and in greater numbers over the course of the Ming and Qing to exploit a fixed canon of texts to the greatest possible extent. In this sense, the eight-legged essay anticipates the contemporary college entrance examination process, as well as the never-ending race to acquire higher-level credentials. Even the gendered dimensions of the parent-child dynamics are similar: in the Ming as in the twenty-first century, mothers are transformed into frontline managers of the education process.[20]

Nor did the examiners escape this intensification: the topics selected become more granular, as large topic questions that ask candidates to respond to a full paragraph or even section of a classic text increasingly yield to small topic questions that focus more closely on a single phrase or even a single character.[21] Examiners were tasked both with coming up with these more circumscribed topics and with monitoring the essays produced to insure that candidates did not stray beyond the bounds to draw from the phrases preceding or following the defined fragment. The diligence and effort required of all involved was much remarked upon not only by Ming and Qing critics but also by their contemporaries in Western Europe, for whom a society in which elites too were expected to toil was a shocking, and in some cases, quite welcome prospect.[22]

. . . . .

Does diligence in service of diminishing returns in one sector serve as an indicator that the society as a whole is stuck in a "high-level equilibrium trap," in Mark Elvin's memorable formulation? Early in this century, there was a famous debate in the pages of the *Journal of Asian Studies* over the extent to which development in early modern Europe and China diverged. To put it simply, Philip C. C. Huang maintained that the early modern Yangzi Delta saw involution rather than development, differing in this regard from Western Europe. Kenneth Pomeranz, in contrast, saw both characteristics manifesting at different points in time and in different spheres *both* in Western Europe *and* in the Yangzi Delta. One of the key points to note is that at certain moments the two scholars cannot even come to agreement on whether a given data set is evidence of involution or of positive development.[23]

As Dietrich Vollrath has persuasively argued, however, introducing *involution* as an explanatory term here does not add anything of significance to Malthus's familiar analysis of the relationship among population size, living standards, and population growth. In the classic Malthusian model, good times lead to population growth, which increases population size, which reduces living standards. Bad times cause the reverse. When technological progress, leading to increased productivity, is added to the equation, continued population growth can be maintained, but living standards remain stagnant. Vollrath argues that increases in productivity in early modern Europe lead to negative Malthusian effects much more quickly than in the contemporaneous Yangzi Delta, due primarily to differences in the amount of additional labor that can be invested in grain production (wet-rice cultivation absorbing extra labor more readily than wheat cultivation).[24] The slower return to equilibrium characteristic of high-intensity agriculture like wet-rice cultivation means that the decline in living standards is much slower but also that much more prolonged, giving an *impression* of stagnation. The differences that can be seen between Western Europe and the Yangzi Delta between 1500 and 1850, then, are contingent and historically specific manifestations of the Malthusian dynamic, not an essential distinction between two fundamentally different modes of economic organization.

Looking at the use of *neijuan* (involution) in contemporary social media, the anthropologist Xiang Biao 項飆 draws a distinction between the Sinological uses of the term in the study of the Qing economy and early twentieth-century state building on one hand and contemporary uses of the term by online commentators on the other. Despite the differences between these two uses, he insists on seeing involution as specifically Chinese in *both* of its guises, as do many of the internet social critics that he references.[25] When we look more closely at these contemporary uses, however, as they highlight an increasingly competitive society that has no legitimate "exit ramp," we find that far from manifesting evidence of "Chinese characteristics," the complaints find ready echoes in critiques of twenty-first-century European and North American society. To cite just a single example of the latter, we may note the shift from single-earner households to dual-earner households over the last half of the twentieth century in the United States; the fact that it now often takes two workers to support a lifestyle that once was attainable on a single salary alone stands as precisely the kind of decreasing returns per unit of labor expended that is supposed to be characteristically involutionary. There is no need to hypothesize an "involution" that is rooted in Chinese culture when the problems identified stem so clearly from the global process by which capital expropriates the accomplishments of labor. This expropriation, which heightens social contradictions and extends their effect by the day, is precisely what Marx hypothesized and what Piketty has so thoroughly documented.[26]

Indeed, it is worth noting that Geertz's *Agricultural Involution*, the locus classicus for socioeconomic uses of the term, highlights the importance of uneven global capitalist development (in this case, in the form of Dutch colonialist extraction from Indonesia) as the broader context within which agricultural involution takes place in nineteenth-century Java. Among the distinctions that Geertz draws between Java and Japan in this period, one of the most crucial is the fact that capital generated in Java was removed to the Netherlands rather than reinvested in Java, while this same dynamic did not appear in Japan.[27] "Involution" in nineteenth-century Java and "involution" in twenty-first-century China turn out to be contingent variants of the general relationship between capital and labor rather than essential characteristics of the societies in question.

The shifting nature of the textual structure typical of the examination essay genre can teach us to appreciate the contingency of Malthusian dynamics, which show historians the face of progress *and* the face of regression, depending on the observer's perspective and preferred timescale, as well as the geographical range of the object of investigation. Even the figures themselves are subject to interpretation, as scholars on the two sides of the controversy over the nineteenth-century "divergence" between China and Europe come to different conclusions from the same data. As a historian, one is never granted the privileged perspective on one's object that the literary critic who has read an entire essay through— often more than once—enjoys. Rather, we are stuck forming our assessments of social processes as "involution" on one hand or "development" on the other on the model of a reader still in the midst of that essay, attempting to properly categorize paragraphs that shift in and out of parallelism as one reads them. At the same time, we must remain attentive to the ways in which paradigms like involution, which can continue to be read as "essentially Chinese" in their form even as their content changes dramatically—from agricultural economics to the internet gig economy—reify these dynamics and obscure their sources.[28]

. . . . .

And yet, is it possible that involution does yet have something to say of its own that is not necessarily China-specific, as a tool of analysis with more general relevance, about this new global regime under which we now begin to labor, of surveillance capitalism?[29] The innovative approaches to time management and subjectivity characteristic of the Ming examination writing suggest that it may; involution also has its productive aspect.

The diligent preparation for which examination candidates were known depended in part on a granular approach to textual study, in which careful ledgers were kept of time spent and the individual written characters (*zi* 字) of the canonical texts served to denominate investments of time and effort; it is no accident that Cherishing Time Associations (*xiyin hui* 惜陰會) and Cherishing Written Character Associations (*xizi hui* 惜字會) flourished during the Ming and Qing.[30] At the same time, "leisure" pursuits such as novel reading, writing occasional classical prose to share with one's friends, and even drinking games could be seen in instrumental terms as means to further one's examination preparation.[31] This ever finer subdivision of temporal periods so that they can be exploited more effectively not only reminds us of the relentless involution of the rice paddy, it also foreshadows our own contemporary attention economy, in which smart devices make it possible to divide time up and multitask, in the process allowing work time and leisure time to interpenetrate in new ways.

Indeed, whether we are located in Shanghai or San Francisco, it is perhaps not only the competitiveness of the higher education selection process that should be our primary focus of concern, nor only the oppressiveness of our work environment, but also the alchemy by which our "free time" activity is transmuted into labor that contributes to the profitable accumulation of data.[32] Like a nautilus building its own comfortable shell, we participate in the construction and operation of algorithms that work to narrow our vision and make our choices increasingly predictable.[33] In Goldenweiser's telling, the constraining frame is integral to the very process of involution; later scholars' diagnosis of involution as problematic stems in part from the imbrication of exterior and interior they understand to be typical of the phenomenon.[34]

The real involution is not, then, in the economics of the outside world and the hard imperatives of the office but rather in the mechanics of subjectivity construction—the folding of "exterior" and "interior" together in complicated ways—that are most effective when they appear to be voluntary. From this perspective, it certainly makes sense that the Ming eight-legged examination essay sets off an explosion of other texts that insistently identify themselves as first-person writing, from classical prose prefaces to *xiaopin wen* 小品文, in the sixteenth and seventeenth centuries.[35] The struggles that essay writers went through as they attempted simultaneously to "speak for the Sages and Worthies" (*dai shengxian liyan* 代聖賢立言) and to advocate for themselves as individuals uniquely deserving of selection provided a rigorous course of training in the tactics through which an "individual voice" could assert itself.[36] Similarly, it is precisely among those examination essay authors most committed to the inward turn in form that we also find a fascination with inwardness as *content*, whether expressed in terms of Wang Yangming's *liangzhi*, Daoist approaches to "fasting of the mind" (*xinzhai* 心齋), or investigations of consciousness and enlightenment that clearly find their inspiration in Chan Buddhism.[37] This interiority is not so much found as it is constructed, step by step, through an examination preparation process that does have its mechanical and repetitive aspects. Thus we are not surprised to find Zhu Xie's enthusiastic endorsement of *liangzhi* couched in terms of its interiority—"the marvelous effect of clear comprehension that does not originate in external discipline"—and also not surprised to find that endorsement tucked into the folds of his involuted text. The harsh condemnations of this "unorthodox" fascination with interiority that would fly thick and fast in the late Ming are evidence not of the formal or intellectual conservatism of the eight-legged essay genre but rather of the deep anxieties aroused by its industrialization of the subjectivity production process. There is no national or cultural configuration that has a monopoly on the contemporary echoes of these anxieties.

 ALEXANDER DES FORGES   戴沙迪
University of Massachusetts—Boston
alex.desforges@umb.edu

Acknowledgments

I would like to thank Zong-qi Cai and Stephen Roddy for their kind invitation to present the original version of this article as a paper at the conference "Critical Theory and Pre-modern Chinese Literature" in July 2021, as well as the other participants for their suggestions and criticisms.

Notes

1. Geertz, *Agricultural Involution*, 80.
2. Hegel, *Philosophy of History*, 116–38; Marx, *Grundrisse*, 472–73, and *A Contribution to the Critique of Political Economy*, 21; Wittfogel, *Oriental Despotism*. In addition to these works, Gates's *China's Motor* stands out for its intellectual rigor and historical specificity.

3. Prasenjit Duara draws a contrast between "state making" in Europe and "state involution" in early twentieth–century China. Duara, *Culture, Power, and the State*, 73–77. See also Siu, *Agents and Victims in South China*, chap. 12. Worth noting is Elizabeth Remick's critique of the state involution paradigm; she argues that Duara's characterization holds true only for a limited time period in the Hebei area and is not relevant to other regions and other periods of modern Chinese history. Remick, *Building Local States*, 239–42. In economic and social history, see the lengthy dispute between Philip C. C. Huang and Kenneth Pomeranz in the *Journal of Asian Studies* 61, no. 2 and 62, no. 1, a dispute that drew in a number of other scholars in the field. For each of the participants in this conversation, involution and development are taken to be settled terms; the debate for them is centered on the question of which societies display these traits in what combination at which point in time. Huang, "Development or Involution in Eighteenth-Century Britain and China?"; Pomeranz, "Beyond the East-West Binary"; Brenner and Isett, "England's Divergence from China's Yangzi Delta"; Lee, Campbell, and Wang, "Positive Check or Chinese Checks?"; Huang, "Further Thoughts on Eighteenth-Century Britain and China"; Pomeranz, "Facts Are Stubborn Things."

4. Xiang Biao says of *neijuan*: "Ta shi you yi dian Zhongguo tese de" 他是有一點中國特色的 (There's something characteristically Chinese about it). Wang and Ge, "Renlei xue jia Xiang Biao tan neijuan." (A partial translation of this interview appears in Wang and Ge, "How One Obscure Word Captures Urban China's Unhappiness.")

5. Geertz, *Agricultural Involution*; Huang, "Development or Involution in Eighteenth-Century Britain and China?" and "Further Thoughts on Eighteenth-Century Britain and China"; Pomeranz, "Beyond the East-West Binary" and "Facts Are Stubborn Things"; Duara, *Culture, Power, and the State*.

6. Geertz, *Agricultural Involution*, 79. See also Mark Elvin's discussion of the "high-level equilibrium trap" in *Pattern of the Chinese Past*, 285–319.

7. Goldenweiser, "Loose Ends of Theory on the Individual, Pattern, and Involution in Primitive Society," 102–3; see also Geertz, *Agricultural Involution*, 81; and Des Forges, *Testing the Literary*, 185–87.

8. Des Forges, *Testing the Literary*, 4, 202n13.

9. "In China, we have the reality of absolute equality, and all the differences that exist are possible only in connection with that administration, and in virtue of the worth which a person may acquire, enabling him to fill a high post in the Government." Hegel, *Philosophy of History*, 124.

10. Des Forges, *Testing the Literary*, 6–11, 60, 85–90.

11. Ibid., 97–103.

12. For a discussion of involutionary parallelism in the broader context of parallelism in the essay genre, see Des Forges, *Testing the Literary*, 90–97.

13. *Qinding sishu wen jiaozhu*, 170–71; Johnston and Wang, *Daxue and Zhongyong*, 241.

14. For a few other examples of involutionary parallelism, see *Qinding sishu wen jiaozhu*, 21, 23, 25, 27–28, 31, 32–33, 34, 170, 201, 674–76.

15. The essay as a whole is organized around the *liangzhi* / *liangneng* 良能 pair, from Mencius 7A.15. For more detail on the uses of Wang Yangming's writings—as well as Buddhist and Daoist texts—as inspiration for examination essays in the sixteenth and seventeenth centuries, see Des Forges, *Testing the Literary*, 62–71, 80–81.

16. Tambiah, "Galactic Polity in Southeast Asia," 524.

17. Liang, *Zhiyi conghua*, 111.
18. See, for example, ibid., 41; Gao, "Wenfa jishuo," 3b; *Huayang jijin* 1.49a.
19. de Certeau, *Practice of Everyday Life*, 97.
20. Des Forges, "Industry and Its Motivations," 99–119; Yang, "How China's Middle-Class Moms Became Their Kids' 'Agents.'"
21. On small topic questions, see Des Forges, "Industry and Its Motivations," 88–91.
22. On diligence and class distinctions, see Des Forges, *Testing the Literary*, 173–78.
23. Huang, "Development or Involution in Eighteenth-Century Britain and China?"; Huang, "Further Thoughts on Eighteenth-Century Britain and China"; Pomeranz, "Beyond the East-West Binary"; Pomeranz, "Facts Are Stubborn Things."
24. Vollrath, "Involution and Growth."
25. Wang and Ge, "Renlei xue jia Xiang Biao tan neijuan."
26. Piketty, *Capital in the Twenty-First Century*.
27. Geertz, *Agricultural Involution*, 130–43.
28. On the special power of fixed terms that are attributed a succession of different meanings over the course of intellectual paradigm shifts, see Des Forges, "Rhetorics of Modernity and the Logics of the Fetish," 24–25.
29. Zuboff, "Digital Declaration."
30. Des Forges, *Testing the Literary*, 116–17.
31. Liangyan Ge argues for the relevance of what he calls "the examination complex" to leisure culture in *Scholar and the State*. Moving in the other direction, Zhou Zuoren sees the initial "topic-breaker" section of the essay to function according to the logic of the lantern riddle. Zhou, *Zhongguo xin wenxue de yuanliu*, 32. Kurahashi Keiko makes a strong case for the connection between apparently dilettantish cultural practices and examination success in *Chūgoku dentō shakai no erītotachi*.
32. Goldhaber, "Attention Economy and the Net"; Wu, *Attention Merchants*.
33. On the intriguing question of the authorship of algorithms, see Amoore, *Cloud Ethics*, 85–107.
34. Goldenweiser, "Loose Ends of Theory on the Individual, Pattern, and Involution in Primitive Society," 102–3.
35. "To argue that the examination system is merely the inert ground against which a lively new voice can distinguish itself only through a radical break would be to overlook the ways in which the practice of that voice manifests itself as a consequence of the examination essay form, as well as the extent to which the very idea of a distinctive individual voice functions as a bureaucratic requirement within the examination system." Des Forges, *Testing the Literary*, 149. See also Des Forges, "Who Am 'I' in the Ming and Qing?"
36. Des Forges, *Testing the Literary*, 130–49.
37. Ibid., 54–68, 139–49.

References

Amoore, Louise. *Cloud Ethics: Algorithms and the Attributes of Ourselves and Others*. Durham, NC: Duke University Press, 2020.

Brenner, Robert, and Christopher Isett. "England's Divergence from China's Yangzi Delta: Property Relations, Microeconomics, and Patterns of Development." *Journal of Asian Studies* 61, no. 2 (2002): 609–62.

de Certeau, Michel. *The Practice of Everyday Life.* Translated by Steven Rendall. Berkeley: University of California Press, 1984.

Des Forges, Alexander. "Industry and Its Motivations: Reading Tang Xianzu's Examination Essay on the Problem of Excess Cloth." *Harvard Journal of Asiatic Studies* 80, no. 1 (2020): 85–122.

————. "The Rhetorics of Modernity and the Logics of the Fetish." In *Contested Modernities of Chinese Literature*, edited by Charles A. Laughlin, 17–31. New York: Palgrave Macmillan, 2005.

————. *Testing the Literary: Prose and the Aesthetic in Early Modern China.* Cambridge, MA: Harvard University Asia Center Publications, 2021.

————. "Who Am 'I' in the Ming and Qing? First-Person Dynamics in Modern Prose (*shiwen*) Examination Essays and Classical Prose (*guwen*) Prefaces." *East Asian Journal of Sinology* 15 (2021): 9–46.

Duara, Prasenjit. *Culture, Power, and the State: Rural North China 1900–1942.* Stanford: Stanford University Press, 1988.

Elvin, Mark. *The Pattern of the Chinese Past.* Stanford: Stanford University Press, 1973.

Gao Dang 高崵. "Wenfa jishuo" 文法集說 (Collected Explanations of Literary Technique). In *Lunwen jichao* 論文集鈔 (A Collection of Discussions of Literary Writing). 1788 edition. Reprint, Beijing: Beijing tushuguan chubanshe, 2006.

Gates, Hill. *China's Motor: A Thousand Years of Petty Capitalism.* Ithaca: Cornell University Press, 1996.

Ge, Liangyan. *The Scholar and the State: Fiction as Political Discourse in Late Imperial China.* Seattle: University of Washington Press, 2015.

Geertz, Clifford. *Agricultural Involution: The Process of Ecological Change in Indonesia.* Berkeley: University of California Press, 1963.

Goldenweiser, Alexander. "Loose Ends of Theory on the Individual, Pattern, and Involution in Primitive Society." In *Essays in Anthropology Presented to A. L. Kroeber*, edited by J. Lowie, 99–104. Berkeley: University of California Press, 1936.

Goldhaber, Michael. "The Attention Economy and the Net." *First Monday* 2, no. 4 (1997). https://firstmonday.org/ojs/index.php/fm/article/view/519/440/.

Hegel, Georg Wilhelm Friedrich. *The Philosophy of History.* Translated by J. Sibree. New York: Dover, 1956.

Huang, Philip C. C. "Development or Involution in Eighteenth-Century Britain and China? A Review of Kenneth Pomeranz's *The Great Divergence: China, Europe, and the Making of the Modern World Economy.*" *Journal of Asian Studies* 61, no. 2 (2002): 501–38.

————. "Further Thoughts on Eighteenth-Century Britain and China: Rejoinder to Pomeranz's Response to My Critique." *Journal of Asian Studies* 62, no. 1 (2003): 157–67.

Huayang jijin 花樣集錦 (A Collection of Patterned Embroidery). Taipei: National Central Library, 1844.

Johnston, Ian, and Wang Ping, trans. *Daxue and Zhongyong: Bilingual Edition.* Hong Kong: Chinese University Press, 2012.

Kurahashi Keiko 倉橋圭子. *Chūgoku dentō shakai no erītotachi: bunkateki saiseisan to kaisō shakai no dainamizumu* 中国伝統社会のエリート達：文化的再生産と階層社会のダイナミズム (Elites in Traditional Chinese Society: Cultural Reproduction and Dynamism of Class Society). Tokyo: Fūkyōsha, 2011.

Lee, James, Cameron Campbell, and Wang Feng. "Positive Check or Chinese Checks?" *Journal of Asian Studies* 61, no. 2 (2002): 591–607.

Liang Zhangju 梁章鉅. *Zhiyi conghua Shilü conghua* 制義叢話試律叢話 (Collected Words on Examination Essays; Collected Words on Examination Poetry). Reprint, Shanghai: Shanghai shudian, 2001.

Marx, Karl. *A Contribution to the Critique of Political Economy*. Translated by S. W. Ryazanskaya. Moscow: Progress, 1970.

———. *Grundrisse: Foundations of the Critique of Political Economy*. Translated by Martin Nicolaus. New York: Vintage Books, 1973.

Piketty, Thomas. *Capital in the Twenty-First Century*. Cambridge, MA: Harvard University Press, 2017.

Pomeranz, Kenneth. "Beyond the East-West Binary: Resituating Development Paths in the Eighteenth-Century World." *Journal of Asian Studies* 61, no. 2 (2002): 539–90.

———. "Facts Are Stubborn Things: A Response to Philip Huang." *Journal of Asian Studies* 62, no. 1 (2003): 167–81.

Qinding sishu wen jiaozhu 欽定四書文校注 (Annotated Edition of the *Imperially Authorized Essays on the Four Books*). Wuhan: Wuhan daxue chubanshe, 2009.

Remick, Elizabeth. *Building Local States: China During the Republican and Post-Mao Eras*. Cambridge, MA: Harvard University Asia Center Publications, 2004.

Siu, Helen. *Agents and Victims in South China: Accomplices in Rural Revolution*. New Haven: Yale University Press, 1989.

Tambiah, Stanley Jeyaraja. "The Galactic Polity in Southeast Asia." *HAU: Journal of Ethnographic Theory* 3 (2013): 503–34.

Vollrath, Dietrich. "Involution and Growth." October 15, 2018. https://growthecon.com/blog/Involution/.

Wang Qianni 王芊霓, and Ge Shifan 葛詩凡. "Renlei xue jia Xiang Biao tan neijuan: yizhong bu yunxu shibai he tuichu de jingzheng" 人類學家項飆談內卷：一種不允許失敗和退出的競爭 (Anthropologist Xiang Biao Discusses Involution: A Competition That Does Not Permit Failure and Withdrawal). *The Paper* 澎湃, October 22, 2020. https://www.thepaper.cn/newsDetail_forward_9648585.

Wang Qianni 王芊霓, and Ge Shifan 葛詩凡. "How One Obscure Word Captures Urban China's Unhappiness." *Sixth Tone*, November 4, 2020. https://www.sixthtone.com/news/1006391/how-one-obscure-word-captures-urban-chinas-unhappiness.

Wittfogel, Karl. *Oriental Despotism: A Comparative Study of Total Power*. New Haven: Yale University Press, 1957.

Wu, Tim. *The Attention Merchants: The Epic Scramble to Get Inside Our Heads*. New York: Knopf, 2016.

Yang, Ke. "How China's Middle-Class Moms Became their Kids' 'Agents.'" *Sixth Tone*, August 21, 2018. https://www.sixthtone.com/news/1002799/how-chinas-middle-class-moms-became-their-kids-agents.

Zhou Zuoren 周作人. *Zhongguo xin wenxue de yuanliu* 中國新文學的源流 (The Origins of China's New Literature). Reprint, Shijiazhuang: Hebei jiaoyu chuban she, 2002.

Zuboff, Shoshanna. "A Digital Declaration: Big Data as Surveillance Capitalism." September 15, 2014. https://opencuny.org/pnmarchive/files/2019/01/Zuboff-Digital-Declaration.pdf.

Contributors

ALEXANDER DES FORGES is professor of Chinese and chair of the Department of Modern Languages, Literatures, and Cultures at the University of Massachusetts Boston. He is the author of *Mediasphere Shanghai: The Aesthetics of Cultural Production* (2007) and *Testing the Literary: Prose and the Aesthetic in Early Modern China* (2021). His current research interests include comparative literary theory and cultural studies in the early modern and modern periods (fifteenth through twentieth centuries).

GRACE S. FONG is professor of Chinese literature at McGill University. Her research focuses on classical Chinese poetry and women's literature of the Ming and Qing periods. She has directed the development of the Ming Qing Women's Writings digital archive and database (digital.library.mcgill.ca/mingqing/) since 2003. She is the author of *Herself an Author: Gender, Agency, and Writing in Late Imperial China* (2008, 2016) and coeditor of *The Inner Quarters and Beyond: Women Writers from Ming through Qing* (2010) and *Representing Lives in China: Forms of Biography in the Ming-Qing Period 1368–1911* (2018).

MARTIN KERN, the Joanna and Greg '84 P13 P18 Zeluck Professor in Asian Studies at Princeton University, specializes in the study of Chinese antiquity, with a focus on early Chinese poetry. Working across the disciplines of literature, philology, history, religion, and art, he is particularly interested in the practices of textual composition, transmission, and hermeneutics in the Chinese manuscript culture of the first millennium BCE. His current book projects include *Performance, Memory, and Authorship in Ancient China: The Formation of the Poetic Tradition* and *The Shijing (Classic of Poetry) in Ancient Manuscripts: Studies in Poetry, Poetics, and the Sociology of Text*. At Princeton, Kern directs Comparative Antiquity: A Humanities Council Global Initiative; at Renmin University of China (Beijing), he leads the International Center for the Study of Ancient Text Cultures. Kern also serves as coeditor of *T'oung Pao*.

LUCAS KLEIN is a father, writer, translator, and associate professor of Chinese at Arizona State University. He is executive editor of the Hsu-Tang Library of Classical Chinese Literature (Oxford), author of *The Organization of Distance* (2018), coeditor of *Chinese Poetry and Translation* (2019), and translator of *Li Shangyin* (2018); Mang Ke, *October Dedications* (2018); Duo Duo, *Words as Grain* (2021), and Xi Chuan, *Notes on the Mosquito* (2012) and *Bloom and Other Poems* (2022).

XINDA LIAN is professor of Chinese language and literature at Denison University. He received his PhD from the University of Michigan in 1995 and has been teaching at Denison since 1994. His research interests include Song dynasty literature, the stylistic

The Journal of Chinese Literature and Culture • 9:1 • April 2022
DOI 10.1215/23290048-9681254 • © 2022 by Duke University Press

analysis of the *Zhuangzi* text, and the study of literary criticism. He is the author of *The Wild and Arrogant: Expression of Self in Xin Qiji's Song Lyrics* (1999) and a variety of book chapters and journal articles on Song dynasty literature and the study of the *Zhuangzi*.

MANLING LUO is associate professor of Chinese literature at Indiana University. She received her PhD in Chinese and comparative literature from Washington University in St. Louis. Her primary research interests include the social life of narratives, literati culture, gender, and religious literature. Her first monograph, *Literati Storytelling in Late Medieval China* (2015), examines how both the literary and the social dimensions of stories intersected, making storytelling a powerful medium for educated men of the mid-eighth to the mid-tenth centuries to redefine themselves in response to sociopolitical transformations. She has also published a range of research articles in English and Chinese.

CHRISTOPHER M. B. NUGENT, professor of Chinese at Williams College, earned his doctorate at Harvard University under the direction of Stephen Owen. He is the author of *Manifest in Words, Written on Paper: Producing and Circulating Poetry in Tang Dynasty China* (winner 2012 Joseph Levenson Book Prize, Pre-1900 Category) and an editor of and contributor to the edited volume *Literary Information in China: A History*. His main research areas are the literary culture of the Tang period (7th–10th cent.), manuscript culture, textual memory and memorization, and medieval educational manuscripts from Dunhuang.

STEPHEN RODDY is professor of languages, literatures, and cultures at the University of San Francisco. His research has focused on intersections of institutional change and literary expression in late premodern China and Japan. Recent publications include a translation (with Ying Wang) of a 1651 *chuanqi* drama *Lianxiangban* 憐香伴 (The Fragrant Companions) and studies of poetry and prose essays by Ji Yun 紀昀 (1724–1805), Gong Zizhen 龔自珍 (1793–1841), Yu Yue 俞樾 (1821–1907), and Yanagawa Seigan 梁川星巌 (1789–1858).

PATRICIA SIEBER is associate professor in the Department of East Asian Languages and Literatures at The Ohio State University. Her research interests encompass Chinese drama, song culture, translation studies, and gender studies. She is the author of *Theaters of Desire: Authors, Readers, and the Reproduction of Early Chinese Song-Drama* (2003); lead editor (with Regina S. Llamas) of *How To Read Chinese Drama: A Guided Anthology* (2022); coeditor (with Li Guo and Peter Kornicki) of *Ecologies of Translation in East and South East Asia, 1600–1900* (forthcoming 2022); and coeditor (with Guo Yingde, Wenbo Chang, and Xiaohui Zhang) of *How to Read Chinese Drama in Chinese: A Language Companion* (forthcoming 2023). She guest-edited a special issue, "The Protean World of *Sanqu* Songs," for the *Journal of Chinese Literature and Culture* 8, no. 1 (2021). Her essays on Chinese drama and song culture have appeared in *Modern Chinese Literature and Culture, Journal of Chinese Literature and Culture, Monumenta Serica, Journal of Chinese Religions*, and *Ming Studies*, among others.

PAULA VARSANO, professor of Chinese literature at the University of California, Berkeley, specializes in classical poetry and poetics from the third through the eleventh centuries, with particular interest in literature and subjectivity, the evolution of spatial representation in poetry, the history and poetics of traditional literary criticism, and the theory and practice of translation. She is the author of *Tracking the Banished Immortal: The Poetry of Li Bo and Its Critical Reception* (2003), translator of François Jullien's *Eloge de la fadeur* (2004), and editor of *The Rhetoric of Hiddenness in Traditional Chinese Culture* (2016). Her book *Knowing and Being Known: The Lyric Subject in Traditional Chinese Poetry and Poetics* is forthcoming.

Keep up to date on new scholarship

Issue alerts are a great way to stay current on all the cutting-edge scholarship from your favorite Duke University Press journals. This free service delivers tables of contents directly to your inbox, informing you of the latest groundbreaking work as soon as it is published.

To sign up for issue alerts:

1. Visit **dukeu.press/register** and register for an account. You do not need to provide a customer number.

2. After registering, visit **dukeu.press/alerts**.

3. Go to "Latest Issue Alerts" and click on "Add Alerts."

4. Select as many publications as you would like from the pop-up window and click "Add Alerts."

read.dukeupress.edu/journals